THE BIG BOOK OF BUSINESS CARDS

THE BIG BOOK OF BUSINESS CARDS

DAVID E. CARTER

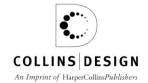

COLLINS | DESIGN

An Imprint of HarperCollinsPublishers

HarperCollins books may be purchased for educational, business, or sales promotional use. For information, please write: Special Markets Department, HarperCollins Publishers Inc., 10 East 53rd Street, New York, NY 10022.

First Edition

First published in 2005 by:
Collins Design
An Imprint of HarperCollins*Publishers*
10 East 53rd Street
New York, NY 10022
Tel: (212) 207-7000
Fax: (212) 207-7654
collinsdesign@harpercollins.com
www.harpercollins.com

Distributed throughout the world by:
HarperCollins*Publishers*
10 East 53rd Street
New York, NY 10022
Fax: (212) 207-7654

Book design by Designs on You!
Suzanna and Anthony Stephens

Library of Congress Control Number: 2005928941

ISBN: 0-06-083409-8

Printed in China by Everbest Printing Company through Crescent Hill Books, Louisville, Kentucky.

First Printing, 2005

Business cards have changed.

Once they were designed almost as an afterthought, and made to match the letterhead and envelope.

Now that business mail has become almost extinct as e-mail takes over, business cards have a new level of importance.

Business transactions have become much more impersonal—automated voice customer service and orders completed totally online, for example. This lack of personal contact has made the rare one-to-one contact more important than ever. How to capitalize on that contact? Leave a business card.

But the business card that is given to someone must impact. It must connect the card with the person, and the old one-color, one-sided business card is no longer worth the paper it is printed on.

The new business card is a business tool, but only if it stands out. Increasingly, businesses are printing on both sides of the card. A few years ago, this technique was rare; now, it's common.

Yes, business cards have changed. And firms who create brand identities need to see just what's happening in the world of business cards. They need to see outstanding cards from large and small companies from around the world.

And that's the whole purpose of this book.

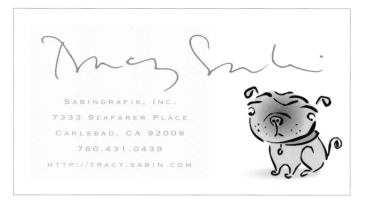

SABINGRAFIK, INC.
7333 SEAFARER PLACE
CARLSBAD, CA 92009
760.431.0439
HTTP://TRACY.SABIN.COM

1.

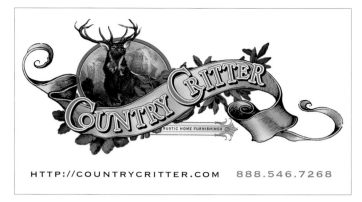

HTTP://COUNTRYCRITTER.COM   888.546.7268

2.

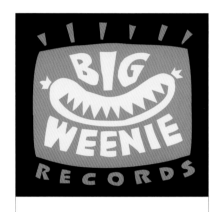

18755 Grahams Drive
Abington, VA 24211

276.628.2818

3.

HELEN WOODWARD
ANIMAL CENTER

P.O. Box 64
6461 El Apajo Road
Rancho Santa Fe, CA 92067

(858) 756-4117
Fax: (858) 756-1466

4.

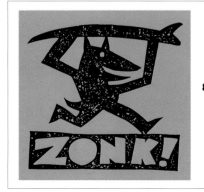

Greg Sabin

Zonk International
818 South Dakota Street
Seattle, WA 98108

206.340.1296
f 206.545.7241

5.

(1-5)
Design Firm **Sabingrafik, Inc.**

1.
Client   Sabingrafik, Inc.
Designer   Tracy Sabin
2.
Client   Country Critter
Designer   Tracy Sabin
3.
Client   Big Weenie Records
Designer   Tracy Sabin
4.
Client   Helen Woodward
                 Animal Center
Designers   Tracy Sabin,
                 Lesley Gunr
5.
Client   Zonk!
Designer   Tracy Sabin

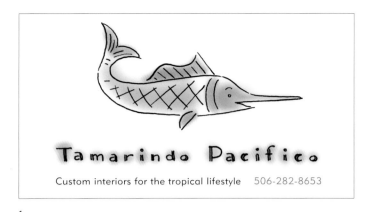

1.

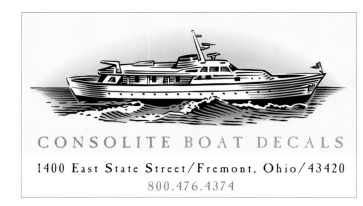

2.

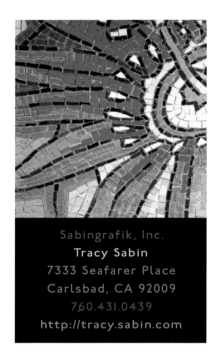

3.

Sabingrafik, Inc.
Tracy Sabin
7333 Seafarer Place
Carlsbad, CA 92009
760.431.0439
http://tracy.sabin.com

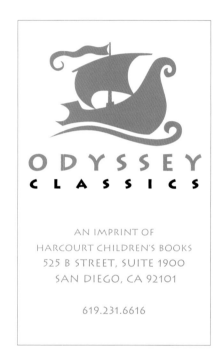

4.

ODYSSEY
CLASSICS

AN IMPRINT OF
HARCOURT CHILDREN'S BOOKS
525 B STREET, SUITE 1900
SAN DIEGO, CA 92101

619.231.6616

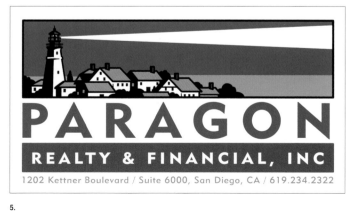

5.

PARAGON
REALTY & FINANCIAL, INC
1202 Kettner Boulevard / Suite 6000, San Diego, CA / 619.234.2322

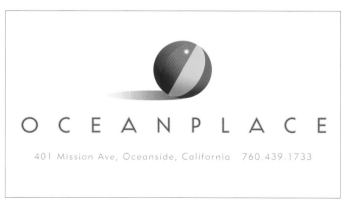

6.

OCEANPLACE

401 Mission Ave, Oceanside, California   760.439.1733

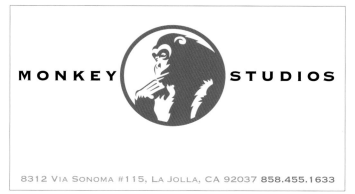

M O N K E Y 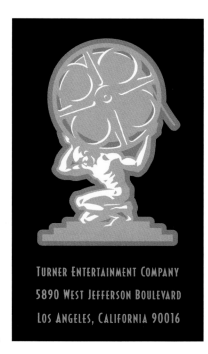 **S T U D I O S**

8312 VIA SONOMA #115, LA JOLLA, CA 92037 858.455.1633

7.

9665 CHESAPEAKE DRIVE, SUITE 300, SAN DIEGO, 92123   800 227-6225

8.

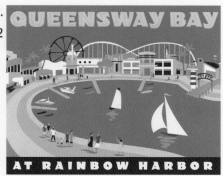

300 East Ocean Blvd.
Long Beach, CA 90802

Tel: 562-436-3636

9.

TURNER ENTERTAINMENT COMPANY

5890 WEST JEFFERSON BOULEVARD

LOS ANGELES, CALIFORNIA 90016

10.

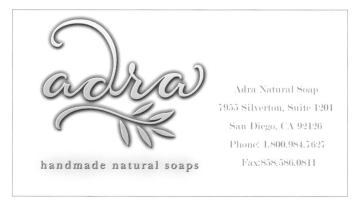

adra

handmade natural soaps

Adra Natural Soap
7955 Silverton, Suite 1201
San Diego, CA 92126
Phone: 1.800.984.7627
Fax:858.586.0811

11.

(1-11)
Design Firm **Sabingrafik, Inc.**

1.
Client	Tamarindo Pacifico
Designer	Tracy Sabin

2.
Client	Consolite Boat Decals
Designer	Tracy Sabin

3.
Client	Sabingrafik, Inc.
Designer	Tracy Sabin

4.
Client	Odyssey Classics
Designer	Tracy Sabin

5.
Client	Paragon Realty & Financial, Inc.
Designer	Tracy Sabin

6.
Client	Oceanplace
Designer	Tracy Sabin

7.
Client	Monkey Studios
Designers	Tracy Sabin, Russell Sabin

8.
Client	San Pacifico
Designer	Tracy Sabin

9.
Client	Queensway Bay
Designer	Tracy Sabin

10.
Client	Turner Entertainment Company
Designer	Tracy Sabin

11.
Client	Adra
Designer	Tracy Sabin

The Park Manor

HOTEL · BALBOA · PARK

25 Spruce Street, San Diego, CA 92103
800-874-2649 or 619-291-0999

1.

PACIFIC MARINE
CREDIT UNION

MCRD, Building 9
P.O. Box 400144
San Diego, CA 92140

Hours:
8:30am-4:30pm
Monday-Friday

800.736.4500
f 619.298.9405

2.

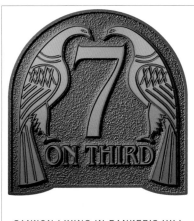

7 ON THIRD

CANYON LIVING IN BANKER'S HILL

9683 TIERRA GRANDE STREET
SUITE 201
SAN DIEGO, CA 92126
619.685.2148

3.

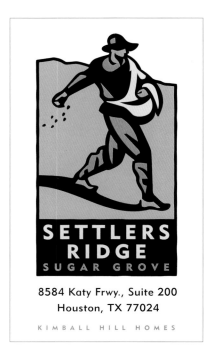

SETTLERS RIDGE
SUGAR GROVE

8584 Katy Frwy., Suite 200
Houston, TX 77024

KIMBALL HILL HOMES

4.

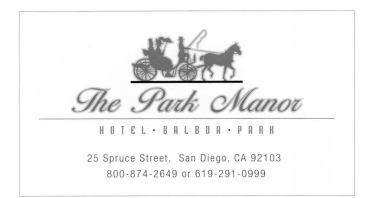

Brightwater Ranch
A Centex Homes Community

1815 Aston Ave.
Suite 101
Carlsbad, CA 92008
760.431.1211
f 760.431.5511

5.

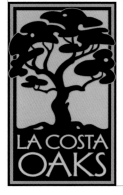

LA COSTA OAKS

7411 CIRCULO SEQUOIA
LA COSTA, CA 92009

PHONE: 760-633-0118
FAX: 760-633-1662

CENTEX HOMES|CENTEX CORPORATION

6.

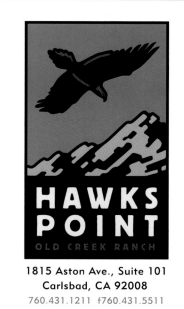

HAWKS POINT
OLD CREEK RANCH

1815 Aston Ave., Suite 101
Carlsbad, CA 92008
760.431.1211 f760.431.5511
A CENTEX HOMES COMMUNITY

7.

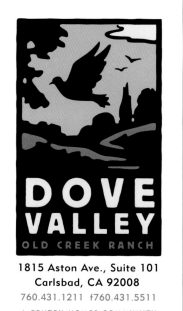

DOVE VALLEY
OLD CREEK RANCH

1815 Aston Ave., Suite 101
Carlsbad, CA 92008
760.431.1211 f760.431.5511
A CENTEX HOMES COMMUNITY

8.

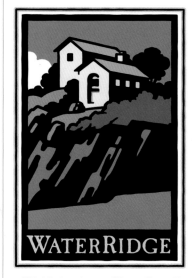

WATERRIDGE

2734 Loker Avenue West, Suite K
Carlsbad, CA 92008
A BREHM COMMUNITIES HOME

9.

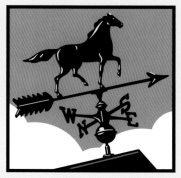

Flying Horse Ranch

1002 Meadowrun Road

Encinitas, CA 92024

10.

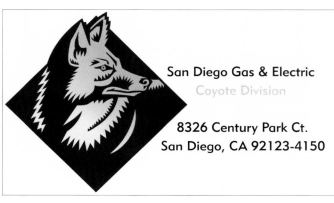

San Diego Gas & Electric
Coyote Division

8326 Century Park Ct.
San Diego, CA 92123-4150

11.

(1)
    Design Firm **Sabingrafik, Inc.**
(2,3)
    Design Firm **McNulty Creative**
(4-10)
    Design Firm **Roni Hicks & Assoc.**
(11)
    Design Firm **Franklin Stoorza**

1.
    Client   The Park Manor
    Designer   Tracy Sabin
2.
    Client   Pacific Marine Credit Union
    Designers   Tracy Sabin, Mary McNulty
3.
    Client   7 On Third
    Designers   Tracy Sabin, Mary McNulty
4.
    Client   Settlers Ridge
    Designers   Tracy Sabin, Paige Cleveland,
                Danny Zaludek

5.
    Client   Brightwater Ranch
    Designers   Tracy Sabin, Danny Zaludek
6.
    Client   La Costa Oaks
    Designers   Tracy Sabin, Steve Sharp
7.
    Client   Hawks Point
    Designers   Tracy Sabin, Steve Sharp
8.
    Client   Dove Valley
    Designers   Tracy Sabin, Steve Sharp
9.
    Client   WaterRidge
    Designers   Tracy Sabin, Steve Sharp
10.
    Client   Flying Horse Ranch
    Designers   Tracy Sabin, Danny Zaludek
11.
    Client   San Diego Gas & Electric
    Designers   Tracy Sabin, Craig Fuller

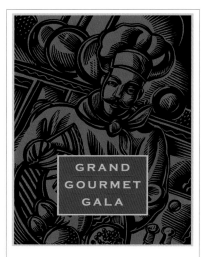

1.

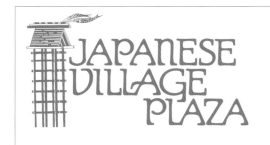

350 East First Street, Los Angeles, CA 90012

2.

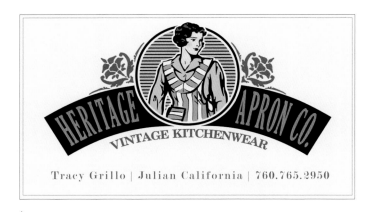

HORTON FARMER'S MARKET
ONE HORTON PLAZA
SAN DIEGO, CA 92101

619.696.7766

3.

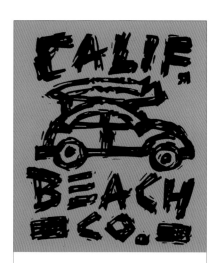

2560 Progress Street
Vista, Ca 92083

760.598.7000

4.

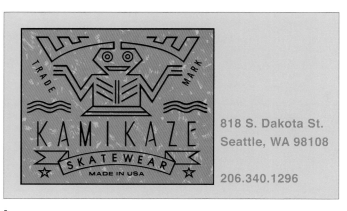

818 S. Dakota St.
Seattle, WA 98108

206.340.1296

5.

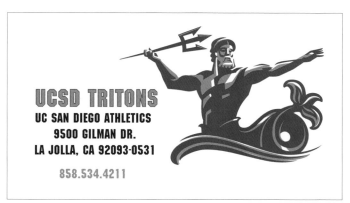

UCSD TRITONS
UC SAN DIEGO ATHLETICS
9500 GILMAN DR.
LA JOLLA, CA 92093-0531

858.534.4211

6.

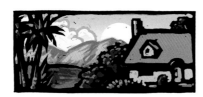

R I V E R B E N D

12522 Feather Drive, Riverside County, CA (951) 582-0816

7.

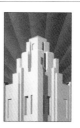

THE PARAMOUNT

TOWNHOMES IN THE CULTURAL HEART OF ESCONDIDO

Barratt Urban Development   760.431.0800

8.

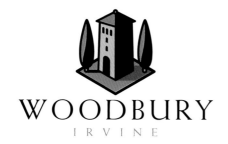

WOODBURY
I R V I N E

The Irvine Company, 550 Newport Center Drive, Newport Beach, CA 92660

9.

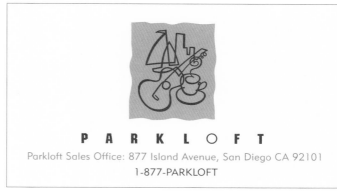

P A R K L O F T

Parkloft Sales Office: 877 Island Avenue, San Diego CA 92101
1-877-PARKLOFT

10.

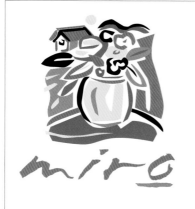

Brookfield Homes
12865 Pointe Del Mar
Suite 200
Del Mar, CA 92014
Phone: 858.481.8500

11.

(1-5)
Design Firm **Sabingrafik, Inc.**
(6)
Design Firm **Design Group West**
(7-11)
Design Firm **Greenhaus**

1.
| Client | Heritage Apron Company |
| Designer | Tracy Sabin |

2.
| Client | Japanese Village Plaza |
| Designer | Tracy Sabin |

3.
| Client | Horton Farmer's Market |
| Designer | Tracy Sabin |

4.
| Client | Calif. Beach Co. |
| Designer | Tracy Sabin |

5.
| Client | Kamikaze Skatewear |
| Designer | Tracy Sabin |

6.
| Client | UCSD Tritons |
| Designers | Tracy Sabin, Jim Naegli |

7.
| Client | Riverbend |
| Designers | Tracy Sabin, Craig Fuller, Sandra Sharp |

8.
| Client | The Paramount |
| Designers | Tracy Sabin, Sandra Sharp, Craig Fuller |

9.
| Client | Woodbury |
| Designers | Tracy Sabin, Craig Fuller |

10.
| Client | Parkloft |
| Designers | Tracy Sabin, Craig Fuller, Sandra Sharp |

11.
| Client | Miro |
| Designers | Tracy Sabin, Craig Fuller, Sandra Sharp |

760.804.8400

La Strada

SeaCountry Homes | 2451 Impala Dr. - Suite A | Carlsbad, CA 92009

1.

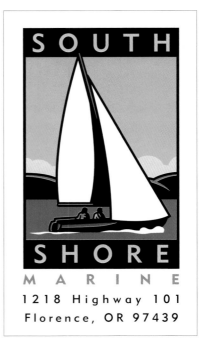

SOUTH
SHORE
MARINE

1218 Highway 101
Florence, OR 97439

2.

AMORE

A BARRATT AMERICAN HOME

5950 PRIESTLY DR.
CARLSBAD, CA 92008
(760) 431-0800

3.

OTAY RANCH
EST·1988

1000 HERITAGE ROAD, CHULA VISTA, CA 91913
(800) 421-9088

4.

THE RIDGE

The Ridge Golf Club
2020 Golf Course Road
Auburn, CA 95602

(530) 888-7888

5.

The Sandhurst Foundation
Old College
The Royal Military Academy Sandhurst
Camberley
Surrey
GU15 4PQ

+44 (0) 1276 412000

6.

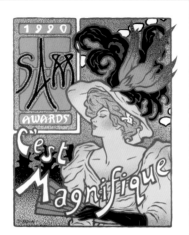

Building Industry Association
6336 Greenwich, Suite A
San Diego, California 92122

858.450.1221

7.

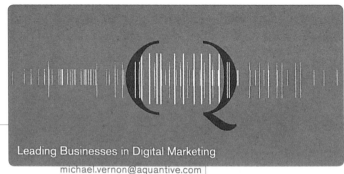

Leading Businesses in Digital Marketing

aquantive.com
avenuea.com
ifrontier.com
atlasdmt.com

michael.vernon@aquantive.com

dir_ 206.816.8599
fax_ 206.816.8502

aQuantive

aQuantive, Inc.
506 Second Avenue
Seattle, Washington 98104

8.

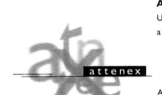

Alan Perry
Unix Specialist
alan@attenex.com

attenex

Attenex Corporation
701 Fifth Avenue, Suite 1450
Seattle, Washington 98104
m: 206.499.5501
f: 206.386.5841

9.

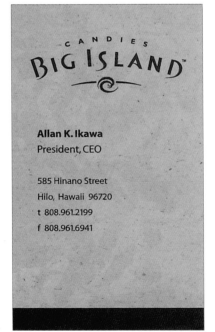

CANDIES
BIG ISLAND

Allan K. Ikawa
President, CEO

585 Hinano Street
Hilo, Hawaii 96720
t 808.961.2199
f 808.961.6941

10.

(1-3)
Design Firm **Greenhaus**
(4)
Design Firm **Tyler Blik Design**
(5)
Design Firm **The Flowers Group**
(6)
Design Firm **MDA Communications**
(7)
Design Firm **Conover**
(8-10)
Design Firm **Hornall Anderson Design Works**

1.
Client   La Strada
Designers   Tracy Sabin, Craig Fuller,
              Sandra Sharp
2.
Client   South Shore Marine
Designers   Tracy Sabin, Craig Fuller
3.
Client   Amore
Designers   Tracy Sabin, Craig Fuller,
              S. Michael Grace, Jerry Sisti
4.
Client   Otay Ranch
Designers   Tracy Sabin, Tyler Blik
5.
Client   The Ridge
Designers   Tracy Sabin, Corey Shehan
6.
Client   The Sandhurst Foundation
Designers   Tracy Sabin, James Dewar

7.
Client   Building Industry Association
Designers   Tracy Sabin, David Conover
8.
Client   aQuantive Corporation
Designers   Jack Anderson, Kathy Saito,
              Henry Yiu, Sonja Max,
              Gretchen Cook
9.
Client   Attenex
Designers   Katha Dalton,
              Jana Wilson Esser
10.
Client   Big Island Candies
Designers   Jack Anderson, Kathy Saito,
              Mary Chin Hutchison,
              Alan Copeland

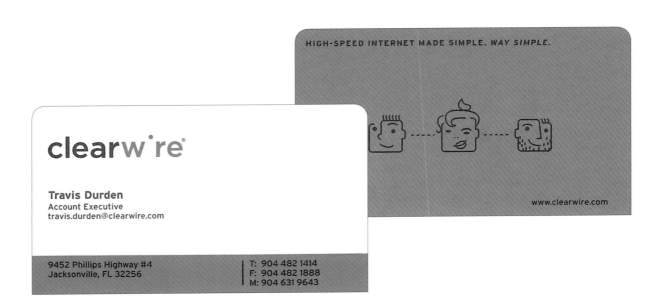

clearw·re

Travis Durden
Account Executive
travis.durden@clearwire.com

9452 Phillips Highway #4
Jacksonville, FL 32256

T: 904 482 1414
F: 904 482 1888
M: 904 631 9643

1.

etrieve™

principal engineer

① 503.533.2300

① 503.533.2301

◉ travis@etrieve.com

ⓦ www.etrieve.com

etrieve™

3000 nw stucki place suite 120

hillsboro, oregon 97124

2.

FREEMOTION FITNESS INC™

Erin Kelly

Inside Sales Representative

Tel 719.955.1100, Ext 117

Fax 719.955.1104

Toll Free 877.363.8449

1096 Elkton Drive, Ste 600

Colorado Springs, Colorado

80907-3573

ekelly@freemotionfitness.com

FREEMOTION FITNESS INC™

3.

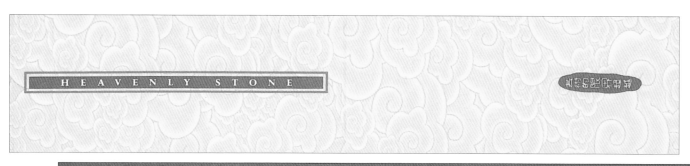

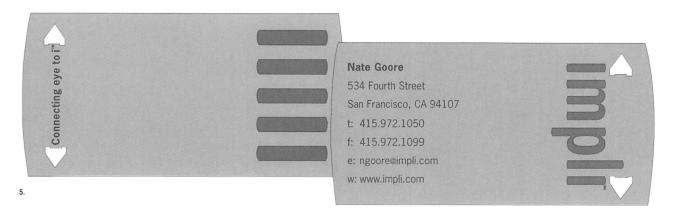

Mary Ann Petro Art Consultant

telephone: 415·749·1948   facsimile: 415·749·1952

2111 Hyde Street Suite 602 San Francisco CA 94109

www.heavenlystone.com   ma_petro@heavenlystone.com

4.

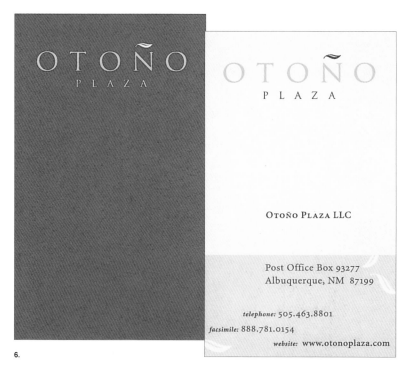

Connecting eye to i™

Nate Goore
534 Fourth Street
San Francisco, CA 94107
t: 415.972.1050
f: 415.972.1099
e: ngoore@impli.com
w: www.impli.com

impli

5.

O T O Ñ O
P L A Z A

O T O Ñ O
P L A Z A

Otoño Plaza LLC

Post Office Box 93277
Albuquerque, NM 87199

telephone: 505.463.8801
facsimile: 888.781.0154

website: www.otonoplaza.com

6.

(1-6)
Design Firm **Hornall Anderson Design Works**

1.
Client   Clearwire
Designers   Jack Anderson, John Anicker,
              Leo Raymundo, Sonja Max,
              Andrew Wicklund

2.
Client   etrieve
Designers   John Hornall, Kathy Saito,
              Henry Yiu, Andrew Smith

3.
Client   FreeMotion
Designers   Jack Anderson, Kathy Saito,
              Sonja Max, Henry Yiu,
              Alan Copeland

4.
Client   Heavenly Stone
Designers   Jack Anderson, Henry Yiu

5.
Client   impli
Designers   Jack Anderson, Sonja Max,
              Kathy Saito, Alan Copeland

6.
Client   Otoño
Designers   John Anicker, Henry Yiu,
              Kathy Saito, Gretchen Cook,
              Sonja Max

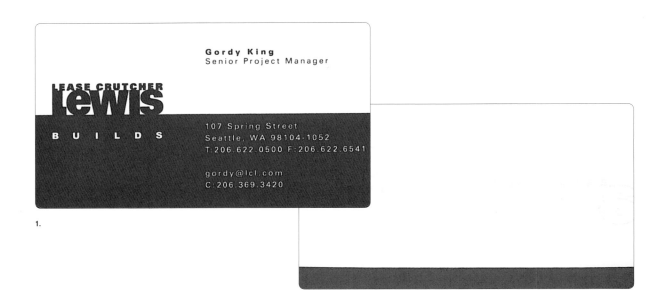

Gordy King
Senior Project Manager

LEASE CRUTCHER
lewis
B U I L D S

107 Spring Street
Seattle, WA 98104-1052
T:206.622.0500 F:206.622.6541

gordy@lcl.com
C:206.369.3420

1.

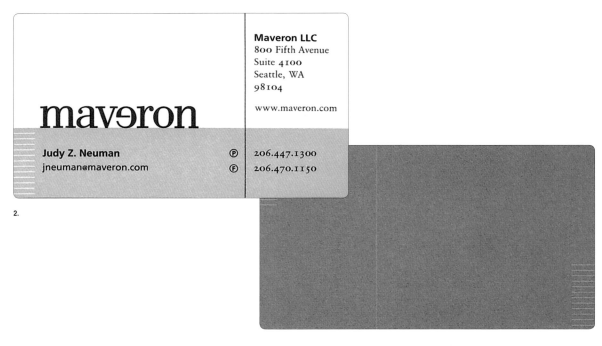

maveron

Maveron LLC
800 Fifth Avenue
Suite 4100
Seattle, WA
98104

www.maveron.com

Judy Z. Neuman   ℗   206.447.1300
jneuman@maveron.com   ℉   206.470.1150

2.

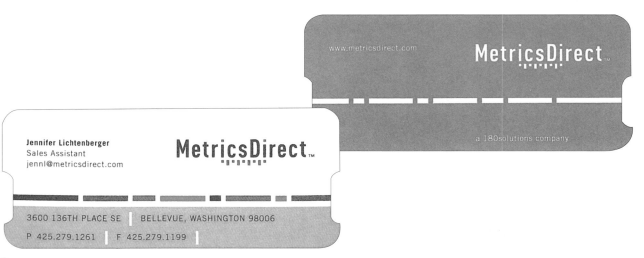

www.metricsdirect.com   **MetricsDirect**™

a 180solutions company

Jennifer Lichtenberger
Sales Assistant
jennl@metricsdirect.com   **MetricsDirect**™

3600 136TH PLACE SE | BELLEVUE, WASHINGTON 98006

P 425.279.1261 | F 425.279.1199

3.

18

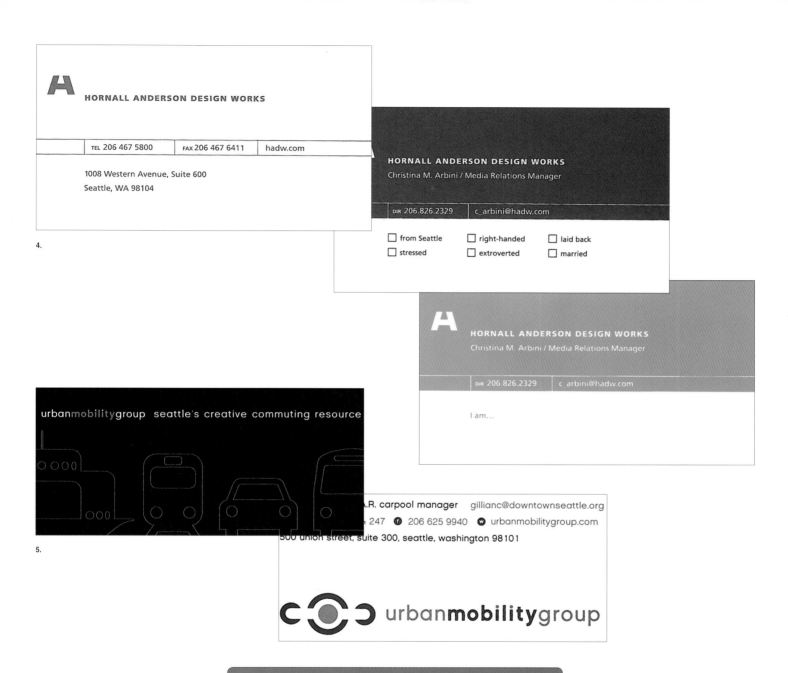

HORNALL ANDERSON DESIGN WORKS

TEL 206 467 5800 | FAX 206 467 6411 | hadw.com

1008 Western Avenue, Suite 600
Seattle, WA 98104

4.

HORNALL ANDERSON DESIGN WORKS
Christina M. Arbini / Media Relations Manager

DIR 206.826.2329 | c_arbini@hadw.com

☐ from Seattle   ☐ right-handed   ☐ laid back
☐ stressed   ☐ extroverted   ☐ married

HORNALL ANDERSON DESIGN WORKS
Christina M. Arbini / Media Relations Manager

DIR 206.826.2329 | c_arbini@hadw.com

I am...

urbanmobilitygroup seattle's creative commuting resource

5.

...A.R. carpool manager   gillianc@downtownseattle.org
...247   206 625 9940   urbanmobilitygroup.com
500 union street, suite 300, seattle, washington 98101

urbanmobilitygroup

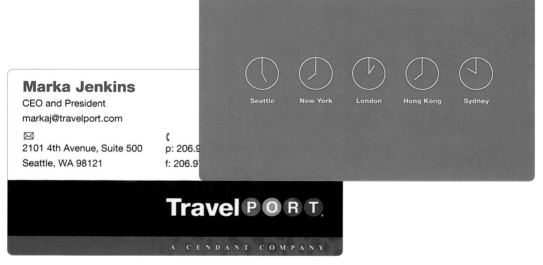

Seattle New York London Hong Kong Sydney

Marka Jenkins
CEO and President
markaj@travelport.com

✉
2101 4th Avenue, Suite 500   p: 206.9...
Seattle, WA 98121   f: 206.9...

TravelP O R T.

A CENDANT COMPANY

6.

(1-6)
Design Firm **Hornall Anderson Design Works**

1.
Client   Lease Crutcher Lewis
Designers   Jack Anderson, Katha Dalton,
             Belinda Bowling, Gretchen Cook,
             Andrew Smith
2.
Client   Maveron
Designers   Jack Anderson, Margaret Long
3.
Client   MetricsDirect
Designers   John Anicker, James Tee,
             Elmer dela Cruz, Kris Delaney
4.
Client   Hornall Anderson Design Works
Designers   John Hornall, Jack Anderson,
             Henry Yiu, Andrew Wicklund,
             Mark Popich
5.
Client   Urban Mobility Group
Designers   Jana Nishi, Belinda Bowling,
             Henry Yiu
6.
Client   Travelport
Designers   Lisa Cerveny, Andrew Wicklund,
             Andrew Smith, Jana Nishi,
             Hillary Radbill

19

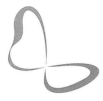

virtutech

Niklas Rudemo
General Manager, EMEA
mobile: +46 708 141 287
niklas@virtutech.com

Virtutech AB
Norrtullsgatan 15, 1tr
SE-113 27 Stockholm
Sweden

phone: +46 8 690 07 27
fax: +46 8 690 07 29
www.virtutech.com

1.

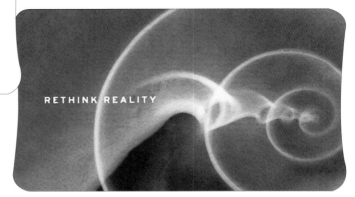

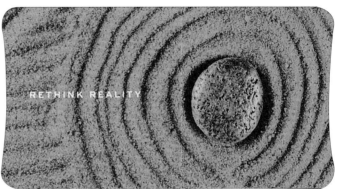

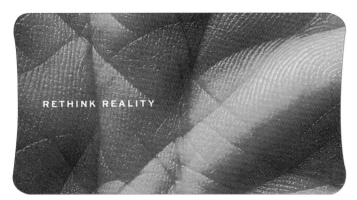

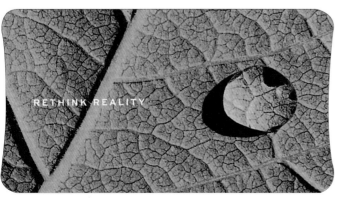

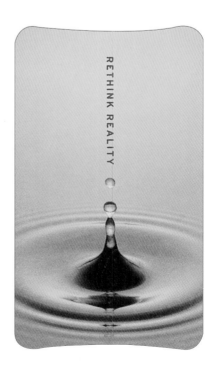

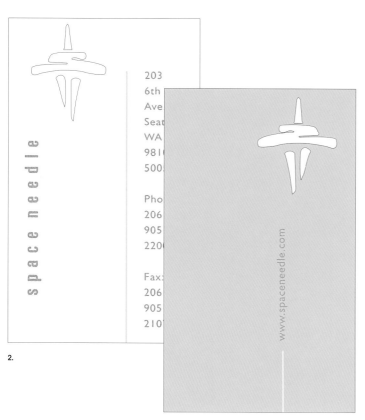

2.

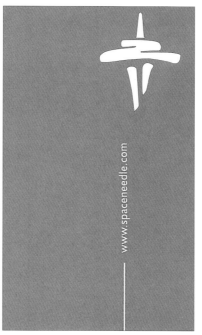

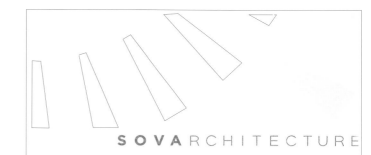

SOVARCHITECTURE

David Sova A.I.A. Principal
m 206 409 7458   **e** d_sova@SOVArchitecture.com

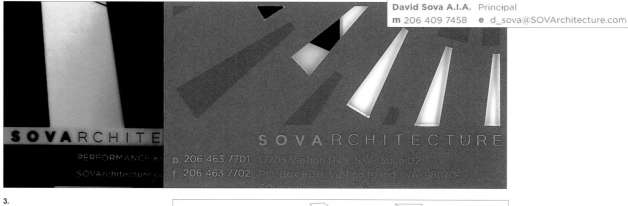

3.

SOVARCHITECTURE

DESIGN ART ARCHITECTURE

(1-3)
Design Firm **Hornall Anderson Design Works**

1.
Client   Virtutech
Designers   Daymon Bruck, Yuri Shvets
2.
Client   Space Needle
Designers   Jack Anderson, Mary Hermes,
             Gretchen Cook, Andrew Smith
3.
Client   SOVArchitecture
Designers   Jack Anderson, Larry Anderson,
             Henry Yiu

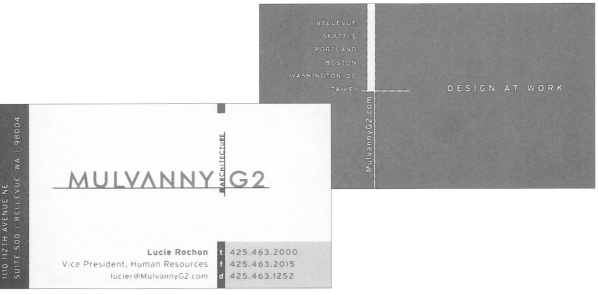

BELLEVUE
SEATTLE
PORTLAND
BOSTON
WASHINGTON, DC
TAIPEI

DESIGN AT WORK

MulvannyG2.com

ARCHITECTURE

MULVANNY G2

1110 112TH AVENUE NE
SUITE 500 | BELLEVUE · WA | 98004

Lucie Rochon
Vice President, Human Resources
lucier@MulvannyG2.com

t 425.463.2000
f 425.463.2015
d 425.463.1252

1.

Don Sorensen
Consultant
dsorensen@aerzone.com

AERZONE.

P.O. Box 610604
2967 N. Airfield Dr., Suite 230
DFW Airport, TX 75261

972 574 3606 Tel
972 574 5375 Fax

www.aerzone.com

2.

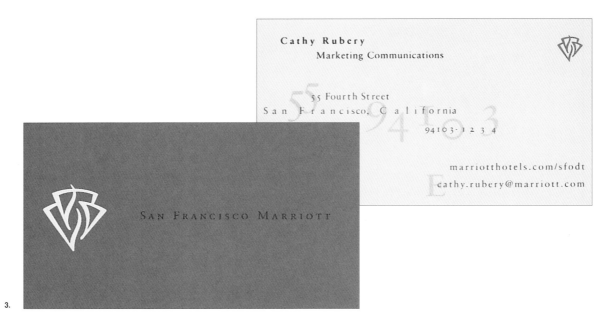

Cathy Rubery
Marketing Communications

55 Fourth Street
San Francisco, California
94103·1234

marriotthotels.com/sfodt
cathy.rubery@marriott.com

SAN FRANCISCO MARRIOTT

3.

Pace International, LLC

Rick Lewis

Service Representative

1403 Hidden Creek Lane   tel 863
Winter Haven, FL 33880   cell 863
rickl@paceint.com   fax 863

Corporate Office:
1011 Western Ave   cust ser
Suite 807   www.pa
Seattle, WA 98104

4.

PaceInternational

seeseattle.org

Seattle's Convention and Visitors Bureau

Darouny Syphachane *Housing Coordinator*

dsyphachane@seeseattle.org

520 Pike Street, Suite 1300, Seattle, WA 98101

T 206 461 5870   F 206 461 5853

5.

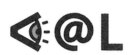

Seed IP

Seed Intellectual Property Law Group PLLC

telephone   206.622.4900
facsimile   206.682.6031
website   SeedIP.com

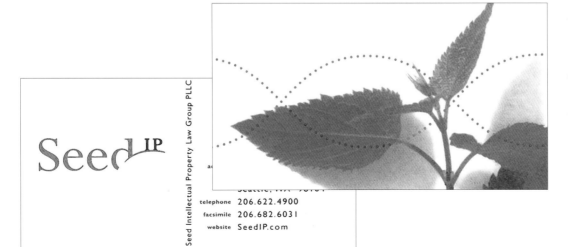

6.

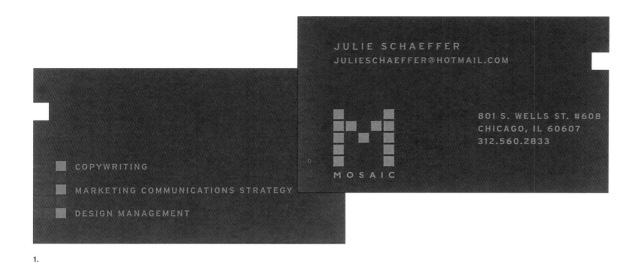

1.

JULIE SCHAEFFER
JULIESCHAEFFER@HOTMAIL.COM

M

MOSAIC

801 S. WELLS ST. #608
CHICAGO, IL 60607
312.560.2833

COPYWRITING

MARKETING COMMUNICATIONS STRATEGY

DESIGN MANAGEMENT

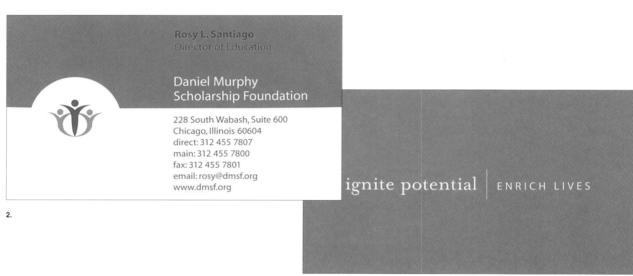

2.

Rosy L. Santiago
Director of Education

**Daniel Murphy
Scholarship Foundation**

228 South Wabash, Suite 600
Chicago, Illinois 60604
direct: 312 455 7807
main: 312 455 7800
fax: 312 455 7801
email: rosy@dmsf.org
www.dmsf.org

ignite potential | ENRICH LIVES

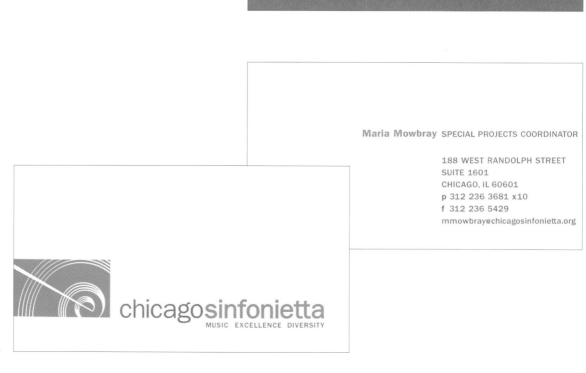

Maria Mowbray SPECIAL PROJECTS COORDINATOR

188 WEST RANDOLPH STREET
SUITE 1601
CHICAGO, IL 60601
p 312 236 3681 x10
f 312 236 5429
mmowbray@chicagosinfonietta.org

chicagosinfonietta
MUSIC EXCELLENCE DIVERSITY

3.

文学博士 ジョン・忠雄・寺本

インディアナポリス美術館
東洋課 学芸員

INDIANAPOLIS MUSEUM OF ART

John Tadao Teramoto, Ph.D.
Associate Curator of Asian Art

4000 Michigan Road
Indianapolis, Indiana U.S.A. 46208-3326
Tel 317-923-1331 **Fax** 317-926-8931
e-mail: jteramoto@ima-art.org
www.ima-art.org

4.

CONSUMER DRIVEN BRAND STRATEGY

ENVISION

SALLY DANCER PARTNER
E sally.dancer@brandenvision.com
V 847 412 5914
F 847 412 5901

630 DUNDEE ROAD SUITE 340
NORTHBROOK ILLINOIS 60062
www.brandenvision.com

5.

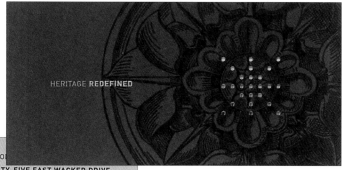

HERITAGE **REDEFINED**

THE O...
THIRTY-FIVE EAST WACKER DRIVE
SUITE 600 CHICAGO ILLINOIS 60601
T 312.726.4260 F 312.977.0919

MORRIS SHOHET PRESIDENT
mshohet@creit.ca

6.

(1-6)
Design Firm **Pressley Jacobs: a design
partnership**

1.
Client   Mosaic
Designer   Sarah Lin
2.
Client   Daniel Murphy Scholarship
            Foundation
Designers   William Lee Johnson,
            Jay Austin
3.
Client   Chicago Sinfonietta
Designer   Kara Kotwas
4.
Client   Indianapolis Museum of Art
Designers   Jay Austin, Kelly Bjork
5.
Client   Envision
Designer   Amy McCarter
6.
Client   Thirty-Five East Wacker Drive
Designer   Amy McCarter

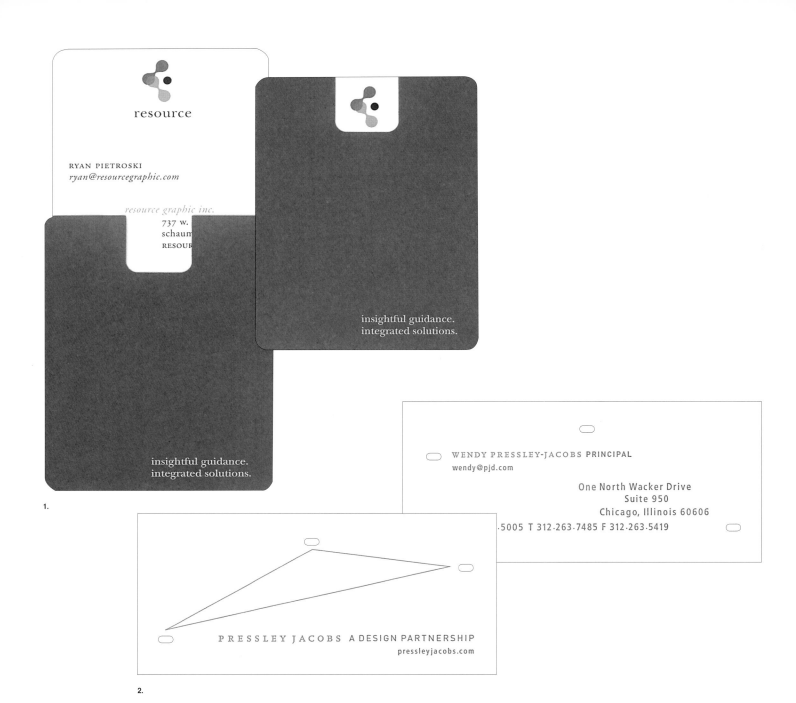

resource

RYAN PIETROSKI
ryan@resourcegraphic.com

resource graphic inc.

737 w.
schaum
RESOUF

insightful guidance.
integrated solutions.

insightful guidance.
integrated solutions.

1.

WENDY PRESSLEY-JACOBS PRINCIPAL
wendy@pjd.com

One North Wacker Drive
Suite 950
Chicago, Illinois 60606

.5005 T 312·263·7485 F 312·263·5419

PRESSLEY JACOBS A DESIGN PARTNERSHIP
pressleyjacobs.com

2.

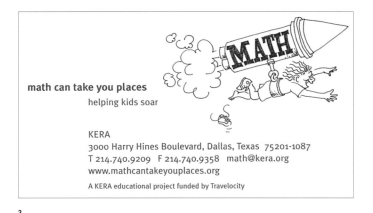

math can take you places

helping kids soar

KERA
3000 Harry Hines Boulevard, Dallas, Texas 75201-1087
T 214.740.9209 F 214.740.9358 math@kera.org
www.mathcantakeyouplaces.org

A KERA educational project funded by Travelocity

3.

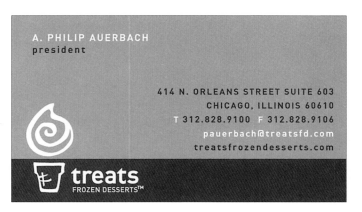

A. PHILIP AUERBACH
president

414 N. ORLEANS STREET SUITE 603
CHICAGO, ILLINOIS 60610
T 312.828.9100 F 312.828.9106
pauerbach@treatsfd.com
treatsfrozendesserts.com

treats
FROZEN DESSERTS™

4.

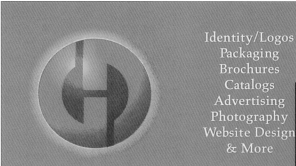

Identity/Logos
Packaging
Brochures
Catalogs
Advertising
Photography
Website Design
& More

5.

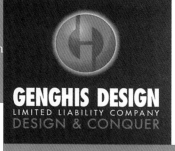

DALE MONAHAN
Creative Director/Designer

303-445-0001
Fax: 303-235-0310

dale@genghis-design.com
www.genghis-design.com

GENGHIS DESIGN
LIMITED LIABILITY COMPANY
DESIGN & CONQUER

2170 Tabor Drive, Lakewood, Colorado 80215

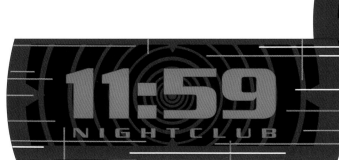

What Time Is It In Your World?

11:59

Charles Vanstrom
1669 Clarkson Street, Denver, CO 80218
Phone: 303.813.1159   Fax: 303.869.4989

11:59
NIGHTCLUB

6.

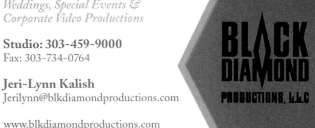

DIGITAL VIDEOGRAPHY -
Weddings, Special Events &
Corporate Video Productions

Studio: 303-459-9000
Fax: 303-734-0764

Jeri-Lynn Kalish
Jerilynn@blkdiamondproductions.com

www.blkdiamondproductions.com
6382 S. Williams St., Littleton, CO 80121

BLACK DIAMOND
PRODUCTIONS, LLC

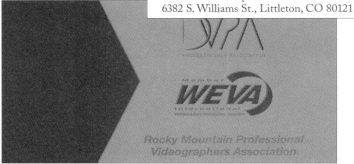

Member
WEVA
International

Rocky Mountain Professional
Videographers Association

7.

(1-4)
Design Firm **Pressley Jacobs: a design partnership**

(5-7)
Design Firm **Genghis Design, LLC**

1.
Client Resource Graphic
Designers Amy McCarter, Sarah Lin

2.
Client Pressley Jacobs: a design partnership
Designer Jef Anderson

3.
Client Math Can Take You Places
Designer Amy McCarter

4.
Client Treats Frozen Desserts
Designer Sarah Lin

5.
Client Genghis Design, LLC
Designer Dale Monahan

6.
Client 11:59 Nightclub
Designer Dale Monahan

7.
Client Black Diamond Productions, LLC
Designer Dale Monahan

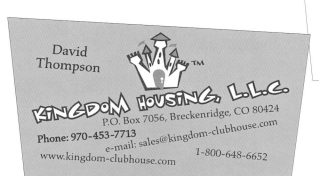

David
Thompson

KINGDOM HOUSING, L.L.C.
P.O. Box 7056, Breckenridge, CO 80424
Phone: 970-453-7713
e-mail: sales@kingdom-clubhouse.com
www.kingdom-clubhouse.com   1-800-648-6652

™

THE CLUBHOUSE, INC.

David
Thompson

P.O. Box 7056, Breckenridge, CO 80424
Phone: 970-453-7713
e-mail: sales@kingdom-clubhouse.com   Fax: 970-453-9060
www.kingdom-clubhouse.com

1.

All Phase
LANDSCAPE

Troy Tinberg

303.914.8370   Fax 303.914.8399
1301 South Pierce Street, Lakewood, Colorado 80

2.

*All Phase Landscape strives to be the most
respected landscape company in Colorado.
When you work with us, we want you to recognize
that our integrity, flexibility and
industry experience are the reasons we are able
to provide superior services and opportunities to our clients,
suppliers and employees.*

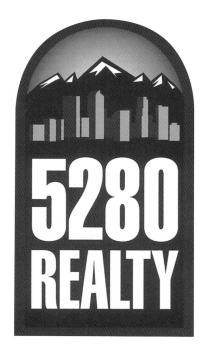

**5280
REALTY**

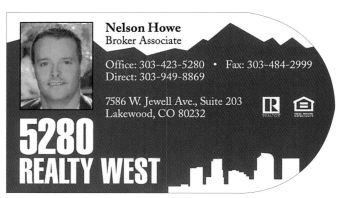

Nelson Howe
Broker Associate

Office: 303-423-5280   •   Fax: 303-484-2999
Direct: 303-949-8869

7586 W. Jewell Ave., Suite 203
Lakewood, CO 80232

**5280
REALTY WEST**

3.

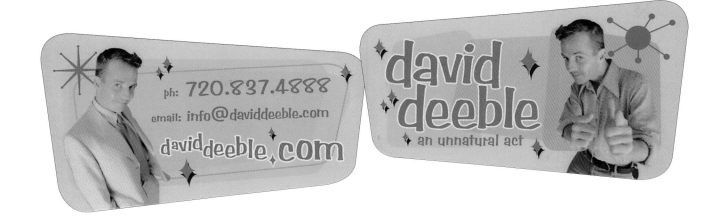

4.

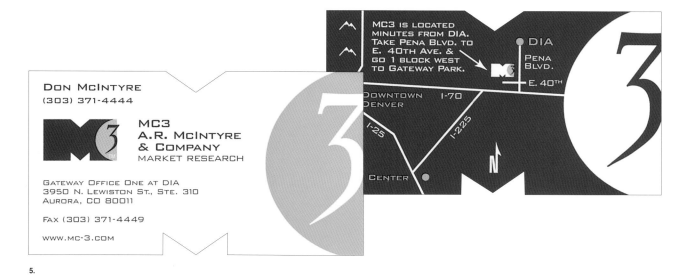

DON McINTYRE
(303) 371-4444

MC3
A.R. McINTYRE
& COMPANY
MARKET RESEARCH

GATEWAY OFFICE ONE at DIA
3950 N. LEWISTON ST., STE. 310
AURORA, CO 80011

Fax (303) 371-4449

www.mc-3.com

MC3 IS LOCATED MINUTES FROM DIA. TAKE PENA BLVD. TO E. 40TH AVE. & GO 1 BLOCK WEST TO GATEWAY PARK.

DIA
PENA BLVD.
E. 40TH
DOWNTOWN DENVER
I-70
I-25
I-225
CENTER

5.

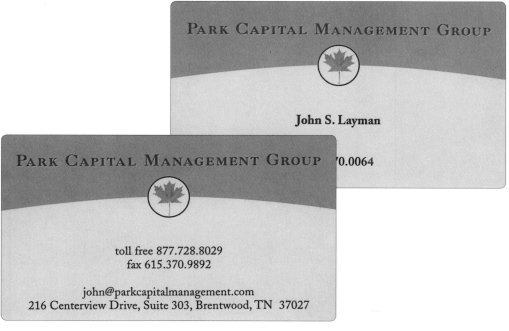

PARK CAPITAL MANAGEMENT GROUP

John S. Layman

70.0064

PARK CAPITAL MANAGEMENT GROUP

toll free 877.728.8029
fax 615.370.9892

john@parkcapitalmanagement.com
216 Centerview Drive, Suite 303, Brentwood, TN 37027

6.

(1-6)
Design Firm **Genghis Design, LLC**

1.
Client   Kingdom Housing,LLC/
             The Clubhouse, Inc.
Designer   Dale Monahan
2.
Client   All Phase Landscape
Designer   Dale Monahan
3.
Client   5280 Realty
Designer   Dale Monahan
4.
Client   David Deeble
Designers   Dale Monahan,
             Brian D'Agosta
5.
Client   MC3, A.R. McIntyre & Company
Designer   Dale Monahan
6.
Client   Park Capital Management Group
Designer   Dale Monahan

29

SERVICES PROVIDED
* COMMERCIAL/RESIDENTIAL
* DESIGN / INSTALLATION
* RADIANT & FORCED AIR HEATING
* CENTRAL AIR CONDITIONING
* AIR FILTRATION / HUMIDIFICATION
* WATER HEATER REPLACEMENTS
* ENDLESS HOT WATER SYSTEMS
* PROFESSIONAL MAINTENANCE SERV
* FLAT RATE, BY THE JOB PRICING
* CONSULTING

1.

TOM WOLVIN

303.346.3466
FAX: 720.344.6688

2277 WEST HYACINTH RD.
HIGHLANDS RANCH, CO 80126
E-MAIL: HORIZONM1@AOL.COM

HORIZON™
MECHANICAL, INC.
HEATING & AIR CONDITIONING
"FOR A COMFORTABLE FUTURE NOW"

DENVER ORAL & MAXILLOFACIAL
SURGERY ASSOCIATES

Mark D. Berman, D.D.S., M.S., P.C.

303-694-1700 • Fax 303-773-6825
8200 E. Belleview Ave., Suite 515E
Greenwood Village, CO 80111

303-948-9663 • Fax 303-773-6825
7325 South Pierce, Suite 204
Littleton, CO 80123
e-mail: denveroms@ibm.net

2.

consulting + development
for creative service firms

pound
interactive

jeremy pound
jeremy@poundi.com

6463 la costa drive # 604
boca raton florida 33433
561.367.8704
www.poundi.com

3.

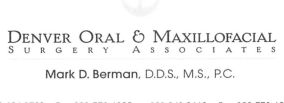

561.302.6525 | info@victoriacave.com

Victoria Cave   interior refiner

Peace, like charity, begins at home.

- Franklin D. Roosevelt

4.

matthew cave
PRINCIPAL

CAVE DESIGN AGENCY
phone 561.417.0780 *fax* 561.417.0490
3500 nw boca raton blvd, 808, boca raton, fl 33431
email matt@cavedesign.com *web* cavedesign.com

5.

cave

Where thinking + feeling live.

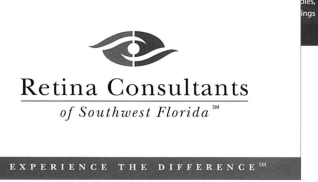

Joseph P. Walker M.D., F.A.C.S.
Glenn L. Wing M.D., F.A.C.S.
Paul A. Raskauskas M.D., F.A.C.S.
Tom Ghuman M.D., F.A.C.S.
Donald C. Fletcher M.D.

info@eye.md

2668 Winkler Ave
Fort Myers, FL 33901
Tel (239) 939.4323
FL (800) 282.8281
Fax (239) 939.4712
www.eye.md

Retina Consultants
of Southwest Florida ℠

EXPERIENCE THE DIFFERENCE ℠

6.

(1,2)
Design Firm **Genghis Design, LLC**
(3-6)
Design Firm **Cave Design Agency**

1.
    Client   Horizon Mechanical, Inc.
    Designer   Dale Monahan
2.
    Client   Denver Oral & Maxillofacial
    Designer   Dale Monahan
3.
    Client   Pound Interactive
    Designers   Matt Cave, David Edmundson
4.
    Client   Victoria Cave
    Designers   Matt Cave, David Edmundson
5.
    Client   Cave Design Agency
    Designers   Matt Cave, David Edmundson
6.
    Client   Retina Consultants of
                Southwest Florida
    Designers   Matt Cave, David Edmundson

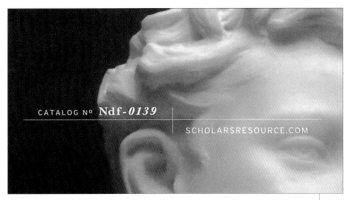

CATALOG Nº *Ndf-0139*

SCHOLARSRESOURCE.COM

1.

SCHOLARS
RESOURCE

KURT WIEDENHOEFT | President / Co-Founder

KURT@SCHOLARSRESOURCE.COM | FIVE HORIZON LANE
FREEPORT, MAINE 04032
TEL 800.688.3040

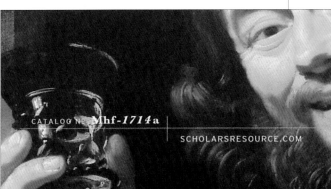

CATALOG Nº *Mhf-1714a*

SCHOLARSRESOURCE.COM

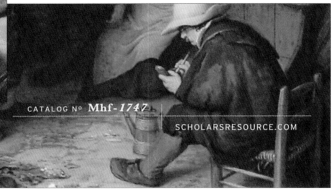

CATALOG Nº *Mhf-1747*

SCHOLARSRESOURCE.COM

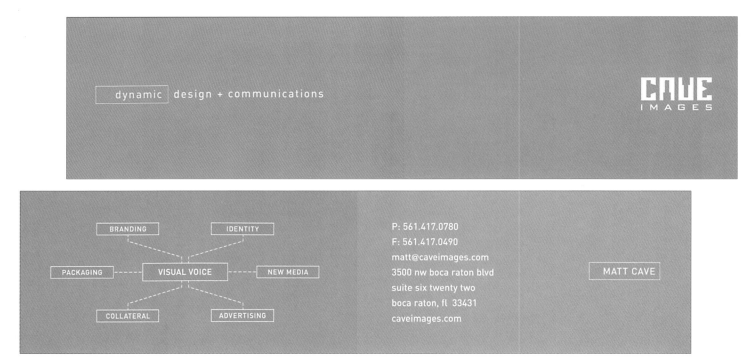

dynamic | design + communications

CAVE
IMAGES

BRANDING   IDENTITY

PACKAGING ---- VISUAL VOICE ---- NEW MEDIA

COLLATERAL   ADVERTISING

P: 561.417.0780
F: 561.417.0490
matt@caveimages.com
3500 nw boca raton blvd
suite six twenty two
boca raton, fl 33431
caveimages.com

MATT CAVE

2.

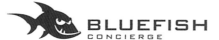

3.

STEVE SIMS
SSIMS@THEBLUEFISH.COM

TEL 866.270.3879 | CELL 561.251.2096 | FAX 775.239.1057
777 E. ATLANTIC AVE SUITE Z251 | DELRAY BEACH FL 33483

WWW.THEBLUEFISH.COM

Marc Holbik
marc@ecoripe.com

ECORIPE TROPICALS
750 Middle River Drive
Fort Lauderdale, FL 33304

P 954 599 0480
F 866 842 8825
www.ecoripe.com

The sweet taste of quality.

4.

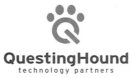

QuestingHound
technology partners

John Boden
Managing Partner

3650 N Federal Hwy, Ste 215
Lighthouse Point, FL 33064

Phone: 954.727.2200 ext: 155
Fax: 954.727.2201

jboden@questinghound.com
www.questinghound.com

5.

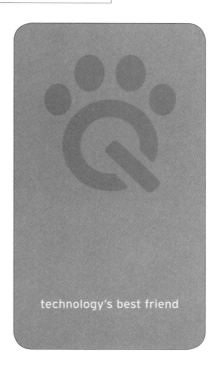

technology's best friend

Apple Valley Villa
14610 Garrett Avenue
Apple Valley, Minnesota
55124-7518

marketing@applevalleyvilla.com
tel: 952.431.8016
fax: 952.431.9923
www.applevalleyvilla.com

1.

Kay Midtvedt
Rental Consultant

Apple Valley Villa
YOUR COMMUNITY

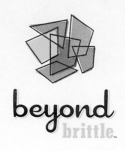

beyond
brittle.™

Scott Walter
President and Mad Brittler

P.O. Box 47185
Plymouth MN 55447
612 804 6664
scott@beyondbrittle.com

smart copy that moves

brain **traffic**

3.

KRISTINA HALVORSON
copywriter

2392 doswell avenue
saint paul, mn 55108

tel 651 646 7500

cel 612 644 3510

khalvorson@braintraffic.com

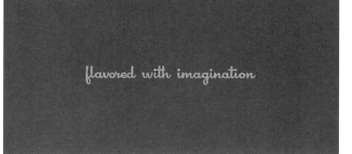

flavored with imagination

2.

4.

_ photo grA

a
ph y

photo grAphy   — — -   one eighty-eight south delAcy Ave
pAsAdena cA 91105
ph_626_440_1974
fx_626_577_8036
ann@cutting.com

Ann e. cutting

w w w . c u t t i n g . c o m

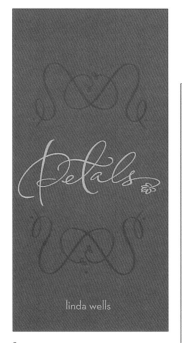

927 nicollet mall minneapolis
minnesota, 54O2
www.petals-floral-design.com

for you

linda wells

5.

telephone {612} 339 OO65
info@petals-floral-design.com
fax {612} 339 1165

Leading Strategically

Insights and Tools for CEOs,
Senior Managers, and HR Leaders

Candy Armstead
registrations

29OO HIGHWOODS BOULEVARD
RALEIGH, NC 27604-1O6O

919-878-9222 (Raleigh) or 336-668-7746 (Greensboro)
www.capital.org

29th
ANNUAL

MANAGEMENT
CONFERENCE

6.

C2 Investment Group

David Silvas
dsilvas@c2ig.com

CORPORATE OFFICE
19901 W. Catawba Ave.
Suite 205
Cornelius, NC 28031
www.c2ig.com

888.327.1422 **TEL**
704.987.8730 **FAX**

7.

(1-5)
Design Firm **Graphiculture, Inc.**
(6,7)
Design Firm **CAI Communications**

1.
Client   Apple Valley Villa
Designer   Chad Olson
2.
Client   Beyond Brittle
Designer   Lindsay Little
3.
Client   Brain Traffic
Designer   Lindsay Little
4.
Client   Ann E. Cutting
Designer   Chad Olson
5.
Client   Petals
Designer   Chad Olson
6.
Client   Capital Associated Industries
Designer   Beth Greene
7.
Client   C2 Investment Group
Designers   Steve McCulloch, Debra Rezeli

henry vizcarra
creative director

henry@30sixtydesign.com

2801 cahuenga blvd. west
los angeles, california 90068
voice 323 850 5311
fax 323 850 6638
www.30sixtydesign.com

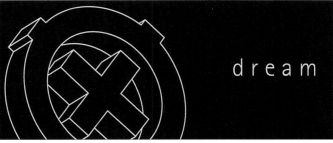

dream

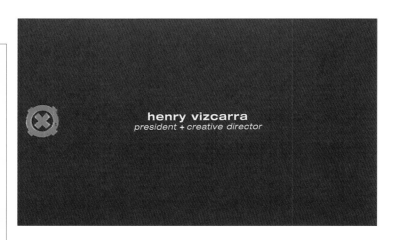

explore

navigate

1.

30sixtyadvertising+design

2801 cahuenga blvd west
los angeles california 90068

ph + 323 850 5311
cl + 213 810 4222
fx + 323 850 6638

par@30sixtydesign.com
www.30sixtydesign.com

2.

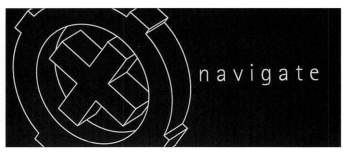

henry vizcarra
president + creative director

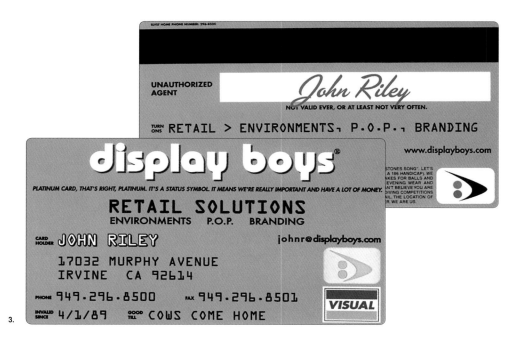

ELVIS' HOME PHONE NUMBER: 296-8500

UNAUTHORIZED
AGENT

John Riley

NOT VALID EVER, OR AT LEAST NOT VERY OFTEN.

TURN
ONS RETAIL > ENVIRONMENTS, P.O.P., BRANDING

www.displayboys.com

display boys®

PLATINUM CARD, THAT'S RIGHT, PLATINUM. IT'S A STATUS SYMBOL. IT MEANS WE'RE REALLY IMPORTANT AND HAVE A LOT OF MONEY.

RETAIL SOLUTIONS
ENVIRONMENTS   P.O.P.   BRANDING

CARD
HOLDER JOHN RILEY

17032 MURPHY AVENUE
IRVINE CA 92614

PHONE 949.296.8500   FAX 949.296.8501

INVALID
SINCE 4/1/89   GOOD
TILL COWS COME HOME

johnr@displayboys.com

VISUAL

3.

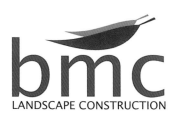

bmc
LANDSCAPE CONSTRUCTION

80 Tannock Street Balwyn North Victoria 3104
www.bmclandscape.com

Bernard McInerney
0418 173 358
bernie@bmclandscape.com

QUALITY WORK BY PROFESSIONALS
OUTDOOR LIGHTING | DECKING
PERGOLAS | PAVING | LAWNS
RETAINING WALLS
WATER FEATURES
COURTYARDS

4.

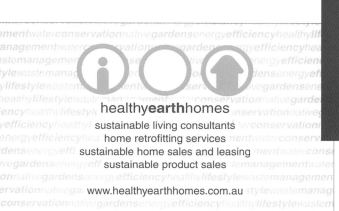

healthy**earth**homes

sustainable living consultants
home retrofitting services
sustainable home sales and leasing
sustainable product sales

www.healthyearthhomes.com.au

5.

daniel **pleiter**

p 03 9789 2626
m 0407 026 025
w www.healthyearthhomes.com.au
e dan@healthyearthhomes.com.au

healthy**earth**homes

change for a healthy earth, home and lifestyle...

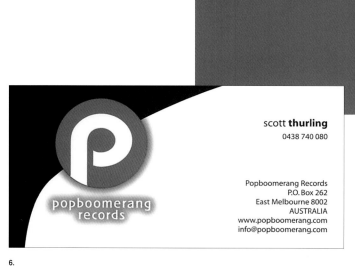

scott **thurling**

0438 740 080

Popboomerang Records
P.O. Box 262
East Melbourne 8002
AUSTRALIA
www.popboomerang.com
info@popboomerang.com

6.

(1-2)
Design Firm **30sixty advertising+design**
(3)
Design Firm **Display Boys**
(4-6)
Design Firm **At First Sight**

1, 2.
Client   30sixty advertising+design
Designers   Henry Vizcarra, Pär Larsson,
           Kae Singhaseni
3.
Client   Display Boys
Designers   Darin Rassmussen, John Riley
4.
Client   BMC Landscape Construction
Designers   Olivia Brown, Barry Selleck
5.
Client   Healthy Earth Homes
Designers   Olivia Brown, Barry Selleck
6.
Client   Popboomerang Records
Designers   Olivia Brown, Barry Selleck

1.

■ wpi **finance**

| homes | personal | business

■ wpi **building**

| domestic | commercial

■ wpi **investment**

| property | shares | opportunities

your **next** appointment _____

■ ray **tweedly**
manager
construction

26a upton street
altona victoria 3018
australia

t +61 1300 882 002
f +61 1300 882 001
m 0401 038 957

i www.werwpi.com
e ouroffice@werwpi.com

ACN 097 694 525

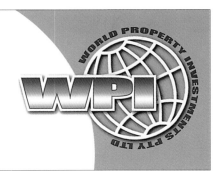

2.

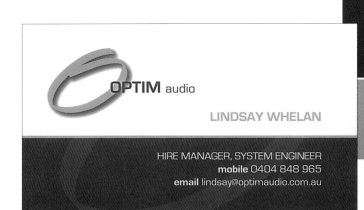

OPTIM audio

LINDSAY WHELAN

HIRE MANAGER, SYSTEM ENGINEER
mobile 0404 848 965
email lindsay@optimaudio.com.au

HIRE | SALES
SERVICE | INSTALLATION
LIVE DIGITAL (O/B) RECORDING
SCHOOL AND THEATRE PRODUCTIONS
CORPORATE AND AUDIO/VISUAL THEMING
COMMUNITY EVENTS

Factory One, 34 Cumberland Drive (P.O.Box 2174) Seaford VIC 3198
phone +61 3 8796 3954
fax +61 3 8796 3957
www.optimaudio.com.au

3.

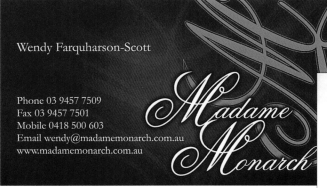

Wendy Farquharson-Scott

Phone 03 9457 7509
Fax 03 9457 7501
Mobile 0418 500 603
Email wendy@madamemonarch.com.au
www.madamemonarch.com.au

Madame Monarch

Designer Silk Masquerade Masks

Magical Silk Wings

Hand Crafted In Australia

Unique Art For Use & Display

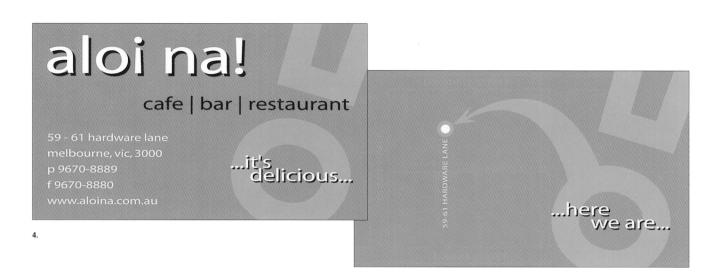

aloi na!

cafe | bar | restaurant

59 - 61 hardware lane
melbourne, vic, 3000
p 9670-8889
f 9670-8880
www.aloina.com.au

...it's delicious...

59-61 HARDWARE LANE

...here we are...

4.

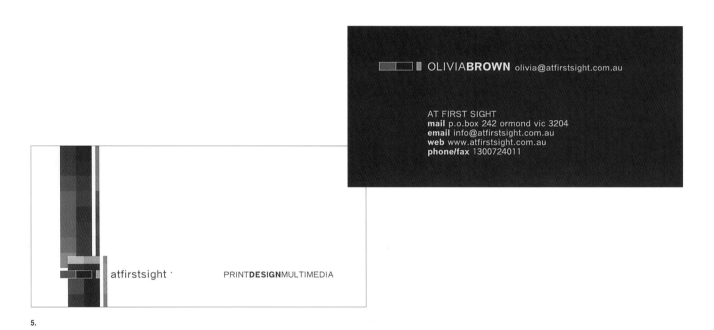

OLIVIA**BROWN** olivia@atfirstsight.com.au

AT FIRST SIGHT
mail p.o.box 242 ormond vic 3204
email info@atfirstsight.com.au
web www.atfirstsight.com.au
phone/fax 1300724011

atfirstsight · PRINT**DESIGN**MULTIMEDIA

5.

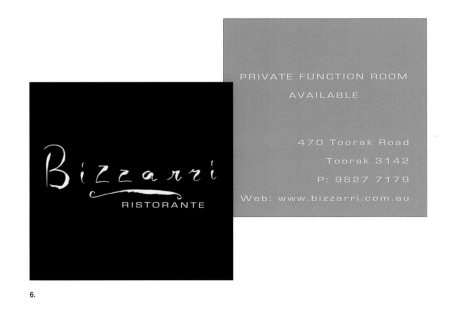

PRIVATE FUNCTION ROOM

AVAILABLE

470 Toorak Road

Toorak 3142

P: 9827 7179

Web: www.bizzarri.com.au

Bizzarri RISTORANTE

6.

(1-6)
Design Firm **At First Sight**

1.
Client   World Property Investments
Designers   Olivia Brown, Barry Selleck
2.
Client   Optim Audio
Designers   Olivia Brown, Barry Selleck
3.
Client   Madame Monarch
Designers   Olivia Brown, Barry Selleck
4.
Client   Aloi Na!
Designers   Olivia Brown, Barry Selleck
5.
Client   At First Sight
Designers   Olivia Brown, Barry Selleck
6.
Client   Bizzarri Ristorante
Designers   Olivia Brown, Barry Selleck

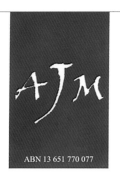

1.

A.J. (Tony) McInerney

1685 Malvern Road, Glen Iris,
Victoria, 3124

mobile) 0408 831 946

email) tony.mcinerney@telstra.com

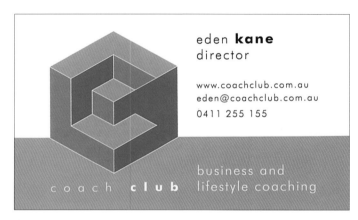

K5 Trading
licenced second-hand dealers
Eden & Jo 03 9773 9547 or 0411 255 155
We buy and sell second-hand goods...
...antiques, old wares, furniture, collectables, house lots

2.

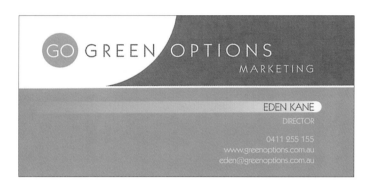

GO GREEN OPTIONS
MARKETING

EDEN KANE
DIRECTOR

0411 255 155
www.greenoptions.com.au
eden@greenoptions.com.au

3.

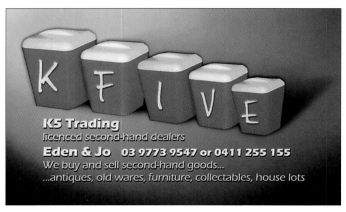

eden **kane**
director

www.coachclub.com.au
eden@coachclub.com.au
0411 255 155

coach club   business and
lifestyle coaching

4.

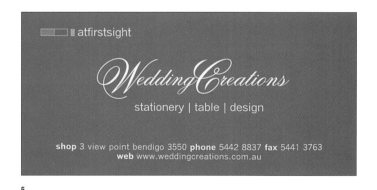

■ atfirstsight

Wedding Creations

stationery | table | design

shop 3 view point bendigo 3550 **phone** 5442 8837 **fax** 5441 3763
web www.weddingcreations.com.au

5.

Gabriel Sponsler
Technical Specialist

411 Pacific Street
Suite 307
Monterey, CA 93940
Tel 831-648-8111
Fax 831-648-8113
www.montereybay.com
Email gabe@montereybay.com

montereybay.com

6.

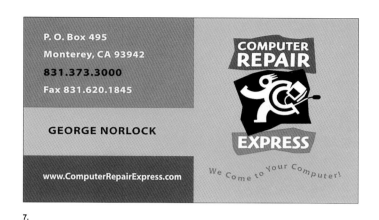

7.

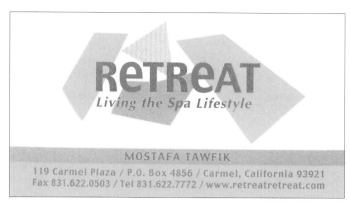

8.

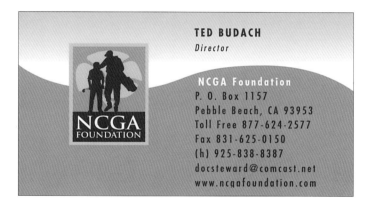

9.

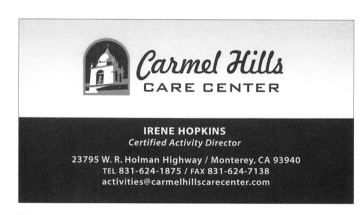

10.

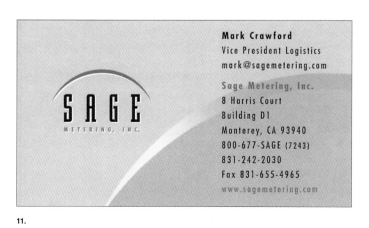

11.

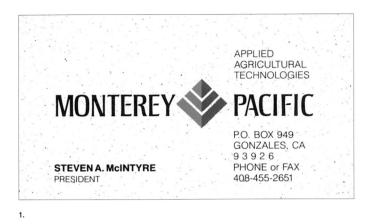

APPLIED
AGRICULTURAL
TECHNOLOGIES

MONTEREY PACIFIC

P.O. BOX 949
GONZALES, CA
93926
PHONE or FAX
408-455-2651

STEVEN A. McINTYRE
PRESIDENT

1.

RICHARD P. DeMARCO
President /CEO

AQUAFUTURE

THE AQUAFUTURE CORPORATION
5-B HARRIS COURT
MONTEREY, CA 93940
TEL 408-648-1998
FAX 408-648-1968
rdemarco@aquafuturecorp.com

2.

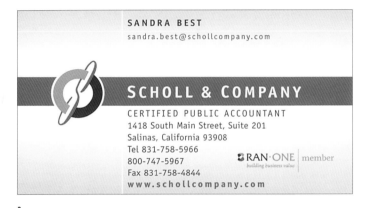

SANDRA BEST
sandra.best@schollcompany.com

SCHOLL & COMPANY

CERTIFIED PUBLIC ACCOUNTANT
1418 South Main Street, Suite 201
Salinas, California 93908
Tel 831-758-5966
800-747-5967
Fax 831-758-4844
www.schollcompany.com

RAN·ONE | member
building business value

3.

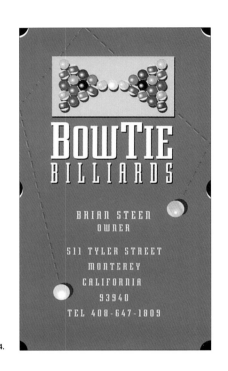

BOWTIE
BILLIARDS

BRIAN STEEN
OWNER

511 TYLER STREET
MONTEREY
CALIFORNIA
93940
TEL 408-647-1809

4.

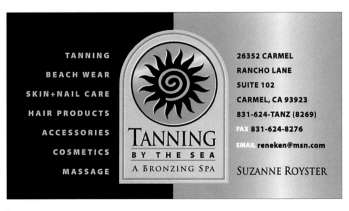

TANNING
BEACH WEAR
SKIN+NAIL CARE
HAIR PRODUCTS
ACCESSORIES
COSMETICS
MASSAGE

TANNING
BY THE SEA
A BRONZING SPA

26352 CARMEL
RANCHO LANE
SUITE 102
CARMEL, CA 93923
831-624-TANZ (8269)
FAX 831-624-8276
EMAIL reneken@msn.com

SUZANNE ROYSTER

5.

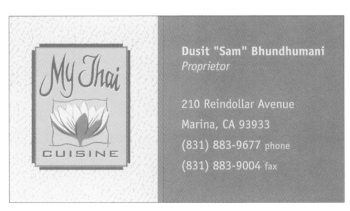

My Thai
CUISINE

Dusit "Sam" Bhundhumani
Proprietor

210 Reindollar Avenue
Marina, CA 93933
(831) 883-9677 phone
(831) 883-9004 fax

6.

42

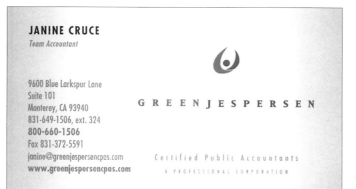

JANINE CRUCE
Team Accountant

9600 Blue Larkspur Lane
Suite 101
Monterey, CA 93940
831-649-1506, ext. 324
800-660-1506
Fax 831-372-5591
janine@greenjespersencpas.com
www.greenjespersencpas.com

GREEN JESPERSEN

Certified Public Accountants
A PROFESSIONAL CORPORATION

7.

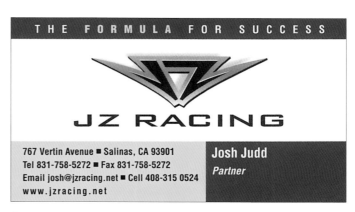

CULINARY CENTER OF MONTEREY

Mary Pagan CHEF/OWNER

625 CANNERY ROW / MONTEREY, CA 93940
TEL 831-333-2133 / FAX 831-333-2127
info@culinarycenterofmonterey.com
www.culinarycenterofmonterey.com

8.

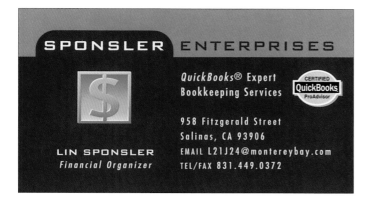

SPONSLER ENTERPRISES

QuickBooks® Expert
Bookkeeping Services

CERTIFIED
QuickBooks
ProAdvisor

958 Fitzgerald Street
Salinas, CA 93906
EMAIL L21J24@montereybay.com
TEL/FAX 831.449.0372

LIN SPONSLER
Financial Organizer

9.

THE FORMULA FOR SUCCESS

JZ RACING

767 Vertin Avenue ■ Salinas, CA 93901
Tel 831-758-5272 ■ Fax 831-758-5272
Email josh@jzracing.net ■ Cell 408-315 0524
www.jzracing.net

Josh Judd
Partner

10.

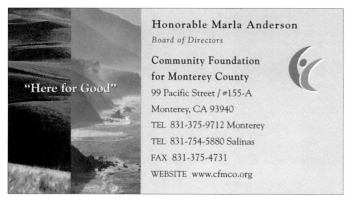

"Here for Good"

Honorable Marla Anderson
Board of Directors

**Community Foundation
for Monterey County**
99 Pacific Street / #155-A
Monterey, CA 93940
TEL 831-375-9712 Monterey
TEL 831-754-5880 Salinas
FAX 831-375-4731
WEBSITE www.cfmco.org

11.

(1-11)
Design Firm **The Wecker Group**

1.
Client Monterey Pacific
Designer Robert Wecker
2.
Client Aquafuture
Designer Robert Wecker
3.
Client Scholl & Company
Designer Robert Wecker
4.
Client Bow Tie Billiards
Designers Matt Gnibus, Robert Wecker
5.
Client Tanning by the Sea
Designers Matt Gnibus, Robert Wecker
6.
Client My Thai Cuisine
Designers Kevin Wecker, Robert Wecker

7.
Client Green Jespersen CPA
Designers Robert Wecker, Tremayne Cryer,
Sponsler Enterprises
8.
Client Culinary Center of Monterey
Designer Robert Wecker
9.
Client MontereyBay.com
Designer Robert Wecker
10.
Client JZ Racing
Designers Matt Gnibus, Robert Wecker
11.
Client Community Foundation for
Monterey County
Designer Robert Wecker

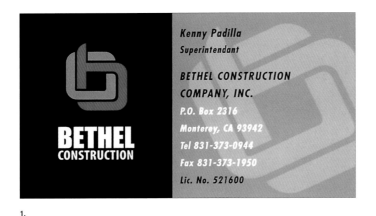

Kenny Padilla
Superintendant

**BETHEL CONSTRUCTION
COMPANY, INC.**

P.O. Box 2316
Monterey, CA 93942
Tel 831-373-0944
Fax 831-373-1950
Lic. No. 521600

1.

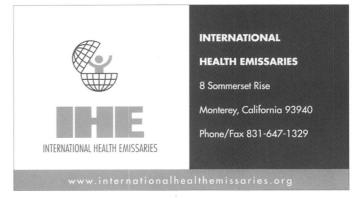

**INTERNATIONAL
HEALTH EMISSARIES**

8 Sommerset Rise

Monterey, California 93940

Phone/Fax 831-647-1329

www.internationalhealthemissaries.org

2.

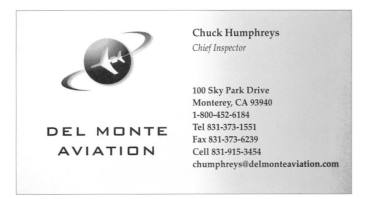

Chuck Humphreys
Chief Inspector

100 Sky Park Drive
Monterey, CA 93940
1-800-452-6184
Tel 831-373-1551
Fax 831-373-6239
Cell 831-915-3454
chumphreys@delmonteaviation.com

DEL MONTE
AVIATION

3.

John Bigham

P.O. BOX

223201

CARMEL,

CALIFORNIA

93922

408-624-7338

FAX 408-624-7127

4.

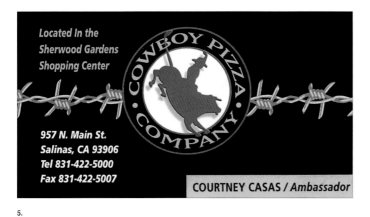

Located In the
Sherwood Gardens
Shopping Center

957 N. Main St.
Salinas, CA 93906
Tel 831-422-5000
Fax 831-422-5007

COURTNEY CASAS / Ambassador

5.

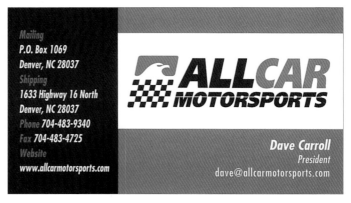

Mailing
P.O. Box 1069
Denver, NC 28037
Shipping
1633 Highway 16 North
Denver, NC 28037
Phone 704-483-9340
Fax 704-483-4725
Website
www.allcarmotorsports.com

Dave Carroll
President
dave@allcarmotorsports.com

6.

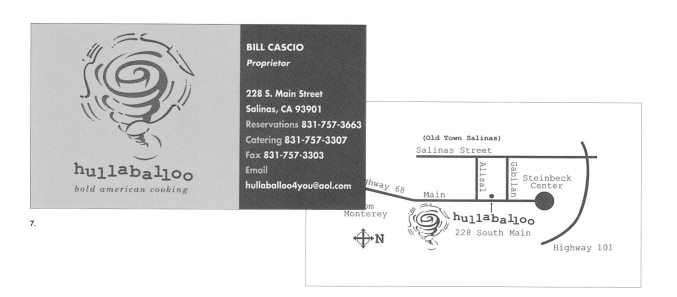

BILL CASCIO

Proprietor

228 S. Main Street
Salinas, CA 93901
Reservations 831-757-3663
Catering 831-757-3307
Fax 831-757-3303
Email
hullaballoo4you@aol.com

hullaballoo

bold american cooking

(Old Town Salinas)
Salinas Street
Highway 68
Main
Monterey
N
Alisal
Gabilan
Steinbeck Center
hullaballoo
228 South Main
Highway 101

7.

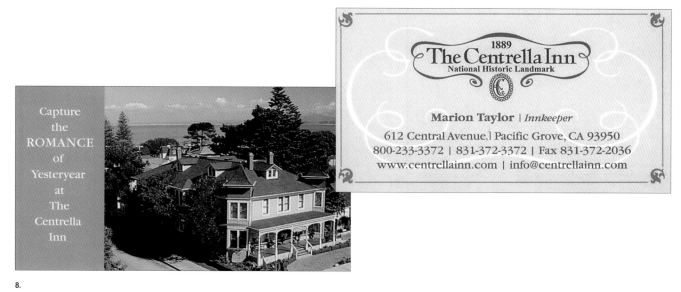

Capture
the
ROMANCE
of
Yesteryear
at
The
Centrella
Inn

1889
The Centrella Inn
National Historic Landmark

Marion Taylor | *Innkeeper*
612 Central Avenue | Pacific Grove, CA 93950
800-233-3372 | 831-372-3372 | Fax 831-372-2036
www.centrellainn.com | info@centrellainn.com

8.

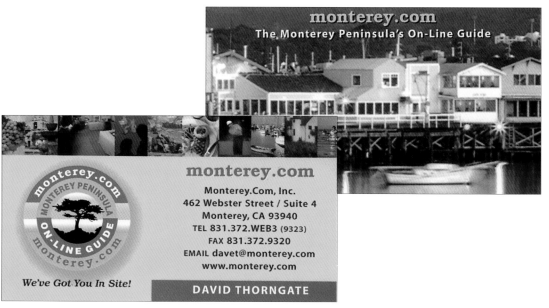

monterey.com
The Monterey Peninsula's On-Line Guide

MONTEREY PENINSULA
ON-LINE GUIDE
monterey.com

We've Got You In Site!

monterey.com

Monterey.Com, Inc.
462 Webster Street / Suite 4
Monterey, CA 93940
TEL 831.372.WEB3 (9323)
FAX 831.372.9320
EMAIL davet@monterey.com
www.monterey.com

DAVID THORNGATE

9.

(1-9)
Design Firm **The Wecker Group**

1.
Client   Bethel Construction
Designer   Robert Wecker
2.
Client   International Health Emissaries
Designer   Robert Wecker
3.
Client   Del Monte Aviation
Designers   Matt Gnibus, Robert Wecker
4.
Client   John Bigham Racing
Designer   Robert Wecker
5.
Client   Cowboy Pizza Company
Designers   Robert Wecker, Courtney Casas,
                Tremayne Cryer
6.
Client   Allison Carroll Motorsports
Designer   Robert Wecker
7.
Client   Hullaballoo
Designers   Robert Wecker, Tremayne Cryer
8.
Client   The Centrella Inn
Designers   Robert Wecker, Matt Gnibus
9.
Client   Monterey.com
Designer   Robert Wecker

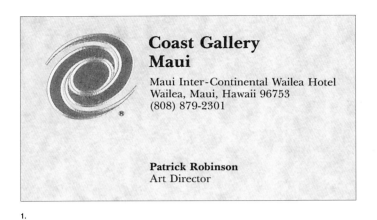

**Coast Gallery
Maui**

Maui Inter-Continental Wailea Hotel
Wailea, Maui, Hawaii 96753
(808) 879-2301

Patrick Robinson
Art Director

1.

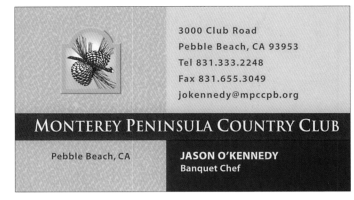

3000 Club Road
Pebble Beach, CA 93953
Tel 831.333.2248
Fax 831.655.3049
jokennedy@mpccpb.org

MONTEREY PENINSULA COUNTRY CLUB

Pebble Beach, CA

JASON O'KENNEDY
Banquet Chef

2.

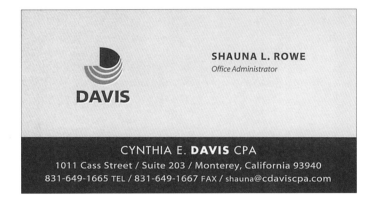

SHAUNA L. ROWE
Office Administrator

DAVIS

CYNTHIA E. DAVIS CPA
1011 Cass Street / Suite 203 / Monterey, California 93940
831-649-1665 TEL / 831-649-1667 FAX / shauna@cdaviscpa.com

3.

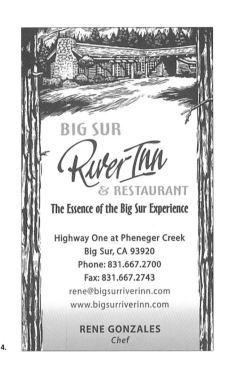

BIG SUR
River Inn
& RESTAURANT

The Essence of the Big Sur Experience

Highway One at Pheneger Creek
Big Sur, CA 93920
Phone: 831.667.2700
Fax: 831.667.2743
rene@bigsurriverinn.com
www.bigsurriverinn.com

RENE GONZALES
Chef

4.

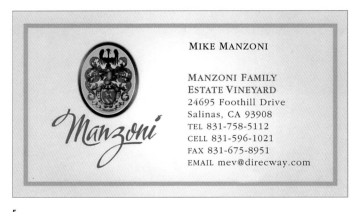

MIKE MANZONI

MANZONI FAMILY
ESTATE VINEYARD
24695 Foothill Drive
Salinas, CA 93908
TEL 831-758-5112
CELL 831-596-1021
FAX 831-675-8951
EMAIL mev@direcway.com

5.

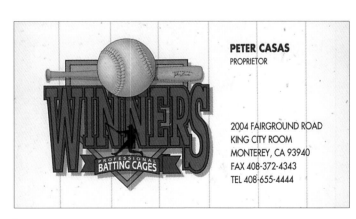

PETER CASAS
PROPRIETOR

WINNERS
PROFESSIONAL
BATTING CAGES

2004 FAIRGROUND ROAD
KING CITY ROOM
MONTEREY, CA 93940
FAX 408-372-4343
TEL 408-655-4444

6.

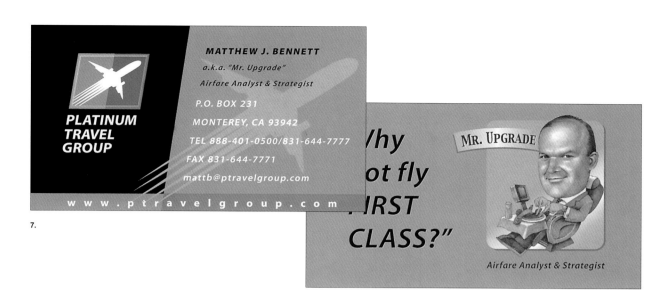

MATTHEW J. BENNETT

a.k.a. "Mr. Upgrade"

Airfare Analyst & Strategist

P.O. BOX 231

MONTEREY, CA 93942

TEL 888-401-0500/831-644-7777

FAX 831-644-7771

mattb@ptravelgroup.com

www.ptravelgroup.com

Why not fly FIRST CLASS?"

MR. UPGRADE

Airfare Analyst & Strategist

7.

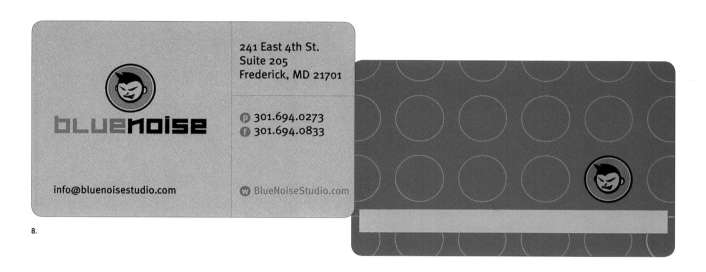

241 East 4th St.
Suite 205
Frederick, MD 21701

bluenoise

301.694.0273
301.694.0833

info@bluenoisestudio.com

BlueNoiseStudio.com

8.

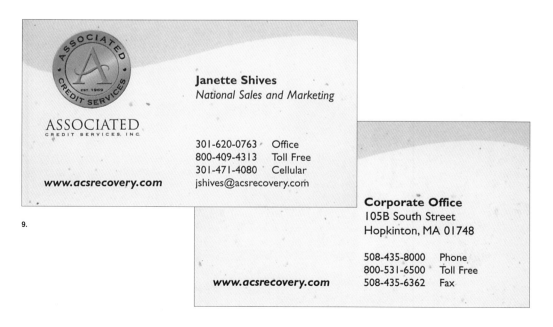

Janette Shives

National Sales and Marketing

ASSOCIATED
CREDIT SERVICES, INC.

301-620-0763   Office
800-409-4313   Toll Free
301-471-4080   Cellular

www.acsrecovery.com

jshives@acsrecovery.com

Corporate Office
105B South Street
Hopkinton, MA 01748

508-435-8000   Phone
800-531-6500   Toll Free
508-435-6362   Fax

www.acsrecovery.com

9.

(1-7)
Design Firm **The Wecker Group**
(8,9)
Design Firm **Octavo Designs**

1.
Client   Coast Gallery Maui
Designer   Terri Borucki
2.
Client   Monterey Peninsula Country Club
Designer   Robert Wecker
3.
Client   Cynthia Davis, CPA
Designers Matt Gnibus, Robert Wecker
4.
Client   Big Sur River Inn
Designers Kevin Wecker, Robert Wecker
5.
Client   Manzoni Family Estate Vineyard
Designer   Robert Wecker
6.
Client   Winners Batting Cages
Designers Robert Wecker, Matt Gnibus
7.
Client   Platinum Travel Group
Designers Robert Wecker, Matt Gnibus
8.
Client   Blue Noise
Designers Sue Hough, Mark Burrier
9.
Client   Associated Credit Services
Designer   Sue Hough

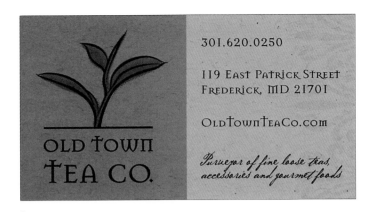

1.

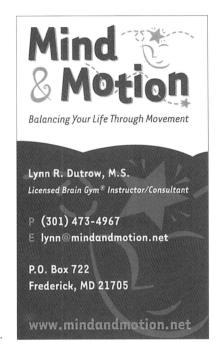

2.

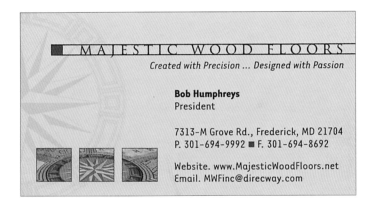

3.

4.

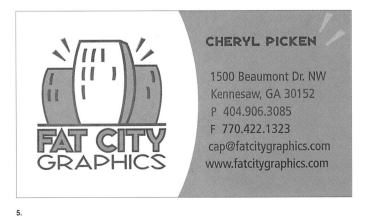

5.

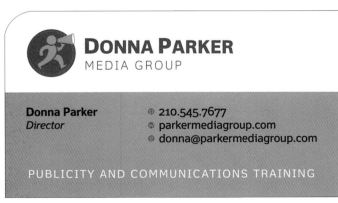

6.

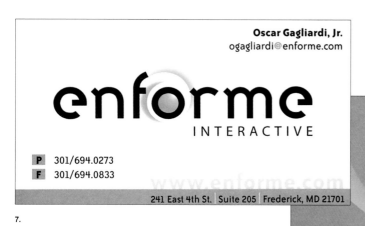

Oscar Gagliardi, Jr.
ogagliardi@enforme.com

enforme
INTERACTIVE

P 301/694.0273
F 301/694.0833

241 East 4th St. | Suite 205 | Frederick, MD 21701

Giving Form to Electronic Information

7.

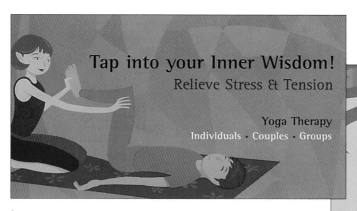

Tap into your Inner Wisdom!
Relieve Stress & Tension

Yoga Therapy
Individuals · Couples · Groups

no prior yoga experience needed

Heather K. Whittington
Certified Phoenix Rising Yoga Therapy Practitioner

240.446.3030
E-Mail: heather@marylandyogatherapy.com

PHOENIX RISING
yoga therapy

www.marylandyogatherapy.com

8.

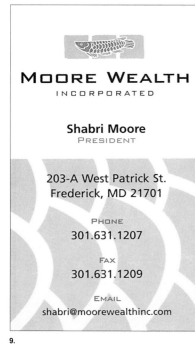

MOORE WEALTH
INCORPORATED

Shabri Moore
PRESIDENT

203-A West Patrick St.
Frederick, MD 21701

PHONE
301.631.1207

FAX
301.631.1209

EMAIL
shabri@moorewealthinc.com

9.

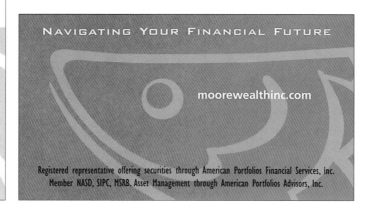

NAVIGATING YOUR FINANCIAL FUTURE

moorewealthinc.com

Registered representative offering securities through American Portfolios Financial Services, Inc.
Member NASD, SIPC, MSRB. Asset Management through American Portfolios Advisors, Inc.

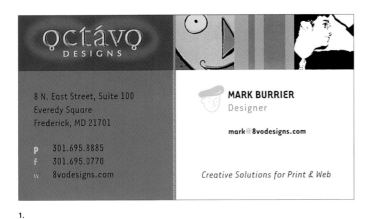

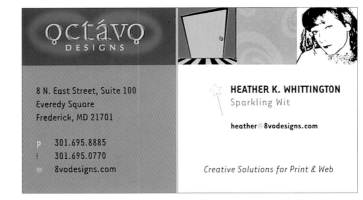

1.

2.

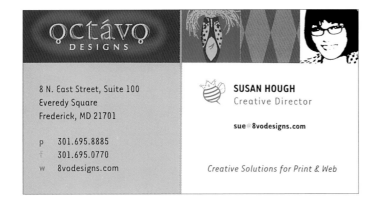

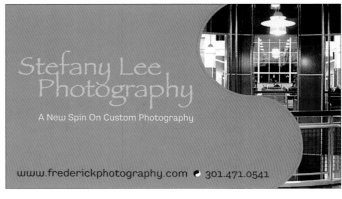

3.

4.

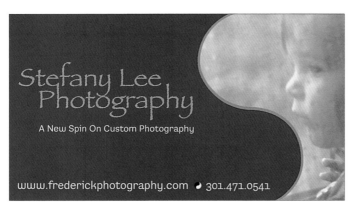

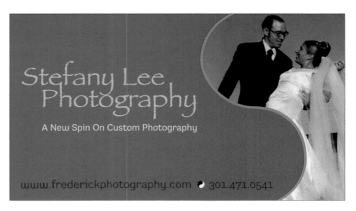

5.

6.

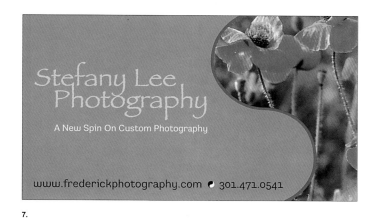

Stefany Lee Photography

A New Spin On Custom Photography

www.frederickphotography.com 301.471.0541

7.

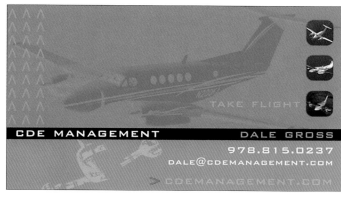

CDE MANAGEMENT   DALE GROSS

TAKE FLIGHT

978.815.0237
dale@cdemanagement.com

> CDEMANAGEMENT.COM

8.

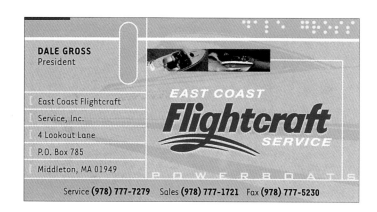

DALE GROSS
President

East Coast Flightcraft
Service, Inc.
4 Lookout Lane
P.O. Box 785
Middleton, MA 01949

EAST COAST
Flightcraft
SERVICE

POWERBOATS

Service **(978) 777-7279**   Sales **(978) 777-1721**   Fax **(978) 777-5230**

9.

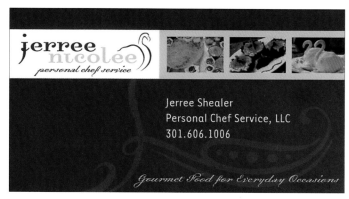

jerree
nicolee
personal chef service

Jerree Shealer
Personal Chef Service, LLC
301.606.1006

Gourmet Food for Everyday Occasions

10.

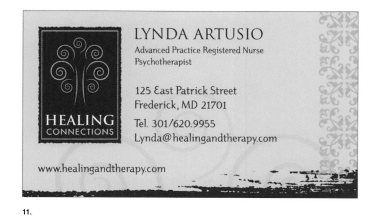

LYNDA ARTUSIO

Advanced Practice Registered Nurse
Psychotherapist

125 East Patrick Street
Frederick, MD 21701

Tel. 301/620.9955

Lynda@healingandtherapy.com

HEALING
CONNECTIONS

www.healingandtherapy.com

11.

1.

49 Locust Avenue
New Canaan, CT 06840
203 966-7015

 Argyle Associates, Inc.

Roger G. Langevin
President

2.

The Complete Research Resource

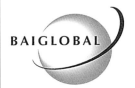 BAIGLOBAL

Clare Reilly
Marketing Coordinator

BAIGlobal Inc.
580 White Plains Road
Tarrytown, NY 10591

Tel: 914 332-5300
Fax: 914 631-8300
E-mail: creilly@baiglobal.com

3.

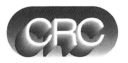 CRC

John F. Keane, Jr.
President

Capitol Risk Concepts, Ltd.
Insurance Brokers
One Water Street Suite 230
White Plains, NY 10601-1009

Tel. 914 946-7161
NYC 212 868-8000
FAX 914 683-8048

4.

For Games That Fill The House

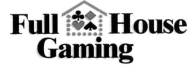 Full House Gaming

Hal Rubin

Full House Gaming, Inc.
4 Dann Farm Road
Pound Ridge, NY 10576

Telephone: 914 764 9494
E-mail: hrubin@optonline.com
www.fullhousegaming.com

5.

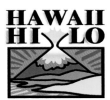 HAWAII HI LO

The Explosive New Game!

Hal Rubin Full House Gaming 4 Dann Farm Road, Pound Ridge, NY 10576
Tel: 914 764 9494 E-mail: hrubin@optonline.com www.fullhousegaming.com

6.

Bob Lee
President

Lee Communications, Inc.

Offices in New York City
and Westchester

11 Conant Valley Road
Pound Ridge, NY 10576
914 533 2325

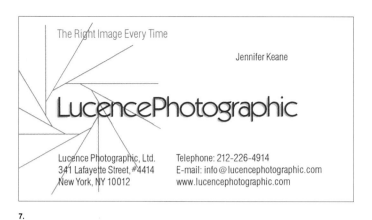

The Right Image Every Time

Jennifer Keane

LucencePhotographic

Lucence Photographic, Ltd.
341 Lafayette Street, #4414
New York, NY 10012

Telephone: 212-226-4914
E-mail: info@lucencephotographic.com
www.lucencephotographic.com

7.

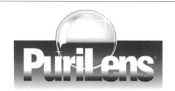

Ron McGhay
President & CEO

COMPLETE CONTACT LENS CARE

Two Principal Road
Scarborough, Ontario,
Canada M1R 4Z3

Tel: 416 285-1024
Tel: 800 387-3301
Fax: 416 285-5140

8.

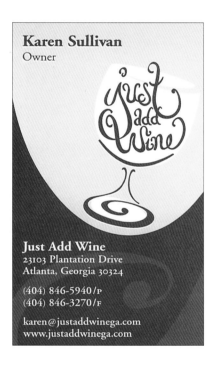

Karen Sullivan
Owner

Just Add Wine
23103 Plantation Drive
Atlanta, Georgia 30324

(404) 846-5940/P
(404) 846-3270/F

karen@justaddwinega.com
www.justaddwinega.com

9.

BCDS

Beaver Country Day School

791 Hammond Street
Chestnut Hill, MA 02467.2300
www.bcdschool.org

Peter Hutton
Head of School
Tel: 617.738.2730
Fax: 617.738.2703
phutton@bcdschool.org

10.

William Wilson | Associated Architects Inc.

William F. Wilson, AIA
Principal

374 Congress Street Suite 400
Boston, MA 02210

617.338.5990 Tel
617.338.5991 Fax
wilson@wilsonarch.com Email

11.

(1-8)
Design Firm **Lee Communications, Inc.**
(9)
Design Firm **The Fluid Group**
(10-11)
Design Firm **kor group**

1.
  Client   Argyle Associates, Inc.
  Designer Bob Lee
2.
  Client   BAIGlobal, Inc.
  Designer Bob Lee
3.
  Client   Capitol Risk Concepts, Ltd.
  Designer Bob Lee
4.
  Client   Full House Gaming
  Designer Bob Lee
5.
  Client   Hawaii Hi-Lo
  Designer Bob Lee
6.
  Client   Lee Communications, Inc.
  Designer Bob Lee
7.
  Client   Lucence Photographic, Ltd.
  Designer Bob Lee

8.
  Client   PuriLens, Inc.
  Designer Bob Lee
9.
  Designer Kyle Phillips
10.
  Client   Beaver Country Day School
  Designers MB Jarosik, Jim Gibson,
              Anne Callahan
11.
  Client   William Wilson Associated Architects
  Designers Karen Dendy Smith

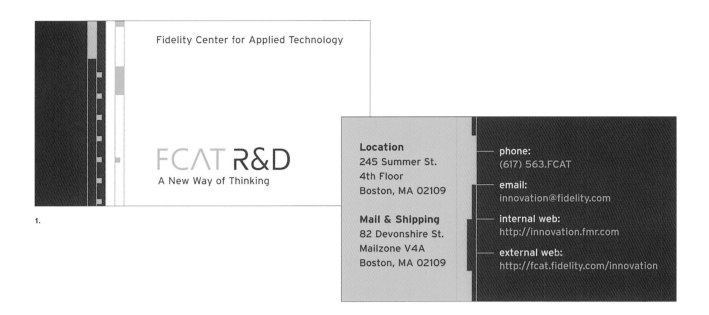

Fidelity Center for Applied Technology

FCAT R&D
A New Way of Thinking

Location
245 Summer St.
4th Floor
Boston, MA 02109

Mail & Shipping
82 Devonshire St.
Mailzone V4A
Boston, MA 02109

phone:
(617) 563.FCAT

email:
innovation@fidelity.com

internal web:
http://innovation.fmr.com

external web:
http://fcat.fidelity.com/innovation

1.

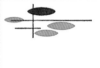

Marketing & Communications

NICOLE F. CHABAT

264 Montgomery Avenue
Haverford, PA 19041
telephone: 610.649.1049
email: nchabat@comcast.net

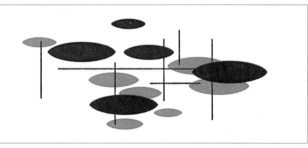

2.

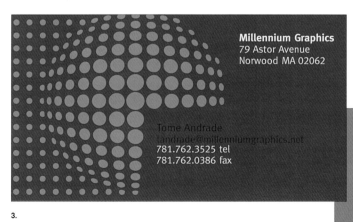

Millennium Graphics
79 Astor Avenue
Norwood MA 02062

Tome Andrade
tandrade@millenniumgraphics.net
781.762.3525 tel
781.762.0386 fax

MILLENNIUM

3.

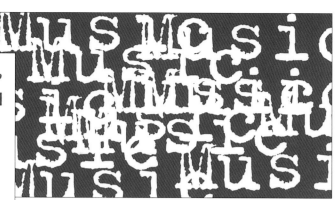

MUSIC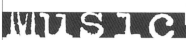

The Jerry Brenner Group

consulting marketing promotion retail

Jonathan R. Lev

T 617•713•0400
F 617•713•3818
JBGlev@aol.com

233 Harvard Street Suite 11 Brookline, MA 02446

4.

kor group
visual communications

One Design Center Place Boston MA 02210

5.

kor

617 330 1007 tel
617 330 1004 fax
alison@kor.com

Alison Noble
Marketing Manager

APPLIANCE + LIGHTING

YALE

**Rogerio Pontes
Lighting Consultant**

296 Freeport Street
Boston, MA 02122

T 617•825•YALE
F 617•825•6541
www.yaleappliance.com
rogerio.pontes@yaleappliance.com

6.

TURN IT ON!

(1-6)
Design Firm **kor group**

1.
Client   Fidelity FCAT
Designers Kjerstin Westgaard
2.
Client   Nicole Chabat
Designers Karen Dendy Smith,
              Brian Azer
3.
Client   Millennium Graphics
Designer   Kjerstin Westgaard
4.
Client   Jerry Brenner Promotions
Designer   MB Jarosik
5.
Client   kor group
Designers Anne Callahan, Karen Dendy Smith,
              MB Jarosik
6.
Client   Yale Appliance + Lighting
Designers Karen Dendy Smith, James Grady

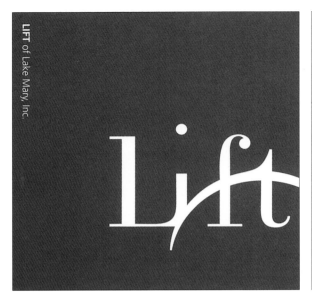

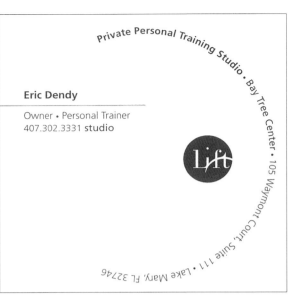

1.

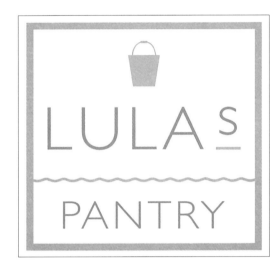

2.

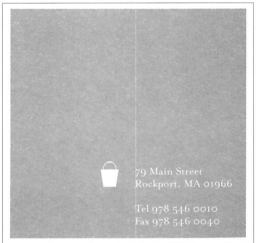

3.

Pure data Pure results

Carleton

Steven L. Thimjon
Vice President &
Chief Financial Officer

10729 Bren Road East
Minnetonka, MN 55343

Main 612.238.4000
Tel 612.238.4068
Fax 612.238.4020
steve.thimjon@carleton.com

www.carleton.com

4.

 newmediary·com

Scott Ormiston
Business Development Manager
scottormiston@newmediary.com

313 Washington Street	Main	617 · 395 · 7900
Suite 260	Direct	617 · 395 · 7916
Newton · MA 02458	Fax	617 · 928 · 5080
USA	Cell	617 · 590 · 0655

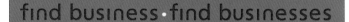 find business·find businesses

5.

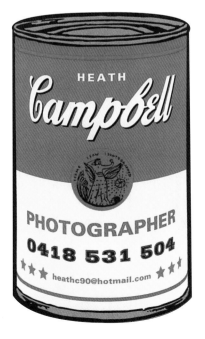
6.

(1-5)
Design Firm **kor group**
(6)
Design Firm **Mono Design**

1.
Client | Lift
Designers | Karen Dendy Smith,
Kjerstin Westgaard

2.
Client | Lula's Pantry
Designers | Jim Gibson,
James Grady

3.
Client | Prince, Lobel, Glovsky & Tye
Designers | Karen Dendy Smith,
Kjerstin Westgaard

4.
Client | Carleton Corporation
Designer | MB Jarosik

5.
Client | Newmediary
Designers | Kjerstin Westgaard,
James Grady

6.
Client | Heath Campbell Photographer
Designer | Matt Clare

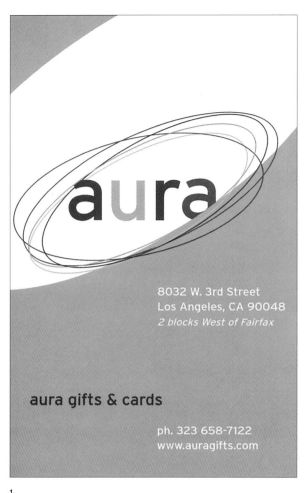

1.

DESIRE : People with red auras tend to have the urge to win, a sense of adventure, and the survival instinct; the majority of them are young children and teenage boys

DEVOTION : People with purple auras appreciate tenderness and kindness in others, are not especially practical and tend to be entertainers, movie stars, free thinkers, visionaries and revolutionaries

CREATIVITY : Many sales people, entrepreneurs, and people who deal with the public have orange auras

HAPPINESS : People with yellow auras encourage and support others; they have a great ability to analyze complex concepts

TRUST : People with blue auras tend to be poets, writers, musicians, philosophers, serious students, spiritual seekers, and people looking for the truth, justice, and beauty in everything

PATIENCE : People with green auras are dedicated parents, social workers, counselors, psychologists, and focus on creating positive change in the world

living and breathing design™

oxygen SPACE

Alex Wigington
PRINCIPAL

401 Richmond St W, Suite 430   t 416 506 0₂0₂ x27
Toronto, ON M5V 3A8   f 416 506 170₂
oxygen.ca   alex@oxygen.ca

2.

CAPIC

THE CANADIAN ASSOCIATION OF PHOTOGRAPHERS AND ILLUSTRATORS IN COMMUNICATIONS
We represent the best in photography and illustration in Canada. Through best business practices, our
code of ethics, education and marketing we help our members achieve excellence in their craft and
success in the global marketplace. CAPIC is committed to protecting the rights of visual creators in Canada.
L'ASSOCIATION CANADIENNE DES PHOTOGRAPHES ET ILLUSTRATEURS EN COMMUNICATIONS
Nous représentons les meilleurs photographes et illustrateurs au Canada. Par la promotion de pratiques
professionnelles de haut niveau et d'un Code de déontologie ainsi que par nos initiatives en matière de formation
et en marketing, nous aidons nos membres à atteindre l'excellence dans leur métier et à connaître le succès
au sein du marché international. La CAPIC s'engage à protéger les droits des créateurs visuels au Canada.

RANDY HARQUAIL   55 MILL STREET THE CASE GOODS BLDG
PRESIDENT   SUITE 302 TORONTO ON M5A 3C4
                        TEL 613.237.4268
                        EMAIL RANDY@HARQUAILPHOTO.COM
                        CAPIC.ORG

3.

+ stacey

+ everything you need in a photographer

stacey brandford photography
9 davies ave, studio 103, toronto on m4m 2a6
let's talk 416.463.8877 my cell 416.712.7788
drop me a line sbrandford@bellnet.ca
check out my site staceybrandford.com

4.

Susie Adelson
Director, Business Development

401 richmond st west, suite 430
toronto, on m5v 3a8
tel 416.599.TRIP [8747] EXT.#42
fax 416.599.8116
susie@weekendtrips.com

weekendtrips.com

what are you doing this weekend?

weekendtrips.com

5.

(1)
Design Firm **kor group**
(2-5)
Design Firm **oxygen design + communications**

1.
Client   Aura
Designers   MB Jarosik,
            Jim Gibson
2.
Client   Oxygen Space
Designer   Alex Wigington
3.
Client   Capic
Designers   Alex Wigington,
            Blake Morrow
4.
Client   Stacey
Designer   Alex Wigington
5.
Client   Weekendtrips.com
Designer   Alex Wigington

damir gusic

554 college st. toronto
ontario canada M6G 1B1

GIVE US A RING 416 925 1818
TOLL FREE 888 238 8244
SEND A FAX 416 927 9893
DROP MAIL dgusic@motoretta.ca
SURF motoretta.ca

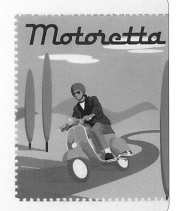

1.

554 college st. toronto
ontario canada M6G 1B1

GIVE US A RING 416 925 1818
TOLL FREE 888 238 8244
SEND A FAX 416 927 9893
DROP MAIL info@motoretta.ca
SURF motoretta.ca

2.

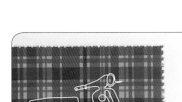

scooters authentic + true

parts
service
paraphernalia

3.

jason girard

554 college st. toronto
ontario canada M6G 1B1

GIVE US A RING 416 925 1818
TOLL FREE 888 238 8244
SEND A FAX 416 927 9893
DROP MAIL jgirard@motoretta.ca
SURF motoretta.ca

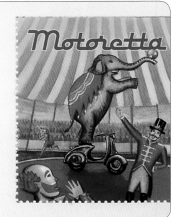

4.

steve petridis

554 college st. toronto
ontario canada M6G 1B1

GIVE US A RING 416 925 1818
TOLL FREE 888 238 8244
SEND A FAX 416 927 9893
DROP MAIL spetridis@motoretta.ca
SURF motoretta.ca

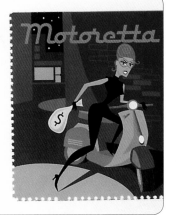

5.

giancarlo serrafero

554 college st. toronto
ontario canada M6G 1B1

GIVE US A RING 416 925 1818
TOLL FREE 888 238 8244
SEND A FAX 416 927 9893
DROP MAIL gserrafero@motoretta.ca
SURF motoretta.ca

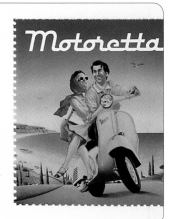

5.

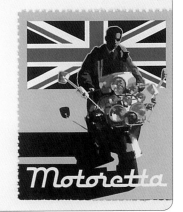

vicki boutin creative director/buyer
40 ridgevalley crescent. toronto canada M9A 3J6

tel 905 681 9285 fax 416 236 0024
1 800 393 2151 • vicki@scraptivity.com

scraptivity.com

scraptiv!ty™

A CLUB FOR
SCRAPBOOKING MEMORIES™

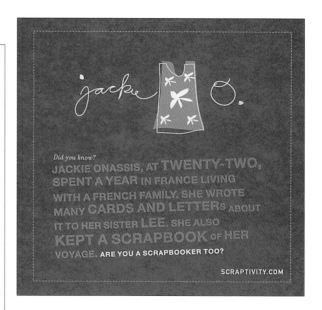

Did you know?
JACKIE ONASSIS, AT TWENTY-TWO,
SPENT A YEAR IN FRANCE LIVING
WITH A FRENCH FAMILY. SHE WROTE
MANY CARDS AND LETTERs ABOUT
IT TO HER SISTER LEE. SHE ALSO
KEPT A SCRAPBOOK OF HER
VOYAGE. ARE YOU A SCRAPBOOKER TOO?

SCRAPTIVITY.COM

6.

oxygen design +
communications

401 Richmond St W
Suite 430, Toronto
Ontario M5V 3A8

tel 416 506 0_20_2 x46
fax 416 506 170_2
karolina@oxygen.ca
oxygen.ca

Karolina Loboda
DESIGNER

oxygen

living and breathing design™

7.

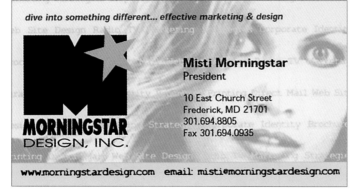

dive into something different... effective marketing & design

MORNINGSTAR DESIGN, INC.

Misti Morningstar
President

10 East Church Street
Frederick, MD 21701
301.694.8805
Fax 301.694.0935

www.morningstardesign.com email: misti@morningstardesign.com

8.

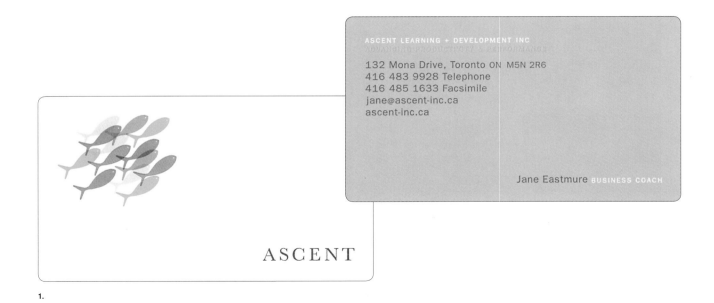

ASCENT LEARNING + DEVELOPMENT INC

132 Mona Drive, Toronto ON M5N 2R6
416 483 9928 Telephone
416 485 1633 Facsimile
jane@ascent-inc.ca
ascent-inc.ca

Jane Eastmure BUSINESS COACH

ASCENT

1.

John-Paul Loseto
Assistant Property Manager

141 E. Madison
Saint Louis, Missouri 63122
Telephone 314.775.2921
Facsimile 314.775.2920
stationplazaleasing@mlpllc.com

2.

Julie Shearburn

WilliamShearburnGallery

4735 McPherson Avenue
Saint Louis, Missouri 63108 USA
Telephone 314.367.8020
Facsimile 314.367.4010
julie@shearburngallery.com
shearburngallery.com

3.

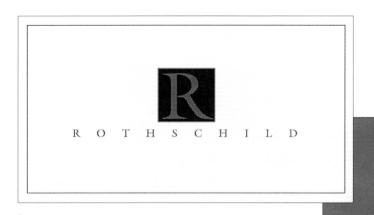

R O T H S C H I L D

4.

Rebecca Totty Corrington
Commercial Property Specialist

Rothschild Realty Inc.
4746 McPherson Avenue ▪ St. Louis, Missouri 63108 USA
Telephone 314.367.7787 ext 121 ▪ Facsimile 314.754.1106
Cel 314.640.3296 ▪ Email rebcorrington@hotmail.com
Internet www.rothschildrealty.com

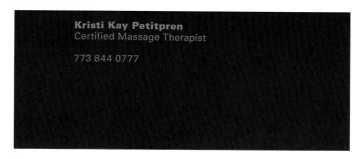

NN

NORTHWESTERN NASAL + SINUS

Daniel G. Carothers, M.D.

676 North Saint Clair, Suite 1575 Chicago, IL 60611
t 800.313.NOSE t 312.266.NOSE f 312.266.3680
dcarothers@nwnasalsinus.com

5.

Kristi Kay Petitpren
Certified Massage Therapist

773 844 0777

6.

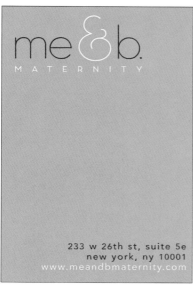

me&b.
MATERNITY

233 w 26th st, suite 5e
new york, ny 10001
www.meandbmaternity.com

7.

MR BIG FILM

LISA DELEO
PRODUCER
LISA@MRBIGFILM.COM

MR BIG FILM | 1147 WEST OHIO CHICAGO ILLINOIS 60622
TEL 312 492 9900 | FAX 312 492 9902 | WWW.MRBIGFILM.COM

8.

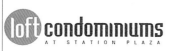

Nina Esson
Sales Manager

loft condominiums
AT STATION PLAZA

141 East Madison
Saint Louis, Missouri 63122
Telephone 314.775.2921
Facsimile 314.775.2920
Cell   314.504.1171
Email stationplazaloft@mlpllc.com

www.station-plaza.com

9.

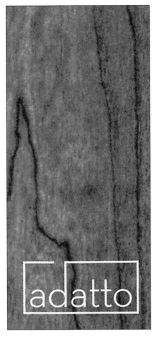

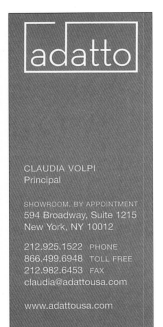

adatto

CLAUDIA VOLPI
Principal

SHOWROOM, BY APPOINTMENT
594 Broadway, Suite 1215
New York, NY 10012

212.925.1522 PHONE
866.499.6948 TOLL FREE
212.982.6453 FAX
claudia@adattousa.com

www.adattousa.com

1.

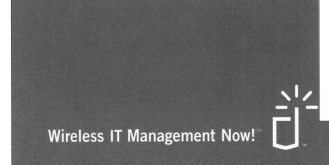

hazen | keay   ART ADVISORY

212.255.4198
ART@HAZENKEAY.COM

LONDON TERRACE STATION
PO BOX #20136
NEW YORK, NEW YORK
10011

ANDREA HAZEN

2.

Ari Kaplan
Founder and CEO
ari.kaplan@XB.com

Expand Beyond
640 N. LaSalle Street
Suite 330
Chicago, IL 60610

T 312.587.9990
F 312.587.8510
www.XB.com

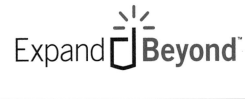

Wireless IT Management Now!

3.

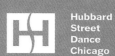

Hubbard **Hubbard** Lou HSDC
Street **Street** Conte Education
Dance **2** Dance & Community
Chicago Studio Programs

4.

Hubbard Street Dance Chicago

1147 West Jackson Boulevard
Chicago, IL 60607-2905 USA
t 312.850.9744
f 312.455.8240
hubbardstreetdance.com

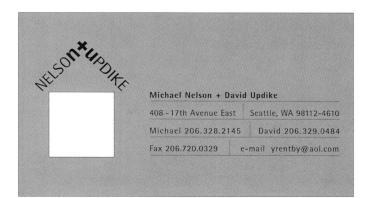

NELSON+UPDIKE

Michael Nelson + David Updike

408 - 17th Avenue East | Seattle, WA 98112-4610

Michael 206.328.2145 | David 206.329.0484

Fax 206.720.0329 | e-mail yrentby@aol.com

5.

PRODUCT

DESIGN

DEVELOPMENT

DELIVERY

LYNN ANDERSON

PD3, INC. - 4112 55TH AVE SW - SEATTLE, WA 98116

P: 206 938.1876 - F: 206 923.9939 - **LYNN.PD3@COMCAST.NET**

6.

giorgio davanzo design

232 belmont ave e, no.506   seattle,wa 98102-6306

phone 206 328.5031   fax 206 324.3592

e-mail giorgio@davanzodesign.com

url www.davanzodesign.com

notes

7.

(1-4)
Design Firm **Liska + Associates Inc.**
(5-7)
Design Firm **Giorgio Davanza Design**

1.
Client   Adatto
Designers Tanya Quick,
           Jonathan Seeds
2.
Client   Hazen Keay
Designer   Jonathan Seeds
3.
Client   Expand Beyond
Designers Steve Liska,
           Paul Wong
4.
Client   Hubbard Street Dance Chicago
Designers Steve Liska,
           Sabine Krauss
5.
Client   Nelson + Updike
Designers Giorgio Davanza
6.
Client   pd3
Designer   Giorgio Davanza
7.
Client   Giorgio Davanzo Design
Designer   Giorgio Davanza

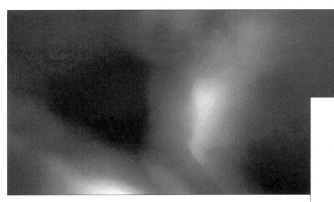

1.

SENOK™
TEA FOR THE SENSES

Landy Pen

126 S Spokane Street | Seattle. WA 98124
P 206.903.0858 | 1.877.736.6583 | F 206.624.3026
lpen@senoktea.com | www.senoktea.com

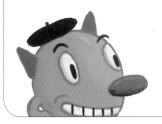

CRANIUM®
play with your brain™

Jacobe Chrisman
Doctor Tick Tock

1511 Third Avenue • Suite 433
Seattle, WA 98101
T 206.652.9708 Ext.116
C 206.963.2229
F 206.652.1483
jacobe@playcranium.com
www.playcranium.com

2.

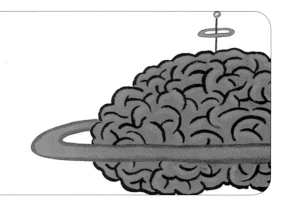

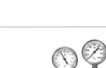
LOOP WORX

JEFF LANGSTON _ LOOPMASTER

25 E 94TH STREET #3 _ NEW YORK, NY 10128 _ WWW.LOOPWORX.COM
P **212.348.1565** _ F 212.348.2886 _ E JLANGSTON@LOOPWORX.COM

3.

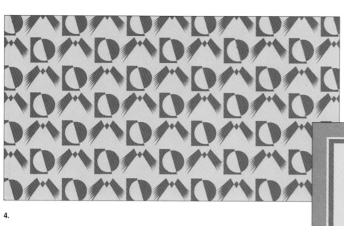

4.

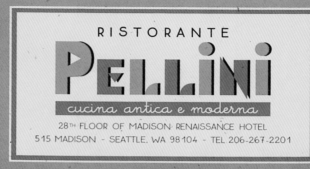

RISTORANTE

PELLINI

cucina antica e moderna

28TH FLOOR OF MADISON RENAISSANCE HOTEL
515 MADISON - SEATTLE, WA 98104 - TEL 206-267-2201

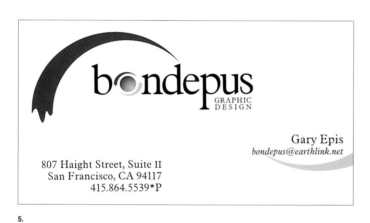

b**o**ndepus
GRAPHIC
DESIGN

Gary Epis
bondepus@earthlink.net

807 Haight Street, Suite II
San Francisco, CA 94117
415.864.5539★P

5.

Sports

Chiropractic

create

Dr. Scott Snow
DC CCSP

510-543-8286 Cell

Golds Gym Oakland
600 Grand Avenue
Oakland, CA 94610

6.

J&B PROPERTIES

Barbara Epis
General Manager

P.O. Box 2624
Sunnyvale, CA 94087

650 941- 6422
Fax 941- 6453

7.

(1-4)
Design Firm **Giorgio Davanzo Design**
(5-7)
Design Firm **Bondepus Graphic Design**

1.
Client   Senok
Designer   Giorgio Davanza
2.
Client   Cranium
Designer   Giorgio Davanza
3.
Client   Loop Worx
Designer   Giorgio Davanza
4.
Client   Pellini
Designer   Giorgio Davanza
5.
Client   Bondepus Graphic Design
Designers   Gary Epis,
            Amy Bond
6.
Client   Sports Chiropractic
Designers   Gary Epis,
            Amy Bond
7.
Client   J&B Properties
Designers   Gary Epis,
            Amy Bond

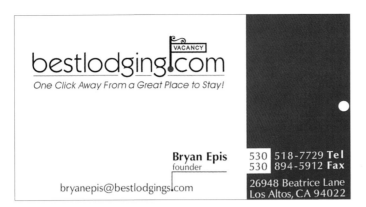

bestlodging.com
One Click Away From a Great Place to Stay!

Bryan Epis
founder

530 | 518-7729 **Tel**
530 | 894-5912 **Fax**

bryanepis@bestlodgings.com

26948 Beatrice Lane
Los Altos, CA 94022

1.

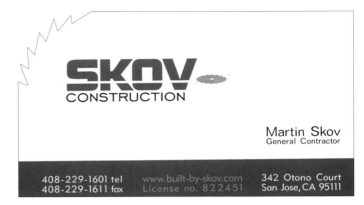

SKOV
CONSTRUCTION

Martin Skov
General Contractor

408-229-1601 tel
408-229-1611 fax

www.built-by-skov.com
License no. 822451

342 Otono Court
San Jose, CA 95111

2.

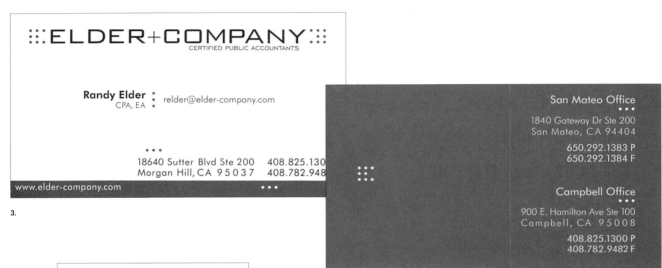

:::**ELDER+COMPANY**:::
CERTIFIED PUBLIC ACCOUNTANTS

Randy Elder
CPA, EA

relder@elder-company.com

• • •

18640 Sutter Blvd Ste 200
Morgan Hill, CA 95037

408.825.130
408.782.948

www.elder-company.com
• • •

San Mateo Office
• • •
1840 Gateway Dr Ste 200
San Mateo, CA 94404

650.292.1383 P
650.292.1384 F

Campbell Office
• • •
900 E. Hamilton Ave Ste 100
Campbell, CA 95008

408.825.1300 P
408.782.9482 F

3.

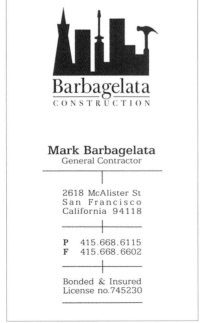

Barbagelata
CONSTRUCTION

Mark Barbagelata
General Contractor

2618 McAlister St
San Francisco
California 94118

P 415.668.6115
F 415.668.6602

Bonded & Insured
License no.745230

4.

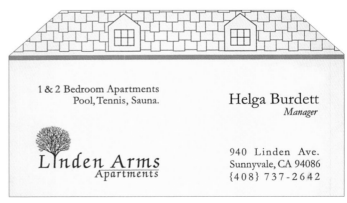

1 & 2 Bedroom Apartments
Pool, Tennis, Sauna.

Helga Burdett
Manager

Linden Arms
Apartments

940 Linden Ave.
Sunnyvale, CA 94086
{408} 737-2642

5.

Michael K. De Neve
Principal

945 Airport Drive
Reply: P.O. Box 14143
San Luis Obispo, CA 93406

T 805.543.7474
F 805.541.0806

6.

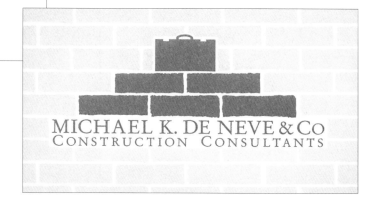

MICHAEL K. DE NEVE & Co
CONSTRUCTION CONSULTANTS

GARY KIRKE
CHAIRMAN

gary.kirke@wildroseresorts.com

WILD ROSE ENTERTAINMENT L.L.C.
P.O. Box 93595 • DES MOINES, IA 50393-3595
(515) 248-1776 • FAX: (515) 243-5202
www.wildroseresorts.com

7.

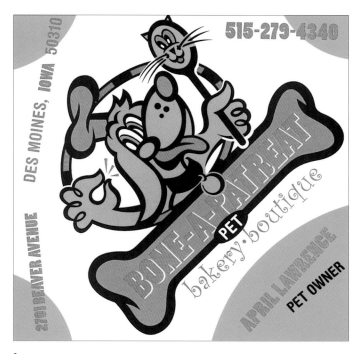

8.

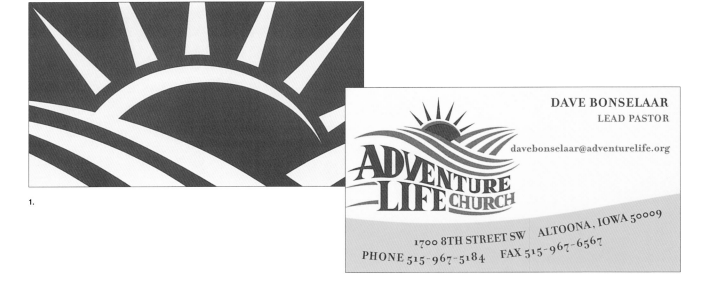

1.

DAVE BONSELAAR
LEAD PASTOR

davebonselaar@adventurelife.org

ADVENTURE LIFE CHURCH

1700 8TH STREET SW   ALTOONA, IOWA 50009
PHONE 515-967-5184   FAX 515-967-6567

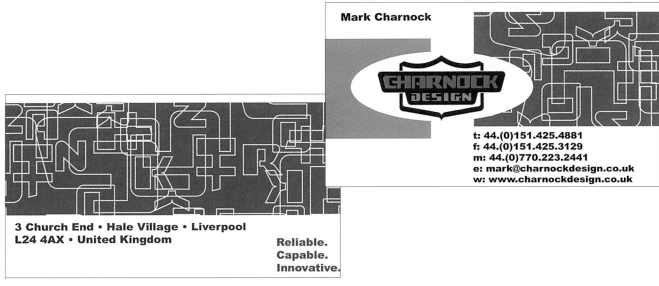

Mark Charnock

CHARNOCK DESIGN

t: 44.(0)151.425.4881
f: 44.(0)151.425.3129
m: 44.(0)770.223.2441
e: mark@charnockdesign.co.uk
w: www.charnockdesign.co.uk

3 Church End • Hale Village • Liverpool
L24 4AX • United Kingdom

Reliable.
Capable.
Innovative.

2.

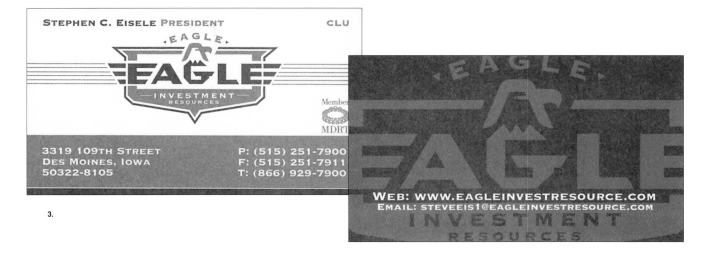

STEPHEN C. EISELE PRESIDENT   CLU

EAGLE
EAGLE
INVESTMENT
RESOURCES

Member
MDRT

3319 109TH STREET
DES MOINES, IOWA
50322-8105

P: (515) 251-7900
F: (515) 251-7911
T: (866) 929-7900

EAGLE
EAGLE
INVESTMENT
RESOURCES

WEB: WWW.EAGLEINVESTRESOURCE.COM
EMAIL: STEVEEIS1@EAGLEINVESTRESOURCE.COM

3.

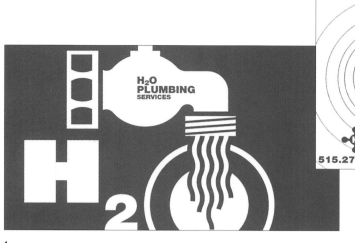

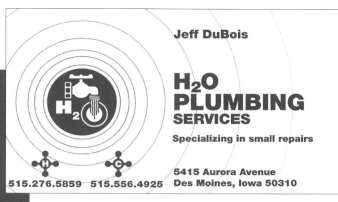

Jeff DuBois

H₂O PLUMBING SERVICES

Specializing in small repairs

**5415 Aurora Avenue
Des Moines, Iowa 50310**

515.276.5859 515.556.4925

4.

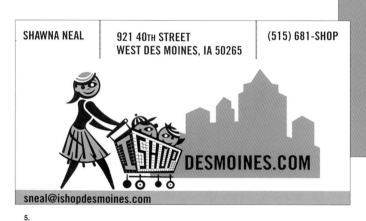

SHAWNA NEAL | **921 40TH STREET
WEST DES MOINES, IA 50265** | **(515) 681-SHOP**

sneal@ishopdesmoines.com

ISHOPDESMOINES.COM
www.ishopdesmoines.com

5.

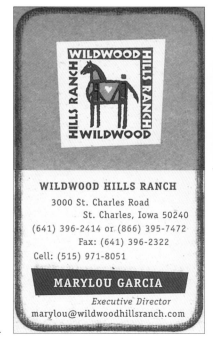

WILDWOOD HILLS RANCH

3000 St. Charles Road
St. Charles, Iowa 50240
(641) 396-2414 or (866) 395-7472
Fax: (641) 396-2322
Cell: (515) 971-8051

MARYLOU GARCIA

Executive Director
marylou@wildwoodhillsranch.com

6.

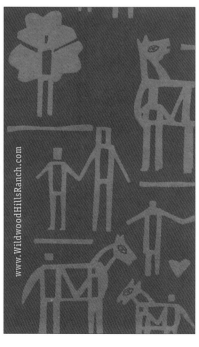

www.WildwoodHillsRanch.com

(1-6)
Design Firm **Sayles Graphic Design**

1.
Client Adventure Life Church
Designer John Sayles
2.
Client Charnock Design
Designer John Sayles
3.
Client Eagle Investment Resources
Designer John Sayles
4.
Client H2O Plumbing Services
Designer John Sayles
5.
Client IshopDesMoines.com
Designer John Sayles
6.
Client Wildwood Hills Ranch
Designer John Sayles

COMMERCIAL • RESIDENTIAL • INTERIOR • EXTERIOR
NEW CONSTRUCTION • REMODELS

SLOAN BROTHERS
PAINTING, INC.

strokes of brilliance

1.

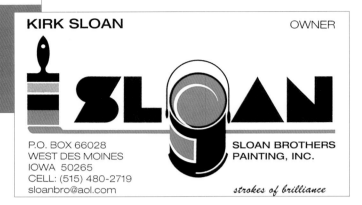

KIRK SLOAN   OWNER

SLOAN

P.O. BOX 66028
WEST DES MOINES
IOWA 50265
CELL: (515) 480-2719
sloanbro@aol.com

SLOAN BROTHERS
PAINTING, INC.

strokes of brilliance

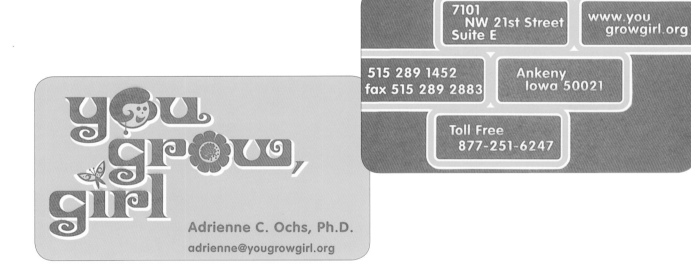

you grow, girl

Adrienne C. Ochs, Ph.D.
adrienne@yougrowgirl.org

7101
NW 21st Street
Suite E

www.you
growgirl.org

515 289 1452
fax 515 289 2883

Ankeny
Iowa 50021

Toll Free
877-251-6247

2.

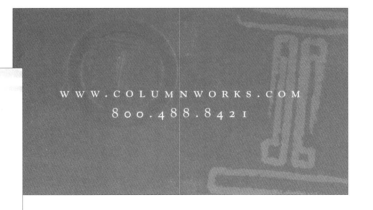

COLUMN WORKS
PREBUILT MASONRY

JAMES W. GOSSETT | PRINCIPAL

COLUMNWORKS WEST

T 530.243.0796 • F 530.243.0736
4780 CATERPILLAR ROAD, BLG. C • REDDING, CALIFORNIA 96003 U.S.A.
JGOSSETT@COLUMNWORKS.COM | WWW.COLUMNWORKS.COM

WWW.COLUMNWORKS.COM
800.488.8421

3.

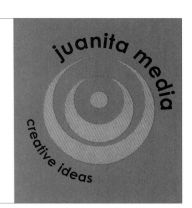

Juanita Ramos
Proprietor

T. 530.242.6568
F. 530.241.8616
juanitamedia@aol.com

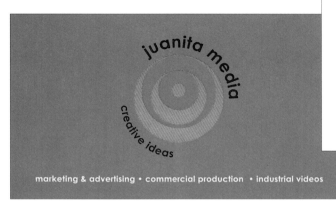

marketing & advertising • commercial production • industrial videos

4.

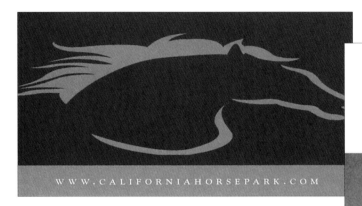

WWW.CALIFORNIAHORSEPARK.COM

5.

CALIFORNIA HORSE PARK
A STATE OF THE ART EQUINE SHOW FACILITY

DAVE DAWSON | DIRECTOR OF DEVELOPMENT

T | 530.226.6237   F | 530.226.6210   C | 530.200.5979
PO BOX 992380   REDDING, CALIFORNIA 96099-2380
londavdaws@aol.com
WWW.CALIFORNIAHORSEPARK.COM

Rachel Andras

PROFESSIONAL FLYFISHING GUIDE AND INSTRUCTOR

2384 HAWN AVENUE
REDDING, CALIFORNIA 96002
530.227.4837
RACHEL@RACHELFISHING.COM
WWW.RACHELFISHING.COM

licenced • bon

6.

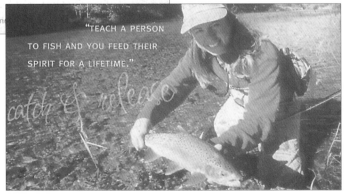

"TEACH A PERSON
TO FISH AND YOU FEED THEIR
SPIRIT FOR A LIFETIME."

catch & release

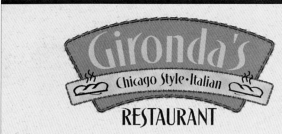

Jim Gironda
1100 Center Street · Redding · California · 96001
t) 530.244.7663 · f) 530.244.7677 · jim@girondas.com · www.girondas.com

1.

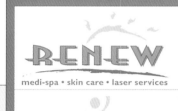

dining · carry out · drive thru · meeting room

Chicago Style

RENEW
medi-spa · skin care · laser services

RENEW FOR 2
a pregnancy spa

Jami Kay Foltz, Aesthetician

2626 Edith Ave. Suite D
Redding, CA 96001
voice 530.241.7772
fax 530.241.7786
jami@renewlaserskincare.com
www.renewlaserskincare.com

You have an appointment with:
Date: Time:
If you're unable to make your appointment, kindly give us 24 hours notice. Thanks!

2.

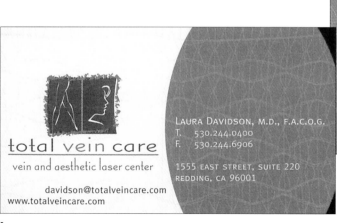

total vein care
vein and aesthetic laser center

davidson@totalveincare.com
www.totalveincare.com

LAURA DAVIDSON, M.D., F.A.C.O.G.
T.   530.244.0400
F.   530.244.6906

1555 EAST STREET, SUITE 220
REDDING, CA 96001

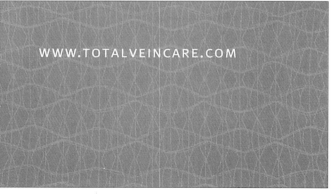

WWW.TOTALVEINCARE.COM

3.

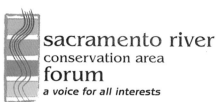

sacramento river
conservation area
forum
a voice for all interests

Pat Brown
Administrative
Assistant

T. 530.528.7435 F. 530.528.7422
pbrown@water.ca.gov · www.sacramentoriver.ca.gov
2440 Main Street · Red Bluff · California · 96080

4.

GALLERYHOTEL

MICHELLE
NATSUMI TAN

Guest Relations Manager

76 Robertson Quay Singapore 238254
Tel (65) 6849 8686 DID (65) 6849 5167
Fax (65) 6235 3590 Hp (65) 9819 8778
www.galleryhotel.com.sg
michelle.natsumi@galleryhotel.com.sg

ギャラリーホテル シンガポール

ミッシェル 夏海
お客様担当マネージャー

5.

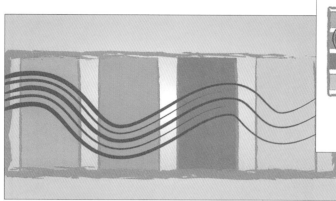

SINGAPORE
THEORIENTALIST
W O V E N   A R T

ABI BAGHERI • Managing Director
Email abi@theorientalist.com

6.

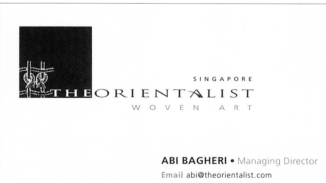

THEORIENTALIST
W O V E N   A R T

1 Nassim Rd #01-00 S258458 **Tel** 6235 3343 **Fax** 6235 9925
Website www.theorientalist.com

(1-4)
Design Firm **Market Street Marketing**
(5,6)
Design Firm **Ukulele Brand**
Consultants Pte Ltd

1.
Client   Gironda's Restaurant
Designer   Kathleen Downs
2.
Client   Renew for 2
Designer   Kathleen Downs
3.
Client   total vein care
Designer   Kathleen Downs
4.
Client   Sacramento River
Designer   Kathleen Downs
5.
Client   Gallery Hotel
Designer   Lynn Lim
6.
Client   The Orientalist Singapore
Designer   Lynn Lim

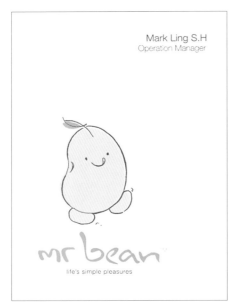

Mark Ling S.H
Operation Manager

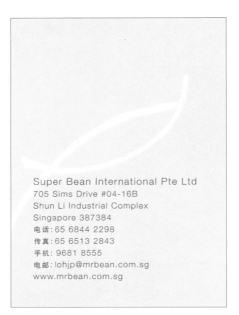

Super Bean International Pte Ltd
705 Sims Drive #04-16B
Shun Li Industrial Complex
Singapore 387384
电话：65 6844 2298
传真：65 6513 2843
手机：9681 8555
电邮：lohjp@mrbean.com.sg
www.mrbean.com.sg

1.

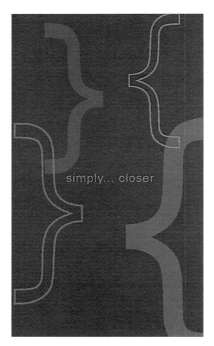

simply... closer

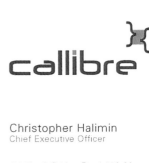

callibre

Christopher Halimin
Chief Executive Officer

111 North Bridge Road #30-00
Peninsula Plaza, Singapore 179098
Tel   65 6416 1302
Fax   65 6338 6588
Mobile 65 9768 9929
Email   chrish@telequam.com

218 Main Street, Suite 102
Kirkland, WA 98033, USA
Tel   1 877 844 1166
Fax   1 425 650 6744

www.callibre.com

2.

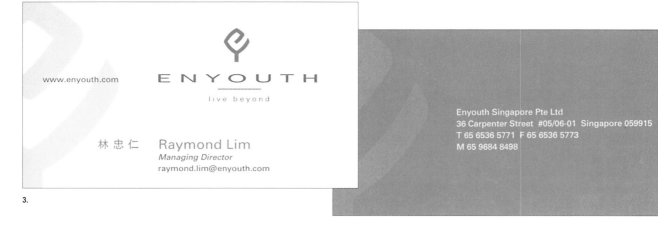

www.enyouth.com

ENYOUTH

live beyond

林忠仁   Raymond Lim
Managing Director
raymond.lim@enyouth.com

Enyouth Singapore Pte Ltd
36 Carpenter Street #05/06-01 Singapore 059915
T 65 6536 5771 F 65 6536 5773
M 65 9684 8498

3.

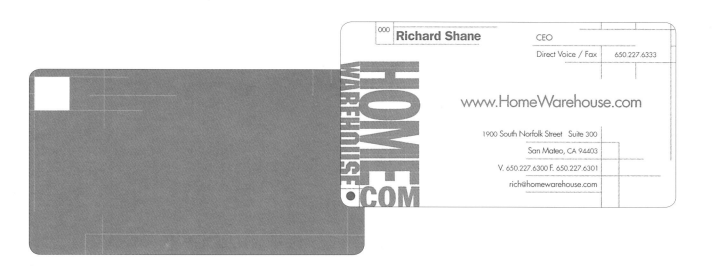

Richard Shane   CEO

Direct Voice / Fax   650.227.6333

www.HomeWarehouse.com

1900 South Norfolk Street   Suite 300

San Mateo, CA 94403

V. 650.227.6300 F. 650.227.6301

rich@homewarehouse.com

000

HOME WAREHOUSE.COM

4.

ROXY

PO BOX 1672 PALO ALTO CA 94302
P 650 324 1529 F 650 324 0259
ROXY@ROXYRAPP.COM

RAPP

PO BOX 1672 PALO ALTO CA 94302
P 650 324 1529 F 650 324 0259
ROXY@ROXYRAPP.COM

5.

WORDS BY DESIGN

NANCY TOMKINS
principal

6.

502 WAVERLEY STREET, SUITE 308
PALO ALTO, CALIFORNIA 94301
TEL 650.322.0390 FAX 650.322.0391
EMAIL sharon@wordsbydesign.com
www.wordsbydesign.com

(1-3)
Design Firm **Ukulele Brand**
Consultants Pte Ltd
(4-6)
Design Firm **Hausman Design**

1.
Client   Super Bean International Pte Ltd
Designers   Lynn Lim, Yohji Neoh
2.
Client   Callibre
Designers   Yohji Neoh, Aliah Hanim
3.
Client   Enyouth Singapore Pte Ltd
Designers   Liu Kar Ming
4.
Client   HomeWarehouse.com
Designers   Joan Hausman, Tammy Tribble
5.
Client   Roxy Rapp & Company
Designer   Joan Hausman
6.
Client   Words by Design
Designer   Joan Hausman

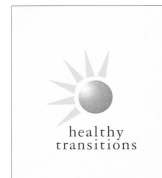

Karen P. Ross, MA, RD
Registered Dietitian, Women's Wellness

555 Bryant Street #497
Palo Alto, CA 94301
P 650 329 8855
F 650 833 0267
karenprrd@aol.com

1.

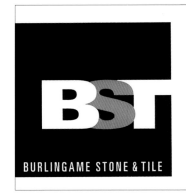

Dave Matovich

Burlingame Stone & Tile, Inc.
1322 Marsten Road
Burlingame, CA 94010
p 650 340 9474
f 650 340 9776
e bstinc@aol.com
Contractor's lic. #C54769913

2.

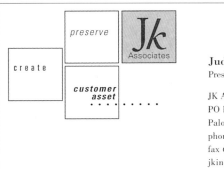

Judith W. Kincaid
President

JK Associates LLC
PO Box 61117
Palo Alto, CA 94306
phone 650.838.9816
fax 650.838.9867
jkincaid@jk-associates.com
www.jk-associates.com

3.

3351 N. Racine #D
Chicago, IL 60657
www.jillphoto.com

tel 773.871.5719
mobile 773.469.5079
jill@jillphoto.com

4.

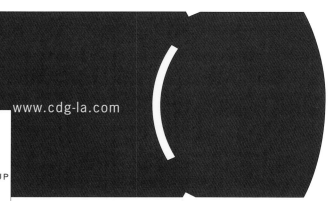

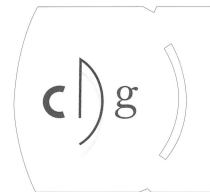

Gary J. Rivera
| *President*

CREATIV DESIGN GROUP
970 W. 190th Street
Suite 440
Torrance, CA 90502

T | 310.525.3200
F | 310.525.3249
C | 310.702.4000
E | gary@cdg-la.com

5.

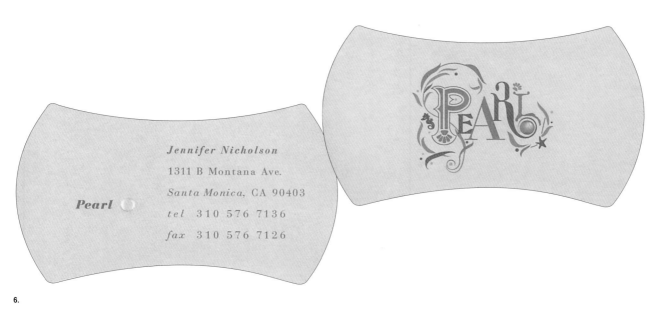

6.

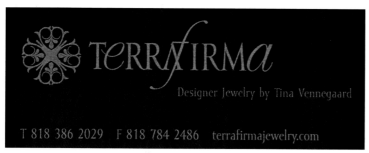

7.

8.

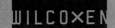

1-866-366-8483

D E S I G N

VINCENT WILCOXEN

5914 BLACKWELDER ST.
CULVER CITY, CA 90232
FAX: 310-559-7922

WWW.WILCOXENDESIGN.COM

1.

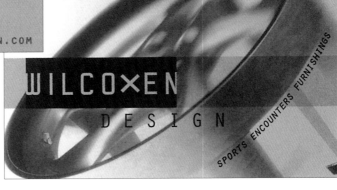

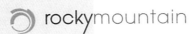

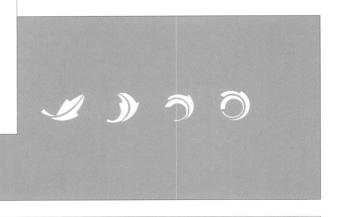

rockymountain

medical spa

KATHLEEN HAYES

Registered Nurse
Practice Manager

715 KENSINGTON AVE.
SUITE 24A
MISSOULA, MT 59801
T/ 406.549.5777
F/ 406.549.5777
kathy@montanamedicalspa.com

montanamedicalspa.com

2.

rockymountain

facial plastic surgery

DAVID M. HAYES, M.D.

h Academy of Facial
nstructive Surgery
Otolaryngology —
Surgery

715 KENSINGTON AVE.
SUITE 24A
MISSOULA, MT 59801
T/ 406.541.7546 (SKIN)
F/ 406.541.3955
info@montanamedicalspa.com

montanamedicalspa.com

A Division of Rocky Mountain Ear, Nose and Throat Center P.C.

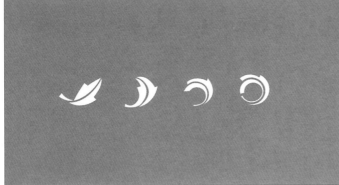

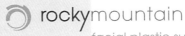

Joy Kovaleski
President

10960 Wilshire Blvd.
Suite 1240
Los Angeles, CA 90024

t 310·478·9700
f 310·478·2823
e jkovaleski@funzoneinc.com

*fun*z**o**ne
INCORPORATED

3.

KROG Studio za arhitekturo in grafično oblikovanje, d.o.o.
Krakovski nasip 22, 1000 Ljubljana
tel.+faks 01/4265 761, GSM 041/780 880

Edi Berk, dipl. ing. arh.
e-mail: edi.berk@krog.si

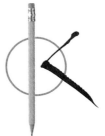

4.

MLINARIČ
Mesarija Mlinarič, d.o.o., Lesce
Železniška ul. 1, 4248 Lesce, Slovenija
T: +386 (0)4 531 83 32
F: +386 (0)4 531 88 72
M: +386 (0)41 721 556
E: joze.mlinaric@mlinaric.si
I: www.mlinaric.si

Jože Mlinarič
univ. dipl. inž. živil. tehnol.
direktor

5.

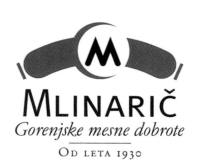

MLINARIČ
Gorenjske mesne dobrote
OD LETA 1930

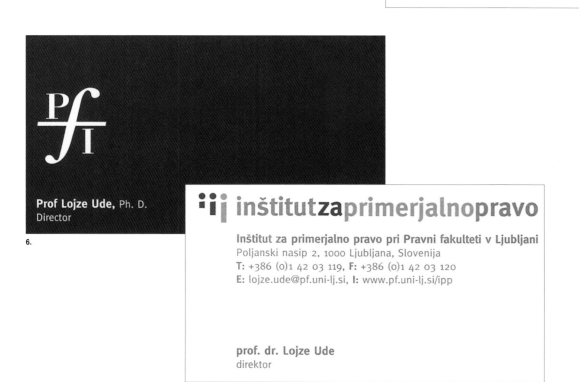

Prof Lojze Ude, Ph. D.
Director

6.

ıiı inštitutzaprimerjalnopravo

Inštitut za primerjalno pravo pri Pravni fakulteti v Ljubljani
Poljanski nasip 2, 1000 Ljubljana, Slovenija
T: +386 (0)1 42 03 119, **F:** +386 (0)1 42 03 120
E: lojze.ude@pf.uni-lj.si, **I:** www.pf.uni-lj.si/ipp

prof. dr. Lojze Ude
direktor

(1-3)
Design Firm **IE Design + Communications**
(4-6)
Design Firm **KROG, Ljubljana**

1.
Client   Wilcoxen Design
Designer   Cya Nelson
2.
Client   Rocky Mountain
Designer   Cya Nelson
3.
Client   Fun Zone
Designer   Marcie Carson
4.
Client   Krog
Designer   Edi Berk
5.
Client   Mlinaric
Designer   Edi Berk
6.
Client   Institut za primerjalno pravo
Designer   Edi Berk

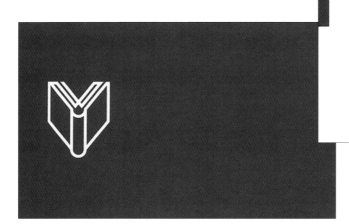

Univerzitetna knjižnica Maribor

Univerza v Mariboru
Univerzitetna knjižnica Maribor
Gospejna ulica 10, 2000 Maribor
tel.: 02/ 250 74 34, 040/261 333
faks: 02/ 252 75 58
e-pošta: vlasta.stavbar@uni-mb.si

mag. Vlasta Stavbar
*prof. zgod. in geog.
bibliotekarka v enoti za
domoznanstvo*

1.

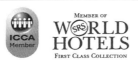

MEMBER OF
W RLD
HOTELS
FIRST CLASS COLLECTION

ICCA
Member

HOTEL MONS

HOTEL IN KONGRESNI CENTER LJUBLJANA

Monsadria, d.o.o., Pot za Brdom 55
SI–1000 Ljubljana, Slovenija
T: +386 (0)1 47 02 730
F: +386 (0)1 47 02 708
Andrea Peters   M: +386 (0)41 605 990
Vodja namestitev   E: andrea.peters@hotel.mons.si
Rooms Division Manager   I: www.hotel.mons.si

2.

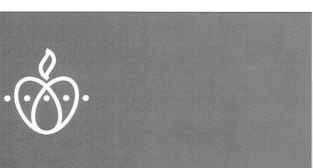

Perger
·1·7·5·7·

Medičarstvo, svečarstvo **Perger Hrabro s.p.**
Glavni trg 34, 2380 Slovenj Gradec
tel. + faks: 02/884 14 96
Galerija: tel.: 02/883 82 91, faks: 883 82 92
GSM: 041/66 88 98
e-pošta: h.perger@sgn.net

Hrabroslav Perger

3.

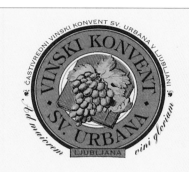

DR. JULIJ NEMANIČ, ENOLOG
Mednarodni pokuševalec vin
Predavatelj

JEREBOVA 14, 8330 METLIKA
TEL.: 01/280 52 43, 07/363 54 31
MOBITEL: 040/242 620
FAKS: 01/280 52 55
E-POŠTA:
JULIJ.NEMANIC@SIOL.NET
JULIJ.NEMANIC@KIS.SI

4.

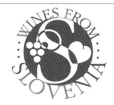

C/o DEBORAH COLLINSON
&
ASSOCIATES
Deborah Collinson
The Garden Flat, 40 Lexham Gardens
London W8 5JE, United Kingdom

Phone: 020 7373 0774
Telefax: 020 7373 0818
E-mail: WinePR@aol.com

5.

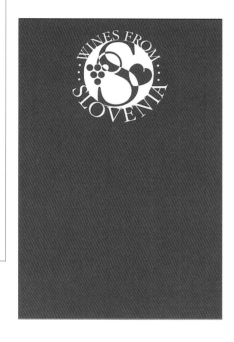

Odvetnik Peter Toš

Beethovnova 12, 1000 Ljubljana, Slovenija
T: +386 (0)1 / 200 17 40, **M:** +386 (0)41 / 733 000
F: +386 (0)1 / 200 17 41, **E:** peter.tos@siol.net

Peter Toš, odvetnik, Attorney at Law

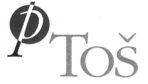

6.

Biro za komunalo

Biro za komunalo, d.o.o.
Projektiranje, inženiring in svetovanje

Dunajska 106, 1000 Ljubljana, Slovenija
tel.: +386 (0)1 5300 682
faks: +386 (0)1 5300 681
e-pošta: kranjc@b-k.si

Anton Kranjc, univ. dipl. ing. grad.
direktor

7.

Grafika¶aradoks

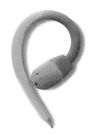

Grafika Paradoks Čopi Marko s.p.
Šmartinska 10, 1000 Ljubljana
Telefon: 01/430 11 20, 430 11 25
Telefaks: 01/430 11 25
Mobitel: 031/344 661
e-mail: grafika.paradoks@siol.net

Marko Čopi
direktor

8.

(1-8)
Design Firm **KROG, Ljubljana**

1.
Client   Univerzitetna knjiznica Maribor
Designer   Edi Berk
2.
Client   Hotel Mons
Designer   Edi Berk
3.
Client   Perger 1757
Designer   Marcie Carson
4.
Client   Vinski konvent sv. Urbana
Designer   Edi Berk
5.
Client   Wines from Slovenia
Designer   Edi Berk
6.
Client   Odvetnik Peter Tos
Designer   Edi Berk
7.
Client   Biro za komunalo
Designer   Edi Berk
8.
Client   Grafika Paradoks
Designer   Edi Berk

restavracija**glažuta**

stekleni dvor, dunajska 119, 1000 ljubljana

robert renninger, vodja restavracije
T: 01 565 43 26
F: 01 565 43 27
M: 031 357 751
E: glazuta@hotel.mons.si

1.

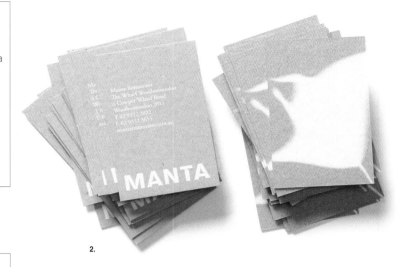

2.

Diana Liacos, MSN, CPNP
www.Perkins.org
617-972-7470

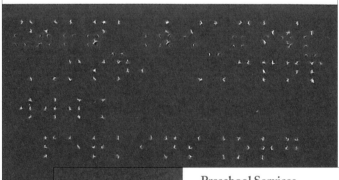

Preschool Services
Infant/Toddler Program and
Preschool Outreach

PreschoolServices@Perkins.org
617-972-7393 phone

175 North Beacon Street
Watertown, MA   02472

www.Perkins.org

617-972-7231 fax

PERKINS
SCHOOL FOR THE BLIND

3.

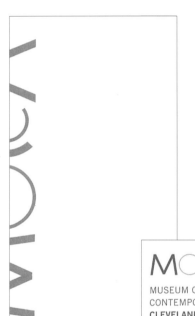

MOCA
MUSEUM OF
CONTEMPORARY ART
CLEVELAND

Heather Young
Visitor Services Manager

8501 Carnegie Avenue
Cleveland, Ohio 44106

www.MOCAcleveland.org

hyoung@MOCAcleveland.org
p 216.421.8671 ext. 42
f 216.421.0737

4.

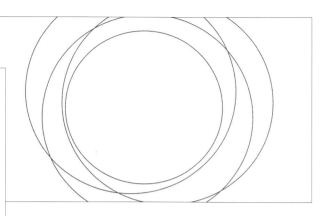

I. James Cavoli
Chief Executive Officer

30775 Bainbridge Road, Suite 270
Cleveland, Ohio 44139

P 440.519.1450
T 877.574.4321
F 440.519.1449
E Jim.Cavoli@LSInsights.com

LifeSettlementInsights.com

5.

Frederick C. Crawford Museum of Transportation and Industry

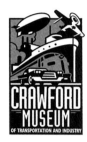

Lisa DeVito Pastor
Campaign Associate

email   lisa@wrhs.org
fax   216.721.8934
10825 East Boulevard   voice   216.721.5722 x289
Cleveland Ohio 44106
www.wrhs.org

6.

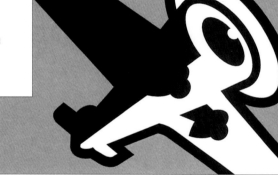

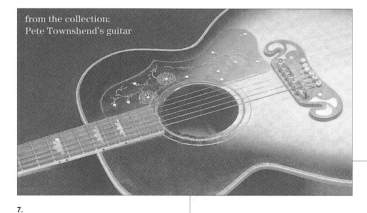

from the collection:
Pete Townshend's guitar

7.

One Key Plaza
Cleveland, Ohio 44114
fax 216 781.1326
216 515.1226

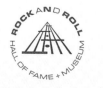

April Tracy
Event Coordinator

1.

Irwin M. Lowenstein, AIA Principal

a 3109 Mayfield Road, Suite 201
Cleveland, Ohio 44118

e irwin@LowensteinDurante.com
w www.LowensteinDurante.com

f 216.932.1891 p 216.932.1890

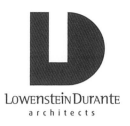

LOWENSTEIN DURANTE
a r c h i t e c t s

Imagination

2.

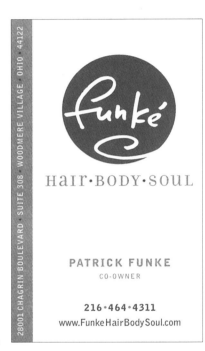

28001 CHAGRIN BOULEVARD • SUITE 308 • WOODMERE VILLAGE • OHIO • 44122

funké
HAIR · BODY · SOUL

PATRICK FUNKE
CO-OWNER

216•464•4311
www.FunkeHairBodySoul.com

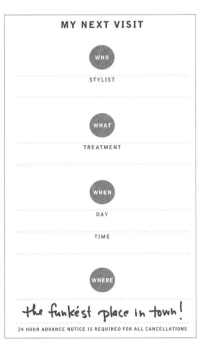

MY NEXT VISIT

WHO
STYLIST

WHAT
TREATMENT

WHEN
DAY

TIME

WHERE

the funkést place in town!

24 HOUR ADVANCE NOTICE IS REQUIRED FOR ALL CANCELLATIONS

3.

jumpstart

Benjamin (Ben) R. Keller
IT Director

JumpStart Inc.
737 Bolivar Road, Suite 3000
Cleveland, Ohio 44115
Ben.Keller@JumpStartInc.org
www.JumpStartInc.org
C 216.299.2989
T 216.363.3434

4.

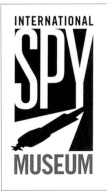

INTERNATIONAL
SPY
MUSEUM

William J. Adams
Group Tour Manager
P] 202.EYE.SPY.U [202.393.7798]
D] 202.207.0220
C] 202.262.7251

International Spy Museum
901 E Street NW Suite 103
Washington, DC 20004
www.spymuseum.org
badams@spymuseum.org
F] 202.393.7797

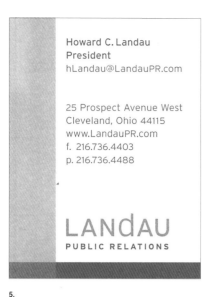

Howard C. Landau
President
hLandau@LandauPR.com

25 Prospect Avenue West
Cleveland, Ohio 44115
www.LandauPR.com
f. 216.736.4403
p. 216.736.4488

LANDAU
PUBLIC RELATIONS

5.

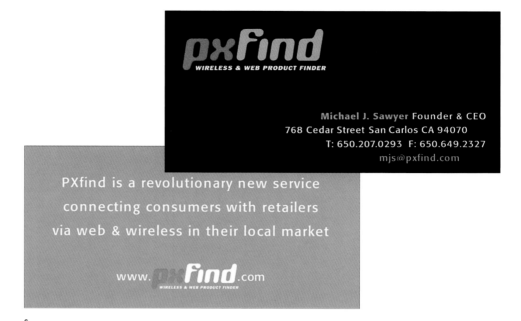

pxfind
WIRELESS & WEB PRODUCT FINDER

Michael J. Sawyer Founder & CEO
768 Cedar Street San Carlos CA 94070
T: 650.207.0293 F: 650.649.2327
mjs@pxfind.com

PXfind is a revolutionary new service
connecting consumers with retailers
via web & wireless in their local market

www. pxfind .com
WIRELESS & WEB PRODUCT FINDER

6.

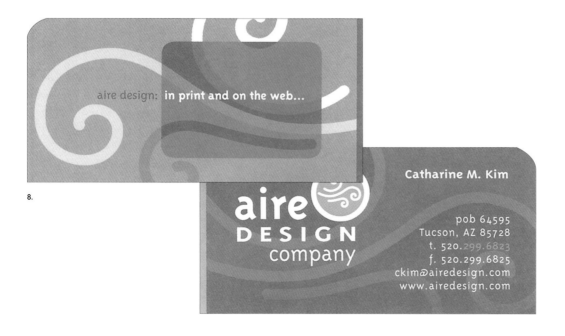

SIMPLY DINNERS

Eastside Location

homecooking made simple

Store: (520) 615-9050
Fax: (520) 232-5483

7865 E. Broadway, Suite 155 • Tucson, Arizona 85710-3975
www.simply-dinners.com • customerservice@simply-dinners.com

7.

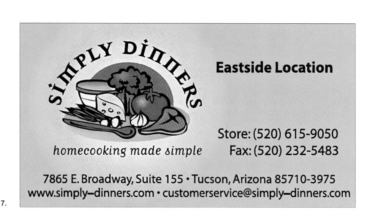

aire design: in print and on the web...

8.

Catharine M. Kim

aire
DESIGN
company

pob 64595
Tucson, AZ 85728
t. 520.299.6823
f. 520.299.6825
ckim@airedesign.com
www.airedesign.com

(1-5)
Design Firm **Nesnadny + Schwartz**
(6)
Design Firm **Sandy Gin Design**
(7,8)
Design Firm **Aire Design Company**

1.
Client   Lowenstein Durante Architects
Designer   Keith Pishnery
2.
Client   Funké Hair Body Soul
Designers   Stacie Ross, Teresa Snow
3.
Client   JumpStart Inc.
Designers   Jamie Finkelhor,
Gregory Oznowich
4.
Client   International Spy Museum
Designers   Mark Schwartz,
Gregory Oznowich
5.
Client   Landau Public Relations
Designers   Joyce Nesnadny,
Michele Moehler
6.
Client   PX Find
Designer   Sandy Gin
7.
Client   Simply Dinners
Designer   Catherine Kim Woodin
8.
Client   Aire Design Company
Designer   Catherine Kim Woodin

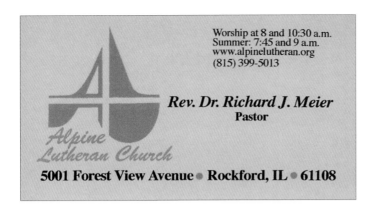

1.

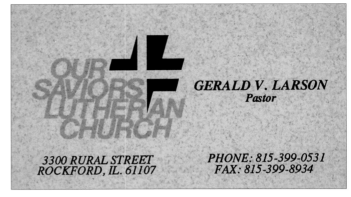

2.

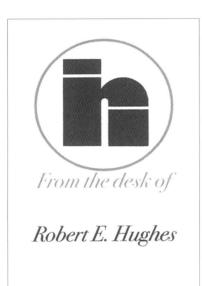

3.

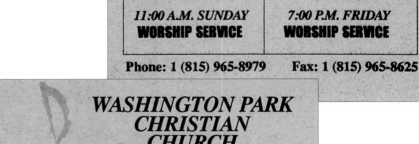

4.

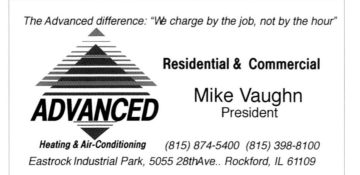

5.

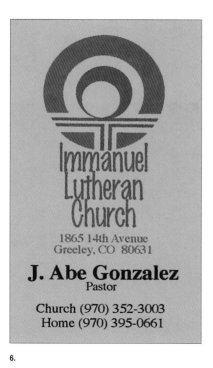

1865 14th Avenue
Greeley, CO 80631

J. Abe Gonzalez
Pastor

Church (970) 352-3003
Home (970) 395-0661

6.

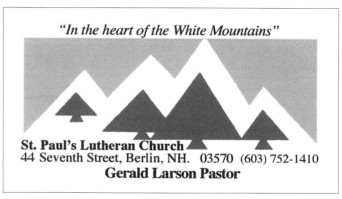

7.

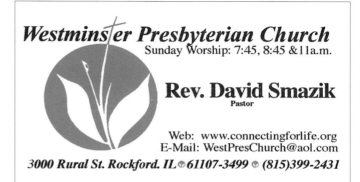

8.

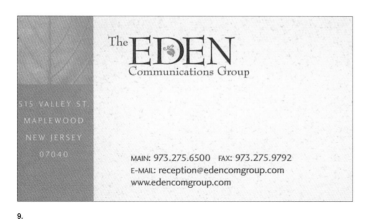

The **EDEN**
Communications Group

515 VALLEY ST.
MAPLEWOOD
NEW JERSEY
07040

MAIN: 973.275.6500   FAX: 973.275.9792
E-MAIL: reception@edencomgroup.com
www.edencomgroup.com

9.

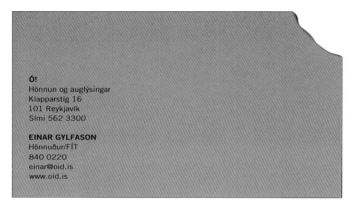

Ó!
Hönnun og auglýsingar
Klapparstig 16
101 Reykjavík
Sími 562 3300

EINAR GYLFASON
Hönnuður/FÍT
840 0220
einar@oid.is
www.oid.is

10.

(1-8)
Design Firm **Larson Logos**
(9)
Design Firm **The Eden**
Communications Group
(10)
Design Firm **Ó!**

1.
Client   Alpine Lutheran Church
Designer   Gerald V. Larson
2.
Client   Our Saviors Lutheran Church
Designer   Gerald V. Larson
3.
Client   Robert E. Hughes
Designer   Gerald V. Larson
4.
Client   Washington Park Christian Church
Designer   Gerald V. Larson
5.
Client   Advanced Heating &
             Air-Conditioning
Designer   Gerald V. Larson
6.
Client   Immanuel Lutheran Church
Designer   Gerald V. Larson

7.
Client   St. Paul's Lutheran Church
Designer   Gerald V. Larson
8.
Client   Westminster Presbyterian Church
Designer   Gerald V. Larson
9.
Client   The Eden Communications Group
Designer   Donna Malik
10.
Client   Ó!
Designer   Einar Gylfason

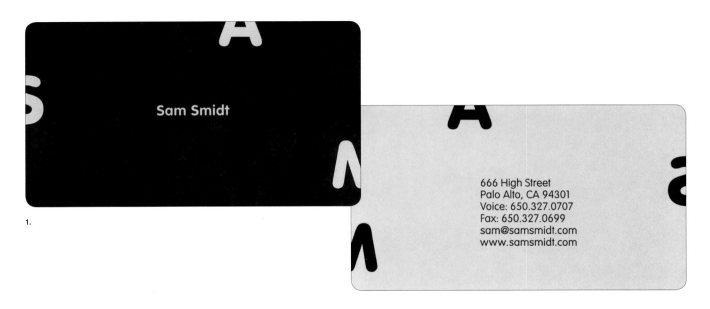

Sam Smidt

666 High Street
Palo Alto, CA 94301
Voice: 650.327.0707
Fax: 650.327.0699
sam@samsmidt.com
www. samsmidt.com

1.

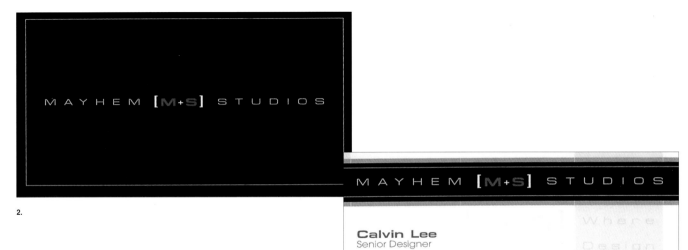

MAYHEM [M+S] STUDIOS

Calvin Lee
Senior Designer

www.mayhemstudios.com

cal@mayhemstudios.com
T: 323.276.9503
C: 323.533.8423

2.

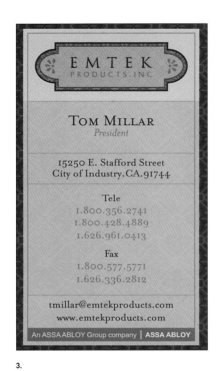

EMTEK
PRODUCTS.INC

TOM MILLAR
President

15250 E. Stafford Street
City of Industry. CA. 91744

Tele
1.800.356.2741
1.800.428.4889
1.626.961.0413

Fax
1.800.577.5771
1.626.336.2812

tmillar@emtekproducts.com
www.emtekproducts.com

An ASSA ABLOY Group company | ASSA ABLOY

3.

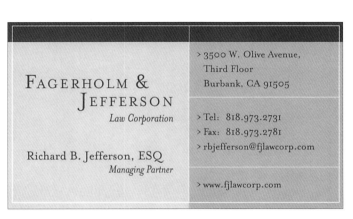

FAGERHOLM &
JEFFERSON
Law Corporation

Richard B. Jefferson, ESQ
Managing Partner

> 3500 W. Olive Avenue,
Third Floor
Burbank, CA 91505

> Tel: 818.973.2731
> Fax: 818.973.2781
> rbjefferson@fjlawcorp.com

> www.fjlawcorp.com

4.

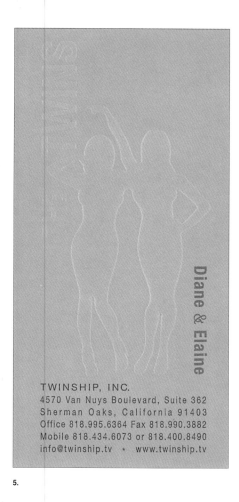

Diane & Elaine

TWINSHIP, INC.
4570 Van Nuys Boulevard, Suite 362
Sherman Oaks, California 91403
Office 818.995.6364 Fax 818.990.3882
Mobile 818.434.6073 or 818.400.8490
info@twinship.tv • www.twinship.tv

5.

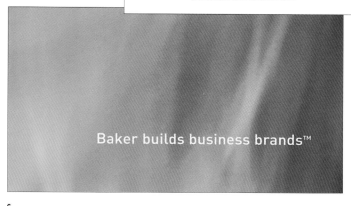

Gary Baker
President & Executive Creative Director

v 310.393.3993 x308
F 310.394.4705
E g.baker@bakerbuilds.com

Baker | Brand Communications℠

725 Arizona Ave. Suite 400 | Santa Monica, CA 90401
www.bakerbuilds.com

Baker builds business brands™

6.

APARTMENT IN PARIS
PRODUCTIONS

HELEN LAYNE
helensAPT@aol.com
646 234 5919

8.

Cari Clark

clark
CReaTiVE
PRINT & GRAPHIC DESIGN

p 912 228 4426
f 912 228 4427

cari@clarkcreativedesign.com

117 Lincoln Street 4A
Savannah, Georgia 31401

7.

LOGO DESIGN

BUSINESS CARDS

CORPORATE IDENTITY

PACKAGE DESIGN

NEWSLETTERS

WEB DESIGN

CATALOGS

www.clarkcreativedesign.com

(1)
Design Firm **Sam Smidt**
(2-4)
Design Firm **Mayhem Studios**
(5)
Design Firm **EPOS, Inc.**
(6)
Design Firm **Baker | Brand Communications**
(7)
Design Firm **Clark Creative
Print & Graphic Design**
(8)
Design Firm **the Mixx no kidding!**

1.
Client   Sam Smidt
Designer   Sam Smidt
2.
Client   Mayhem Studios
Designer   Calvin Lee
3.
Client   Emtek Products, Inc.
Designer   Calvin Lee
4.
Client   Fagerholm & Jefferson Law
                  Corporation
Designer   Calvin Lee

5.
Designers   Gabrielle Raumberger,
                    Christina Landers
6.
Client   Baker | Brand Communications
7.
Client   Clark Creative
Designer   Cari Clark
8.
Client   Apartment in Paris
Designer   Lisa Delaney

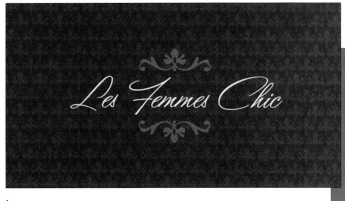

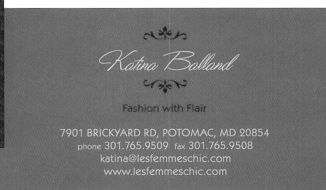

Katina Balland

Fashion with Flair

7901 BRICKYARD RD, POTOMAC, MD 20854
phone 301.765.9509 fax 301.765.9508
katina@lesfemmeschic.com
www.lesfemmeschic.com

1.

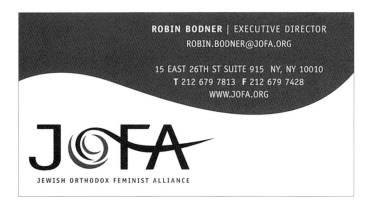

ROBIN BODNER | EXECUTIVE DIRECTOR
ROBIN.BODNER@JOFA.ORG

15 EAST 26TH ST SUITE 915 NY, NY 10010
T 212 679 7813 **F** 212 679 7428
WWW.JOFA.ORG

JEWISH ORTHODOX FEMINIST ALLIANCE

2.

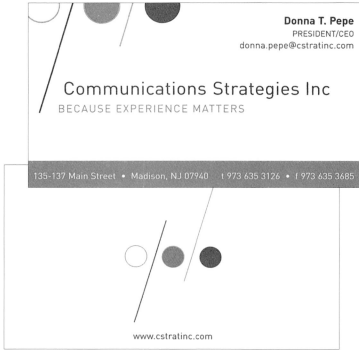

Donna T. Pepe
PRESIDENT/CEO
donna.pepe@cstratinc.com

Communications Strategies Inc
BECAUSE EXPERIENCE MATTERS

135-137 Main Street • Madison, NJ 07940   t 973 635 3126 • f 973 635 3685

www.cstratinc.com

3.

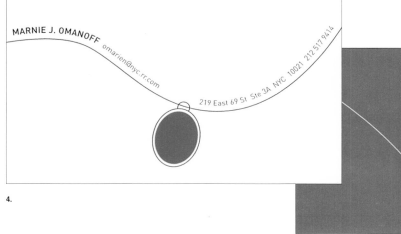

MARNIE J. OMANOFF omarien@nyc.rr.com

219 East 69 St Ste 3A NYC 10021 212 517 9414

4.

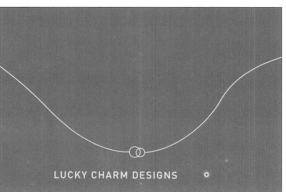

LUCKY CHARM DESIGNS

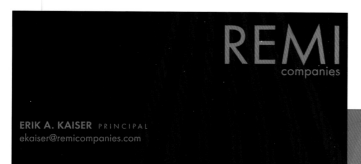

REMI
companies

ERIK A. KAISER PRINCIPAL
ekaiser@remicompanies.com

Real Estate. Real Vision.

Five Marine View Plaza Suite 401 Hoboken, New Jersey 07030
tel 201 420 7142 fax 201 420 7696 www.remicompanies.com

5.

VARSITY
ENTERTAINMENT

David Swartz
Senior Producer
swartz@varsityent.com

450 Park Avenue South

Floor 3

NYC

10016

T

212 779 3999

F

212 779 4999

www.varsityent.com

VARSITY ENTERTAINMENT

6.

Stephanie Astic
PRODUCTIONS

Stephanie Astic George
steph@asticproductions.com
850 Seventh Ave Suite 1102 NYC 10019
T 212.581.1400 F 212.581.1442

7.

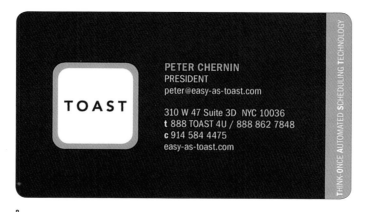

TOAST

PETER CHERNIN
PRESIDENT
peter@easy-as-toast.com

310 W 47 Suite 3D NYC 10036
t 888 TOAST 4U / 888 862 7848
c 914 584 4475
easy-as-toast.com

THINK ONCE AUTOMATED SCHEDULING TECHNOLOGY

8.

(1-8)
Design Firm **themixx**

1.
Client   Les Femmes Chic
Designer Lisa Delaney
2.
Client   JOFA
Designer Lisa Delaney
3.
Client   Communications Strategies
Designer Reed Seifer
4.
Client   Lucky Charm Designs
Designer Lisa Delaney
5.
Client   REMI Companies
Designer Lisa Delaney
6.
Client   Varsity Entertainment
Designer Lisa Delaney
7.
Client   Stephanie Astic Productions
Designer Lisa Delaney
8.
Client   TOAST
Designer Lisa Delaney

1.

antique and contemporary design

info@abhayatribeca.com

a b h a y a

145 hudson street nyc 10013 212.431.6931 f 212.431.6932

 First Quality Maintenance

 Classic Security

 Bright Star Couriers

 Onyx Restoration Works

2.

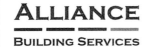 **ALLIANCE**

BUILDING SERVICES

Michael Rodriguez
President

70 West 36th Street New York, NY 10018
T: 212-244-6045 F: 212-947-7833
E: mrodriguez@alliancebuilding.us

CONSIDER IT DONE.

3.

ART JOHNSON, VICE PRESIDENT
art@metrohomesllc.com

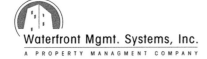 Waterfront Mgmt. Systems, Inc.
A PROPERTY MANAGMENT COMPANY

PO Box 271 Hoboken, NJ
T 201 420 0980 Ext.104 **F** 201 420
www.metrohomesll

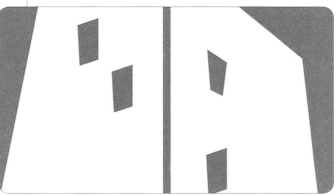

94

Carol Martin **Director, Sales and Operations**
CarolM@footagebank.com

1733 Abbot Kinney Boulevard Suite C
Venice California 90291
tel 310 822 1400 fax 310 822 4100
www.footagebank.com

FootageBank

4.

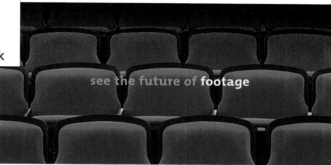

see the future of **footage**

Lisa A. Foti
lisafoti@citura.com

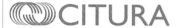CITURA

350 Seventh Avenue | Suite 1503 | NYC 10001
P 212 760 0545 | C 201 401 6839 | F 212 695 6664

5.

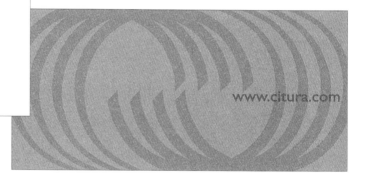

www.citura.com

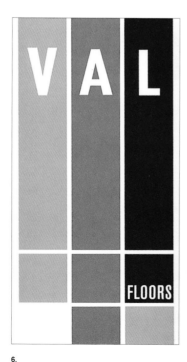

6.

LINDA J. LUPPINO
PROJECT MANAGER
lluppino@valfloors.com

CERAMIC
MARBLE
WOOD
CARPET
RESILIENT

4200 westside avenue
north bergen nj 07047
tel [NJ] 201 617 7900
tel [NYC] 212 690 7688
fax 201 617 0508
www.valfloors.com

(all)
 Design Firm **themixx**

1.
 Client Abhaya
 Designer Lisa Delaney
2.
 Client Alliance Building Services
 Designer Lisa Delaney
3.
 Client Waterfront Mgmt. Systems
 Designer Lisa Delaney
4.
 Client Footage Bank
 Designer Lisa Delaney
5.
 Client Citura
 Designer Liz Bernabe
6.
 Client VAL Floors
 Designer Reed Seifer

1.

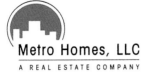

MICHELE BORYCZEWSKI, DIRECTOR OF OPERATIONS

michele@metrohomesllc.com

Metro Homes, LLC

A REAL ESTATE COMPANY

PO Box 271 Hoboken, NJ 07030

T 201 420 0980 Ext.105 **F** 201 420 5134 **P** 800 568 8437

www.metrohomesllc.com

2.

marc leonard.
vice-president, programming.
marc.leonard@logostaff.com

L**O**G**O**
different. together.

1775 Broadway, New York, NY 10019 t 212.767.8544 f 212.767.3943

L**O**G**O**
different. together.

3.

PAUL FRIED, PARTNER

paul@metrohomesllc.com

Waterfront Design Group, LLC

AN INTERIOR DESIGN COMPANY

PO Box 271 Hoboken, NJ 0

T 201 459 0990 **F** 201 459 0910 **P** 800 374

www.metrohomesll

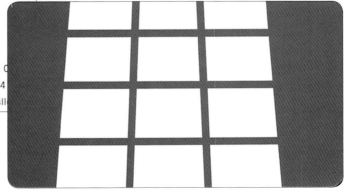

JAMES C. MCKENNA
PRESIDENT
CHIEF EXECUTIVE OFFICER
jmckenna@hunterrobertscg.com

T 212 786 4440

F 212 786 4441

C 917 453 2688

2 World Financial Center, 6th Floor ▮ New York, New York 10281

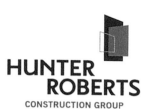

HUNTER
ROBERTS
CONSTRUCTION GROUP

www.hunterrobertscg.com

4.

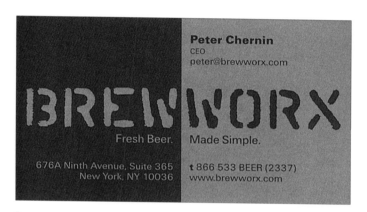

Peter Chernin
CEO
peter@brewworx.com

BREWWORX

Fresh Beer.   Made Simple.

676A Ninth Avenue, Suite 365   t 866 533 BEER (2337)
New York, NY 10036   www.brewworx.com

5.

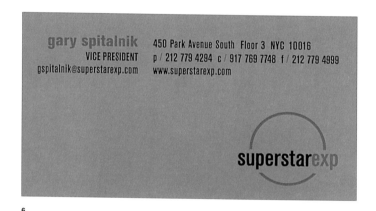

gary spitalnik   450 Park Avenue South Floor 3 NYC 10016
VICE PRESIDENT   p / 212 779 4294 c / 917 769 7748 f / 212 779 4999
gspitalnik@superstarexp.com   www.superstarexp.com

superstarexp

6.

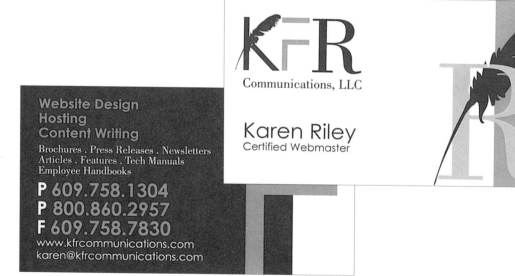

KFR
Communications, LLC

Karen Riley
Certified Webmaster

Website Design
Hosting
Content Writing

Brochures . Press Releases . Newsletters
Articles . Features . Tech Manuals
Employee Handbooks

P 609.758.1304
P 800.860.2957
F 609.758.7830

www.kfrcommunications.com
karen@kfrcommunications.com

7.

(1-6)
    Design Firm **themixx**
(7)
    Design Firm **KFR Communications, LLC**

1.
    Client   Metro Homes
    Designer   Lisa Delaney
2.
    Client   LOGO
    Designer   Lisa Delaney
3.
    Client   Waterfront Design Group
    Designer   Lisa Delaney
4.
    Client   Hunter Roberts
                Construction Group
    Designer   Lisa Delaney
5.
    Client   Brew Worx
    Designer   Lisa Delaney
6.
    Client   Superstar Exp
    Designer   Lisa Delaney
7.
    Client   KFR Communications, LLC
    Designer   Karen Riley

1.

SHARP DESIGNS

Graphics on the Cutting Edge

STEPHANIE SHARP

50 Florence Street
Hamilton, NJ 08610
(609) 392-8724
FAX (609) 392-8725
www.sharpdes.com
stefs@sharpdes.com

2.

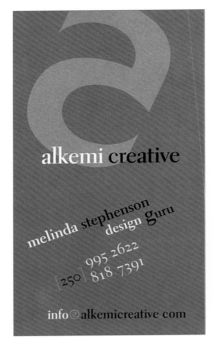
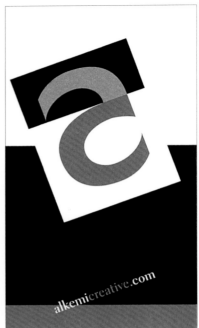

alkemi creative

melinda stephenson
design guru
995 2622
[250] 818 7391

info@alkemicreative.com

alkemicreative.com

3.

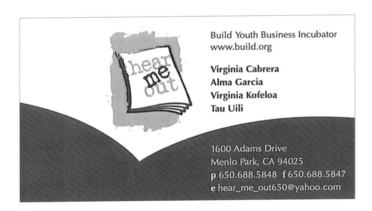

Build Youth Business Incubator
www.build.org

Virginia Cabrera
Alma Garcia
Virginia Kofeloa
Tau Uili

1600 Adams Drive
Menlo Park, CA 94025
p 650.688.5848 f 650.688.5847
e hear_me_out650@yahoo.com

4.

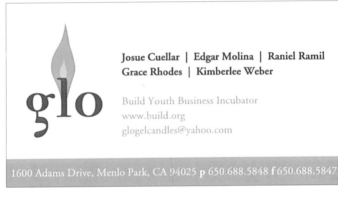

Josue Cuellar | Edgar Molina | Raniel Ramil
Grace Rhodes | Kimberlee Weber

Build Youth Business Incubator
www.build.org
glogelcandles@yahoo.com

1600 Adams Drive, Menlo Park, CA 94025 p 650.688.5848 f 650.688.5847

5.

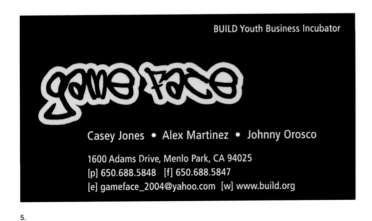

BUILD Youth Business Incubator

Casey Jones • Alex Martinez • Johnny Orosco

1600 Adams Drive, Menlo Park, CA 94025
[p] 650.688.5848 [f] 650.688.5847
[e] gameface_2004@yahoo.com [w] www.build.org

6.

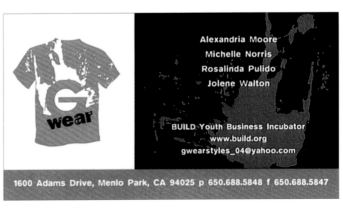

Alexandria Moore
Michelle Norris
Rosalinda Pulido
Jolene Walton

BUILD Youth Business Incubator
www.build.org
gwearstyles_04@yahoo.com

1600 Adams Drive, Menlo Park, CA 94025 p 650.688.5848 f 650.688.5847

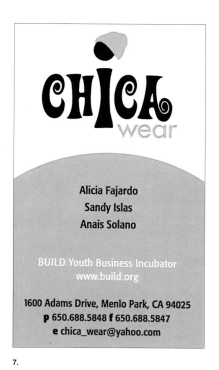

Alicia Fajardo

Sandy Islas

Anais Solano

BUILD Youth Business Incubator
www.build.org

1600 Adams Drive, Menlo Park, CA 94025
p 650.688.5848 **f** 650.688.5847
e chica_wear@yahoo.com

7.

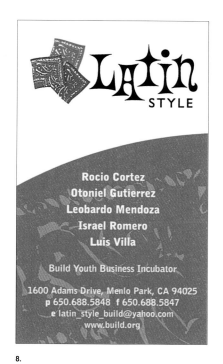

Rocio Cortez
Otoniel Gutierrez
Leobardo Mendoza
Israel Romero
Luis Villa

Build Youth Business Incubator

1600 Adams Drive, Menlo Park, CA 94025
p 650.688.5848 **f** 650.688.5847
e latin_style_build@yahoo.com
www.build.org

8.

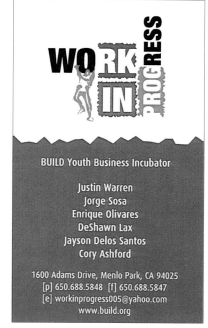

BUILD Youth Business Incubator

Justin Warren
Jorge Sosa
Enrique Olivares
DeShawn Lax
Jayson Delos Santos
Cory Ashford

1600 Adams Drive, Menlo Park, CA 94025
[p] 650.688.5848 [f] 650.688.5847
[e] workinprogress005@yahoo.com
www.build.org

9.

10.

746 Toro Canyon Road, Santa Barbara, CA 93108
Toll Free: 888-394-1333 | Tel: 805-695-0427
E-mail: ritarivest@mindspring.com | www.ritarivest.com

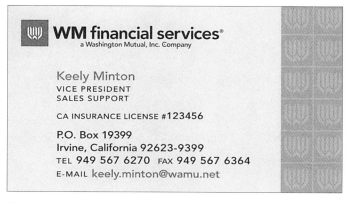

WM financial services®
a Washington Mutual, Inc. Company

Keely Minton
VICE PRESIDENT
SALES SUPPORT

CA INSURANCE LICENSE #123456

P.O. Box 19399
Irvine, California 92623-9399
TEL 949 567 6270   FAX 949 567 6364
E-MAIL keely.minton@wamu.net

11.

(1)
Design Firm **Sharp Designs**
(2)
Design Firm **alkemi creative**
(3-11)
Design Firm **Tajima Creative**

1.
Client   Sharp Designs
Designer   Stephanie Sharp
2.
Client   alkemi creative
Designer   Melinda Stephenson
3-9.
Client   BUILD Youth Business Incubator
Designers Komal Dedhia, Ximena Quijano,
              David Russell, Rich Nelson
10.
Client   Rita Rivest
Designers Komal Dedhia
11.
Client   Washington Mutual
Designers Komal Dedhia, Ellen Roebuck

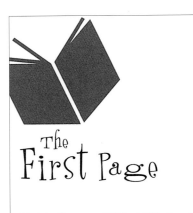

The First Page

Christy Coyne 270 East 17th Street
Suite 10
Costa Mesa
California 92627

Telephone:
949 645-KIDS
Fax:
949 645-5003

theFirstPage.net

1.

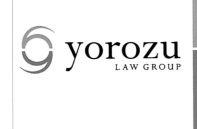
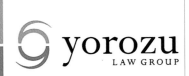

TASHA A. YOROZU
Attorney at Law

26 O'FARRELL ST, 9TH FLOOR
SAN FRANCISCO, CA 94108
PHONE 415.707.5011
FAX 415.707.5050
tyorozu@yorozulaw.com

萬 タシャ
弁護士

萬 グループ 法律事務所

26 O'FARRELL ST, 9TH FLOOR
SAN FRANCISCO, CA 94108
電話 415.707.5011
ファックス 415.707.5050
tyorozu@yorozulaw.com

2.

Chris Pearce
President

Ph: (808) 733-3330
Fax: (808) 733-3340

WORLD SAKE IMPORTS

3465 WAIALAE AVENUE · SUITE 340 · HONOLULU · HAWAII 96816 USA
cpearce@worldsake.com · Honolulu · San Francisco · New York

3.

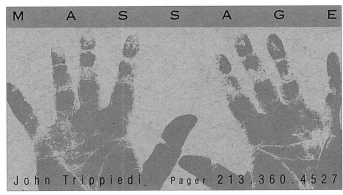

MASSAGE

John Trippiedi.   Pager 213.360.4527

4.

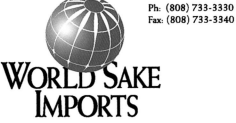

ROBERT FRAIDENBURGH
PRESIDENT

OPTIMET

4970 WINDPLAY DRIVE, SUITE C-6
EL DORADO HILLS, CA 95762
ph: 916-941-7366   fax: 916-941-7369

5.

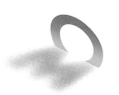

graphic **DesiGN**
michael niblett

Michael Niblett
1716 Hulen Street
Fort Worth, Texas 76110
817-257-7172 fax: 817-257-5814
m.niblett@tcu.edu

6.

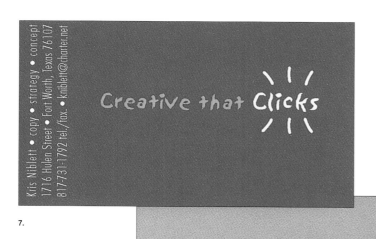

Creative that Clicks

Kris Niblett • copy • strategy • concept
1716 Hulen Street • Fort Worth, Texas 76107
817-731-1792 tel./fax. • kniblett@charter.net

7.

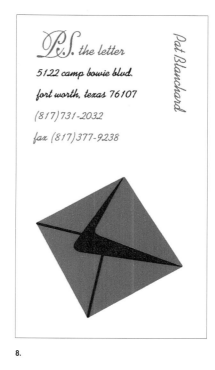

P.S. the letter

5122 camp bowie blvd.
fort worth, texas 76107
(817)731-2032
fax (817)377-9238

Pat Blanchard

8.

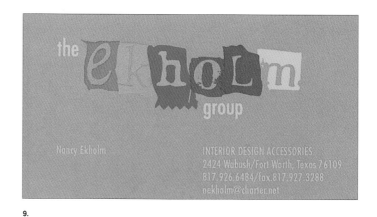

the ekholm group

Nancy Ekholm

INTERIOR DESIGN ACCESSORIES
2424 Wabash/Fort Worth, Texas 76109
817.926.6484/fax.817.927.3288
nekholm@charter.net

9.

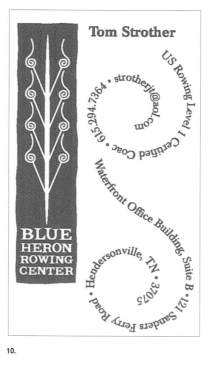

Tom Strother

US Rowing Level 1 Certified Coac • 615.294.7364 • strotherjt@aol.com

Waterfront Office Building, Suite B • 121 Sanders Ferry Road • Hendersonville, TN • 37075

BLUE HERON ROWING CENTER

10.

(1,2)
Design Firm **Tajima Creative**
(3)
Design Firm **UCI Inc/Urano Communication International**
(4,5)
Design Firm **J. Robert Faulkner Advertising**
(6-10)
Design Firm **Michael Niblett Design**

1.
Client   The First Page
Designer   Janice Wong
2.
Client   Yorozu Law Group
Designers   Komal Dedhia, Rich Nelson
3.
Client   World Sake Imports
Designers   Ryo T. Urano, Dwight Irick
4.
Client   John Trippiedi
Designers   John Trippiedi, Bob Faulkner

5.
Client   Optimet
Designers   Robert Fraidenbergh,
            Bob Faulkner
6.
Client   Michael Niblett Design
Designer   Michael Niblett
7.
Client   Creative that Clicks
Designer   Michael Niblett
8.
Client   PS the Letter
Designer   Michael Niblett
9.
Client   The Eckholm Group
Designer   Michael Niblett
10.
Client   Blue Heron Rowing Center
Designer   Michael Niblett

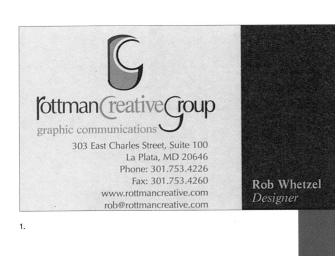

rottmanCreative**Group**
graphic communications

303 East Charles Street, Suite 100
La Plata, MD 20646
Phone: 301.753.4226
Fax: 301.753.4260
www.rottmancreative.com
rob@rottmancreative.com

Rob Whetzel
Designer

The *difference* is in the design.

1.

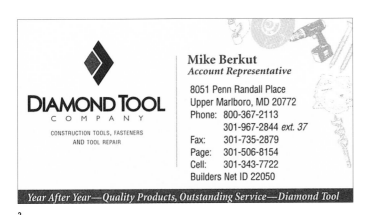

DIAMOND TOOL
C O M P A N Y

CONSTRUCTION TOOLS, FASTENERS
AND TOOL REPAIR

Mike Berkut
Account Representative

8051 Penn Randall Place
Upper Marlboro, MD 20772
Phone: 800-367-2113
            301-967-2844 *ext. 37*
Fax: 301-735-2879
Page: 301-506-8154
Cell: 301-343-7722
Builders Net ID 22050

Year After Year—Quality Products, Outstanding Service—Diamond Tool

2.

P. L. Doyle
I N C O R P O R A T E D
growing alternative & integrative health businesses

Patricia L. Doyle
PRESIDENT

502 Tobacco Quay
Alexandria, VA 22314
Phone: 703-299-0188
Fax: 703-299-1094
Email: pdoyle@pldoyle.com
www.pldoyle.com

3.

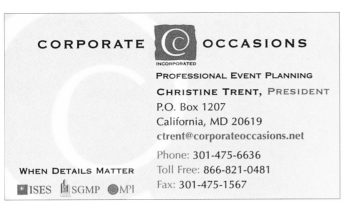

CORPORATE 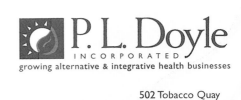 OCCASIONS
INCORPORATED

PROFESSIONAL EVENT PLANNING

CHRISTINE TRENT, PRESIDENT

P.O. Box 1207
California, MD 20619
ctrent@corporateoccasions.net

Phone: 301-475-6636
Toll Free: 866-821-0481
Fax: 301-475-1567

WHEN DETAILS MATTER

ISES SGMP MPI

4.

Atlantic
F I R E S T O P P I N G

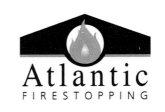

Tim Lancaster
Vice President

8051 Penn Randall Place
Upper Marlboro, MD 20772

Phone: 301-568-7288
Fax :   301-967-0218
Cell: 240-882-7179

Specializing in Firestop Installation Services

5.

6.

Pat Taylor
Graphic Designer
3540 S Street, NW
Washington, DC 20007
202•338•0962

7.

Pat	A	3540
Taylor	Graphic	S Street
Inc.	Design	Northwest
	Company	Washington
		DC 20007

Phone 202.338.0962

Fax 202.338.5630

8.

PAT TAYLOR INC 3540 S STREET NW WASHINGTON DC 20007 (202) 338-0962

9.

PAT TAYLOR		
Graphic	3540	Phone
Designer	S Street	202
	NorthWest	338
	Washington	0962
	DC	Fax
	20007	202
		944
		5471

10.

```
My company name is: Pat Taylor Inc
I'm a graphic design company
My address is: 3540 S Street NW
               Washington DC 20007
My phone number is: 202.338.0962
My facsimile number is: 202.944.5471
I do not have e-mail or a website.
Sorry.
```

(1-5)
Design Firm **Rottman Creative Group, LLC**
(6-10)
Design Firm **Pat Taylor Graphic Designer**

1.
Client Rottman Creative Group, LLC
Designer Gary Rottman
2.
Client Diamond Tool Company
Designer Gary Rottman
3.
Client P.L. Doyle
Designer Gary Rottman
4.
Client Corporate Occasions
Designer Gary Rottman
5.
Client Atlantic Fire Stopping
Designer Gary Rottman
6-10.
Client Pat Taylor Graphic Designer
Designer Pat Taylor

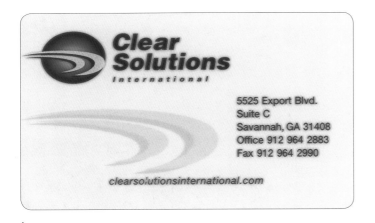

Clear Solutions
International

5525 Export Blvd.
Suite C
Savannah, GA 31408
Office 912 964 2883
Fax 912 964 2990

clearsolutionsinternational.com

1.

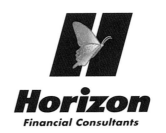

Horizon
Financial Consultants

Carol Whorley
Senior Loan Officer
6205 Abercorn Street
Suite 103
Savannah, GA 31405
912 303 9335 Office
912 303 9747 Processor
912 547 3132 Cell
912 303 9741 Fax

carol@horizonfinancialconsultants.com

2.

Longwater & Company

Elaine Longwater
President

Marketing
Advertising
PR and
Multimedia

619 Tattnall St.
Savannah, GA
31401

Phone
912 233 9200
Fax no.
912 233 1663
e-mail elaine@
longwater.com

3.

GreenerGrass
HAIR COLOR AND DESIGNS, INC.

Teresa Atwell

7373 Hodgson Memorial Drive ◆ Building #2
Savannah, Georgia 31406 ◆ 912-352-0700

4.

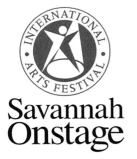

Savannah Onstage

Kim Askey
*Financial Manager/
Competition Coordinator*

26 East Bay Street
Savannah, GA 31401
Post Office Box 8105
Savannah, GA 31412
Phone (912) 236-5745
Fax (912) 236-1989

kim@savannahonstage.org
www.savannahonstage.org

5.

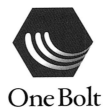

One Bolt

Ralph F. Wackenhut
Secretary & Treasurer

One Bolt, Inc.
333A Choccolocco St.
Oxford, AL 36203
U.S.A.

Phone: 256-835-1393
Fax: 256-831-6349

6.

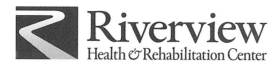

Riverview
Health & Rehabilitation Center

Linda McCorkle
Admissions & Marketing Director

6711 LaRoche Avenue, Savannah, GA 31406
(912) 354 8225 • Fax (912) 790 3238
www.riverviewhealth.net • riverviewhealth@aol.com

7.

Mission Statement

*Riverview Health and Rehabilitation Center has been
founded to provide competent and compassionate care
to meet the ever-changing health care needs of the
community and to provide a physically and emotionally
safe environment that will enrich the
quality of life for the residents.*

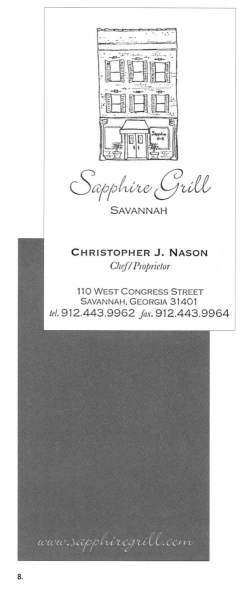

Sapphire Grill
SAVANNAH

CHRISTOPHER J. NASON
Chef/Proprietor

110 WEST CONGRESS STREET
SAVANNAH, GEORGIA 31401
tel. 912.443.9962 *fax.* 912.443.9964

www.sapphiregrill.com

8.

m i c i
~ HANDCRAFTED ITALIAN ~

ADAM VELA OWNER

1531 stout st. #150 denver, co 80202 | 303 629 mici (6424) | cell 720 427 4568
fax 303 629 8552 | adamvela@msn.com
www.miciitalian.com

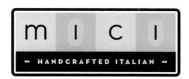
pizza   pasta   panini   vino   gelato

9.

(1-8)
Design Firm **Longwater & Company**
(9)
Design Firm **Ellen Bruss Design**

1.
Client   Clear Solutions International
Designer Kathryn Strozier
2.
Client   Horizon Financial Consultants
Designer Kathryn Strozier
3.
Client   Longwater & Co., Inc.
Designer Kathryn Strozier
4.
Client   Greener Grass
Designer Kathryn Strozier

5.
Client   Savannah Onstage Music &
          Arts Festival
Designer Kathryn Strozier
6.
Client   One Bolt, Inc.
Designer Kathryn Strozier
7.
Client   Riverview Health &
          Rehabilitation Center
Designer Kathryn Strozier
8.
Client   Sapphire Grill
Designers Amy Mason, Patrick Grone
9.
Client   MICI
Designers Ellen Bruss Design Team

ADAM J. LERNER, PhD EXECUTIVE DIRECTOR

THELAB ART+IDEAS

THE LAB AT BELMAR 1430 WYNKOOP NO.100 DENVER. CO 80202
P 303 573 0050 F 303 573 0011 ADAM@BELMARLAB.ORG

1.

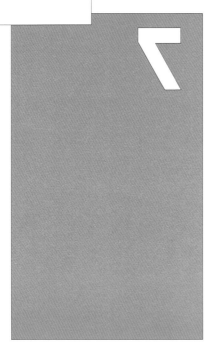

7

Giovanni Stone IDSA
Curator · BLOCK SEVEN
P303·742·1525 F303·742·1526
445 South Saulsbury Street
Lakewood Colorado 80226

2.

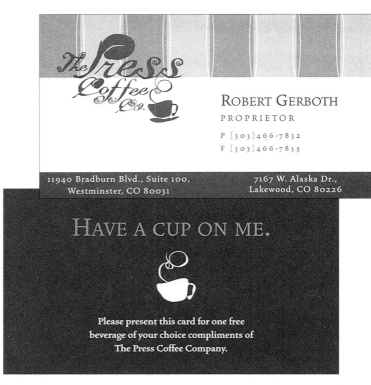

The Press Coffee Co.

ROBERT GERBOTH
PROPRIETOR
P [303]466-7832
F [303]466-7835

11940 Bradburn Blvd., Suite 100,   7167 W. Alaska Dr.,
Westminster, CO 80031   Lakewood, CO 80226

HAVE A CUP ON ME.

Please present this card for one free
beverage of your choice compliments of
The Press Coffee Company.

3.

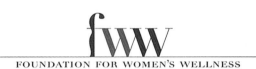

DEE CHIRAFISI KENTWOOD CITY PROPERTIES
1660 SEVENTEENTH STREET SUITE 100 DENVER CO 80202
WWW.REALTOR.COM/DENVER/DEECHIRAFISI
P 303 881 6312 F 303 302 5011

4.

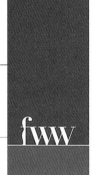

fww
FOUNDATION FOR WOMEN'S WELLNESS

5.

SHARON CRAVITZ
EXECUTIVE DIRECTOR

FOUNDATION FOR WOMEN'S WELLNESS
1000 SOUTH RACE STREET
DENVER, CO 80209
303.548.0595 PHONE
303.744.7759 FAX
SHARONCRAVITZ@THEFWW.ORG
WWW.THEFWW.ORG

fww

K. C. LIM
Chief Executive Officer
H/P: +6 012-202 8889

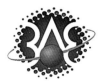

BAE INTERNATIONAL INC. SDN BHD (623691-K)
Level 25, Plaza Pengkalan, 3rd Mile Jalan Ipoh,
51100 Kuala Lumpur, Malaysia.
Tel: +(603) 4043 8889 Fax: +(603) 4043 8899
E-mail: kc13@tm.net.my
Website: www.myBAE.com

6.

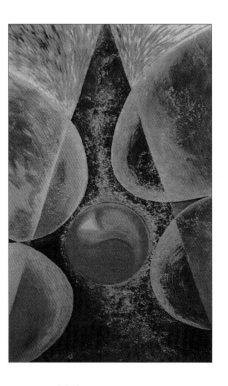

(1-5)
Design Firm **Ellen Bruss Design**
(6)
Design Firm **Truefaces Creation SDN BHD**

1.
Client   The Lab
Designers   Ellen Bruss Design Team
2.
Client   Block 7
Designers   Ellen Bruss Design Team
3.
Client   Press Coffee Company
Designers   Ellen Bruss Design Team
4.
Client   Arthouse
Designers   Ellen Bruss Design Team
5.
Client   Foundation for Women's
                  Wellness
Designers   Ellen Bruss Design Team
6.
Client   BAE International Inc. Sdn Bhd

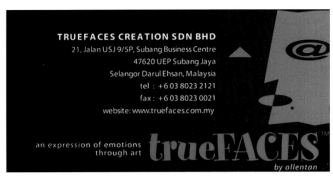

TRUEFACES CREATION SDN BHD
21, Jalan USJ 9/5P, Subang Business Centre
47620 UEP Subang Jaya
Selangor Darul Ehsan, Malaysia
tel : +6 03 8023 2121
fax : +6 03 8023 0021
website: www.truefaces.com.my

an expression of emotions through art **trueFACES**™
by allentan

1.

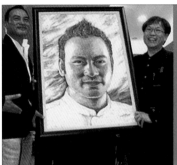

@llentan
mobile +6 012 208 2608
allentan@truefaces.com

TrueFACES paintings are also displayed
@ KIARA-COM SDN BHD
Suite A-0G-03, Block A, Plaza Mont Kiara
2, Jalan Kiara, Mont Kiara, 50480 Kuala Lumpur

Canon

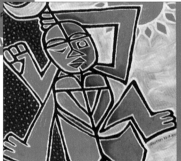

@llentan
mobile +6 012 208 2608
allentan@truefaces.com.my

TrueFACES paintings are also displayed
@ KIARA-COM SDN BHD
Suite A-0G-03, Block A, Plaza Mont Kiara
2, Jalan Kiara, Mont Kiara, 50480 Kuala Lumpur

Canon

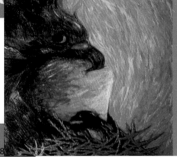

@llentan
mobile +6 012 208 2608
allentan@truefaces.com.my

TrueFACES paintings are also displayed
@ KIARA-COM SDN BHD
Suite A-0G-03, Block A, Plaza Mont Kiara
2, Jalan Kiara, Mont Kiara, 50480 Kuala Lumpur

Canon

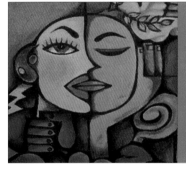

@llentan
mobile +6 012 208 2608
allentan@truefaces.com.my

TrueFACES paintings are also displayed
@ KIARA-COM SDN BHD
Suite A-0G-03, Block A, Plaza Mont Kiara
2, Jalan Kiara, Mont Kiara, 50480 Kuala Lumpur

Canon

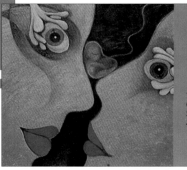

@llentan
mobile +6 012 208 2608
allentan@truefaces.com.my

TrueFACES paintings are also displayed
@ KIARA-COM SDN BHD
Suite A-0G-03, Block A, Plaza Mont Kiara
2, Jalan Kiara, Mont Kiara, 50480 Kuala Lumpur

Canon

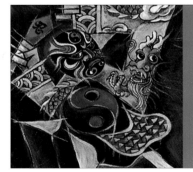

@llentan
mobile +6 012 208 2608
allentan@truefaces.com.my

TrueFACES paintings are also displayed
@ KIARA-COM SDN BHD
Suite A-0G-03, Block A, Plaza Mont Kiara
2, Jalan Kiara, Mont Kiara, 50480 Kuala Lumpur

Canon

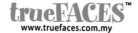

@llentan
+6 012-208 2608

trueFACES™
www.truefaces.com.my

TRUEFACES CREATION SDN BHD

11, Jalan USJ5/3F, UEP Subang Jaya
47610 Subang Jaya, Selangor, Malaysia
Fax : +6 03-5631 0051
Email : allentan@truefaces.com.my

Original paintings also displayed @ KIARA-COM SDN BHD
Suite A-0G-03, Block A, Plaza Mont Kiara, 2, Jalan Kiara, Mont Kiara, 50480 Kuala Lumpur.

2.

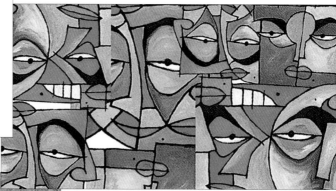

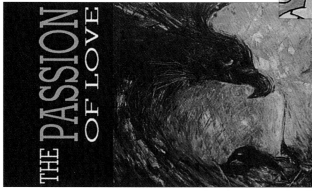

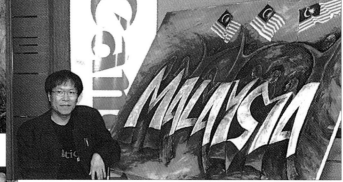

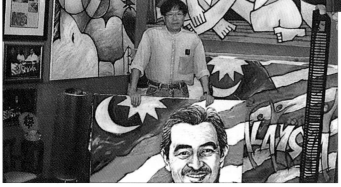

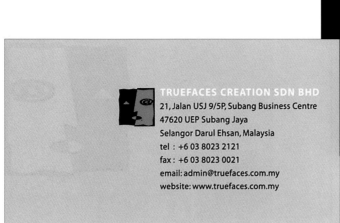

3.

TRUEFACES CREATION SDN BHD
21, Jalan USJ 9/5P, Subang Business Centre
47620 UEP Subang Jaya
Selangor Darul Ehsan, Malaysia
tel : +6 03 8023 2121
fax : +6 03 8023 0021
email: admin@truefaces.com.my
website: www.truefaces.com.my

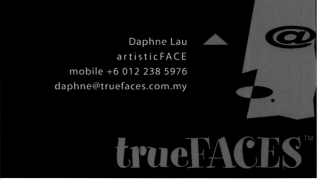

Daphne Lau
artisticFACE
mobile +6 012 238 5976
daphne@truefaces.com.my

trueFACES™

(1-3)
Design Firm **Truefaces Creation Sdn Bhd**

1-3.
Client   Truefaces Creation Sdn Bhd

109

1.

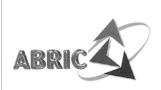

王荣禄
Dato' Albert E.L. Ong
Chief Executive Officer

ABRIC BERHAD
Level 3, Lot 8, Jalan Astaka U8/84
Bukit Jelutong, 40100 Shah Alam
Selangor Darul Ehsan, Malaysia
Tel : +603 7847 5555
Fax: +603 7846 5555
E-mail: albertong@abric.net

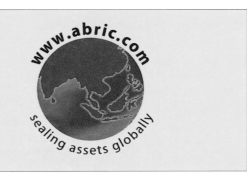

www.abric.com
sealing assets globally

2.

Ali
H/P: 016-278 6642

WE CATER FOR ALL OCCASIONS

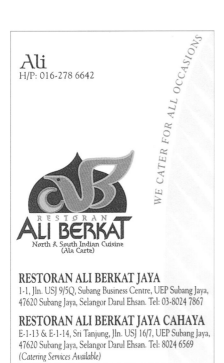

RESTORAN
ALI BERKAT
North & South Indian Cuisine
(Ala Carte)

RESTORAN ALI BERKAT JAYA
1-1, Jln. USJ 9/5Q, Subang Business Centre, UEP Subang Jaya,
47620 Subang Jaya, Selangor Darul Ehsan. Tel: 03-8024 7867

RESTORAN ALI BERKAT JAYA CAHAYA
E-1-13 & E-1-14, Sri Tanjung, Jln. USJ 16/7, UEP Subang Jaya,
47620 Subang Jaya, Selangor Darul Ehsan. Tel: 8024 6569
(Catering Services Available)

3.

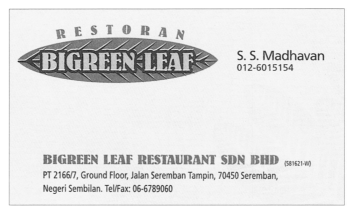

S. S. Madhavan
012-6015154

BIGREEN LEAF RESTAURANT SDN BHD (581621-W)
PT 2166/7, Ground Floor, Jalan Seremban Tampin, 70450 Seremban,
Negeri Sembilan. Tel/Fax: 06-6789060

4.

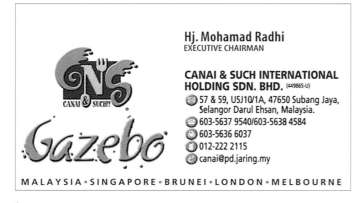

Hj. Mohamad Radhi
EXECUTIVE CHAIRMAN

**CANAI & SUCH INTERNATIONAL
HOLDING SDN. BHD.** (449865-U)
57 & 59, USJ10/1A, 47650 Subang Jaya,
Selangor Darul Ehsan, Malaysia.
603-5637 9540/603-5638 4584
603-5636 6037
012-222 2115
canai@pd.jaring.my

MALAYSIA•SINGAPORE•BRUNEI•LONDON•MELBOURNE

5.

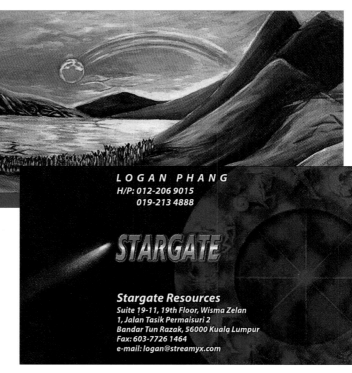

LOGAN PHANG
H/P: 012-206 9015
019-213 4888

STARGATE

Stargate Resources
Suite 19-11, 19th Floor, Wisma Zelan
1, Jalan Tasik Permaisuri 2
Bandar Tun Razak, 56000 Kuala Lumpur
Fax: 603-7726 1464
e-mail: logan@streamyx.com

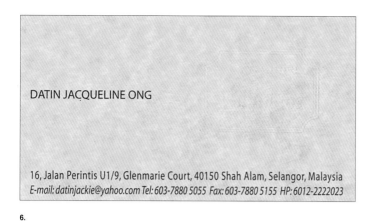

DATIN JACQUELINE ONG

16, Jalan Perintis U1/9, Glenmarie Court, 40150 Shah Alam, Selangor, Malaysia
E-mail: datinjackie@yahoo.com Tel: 603-7880 5055 Fax: 603-7880 5155 HP: 6012-2222023

6.

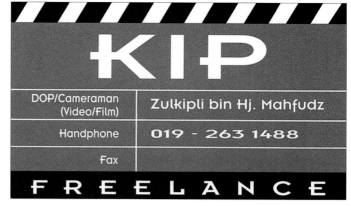

DOP/Cameraman (Video/Film) — Zulkipli bin Hj. Mahfudz
Handphone — 019 - 263 1488
Fax —

7.

kamaltan
019-3710386

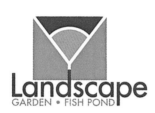

Landscape
GARDEN • FISH POND

10, JALAN USJ 11/3K, UEP SUBANG JAYA
SELANGOR DARUL EHSAN. TEL: 03-5637 2764

8.

CHUNG HON CHEONG
Managing Director

R Link

Reward-Link•com Sdn Bhd
506774-K
19th Floor, Menara Kurnia, No. 9, Jalan PJS 8/9,
46150 Petaling Jaya, Selangor Darul Ehsan.
Tel: +6 03-7875 7266 Fax: +6 03-7875 7070
H/P: +6 012-329 1830   email: hcchung@rexit.com

9.

TING PAI SHIN
012-337 0077

TTL

TTL DISTRIBUTORS SDN BHD
4261B-P
19, Jalan Penyelengara U1/77,
Taman Perindustrian Batu Tiga,
40150 Shah Alam, Selangor.
Tel: 03-5510 9781, 5510 3495
Fax: 03-5510 3512
E-mail: ttldist@tm.net.my
Website: www.ttldistributors.com.my

10.

(1-10)
Design Firm **Truefaces Creation Sdn Bhd**

1.
Client   Abric Berhad
2.
Client   Restoran Ali Berkat Jaya
3.
Client   Bigreen Leaf Restaurant Sdn Bhd
4.
Client   Canai & Such International
          Holding Sdn Bhd
5.
Client   Stargate Resources
6.
Client   Datin Jacqueline Ong
7.
Client   KIP
8.
Client   Landscape
9.
Client   Reward-Link.com Sdn Bhd
10.
Client   TTL Distributors Sdn Bhd

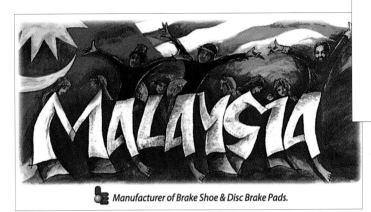

Manufacturer of Brake Shoe & Disc Brake Pads.

1.

PUA YU LEN 潘宥年
DIRECTOR
012-2116129

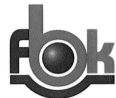

FBK SYSTEMS SDN. BHD.
(376449-D)
No. 5 & 7, Jalan BJ 6,
Taman Perindustrian Belmas Johan,
48000 Rawang, Selangor Darul Ehsan, Malaysia.
Tel: 03-6093 3928, 6093 6468 Fax: 03-6093 1928
E-mail: fbkmal@tm.net.my

Muraleedarren
Principal Facilitator
019 215 6278

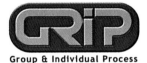

Group & Individual Process

Suite 33-01, 33rd Floor, Menara Keck Seng,
203 Jalan Bukit Bintang, 55100 Kuala Lumpur

Tel: +603 2116 5606   Fax: +603 2116 5888   Email: griptnw@tm.net.my

2.

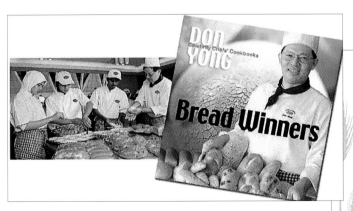

3.

DON YONG
B.Sc., M.Sc. (UK).
CHIEF EXECUTIVE OFFICER
H/P: 019-351 3518

MALAYSIAN INSTITUTE OF BAKING
(Formerly known as English Hotbreads School of Baking (M) Sdn. Bhd.)

11, Jalan 52/8, New Town, 46200 Petaling Jaya, Selangor Darul Ehsan
Tel: 603-7956 9011 / 7956 9043 Fax: 603-7954 1557 / 7955 2457
E-mail: don_yong@tm.net.my / ehbsb@tm.net.my

Muhammad Adam Bin Abdullah
Director of Sales
012-366 0786

MAJU CURRY HOUSE SDN. BHD. (617550-X)
11-1, Jln 45A/26, Taman Sri Rampai, Setapak,
53300 Kuala Lumpur, Malaysia.
Tel: 603-4149 2611 Fax: 603-4142 6211

MARKETING OFFICE:
42-2, Jalan Dagang, SB4/2 Taman Sungai Besi Indah,
43300 Balakong, Selangor Darul Ehsan.
Tel: 603-8941 1786, 8941 2786 Fax: 603-8941 3786

4.

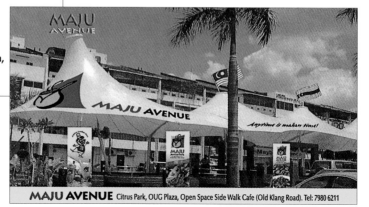

MAJU AVENUE Citrus Park, OUG Plaza, Open Space Side Walk Cafe (Old Klang Road). Tel: 7980 6211

Hala Lim Chin Leong
+6012-538 1557

MAX POWER ADVANTAGE SDN BHD (658767-D)
J-1-17, Jalan PJU 1/43, Aman Suria Damansara,
47301 Petaling Jaya, Malaysia.
e-mail: halatrans2003@yahoo.com

ECO CHARGE
www.eco-charge.jp

5.

I'm Eco-Friendly×Eco-Power

K. Balasubramaniam@Jagen
Managing Director
H/P: 012-339 9442

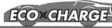

SUBAAHANA
MALAYSIA SDN. BHD.

42-2, Jalan Dagang, SB4/2 Taman Sungai Besi Indah, 43300 Balakong, Selangor Darul Ehsan.
Tel: 03-8941 1786, 8941 2786 Fax: 03-8941 3786

6.

• Interior Design • Renovation • Wall Paper • Customized Cabinets
• Vertical Blind • Wiring • Carpeting • Commission Agent
• Souvenir And Florist Center • Marketing Agent

(1-6)
Design Firm **Truefaces Creation Sdn Bhd**

1.
Client FBK Systems Sdn Bhd
2.
Client Grip Training Workshop
3.
Client Malaysian Institute of Baking
4.
Client Maju Curry House Sdn Bhd
5.
Client Max Power Advantage Sdn Bhd
6.
Client Subaahana Malaysia Sdn Bhd

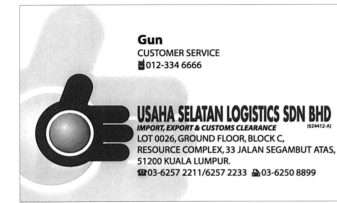

Gun
CUSTOMER SERVICE
📱012-334 6666

USAHA SELATAN LOGISTICS SDN BHD (624412-A)
IMPORT, EXPORT & CUSTOMS CLEARANCE
LOT 0026, GROUND FLOOR, BLOCK C,
RESOURCE COMPLEX, 33 JALAN SEGAMBUT ATAS,
51200 KUALA LUMPUR.
☎03-6257 2211/6257 2233   📠03-6250 8899

1.

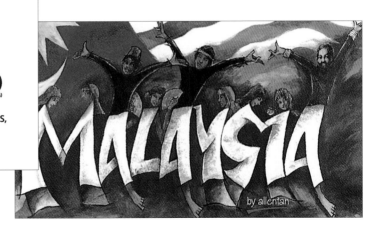

by allenfan

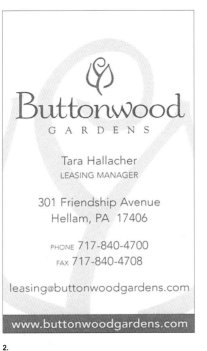

Tara Hallacher
LEASING MANAGER

301 Friendship Avenue
Hellam, PA 17406

PHONE 717-840-4700
FAX 717-840-4708

leasing@buttonwoodgardens.com

www.buttonwoodgardens.com

2.

Randy Farrales
PROPERTY MANAGER

3002-1 Mackenzi Lane
York, PA 17404

PHONE 717-792-4595

pmgr@colonialgardensyork.com

www.colonialgardensyork.com

3.

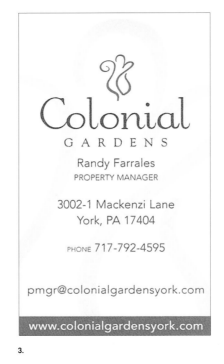

Robert Baylor

530 Hammond Rd.
York, PA 17402

PH (717) 840-9071
FX (717) 840-9073

rbaylor@cad-ware.com
www.cad-ware.com

4.

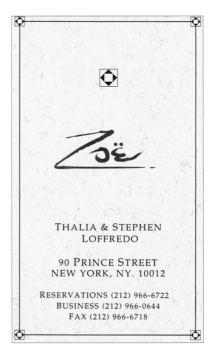

THALIA & STEPHEN
LOFFREDO

90 PRINCE STREET
NEW YORK, NY. 10012

RESERVATIONS (212) 966-6722
BUSINESS (212) 966-0644
FAX (212) 966-6718

5.

Ronald B. Low M.D., F.A.C.S.
EAR, NOSE & THROAT
HEAD AND NECK SURGERY

20 PROSPECT AVENUE, SUITE 909
HACKENSACK, NJ 07601
TEL: 201-489-6520
FAX: 201-489-6530

6.

DAVID SABLE, M.D.
154 West 71st Street
New York, NY 10023
Tel: 212.496.1177
Fax: 212.712.2389
E-Mail: DSable@armtnyc.com

A R M T

ASSISTED REPRODUCTIVE MEDICAL TECHNOLOGIES

7.

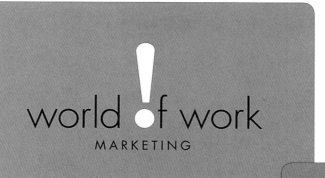

world !of work
MARKETING

8.

Communications Solutions That Mean Business
Claire M. Stoddard, President

!

180 Cabrini Boulevard, Suite 126, New York, NY 10033
T 212.795.6606 F 212.795.6586
claire@worldofworksolutions.com

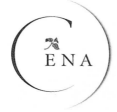

ENA

Albert Melera
Service Manager

12 East 22nd Street
New York, NY 10010

Reservations 212.505.1222
Business 212.253.5647
Fax 212.253.5649

9.

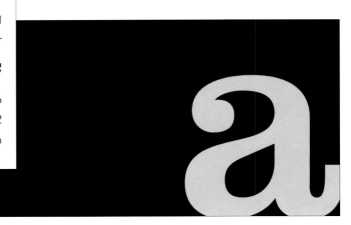

JASON FRIEDMAN
Studio Manager/Senior Photographer

adam raphael photography, LLC

347 Fifth Avenue, #303 New York, NY 10016

Tel: (212) 685-6661 Cell: (917) 861-6030 Fax: (212) 685-6662

user171251@aol.com www.adamraphael.com

1.

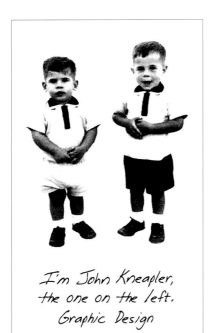

I'm John Kneapler,
the one on the left.
Graphic Design

2.

John Kneapler
President

John Kneapler Design
151 West 19th Street
Suite 11c
New York, NY 10011

Tel 212.463.9774
Fax 212.463.0478

JKneapler@aol.com
www.JohnKneaplerDesign.com

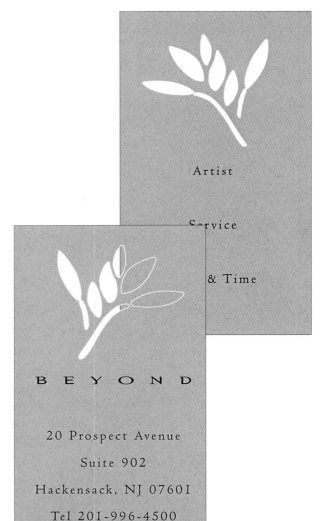

Artist

Service

& Time

B E Y O N D

20 Prospect Avenue

Suite 902

Hackensack, NJ 07601

Tel 201-996-4500

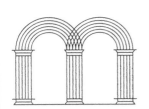

Mann Realty Associates
OWNERS · INVESTORS · MANAGERS

Maurice A. Mann
CHIEF EXECUTIVE OFFICER

1776 Broadway, 23rd Fl. New York, NY 10019
Tel: 212.977.0000 Ext. 222 Fax: 212.977.0086
Email: maurice@mannrealty.com
Licensed Real Estate Broker

3.

4.

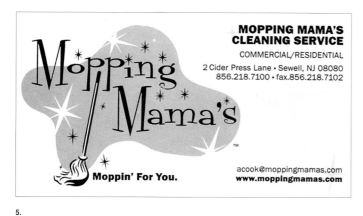

MOPPING MAMA'S CLEANING SERVICE

COMMERCIAL/RESIDENTIAL

2 Cider Press Lane • Sewell, NJ 08080
856.218.7100 • fax.856.218.7102

acook@moppingmamas.com
www.moppingmamas.com

5.

Leigh Maida
Graphic Design

2215 Christian Street Philadelphia, PA 19146
t/215.605.5667   f/419.710.9357   e/info@leighmaidadesign.com

www.leighmaidadesign.com

6.

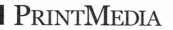

PRINTMEDIA

ABBE LUNGER
PRINTMEDIA, LLC.

Media, Pennsylvania

tel. 610.892.2722
fax. 610.892.2744

alunger3@comcast.net

7.

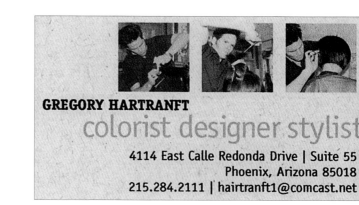

GREGORY HARTRANFT
colorist designer stylist

4114 East Calle Redonda Drive | Suite 55
Phoenix, Arizona 85018
215.284.2111 | hairtranft1@comcast.net

8.

MISS SADIE MAE'S
GOURMET
DOGGIE
BISCUITS

CYNDI NEEDLEMAN / Chef & Owner
PO Box 63725 Philadelphia, PA 19147 · tel.215.726.1931 · fax.952.487.0978
cyndi@sadiesbiscuits.com · **www.sadiesbiscuits.com**

9.

(1-4)
Design Firm **John Kneapler Design**
(5-9)
Design Firm **Leigh Maida Graphic Design**

1.
Client   Adam Raphael Photography
Designers   Colleen Shea,
                   John Kneapler
2.
Client   John Kneapler Design
Designers   John Kneapler,
                   Charles Kneapler
3.
Client   Mann Realty Associates
Designers   John Kneapler, Scot Sterling,
                   Suhita Shirodkar
4.
Client   Beyond Spa
Designers   Colleen Shea,
                   John Kneapler

5.
Client   Mopping Mama's
Designer   Leigh Maida
6.
Client   Leigh Maida Graphic Design
Designer   Leigh Maida
7.
Client   PrintMedia
Designer   Leigh Maida
8.
Client   Gregory Hartranft
Designer   Leigh Maida
9.
Client   Sadiesbiscuits.com
Designer   Leigh Maida

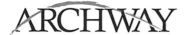

Thomas C. Young
Associate Underwriter

Archway Insurance Group, LLC

1301 Wright's Lane East
West Chester, PA 19380

tel.610.719.0838 x291
fax.610.692.8913

tyoung@archwayins.com
www.archwayins.com

1.

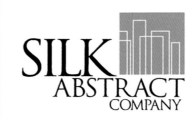

Silk Abstract Company
224 South 20th Street
Philadelphia, PA 19103

tel.215.751.0111
fax.215.751.0112

sparisi@silktitle.com
www.silktitle.com

Susan Parisi

2.

Wilk Brand & Silver
Attorneys at Law
A PROFESSIONAL CORPORATION

Peter O'Hara, Esquire

224 South 20th Street Philadelphia, PA 19103
tel.215.985.1500 | fax.215.751.0112 | pohara@wilkbrand.com
www.wilkbrand.com

3.

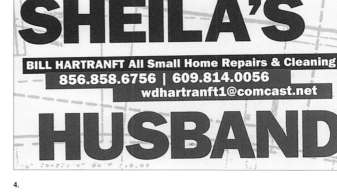

SHEILA'S

BILL HARTRANFT All Small Home Repairs & Cleaning
856.858.6756 | 609.814.0056
wdhartranft1@comcast.net

HUSBAND

4.

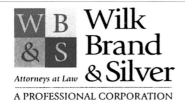

Leigh Maida **Creative Director**

InMarket Partners, LLC
2215 Christian Street, Suite A, Philadelphia, PA 19146-1718
tel.610.408.8022 > cell.215.605.5667 > fax.419.710.9357
leigh@inmarketpartners.com > www.inmarketpartners.com

[s t r a t e g i c   i n s u r a n c e   c o m m u n i c a t i o n s]

5.

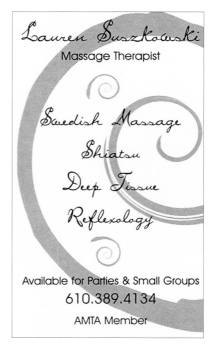

Lauren Suszkowski
Massage Therapist

Swedish Massage

Shiatsu

Deep Tissue

Reflexology

Available for Parties & Small Groups
610.389.4134

AMTA Member

6.

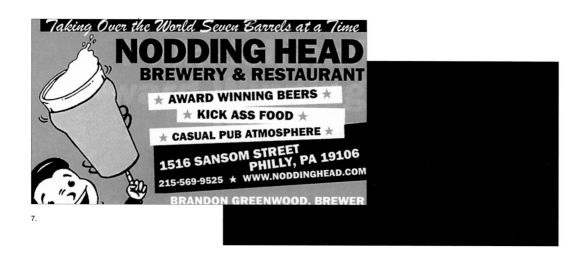

7.

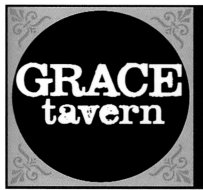

James Fernandes
Tom Peters
Fergus Carey

full menu
11:30am – 2am daily

23rd & South Streets
2229 Grays Ferry Ave
Philadelphia, PA 19146

215.893.9580

a lovingly restored
neighborhood tavern

8.

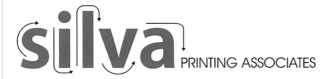 PRINTING ASSOCIATES

John Silva, President

3448 Progress Drive, Suite G
Bensalem, PA 19020

tel.215.633.9901
fax.215.638.8696
cell.215.760.7463

silvaprintingassociates@aol.com

9.

(1-9)
Design Firm **Leigh Maida Graphic Design**

1.
| Client | Archway |
| Designer | Leigh Maida |

2.
| Client | Silk Abstract Company |
| Designer | Leigh Maida |

3.
| Client | Wilk Brand & Silver |
| Designer | Leigh Maida |

4.
| Client | Sheila's Husband |
| Designer | Leigh Maida |

5.
| Client | InMarket Partners, LLC |
| Designer | Leigh Maida |

6.
| Client | Lauren Suszkowski |
| Designer | Leigh Maida |

7.
| Client | Nodding Head Brewery & Restaurant |
| Designer | Leigh Maida |

8.
| Client | Grace Tavern |
| Designer | Leigh Maida |

9.
| Client | Silva Printing Associates |
| Designer | Leigh Maida |

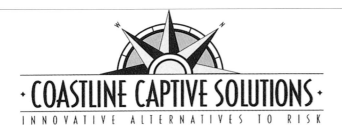

1.

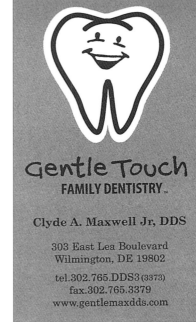

2.

3.

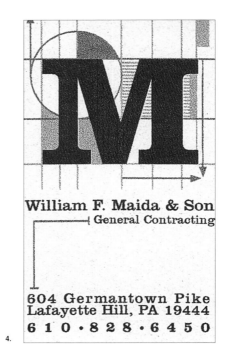

4.

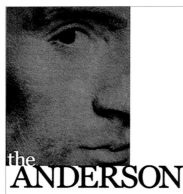

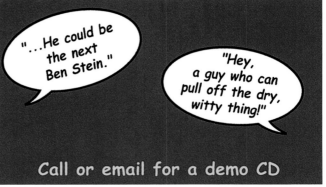

5.

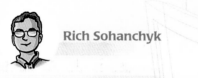

Rich Sohanchyk

PELHAMPRINT.COM

331 Fifth Avenue • Pelham, NY 10803
tel 914.738.6066 • fax 914.738.6073
www.pelhamprint.com

6.

igital • BW & Color Copies
onary • Brochures • Signs
letters • CAD Output
...and more

porate Identity • Logo's
Packaging • Promotional Products
Multimedia • Website Design & Hosting

7.

arts council
of the valley

Robin L. Iten Porter
executive director

p.o. box 1051 Harrisonburg, VA. 22803
p540-801-8779 f540-438-9589
email@valleyarts.org www.valleyarts.org

arts council
of the valley

p.o. box 1051
Harrisonburg, VA. 22803
p540-801-8779
f540-438-9589
email@valleyarts.org
www.valleyarts.org

LINDA B. GENTRY, DDS
10136 Maple Street ᴗ Omaha, Nebraska 68134
(402) 571-3415 ᴗ drgentry@gentrysmiles.com
gentrysmiles.com

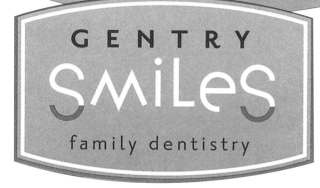

GENTRY
SMiLeS
family dentistry

8.

(1-4)
Design Firm **Leigh Maida Graphic Design**
(5,6)
Design Firm **Gregory Richard Media Group**
(7)
Design Firm **TLC Design**
(8)
Design Firm **emspace design group**

1.
  Client   Coastline Captive Solutions
  Designer Leigh Maida
2.
  Client   Gentle Touch Family Dentistry
  Designer Leigh Maida
3.
  Client   The Anderson
  Designer Leigh Maida

4.
  Client   William F. Maida & Son
  Designer Leigh Maida
5.
  Client   Chris Jobin Voice Over
  Designer Richard Sohanchyk
6.
  Client   PELHAMPRINT.com
  Designer Richard Sohanchyk
7.
  Client   Art Council of the Valley
  Designer Trudy L. Cole
8.
  Client   Gentry Smiles
  Designer Juliane Bautista

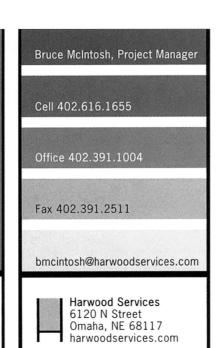

Painting
Wallcovering
Wood Finishing
Shop Finishes
Duroplex
Concrete Staining
Elastomerics
Multi-color Finishes
Special Coatings
Floor Coatings
Waterproofing

HARWOOD
SERVICES COMMERCIAL, INC

Bruce McIntosh, Project Manager

Cell 402.616.1655

Office 402.391.1004

Fax 402.391.2511

bmcintosh@harwoodservices.com

Harwood Services
6120 N Street
Omaha, NE 68117
harwoodservices.com

1.

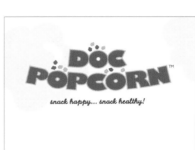

snack happy... snack healthy!

Rob Israel
President

Phone: 212 655 5112
Email: rob@docpopcorn.com
Fax: 212 655 5286

60 Madison Ave. 3rd Floor
New York, NY 10010
www.docpopcorn.com

2.

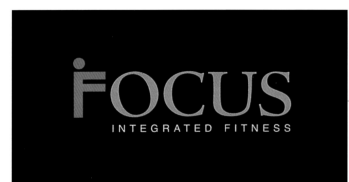

3.

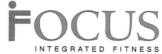

JOE MASIELLO, CPT

25 1/2 E 61 ST, STUDIO 5E
NY, NY 10021
T: 212.319.3816
F: 212.319.3817
C: 917.797.2827
JOE@FOCUSNYC.COM

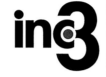

Harvey Appelbaum
Creative Director
happel@inc-3.com
www.inc-3.com
220 East 23rd Street . New York, NY 10010 . P212.213.1130 . F212.532.8022

4.

identity
new media
communications

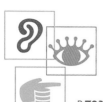

Beth Singer Design, LLC

P **703.469.1900**
info@bethsingerdesign.com

5.

P **703.469.1900** F **703.525.7399**
1408 North Fillmore Street, Suite 6, Arlington, VA 22201
www.bethsingerdesign.com

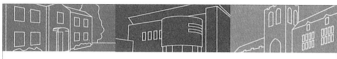

E & G   G R O U P

SARA B. BARNES, HCCP   1350 BEVERLY ROAD, SUITE 200
Senior Property Manager   MCLEAN, VA 22101
                              P 703.893.0303 F 703.893.3273

                              sbarnes@eandggroup.com

6.

E&G Property Services, Inc.
Campus Management, LLC   www.eandggroup.com
Elsinore Group, LLC

Jeff Koch
Regional Director
Central Region East

crebbyo10@aol.com

T 610-435-3571 Ext. 159
F 610-435-2859
702 N. 22nd Street
Allentown, PA 18104

BBYO

B'nai B'rith Youth Organization

7.

(1)
　Design Firm **emspace design group**
(2-4)
　Design Firm **inc3**
(5-7)
　Design Firm **Beth Singer Design, LLC**

1.
　Client   Harwood Services
　Designer Juliane Bautista
2.
　Client   Doc Popcorn
　Designers Harvey Appelbaum,
　 Christofer Nystrom
3.
　Client   Focus
　Designers Harvey Appelbaum,
　 Christofer Nystrom

4.
　Client   inc3
　Designers Harvey Appelbaum,
　 John Sexton
5.
　Client   Beth Singer Design, LLC
　Designer Suheun Yu
6.
　Client   E&G Group
　Designer Chris Hoch
7.
　Client   B'nai B'rith Youth
　 Organization
　Designer Suheun Yu

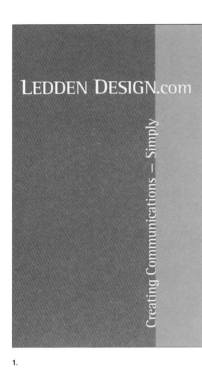

1.

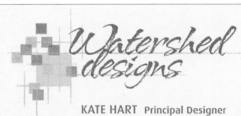

2.

Watershed designs
Inspirational ■ **Innovative** ■ **Interiors** ■

KATE HART Principal Designer

110 Park Street, Toronto, Ontario M1N 2P3

t: 416-267-2642   e: kate@watersheddesigns.ca
c: 416-676-2388   w: watersheddesigns.ca

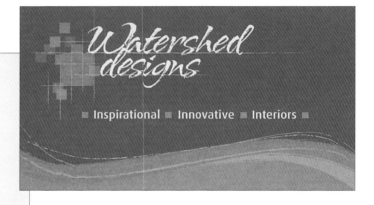

Bill McLean
Software Designer

McLean
SOFTWARE
.com

☎ 416.252.0294
🖳 bill@mcleansoftware.com
✆ 416.252.8185

50 Holbrooke Avenue
Toronto Ontario
Canada M8Y 3B4

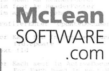

3.

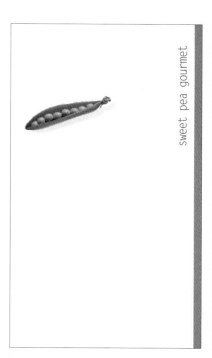
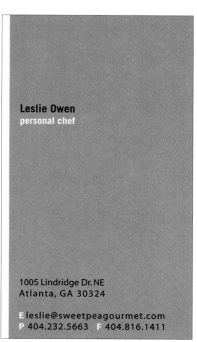

sweet pea gourmet

Leslie Owen
personal chef

1005 Lindridge Dr. NE
Atlanta, GA 30324

E leslie@sweetpeagourmet.com
P 404.232.5663   F 404.816.1411

4.

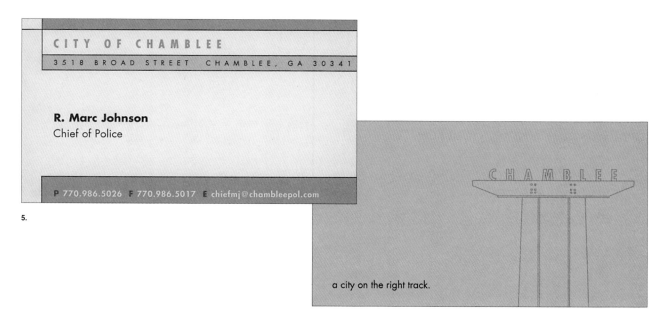

CITY OF CHAMBLEE

3 5 1 8   B R O A D   S T R E E T   C H A M B L E E ,   G A   3 0 3 4 1

R. Marc Johnson
Chief of Police

P 770.986.5026   F 770.986.5017   E chiefmj@chambleepol.com

5.

CHAMBLEE

a city on the right track.

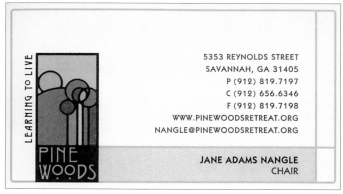

LEARNING TO LIVE

PINE WOODS

5353 REYNOLDS STREET
SAVANNAH, GA 31405
P (912) 819.7197
C (912) 656.6346
F (912) 819.7198
WWW.PINEWOODSRETREAT.ORG
NANGLE@PINEWOODSRETREAT.ORG

JANE ADAMS NANGLE
CHAIR

6.

(1-3)
Design Firm **Ledden Design**
(4-6)
Design Firm **sky design**

1.
Client   Ledden Design
Designer   Cathy Ledden
2.
Client   Watershed Designs
Designer   Cathy Ledden
3.
Client   McLean Software
Designer   Cathy Ledden
4.
Client   Sweet Pea Gourmet
Designer   W. Todd Vaught

5.
Client   City of Chamblee
Designers   W. Todd Vaught,
            Carrie Wallace Brown
6.
Client   Pinewoods
Designers   W. Todd Vaught,
            Carrie Wallace Brown

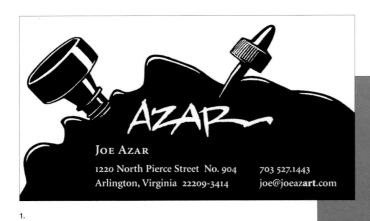

JOE AZAR

1220 North Pierce Street No. 904 703 527.1443
Arlington, Virginia 22209-3414 joe@joeazart.com

1.

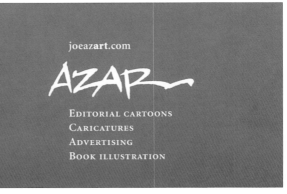

joeaz**art**.com

EDITORIAL CARTOONS
CARICATURES
ADVERTISING
BOOK ILLUSTRATION

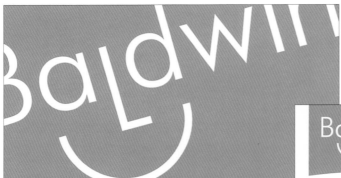

2.

Baldwin
GRAPHICS

1301 Pennsylvania Ave. NW
Mezzanine Level
Washington DC 20004-1701

Eric J. Baldwin
President

202 347.0123 *f* 202 347.0596
eric@baldwingraphics.com
www.baldwingraphics.com

PRINTING · PHOTOCOPYING · DESIGN

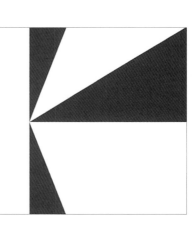

KABEL

Robert J. Kabel

805 15th Street NW Suite 700
Washington DC 20005-2282

+1 **202 312 7408** voice
+1 202 257 0708 cell
+1 202 312 7460 fax

rk@robertkabel.com
www.robertkabel.com

3.

Coldwell Banker Residential Brokerage
Owned and Operated by NRT Incorporated

Jeff Shewey

202 332-3228
move@jeffshewey.com

Four Seasons Plaza
2828 Pennsylvania Avenue NW
Washington DC · 20007-3719
202 333-6100 o · 202 342-9118 f
www.jeffshewey.com

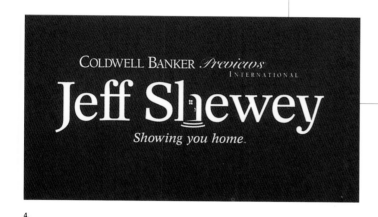

COLDWELL BANKER *Previews*
INTERNATIONAL

Jeff Shewey
Showing you home.

4.

CHR Communications

advertising | design | public relations

Kathy Hourigan

800 N. Milford Rd.
Suite 700
Milford, MI 48381

248.685.9933
248.685.9944 fx

khourigan@chrcommunications.com
www.chrcommunications.com

5.

Karen Mattson
General Manager

57075 Pontiac Trail
New Hudson, MI 48165

(248) 437-4141
(248) 437-3970 Fax
(248) 921-0525 Cell

kmattson@glcylinders.com
www.glcylinders.com

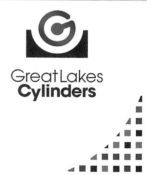

GreatLakes
Cylinders

6.

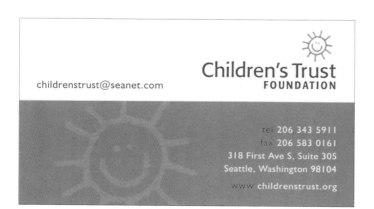

childrenstrust@seanet.com

Children's Trust
FOUNDATION

tel 206 343 5911
fax 206 583 0161
318 First Ave S, Suite 305
Seattle, Washington 98104

www.childrenstrust.org

7.

(1-4)
Design Firm **Eyebeam Creative LLC**
(5,6)
Design Firm **CHR Communications**
(7)
Design Firm **Belyea**

1.
Client   Azar
Designers   Gregory Gersch,
              Joseph Azar
2.
Client   Baldwin Graphics
Designer   Gregory Gersch
3.
Client   Kabel
Designer   Gregory Gersch

4.
Client   Jeff Shewey
Designers   Gregory Gersch,
              Joseph Azar, Richard Lippman
5.
Client   CHR Communications
Designers   Kathy Hourigan,
              Gene Renaker
6.
Client   Great Lakes Cylinders
Designer   Kathy Hourigan
7.
Client   Children's Trust Foundation
Designer   Nick Johnson

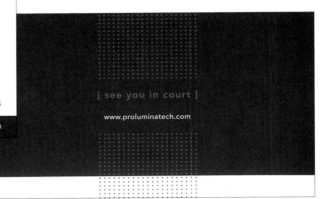

Christian Hazelmann : President and CEO
chazelmann@proluminatech.com

Prolumina
TRIAL TECHNOLOGIES

80 South Washington Suite 200 Seattle Washington 98104

P 206 622 6700 : F 206 467 1777 : W proluminatech.com

[see you in court]

www.proluminatech.com

1.

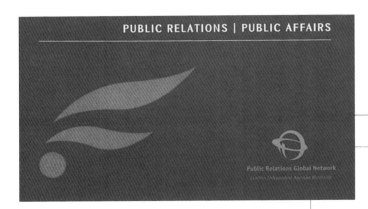

PUBLIC RELATIONS | PUBLIC AFFAIRS

Public Relations Global Network
Leading Independent Agencies Worldwide

2.

Natalie Price SENIOR VICE PRESIDENT

nprice@feareygroup.com
cell 206.790.5282

1809 Seventh Avenue, Suite 1111
Seattle, Washington 98101

T 206.343.1543   F 206.622.5694
www.feareygroup.com

THE **FEAREY** GROUP

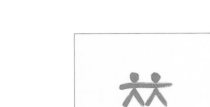

BARRY ACKERLEY
Founder and Co-chair

GINGER & BARRY
Ackerley
FOUNDATION

1301 Fifth Avenue, Suite 3525
Seattle, Washington 98101
206.624.2888
206.623.7853 fax
www.ackerleyfoundation.org

ENSURING THAT EVERY CHILD
RECEIVES A GREAT EDUCATION.

3.

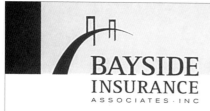

BAYSIDE INSURANCE
A S S O C I A T E S · I N C

Jerry Judge
AGENCY PRINCIPAL

jerry@bayside-insurance.com

1610 Postal Road
PO Box 545
Chester, Maryland 21619
410.643.6641
800.773.0046
Fax 410.604.3571

408 N. Washington Street
PO Box 3087
Easton, Maryland 21601
410.822.2800
866.ERIE.INS
Fax 410.820.0210

4.

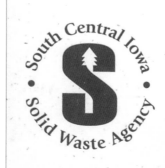

South Central Iowa Solid Waste Agency

Rachel Elgin
Education & Program
Specialist

1736 Highway T17
Tracy, Iowa 50256
Tel: 641-828-8545
Fax: 641-842-3722
E-mail: relgin@sciswa.org

*Serving Lucas, Marion, Monroe
and Poweshiek Counties*

5.

Julia M. Kennedy, LPO
Escrow Manager

FIRST AMERICAN TITLE COMPANY
of Jefferson County

2037 East Sims Way • P.O. Box 598 • Port Townsend, WA 98368
360/385-1322 • 800/401-1001 • Fax 360/385-1877
jkennedy@fatcojc.com

6.

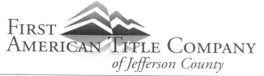

Casey's KETTLE CORN
The Perfect Snack
Lightly Sweet · Lightly Salty

Retail • Wholesale • Fundraisers

Casey & Carolyn Dennis
Owners

P.O. Box 280
Sequim, WA 98382
Phone: (360) 582-1138
Fax: (360) 582-9454

www.caseyskettlecorn.com

7.

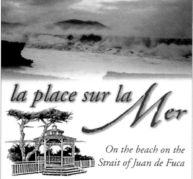

A MAGICAL PLACE...

la place sur la Mer

*On the beach on the
Strait of Juan de Fuca*

Events • Weddings • Special Occasions

Lyndee Lapin, Proprietor

2026 Place Road
Port Angeles, Washington 98363
(360) 565-8030
lyndee@laplacesur-la-mer.com
www.laplacesur-la-mer.com

8.

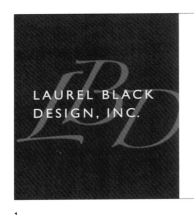

LAUREL BLACK
DESIGN, INC.

246 Patterson Road

Port Angeles, WA 98362

Office: 360.457.0217

Fax: 360.457.8122

Cell: 360.460.1834

info@laurelblack.com

www.laurelblack.com

1.

PERCEPTION IS EVERYTHING.

LAUREL BLACK DESIGN, INC.

GRAPHIC DESIGN • ELECTRONIC DESIGN

IDENTITY CREATION • CREATIVE SERVICES • PROMOTIONAL STRATEGIES

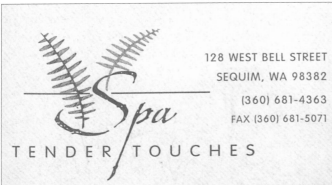

Spa
TENDER / TOUCHES

128 WEST BELL STREET

SEQUIM, WA 98382

(360) 681-4363

FAX (360) 681-5071

2.

YOUR NEXT APPOINTMENT IS

DATE		TIME			SERVICE
MON	TUES	WED	THUR	FRI	SAT

24 HOUR CANCELLATION NOTICE IS REQUIRED

(360) 681-4363

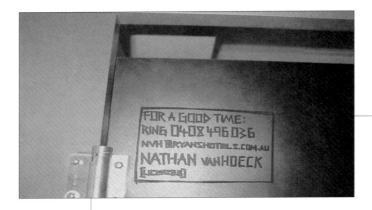

FOR A GOOD TIME:
RING 0408 496 036
NVH@RYANSHOTELS.COM.AU
NATHAN VANHOECK
[LICENSEE]

Call Me!
Nathan Van Hoeck
(Licensee)
0408 496 036
nvh@ryanshotels.com.au

590 Kingsway
Miranda NSW 2228

T. 02 9524 0398
F. 02 9526 2460

www.carmens.com.au   carmens   Split restaurant & bar   MIRANDA HOTEL

3.

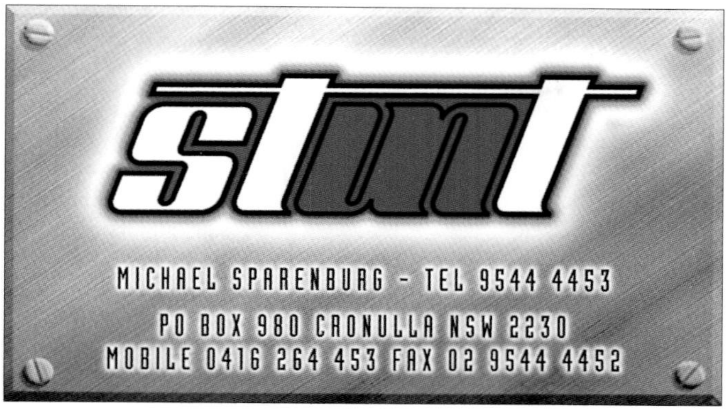

4.

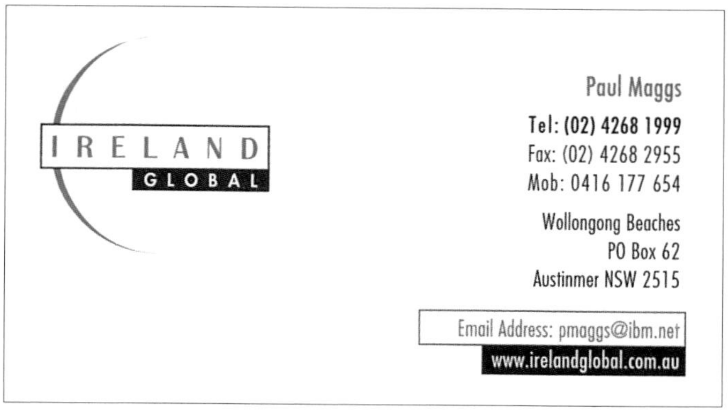

5.

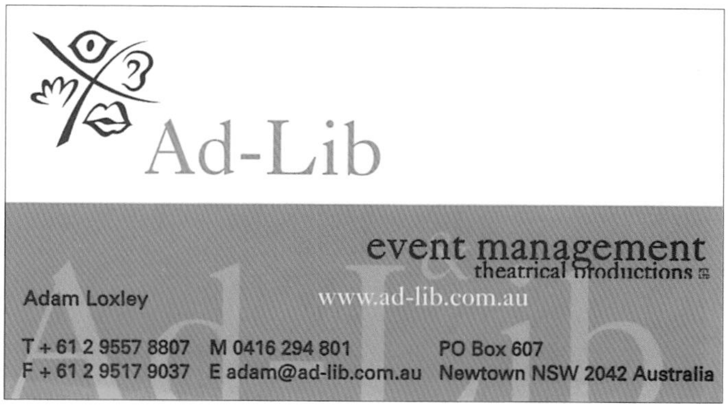

6.

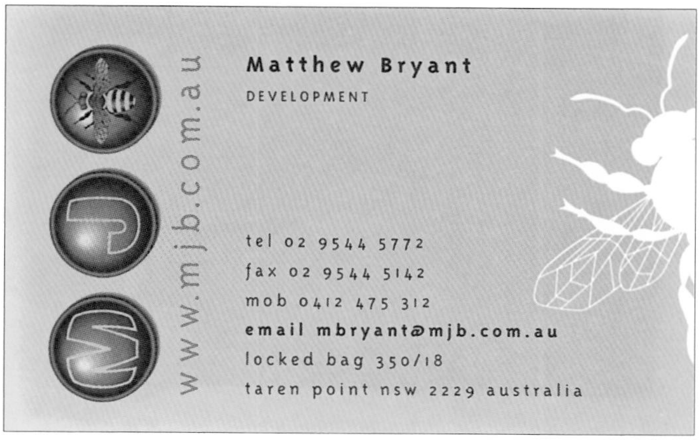

7.

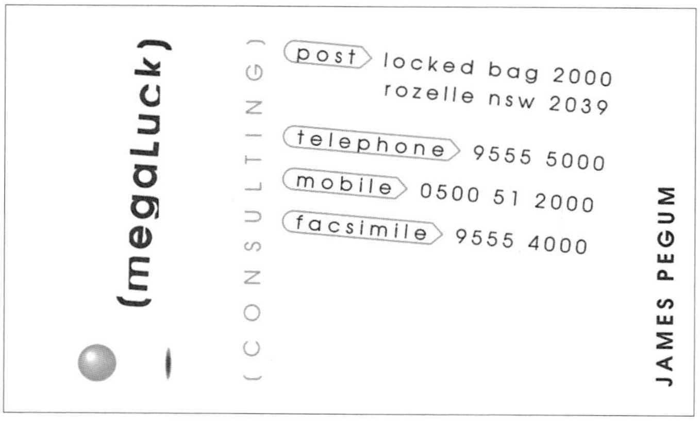

8.

(1,2)
Design Firm **Laurel Black Design, Inc.**
(3-8)
Design Firm **Percept Creative Group**

1.
Client Laurel Black Design, Inc.
Designer Laurel Black

2.
Client Tender Touches Spa
Designer Laurel Black

3.
Client Carmens Nightclub
Designer Lewis Jenkins

4.
Client Stunt Clothing
Designer Lewis Jenkins

5.
Client Ireland Global
Designers Lewis Jenkins, Trent Agnew

6.
Client Ad-Lib Theatrical
Designers Lewis Jenkins, Trent Agnew

7.
Client MJB
Designer Lewis Jenkins

8.
Client Megaluck Consulting
Designer Lewis Jenkins

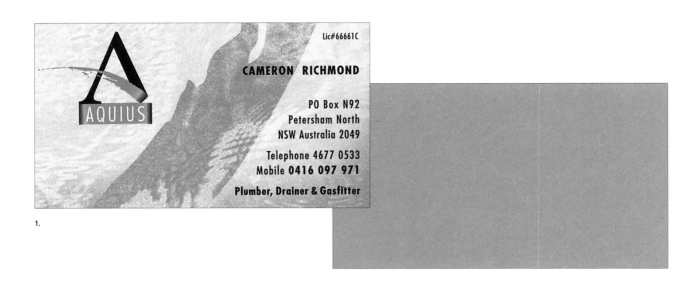

1.

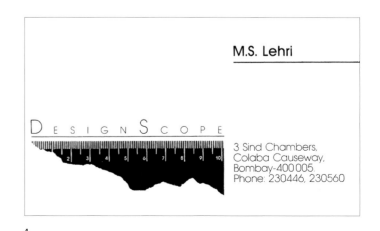

Show them what you're made of.

2.

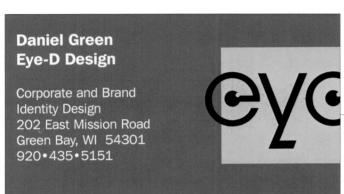

3.

Kumar Thakkar
Publishing Director

MOBILE WORLD TELECOM CONSULTANCY (I) PVT. LTD.
Phone:+91 (22) 498 5000 / 6000 / 8000
Direct:+91 (22) 431 5555 Fax:+91 (22) 498 4428, 436 3722
Email: mobile@bom3.vsnl.net.in
Net: www.worldmobile.com

4.

M.S. Lehri

D E S I G N S C O P E

3 Sind Chambers,
Colaba Causeway,
Bombay-400 005.
Phone: 230446, 230560

Saunak Parikh
Director

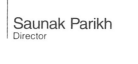

UNIDESIGN JEWELLERY PVT. LTD.
Plot-5 SEEPZ, Andheri East, Bombay 400 096. India
Phone: (+91-22) 837 6506 / 821 1653
Fax: (+91-22) 838 2041

5.

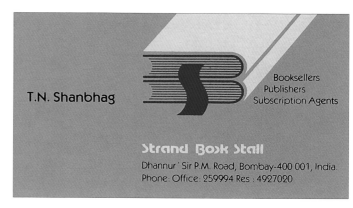

T.N. Shanbhag

Booksellers
Publishers
Subscription Agents

Strand Book Stall
Dhannur ˙ Sir P.M. Road, Bombay-400 001, India.
Phone: Office: 259994 Res : 4927020

6.

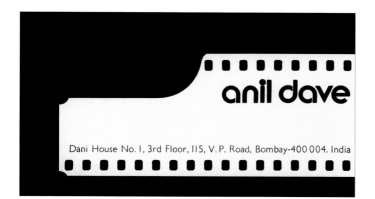

anil dave

Dani House No. I, 3rd Floor, II5, V. P. Road, Bombay-400 004. India

7.

Nitish Jain
Managing Director

Crescent Finstock Limited
DoubleDot Centre
533, Kalbadevi Road, Mumbai 400 002
Phone: 201 9200 / 234 7777
Fax: 201 7880 Email: nitishjain@doubledot.co.in

8.

Sunita Zaveri

Tribhovandas Bhimji Zaveri
Westend
442, Chitrakar Dhurandhar Marg, Khar West
Mumbai 400 052

Phone: +91 (22) 649 0606 Fax: +91 (22) 648 7408

9.

(1)
Design Firm **Percept Creative Group**
(2)
Design Firm **Daniel Green Eye-D Design**
(3-9)
Design Firm **Graphic Communication Concepts**

1.
Client   Aquius
Designer   Lewis Jenkins
2.
Client   Daniel Green Eye-D Design
Designer   Daniel Green
3.
Client   Mobile World Telecom
Designer   Sudarshan Dheer
4.
Client   Design Scope
Designer   Sudarshan Dheer
5.
Client   Unidesign Jewellery
Designer   Sudarshan Dheer

6.
Client   Strand Book Stall
Designer   Sudarshan Dheer
7.
Client   Anil Dave
Designer   Sudarshan Dheer
8.
Client   Crescent Finstock
Designer   Sudarshan Dheer
9.
Client   Tribhovandas Bhimji Zaveri
Designer   Sudarshan Dheer

133

Ramesh Kejriwal
Managing Director

PARKSONS PRESS LTD.
15 Shah Industrial Estate, Off Veera Desai Road, Andheri West
Mumbai 400 053. India
Phone: +91 (22) 636 2344, 633 8624
Fax: +91 (22) 636 0690, 632 9508
Email: parksons@bom2.vsnl.net.in

1.

Vikas Choudhury
Director

18° 55' 35" N, 72° 49' 22" E

Aurovision Pvt. Ltd.
41/42 Atlanta, Nariman Point, Bombay-400 021. India
Phone: +91-22-285 6527/8/9 Fax: +91-22-287 3100
E-mail: vc@aurovision.com Web: www.aurovision.com

2.

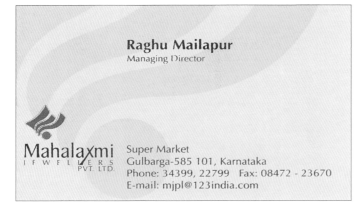

Raghu Mailapur
Managing Director

Super Market
Gulbarga-585 101, Karnataka
Phone: 34399, 22799 Fax: 08472 - 23670
E-mail: mjpl@123india.com

3.

Gopal Narang
Director

EMGEEN
CORP

Emgeen Holdings Pvt. Ltd.

Dwarka, 57 Tagore Road, Santacruz West
Mumbai-400 054, India

Phone:+91 (22) 649 8262 Fax:+91 (22) 604 4644
E-mail: gopal@emgeen.com

4.

Jewelex

Atul Kothari
President

Jewelex New York Ltd
22 West 48th Street, Suite 1500
New York, NY 10036

Phone: (212) 840 6970, (800) 208 9999
Fax: (212) 840 6971
E-mail: akothari@jewelexltd.com

5.

TITAN

Xerxes Desai
Managing Director

TITAN INDUSTRIES LIMITED
Golden Enclave, Tower-A, Airport Road,
Bangalore-560 017, India. Telex: 0845-8683 TITN IN.
Phone: 559 3551 Fax: 080-558 9923

6.

S.S.Godbole
Chief Executive Officer

INTECH

IDBI **INTECH** LIMITED

IDBI Building, Plot: 39-41, Sector-11
CBD Belapur, Navi Mumbai-400 614, India

Phone: +91 (22) 756 2077
Fax: +91 (22) 756 2086

7.

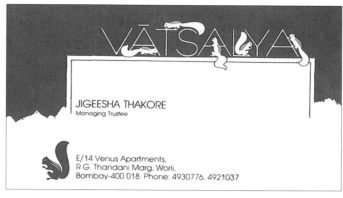

VATSALYA

JIGEESHA THAKORE
Managing Trustee

E/14 Venus Apartments,
R.G. Thandani Marg, Worli,
Bombay-400 018. Phone: 4930776, 4921037

8.

Gyan Jasra

Jasras Digital Pvt. Ltd.
Vijay Bhavan, 7 Bungalows
Versova, Andheri West
Mumbai 400 061- India

Phone:(+91) 98200 10031
Fax:+91(22) 627 0341
E-mail: jasra @bom2.vsnl.net.in

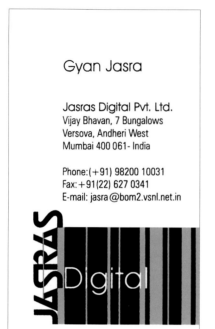

9.

Sharmila Kadle

Corporate
Photography

GuruDutt

22, Saraswat Colony Near Zilla Parishad
Pune – 411 001. India
Phone : (0212) 64 5085 / 62 9277
Fax : (0212) 64 6650

122, Poornanand
62 Banganga Walkeshwar
Bombay – 400 006. India
Phone : 364 3743

10.

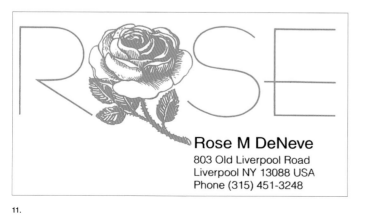

Rose M DeNeve
803 Old Liverpool Road
Liverpool NY 13088 USA
Phone (315) 451-3248

11.

(1-11)
Design Firm **Graphic Communication
Concepts**

1.
Client   Parksons Press
Designer   Sudarshan Dheer
2.
Client   Aurovision
Designer   Sudarshan Dheer
3.
Client   Mahalaxmi Jewellers
Designer   Sudarshan Dheer
4.
Client   Emgeen Holdings
Designer   Sudarshan Dheer
5.
Client   Jewelex New York
Designer   Sudarshan Dheer
6.
Client   Titan Industries
Designer   Sudarshan Dheer

7.
Client   IDBI Intech
Designer   Sudarshan Dheer
8.
Client   Vatsalya
Designer   Sudarshan Dheer
9.
Client   Jasras Digital
Designer   Sudarshan Dheer
10.
Client   Guru Dutt
Designer   Sudarshan Dheer
11.
Client   Rose M DeNeve
Designer   Sudarshan Dheer

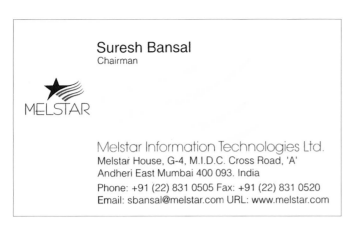

1.

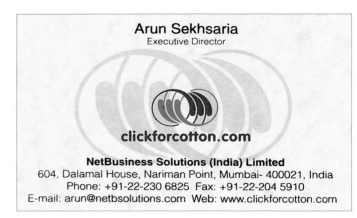

2.

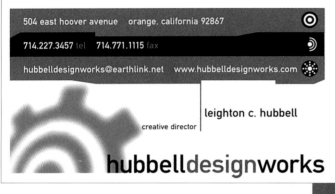

3.

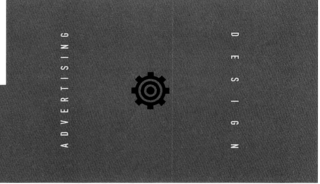

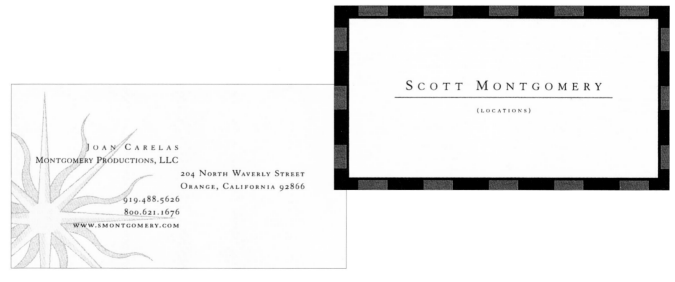

4.

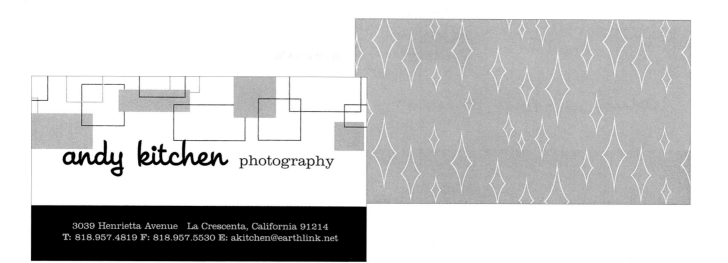

andy kitchen photography

3039 Henrietta Avenue   La Crescenta, California 91214
T: 818.957.4819 F: 818.957.5530 E: akitchen@earthlink.net

5.

IN THE HUNT
CANINE & EQUESTRIAN FARM

6.

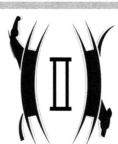

EQUESTRIAN BOARDING

615.368.2443 PH
615.368.2444 FX

WWW.INTHEHUNTFARM.COM

HUNT SEAT LESSONS

8462 COVINGTON ROAD
EAGLEVILLE, TENNESSEE
37060

Ann Reese *photographer*
kids

1280 Bison Avenue Suite B 9596
Newport Beach, California 92660
ph 949.759.1211 fx 949.721.9816

weddings

7.

(1,2)
Design Firm **Graphic Communication Concepts**
(3-7)
Design Firm **Hubbell Design Works**

1.
Client   Melstar Information
Designer   Sudarshan Dheer
2.
Client   NetBusiness Solutions
Designer   Sudarshan Dheer
3.
Client   Hubbell Design Works
Designer   Leighton Hubbell
4.
Client   Montgomery Productions, LLC
Designer   Leighton Hubbell
5.
Client   Andy Kitchen Photography
Designer   Leighton Hubbell
6.
Client   In the Hunt Canine &
             Equestrian Farm
Designer   Leighton Hubbell
7.
Client   Ann Reese Photographer
Designer   Leighton Hubbell

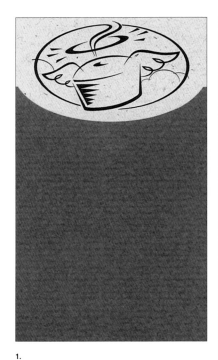

1.

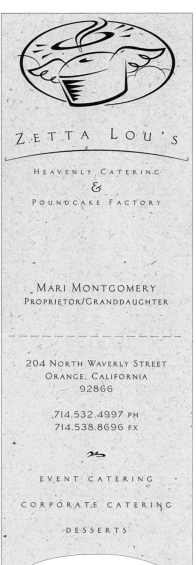

ZETTA LOU'S

HEAVENLY CATERING
&
POUNDCAKE FACTORY

MARI MONTGOMERY
PROPRIETOR/GRANDDAUGHTER

204 NORTH WAVERLY STREET
ORANGE, CALIFORNIA
92866

714.532.4997 PH
714.538.8696 FX

EVENT CATERING

CORPORATE CATERING

DESSERTS

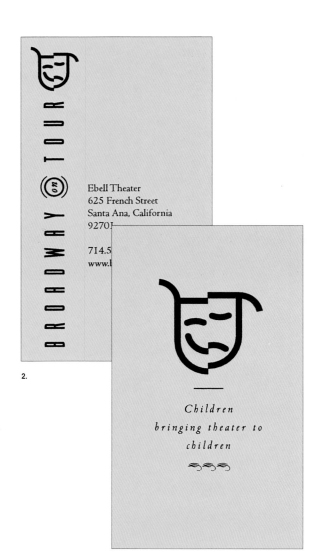

BROADWAY ON TOUR

Ebell Theater
625 French Street
Santa Ana, California
92701

714.5

www.l

2.

*Children
bringing theater to
children*

ELLEN SHAKESPEARE

158 N. GLASSELL STREET

SUITE 203

ORANGE, CALIFORNIA

92866

TEL 714.538.4464

FAX 714.538.4473

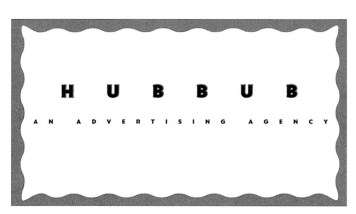

H U B B U B

AN ADVERTISING AGENCY

3.

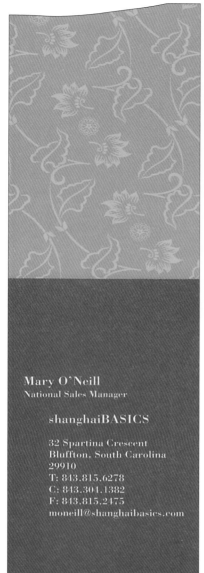

Mary O'Neill
National Sales Manager

shanghaiBASICS

32 Spartina Crescent
Bluffton, South Carolina
29910
T: 843.815.6278
C: 843.304.1382
F: 843.815.2475
moneill@shanghaibasics.com

4.

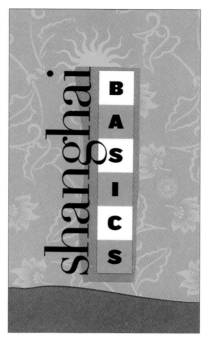

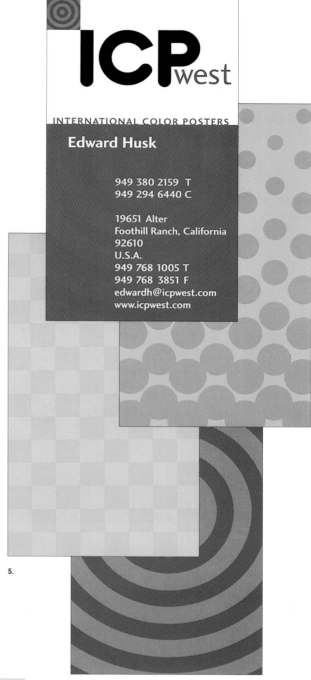

INTERNATIONAL COLOR POSTERS

Edward Husk

949 380 2159 T
949 294 6440 C

19651 Alter
Foothill Ranch, California
92610
U.S.A.
949 768 1005 T
949 768 3851 F
edwardh@icpwest.com
www.icpwest.com

5.

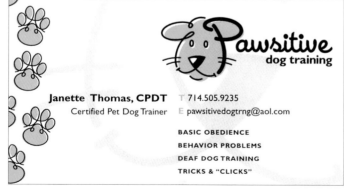

Janette Thomas, CPDT
Certified Pet Dog Trainer

T 714.505.9235
E pawsitivedogtrng@aol.com

BASIC OBEDIENCE
BEHAVIOR PROBLEMS
DEAF DOG TRAINING
TRICKS & "CLICKS"

6.

(1-6)
Design Firm **Hubbell Design Works**

1.
Client   Zetta Lou's Heavenly Catering
Designer   Leighton Hubbell
2.
Client   Broadway on Tour
Designer   Leighton Hubbell
3.
Client   Hubbub Advertising
Designer   Leighton Hubbell
4.
Client   shanghaiBASICS
Designer   Leighton Hubbell
5.
Client   International Color Posters
Designer   Leighton Hubbell
6.
Client   Pawsitive Dog Training
Designer   Leighton Hubbell

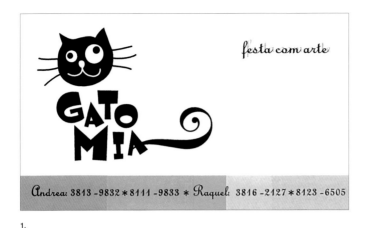

1.

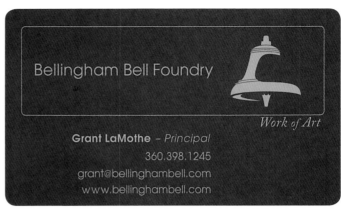

Bellingham Bell Foundry

Work of Art

Grant LaMothe – *Principal*
360.398.1245
grant@bellinghambell.com
www.bellinghambell.com

2.

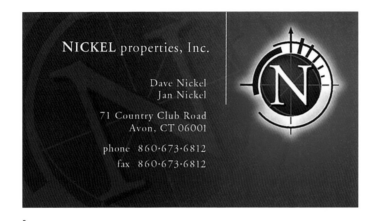

NICKEL properties, Inc.

Dave Nickel
Jan Nickel

71 Country Club Road
Avon, CT 06001

phone 860·673·6812
fax 860·673·6812

3.

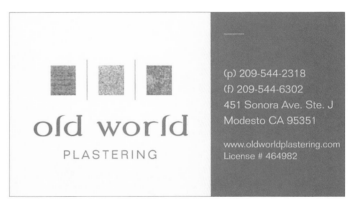

old world
PLASTERING

(p) 209-544-2318
(f) 209-544-6302
451 Sonora Ave. Ste. J
Modesto CA 95351

www.oldworldplastering.com
License # 464982

4.

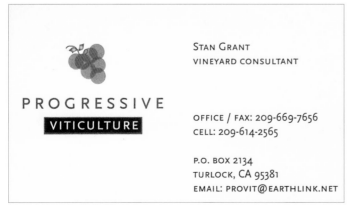

STAN GRANT
VINEYARD CONSULTANT

PROGRESSIVE
VITICULTURE

OFFICE / FAX: 209-669-7656
CELL: 209-614-2565

P.O. BOX 2134
TURLOCK, CA 95381
EMAIL: PROVIT@EARTHLINK.NET

5.

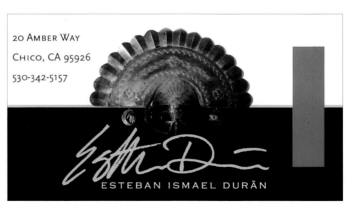

20 AMBER WAY
CHICO, CA 95926

530-342-5157

ESTEBAN ISMAEL DURÃN

6.

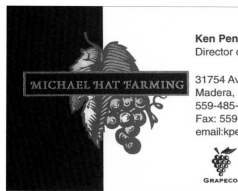

Ken Penfold
Director of Procurement

31754 Avenue 9
Madera, CA 93638
559-485-2760
Fax: 559-674-6676
email:kpenfold@grapeco.com

7.

ST. LUKE'S
FAMILY PRACTICE

Robert A. Forester, M.D.

drf@stlukesfp.org
www.stlukesfp.org
P.O. Box 4517
Modesto, CA 95352-4517

8.

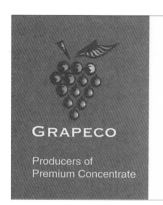

GRAPECO

Producers of
Premium Concentrate

Norm Hammers
Production Foreman

559-485-2760
Fax: 559-674-6676
31754 Avenue 9
Madera, CA 93638

9.

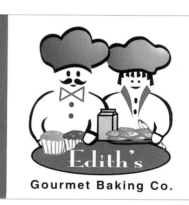

Edith's
Gourmet Baking Co.

George Kosmas

209-522-1220

Fax: 209-522-5133

1-800-262-7755

400 I. Street, Suite 4

Modesto, CA 95351

10.

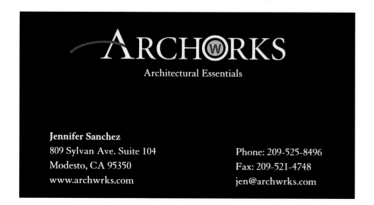

ARCHWORKS
Architectural Essentials

Jennifer Sanchez
809 Sylvan Ave. Suite 104
Modesto, CA 95350
www.archwrks.com

Phone: 209-525-8496
Fax: 209-521-4748
jen@archwrks.com

11.

(1)
Design Firm **Gabriela Gasparini Design**
(2)
Design Firm **Brand Equity Project**
(3)
Design Firm **Todd Nickel**
(4-11)
Design Firm **Marcia Herrmann Design**

1.
Client   Gato Mia
Designer   Gabriela Gasparini
2.
Client   Bellingham Bell Foundry
Designer   Tim Davenport
3.
Client   Nickel Properties, Inc.
Designer   Todd Nickel
4.
Client   Old World Plastering
Designer   Marcia Herrmann

5.
Client   Progressive Viticulture
Designer   Marcia Herrmann
6.
Client   Esteban Ismael Durān
Designer   Marcia Herrmann
7.
Client   Michael Hat Farming
Designer   Marcia Herrmann
8.
Client   St. Luke's Family Practice
Designer   Marcia Herrmann
9.
Client   Grapeco
Designer   Marcia Herrmann
10.
Client   Edith's Gourmet Baking Co.
Designer   Marcia Herrmann
11.
Client   Archworks
Designer   Marcia Herrmann

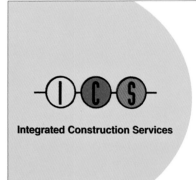

Integrated Construction Services

License #776486

209-656-0640
Fax: 209-669-6891
412 S. Tully Rd.
Turlock, CA 95380

1.

AGILE OAK ORTHOPEDICS

Karen Horrocks, M.A.

1191 E. Yosemite Ave., Suite C
Manteca CA 95336
209-239-5077
Fax: 209-239-5085
e-mail: karen@agileoak.com

2.

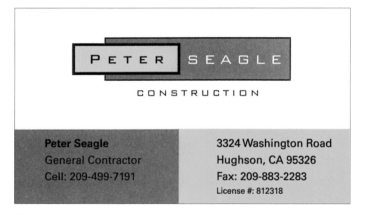

PETER SEAGLE
CONSTRUCTION

Peter Seagle
General Contractor
Cell: 209-499-7191

3324 Washington Road
Hughson, CA 95326
Fax: 209-883-2283
License #: 812318

3.

David Quiñonez

809 Sylvan Ave. Suite 104
Modesto, CA 95350
Office: 209-525-8493
Fax: 209-521-4748

MAMBO
Marketing With A Twist!

4.

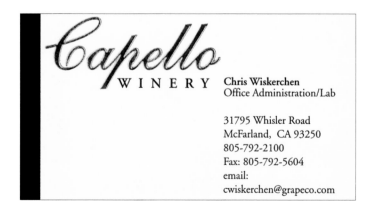

Capello WINERY

Chris Wiskerchen
Office Administration/Lab

31795 Whisler Road
McFarland, CA 93250
805-792-2100
Fax: 805-792-5604
email:
cwiskerchen@grapeco.com

5.

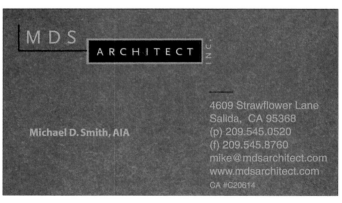

MDS ARCHITECT INC.

Michael D. Smith, AIA

4609 Strawflower Lane
Salida, CA 95368
(p) 209.545.0520
(f) 209.545.8760
mike@mdsarchitect.com
www.mdsarchitect.com
CA #C20614

6.

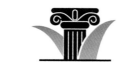

LJM DESIGN GROUP

Landscape Architecture & Planning

530-587-6003 Fax 530-587-6283
15695 Donner Pass Road, Suite 209
Truckee, CA 96161

7.

BR⊙THERS

INTERNATIONAL FOOD CORPORATION

Travis D. Betters

224 Ellicott Street
Batavia, NY 14020
Tele: 585-343-3007
Fax: 585-343-4218

e-mail:cpbetters@2ki.net
www.brothersinternational.com www.grapeco.com

8.

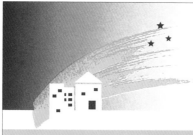

Joni F. Ogden
President

1535 J Street, Suite B
Modesto, CA 95354
Phone: 209-569-0887
Fax: 209-569-0339
jonioggie@sbcglobal.net

GENESIS
Family Enterprises Inc.

9.

NRC INC.

INSURANCE AGENCY

Gloria Cordle

10.

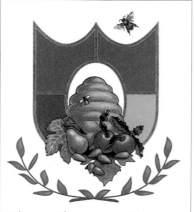

Four Seasons Farms

Ann Blair Endsley
209-599-2234
Fax: 209-599-7548
23073 S. Frederick Rd.
Ripon, CA 95366

11.

(1-11)
Design Firm **Marcia Herrmann Design**

1.
Client   ICS
Designer   Marcia Herrmann
2.
Client   Agile Oak Orthopedics
Designer   Marcia Herrmann
3.
Client   Peter Seagle Construction
Designer   Marcia Herrmann
4.
Client   Mambo
Designer   Marcia Herrmann
5.
Client   Capello Winery
Designer   Marcia Herrmann
6.
Client   MDS Architect
Designer   Marcia Herrmann
7.
Client   LJM Design Group
Designer   Marcia Herrmann

8.
Client   Brothers International
             Food Corporation
Designer   Marcia Herrmann
9.
Client   Genesis Family Enterprises Inc.
Designer   Marcia Herrmann
10.
Client   NRC Inc.
Designer   Marcia Herrmann
11.
Client   Four Seasons Farm
Designer   Marcia Herrmann

143

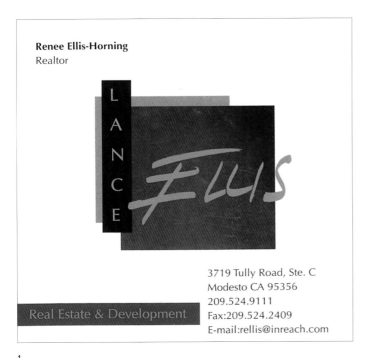

Renee Ellis-Horning
Realtor

3719 Tully Road, Ste. C
Modesto CA 95356
209.524.9111
Fax:209.524.2409
E-mail:rellis@inreach.com

Real Estate & Development

1.

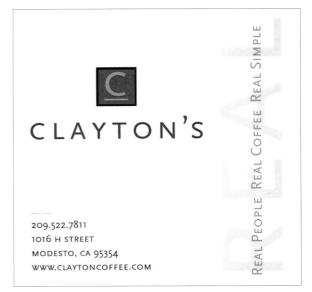

CLAYTON'S

REAL PEOPLE REAL COFFEE REAL SIMPLE

209.522.7811
1016 H STREET
MODESTO, CA 95354
WWW.CLAYTONCOFFEE.COM

2.

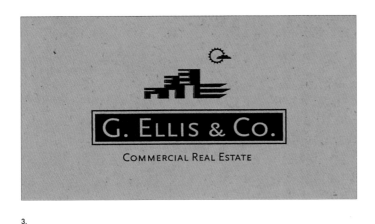

G. ELLIS & CO.

COMMERCIAL REAL ESTATE

3.

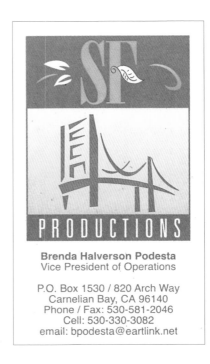

SF PRODUCTIONS

Brenda Halverson Podesta
Vice President of Operations

P.O. Box 1530 / 820 Arch Way
Carnelian Bay, CA 96140
Phone / Fax: 530-581-2046
Cell: 530-330-3082
email: bpodesta@eartlink.net

4.

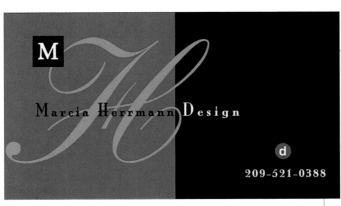

Marcia Herrmann Design

209-521-0388

5.

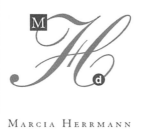

MARCIA HERRMANN

MARCIA HERRMANN DESIGN

809 SYLVAN AVE., SUITE 104
MODESTO, CA 95350
209-521-0388
FAX: 209-521-4748

email: mh@her2man2.com
www.her2man2.com

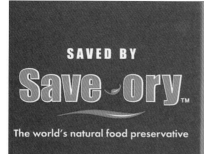

SAVED BY
Save-ory™

The world's natural food preservative

Hirotaka Furukawa, Ph.D.
Technical Manager

Meitetsu U.S.A. Inc.
3450 Arden Road
Hayward, CA 94545-3906

Toll free: 888-211-7233 (SAFE)
Fax #: 510-259-0119
hfurukawa@save-ory.com

NATURAL FOOD

PRESERVATIVE

www.save-ory.com

The **Save-ory**™ Spectrum:

Natural
Thermal stability
Prevents food poisoning
Safe
Easy to use
Odorless
Water soluble
Effective over a wide pH range

Meitetsu U.S.A. Inc.
3450 Arden Road
Hayward, CA 94545-3906

Toll free: 888-211-7233 (SAFE)
Fax #: 510-254-9797
info@save-ory.com

6.

BVNGALOW
BAKING CO.

BARBARA GRANT

P.O. Box 3791
Turlock, CA 95381

Office/Fax: 209-669-7656
Cell: 209-605-4177
WWW.BUNGALOWBAKING.COM

7.

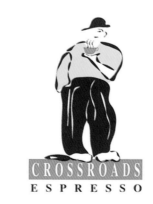

CROSSROADS
E S P R E S S O

Helen M. Russell

1-800-552-4424 Ext. 518
415-342-1111 Fax 415-697-6464
882 Mahler Road Burlingame, CA 94010

8.

Crossroads Espresso

We Know Espresso!

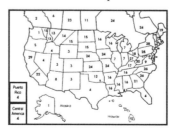

The Company With A
National Service Network

1-800-552-4424

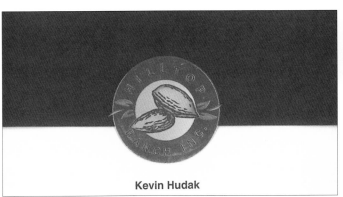

Kevin Hudak

1.

The Experienced Source For California Almonds

C.F.O.

13890 Looney Road ⚡Ballico, CA 95303
Tel: 209-874-1875⚡ Fax: 209-874-1877⚡ www.hilltopranch.com
Pager: 209-569-1633 ⚡ gerrit@hilltopranch.com

Gerrit N. Dorrepaal

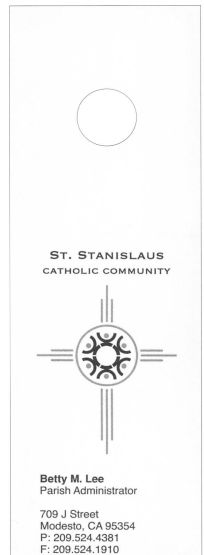

St. Stanislaus
catholic community

Betty M. Lee
Parish Administrator

709 J Street
Modesto, CA 95354
P: 209.524.4381
F: 209.524.1910

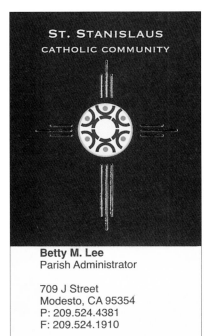

St. Stanislaus
catholic community

Betty M. Lee
Parish Administrator

709 J Street
Modesto, CA 95354
P: 209.524.4381
F: 209.524.1910

2.

146

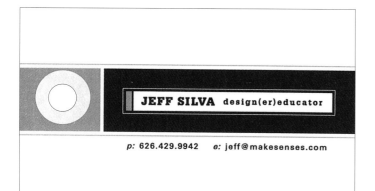

JEFF SILVA design(er)educator

p: 626.429.9942   *e:* jeff@makesenses.com

3.

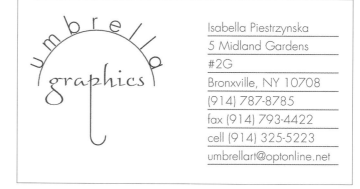

Isabella Piestrzynska
5 Midland Gardens
#2G
Bronxville, NY 10708
(914) 787-8785
fax (914) 793-4422
cell (914) 325-5223
umbrellart@optonline.net

4.

McFarland State Bank

Banking You Can Believe In

E. David Locke
President

Office: 608.838.3141
Direct: 608.838.7400
Fax: 608.838.8916

dlocke@msbonline.com

5990 Hwy. 51, Box 7
McFarland, WI 53558

SINCE 1904

5.

VIBRANT
ENTERPRISE
ASSOCIATES

Tom Fauré
405 Prides Run, Lake in the Hills, IL 60156
tel 847.658.2485   cell 847.331.5970   fax 847.458.9815
faure@vibrantenterprise.com

6.

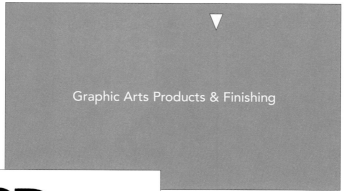

Graphic Arts Products & Finishing

MCD

Imagination Made Real™

Greg Meir
Account Manager

Direct: 608.268.3727 Mobile: 608.444.1362
Email: gmeir@mcd.net
MCD Incorporated, 2547 Progress Road, Madison, WI 53716
800.395.9405 Fax: 608.223.6850 www.mcd.net

7.

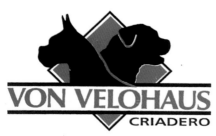

1.

CRUZAS CUIDADOSAMENTE PLANEADAS
PARA PRODUCIR CACHORROS
DE SUPERIOR CALIDAD,
EXCELENTE TEMPERAMENTO
Y CONFORMACION.

VON VELOHAUS
CRIADERO
BOXER◆ ROTTWEILER◆ MALINOIS

MANUEL TORAN TORRES
MANEJADOR

ROMA No. 100 COL. LOS ANGELES
C.P. 60160   TEL-FAX: (452) 3 57 07
URUAPAN, MICHOACAN, MEXICO
E MAIL: cornamen@mail.compusep.com

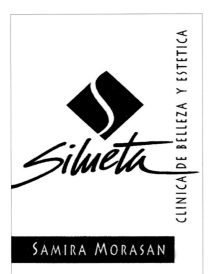

2.

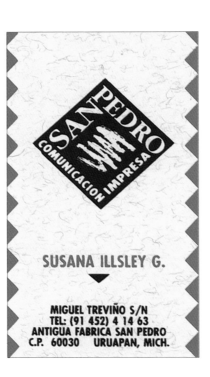

3.

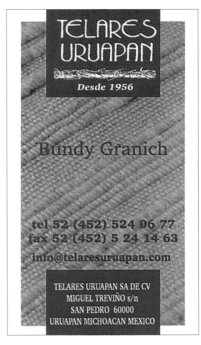

4.

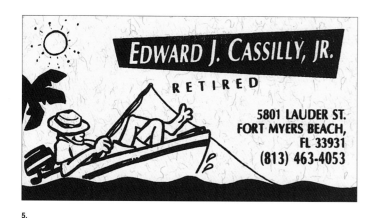

5.

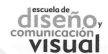
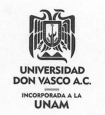

6.

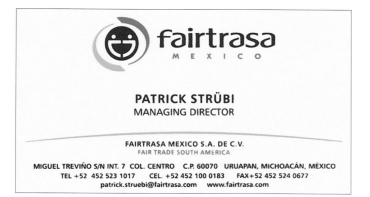

7.

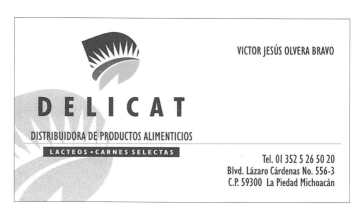

8.

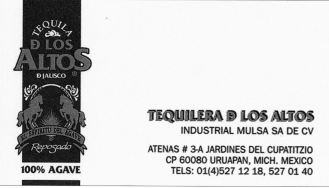

9.

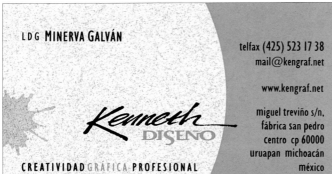

1.

soluciones
visuales
creativas

estrategias efectivas de
imagen y promoción

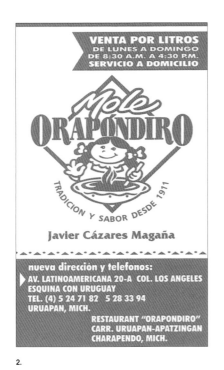

2.

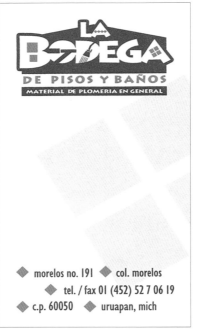

3.

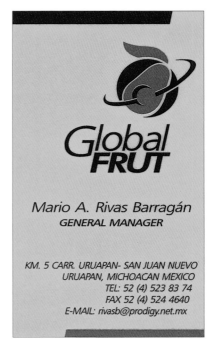

4.

150

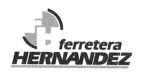

ferretera HERNANDEZ

Ing. Gerardo Alfonso Mancera Huante

JALISCO No. 81 COL. RAMON FARIAS C.P. 60050 TEL. 447-85 FAX 447-90
URUAPAN, MICHOACAN.

5.

Fresh & Spice
I N T E R N A C I O N A L

tel. **+52 (452) 524 0771**, tel./fax **+52 (452) 523 4588**
MANUEL PEREZ CORONADO #5 int. c C.P. 60080 URUAPAN, MICHOACAN, MÉXICO
e-mail: fresh&spice@hotmail.com

6.

DESDE 1986

MIEMBRO FUNDADOR DE
INTEGRAF
COLEGIO DE PROFESIONALES
EN DISEÑO GRAFICO
DE MICHOACAN A C

LOGOTIPOS ■ PAPELERIA ■ FOLLETOS ■ MENUS ■ ILUSTRACION ■ CALIGRAFIA
MASCOTAS ■ CARICATURAS ■ CARTELES ■ ANUNCIOS ■ ETIQUETAS ■ EMPAQUES

7.

LDG **K**ENNETH **T**REVIÑO

FABRICA DE **S**AN PEDRO
MIGUEL **T**REVIÑO **S/N**
CENTRO
CP 60000 **U**RUAPAN MICH.

EMAIL
kenneth@mail.compusep.com

TEL Y **F**AX (452) **3 1738**

Kenneth DISEÑO
CREATIVIDAD GRAFICA PROFESIONAL

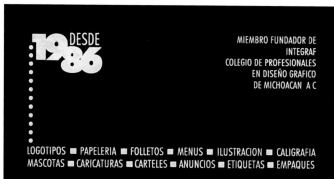

la casa del BEBE

ARTICULOS Y ACCESORIOS
PARA BEBE

Karla Beltrán
de Demerutis

BLVD. GARCIA DE LEON 1785 B
CHAPULTEPEC ORIENTE
CP 58280 MORELIA MICHOACAN

8.

(1-8)
Design Firm **Kenneth Diseño**

1.
Client   Kenneth Diseño
Designers   Kenneth Treviño,
         Minerva Galván
2.
Client   Orapondiro
Designer   Kenneth Treviño
3.
Client   La Bodega
Designers   Minerva Galván,
         Kenneth Treviño
4.
Client   Global Frut
Designer   Kenneth Treviño
5.
Client   Hernandez
Designer   Kenneth Treviño

6.
Client   Fresh & Spice
Designer   Kenneth Treviño
7.
Client   Kenneth Diseño
Designer   Kenneth Treviño
8.
Client   La Casa Del Bebe
Designer   Kenneth Treviño

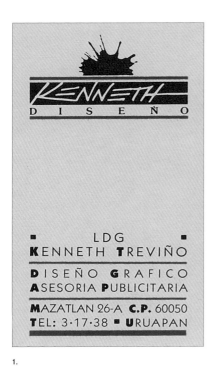

1.

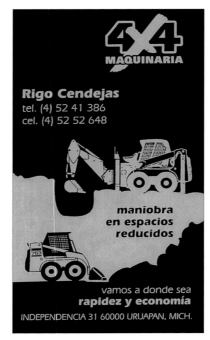

Rigo Cendejas
tel. (4) 52 41 386
cel. (4) 52 52 648

maniobra
en espacios
reducidos

vamos a donde sea
rapidez y economía

INDEPENDENCIA 31 60000 URUAPAN, MICH.

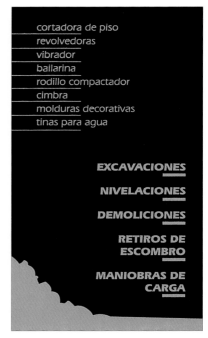

cortadora de piso
revolvedoras
vibrador
bailarina
rodillo compactador
cimbra
molduras decorativas
tinas para agua

EXCAVACIONES

NIVELACIONES

DEMOLICIONES

**RETIROS DE
ESCOMBRO**

**MANIOBRAS DE
CARGA**

2.

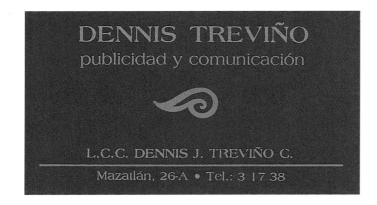

3.

4.

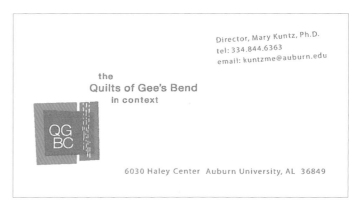

5.

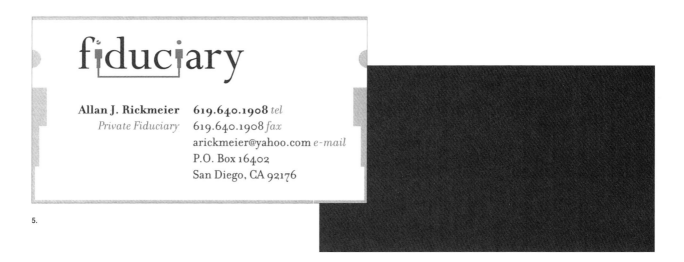

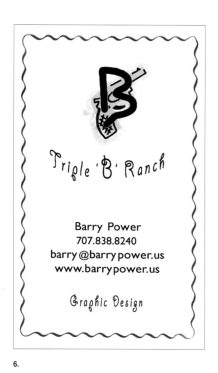

Triple 'B' Ranch

Barry Power
707.838.8240
barry@barrypower.us
www.barrypower.us

Graphic Design

6.

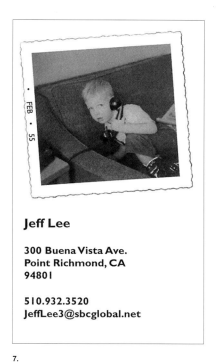

FEB · 55

Jeff Lee

300 Buena Vista Ave.
Point Richmond, CA
94801

510.932.3520
JeffLee3@sbcglobal.net

7.

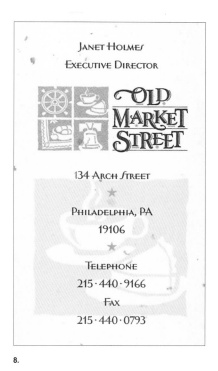

JANET HOLMES
EXECUTIVE DIRECTOR

OLD MARKET STREET

134 ARCH STREET

PHILADELPHIA, PA
19106

TELEPHONE
215·440·9166

FAX
215·440·0793

8.

RANDI WOLF
GRAPHIC DESIGNER

RANDESIGN@ERW-GROUP.COM

Randi Wolf

DESIGN

18 CYPRESS COURT • GLASSBORO, NJ 08028
PHONE 856 582 8181 • FAX 856 582 8187

9.

WWW.RANDIWOLFDESIGN.COM

Randi Wolf

DESIGN

Art Levy

WORDS & *ideas*

405 Lakeside Road
Wynnewood, PA 19096
TEL: 215-658-0250
FAX: 215-658-0251

10.

(1-3)
Design Firm **Kenneth Diseño**
(4)
Design Firm **Kelly Bryant Design**
(5)
Design Firm **incitrio design {brand} media**
(6,7)
Design Firm **Triple 'B' Ranch Design**
(8-10)
Design Firm **Randi Wolf Design**

1.
Client   Kenneth Diseño
Designer   Kenneth Treviño
2.
Client   4 x 4
Designers   Kenneth Treviño,
             Minerva Galván
3.
Client   Dennis Treviño
Designer   Kenneth Treviño

4.
Client   Quilts of Gee's Bend in context
Designer   Kelly Bryant
5.
Client   Allan J. Rickmeier
Designer   Natasha Krochina
6.
Client   Triple 'B' Ranch Design
Designer   Barry Power
7.
Client   Jeff Lee
Designers   Jeff Lee,
             Barry Power
8.
Client   Old Market Street
Designer   Randi Wolf
9.
Client   Randi Wolf Design
Designer   Randi Wolf
10.
Client   Words & Ideas
Designer   Randi Wolf

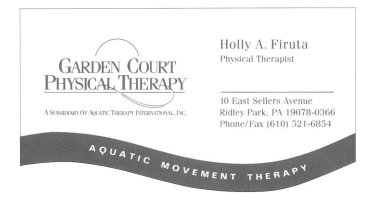

1.

Garden Court Physical Therapy
A Subsidiary Of Aquatic Therapy International, Inc.

Holly A. Firuta
Physical Therapist

10 East Sellers Avenue
Ridley Park, PA 19078-0366
Phone/Fax (610) 521-6854

AQUATIC MOVEMENT THERAPY

2.

Aquatic Therapy
INTERNATIONAL, INC.

- Education
- Consultation
- Rehabilitation
- Wellness

10 East Sellers Avenue
Ridley Park, PA 19078-0366
Phone/Fax (610) 521-6854

AQUATIC MOVEMENT THERAPY

3.

Florence Schiavo
Creative Director
fschiavo@mimco.com

Babbling Brook
LITTLE WORKS OF HEART

420 Benigno Blvd. • Unit H • Bellmawr, NJ 08031
Phone (856)931-8611 • Fax (856)931-4530
www.mybabblingbrook.com

4.

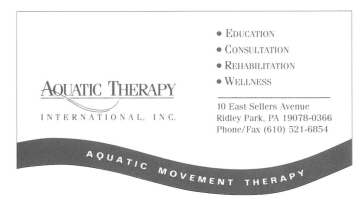

Children's Miracle Network
OF GREATER PHILADELPHIA

Carole Q. Hurst
Executive Director

1650 Market Street, Suite 3050
Philadelphia, Pennsylvania 19103
Telephone: (215) 587-9444
Fax: (215) 587-9732

5.

2200 Norcross Pkwy
Suite 200
Norcross, GA 30071

Bus: (770) 446-2822
ext. 222
Fax: (678) 868-1043
Cell: (770) 329-4083

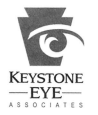
DEPLOYMENT SOLUTIONS

Mitchell Furbush
Managing Principle

mfurbush@depsol.com

6.

KEYSTONE EYE ASSOCIATES, LLC

JENNIFER RISPO-MAGUIRE
Business Manager, Site Supervisor

KEYSTONE
—EYE—
ASSOCIATES

9501 Roosevelt Blvd., Ste. 101
Philadelphia, PA 19114
215-673-1500
215-673-6660 (fax)

6409 Rising Sun Ave.
Philadelphia, PA 19111
215-725-9700
215-725-4973 (fax)

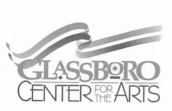

MARK FIELDS
DIRECTOR
(856) 256-4548
fields@rowan.edu

ROWAN UNIVERSITY
GLASSBORO, NJ 08028
FAX: (856) 256-4919
www.rowan.edu/centerarts

7.

Liz Shapiro ♪ Legal Search

226 W. Rittenhouse Square • Suite 613 • Philadelphia, Pennsylvania 19103
Telephone 215-546-3646 • Facsimile 215-546-3645
LShapiro@LizShapiroLegalSearch.com • www.LizShapiroLegalSearch.com

Nationwide Permanent Attorney Placements

8.

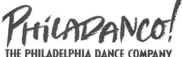

THE PHILADELPHIA DANCE COMPANY

9 North Preston St. • Philadanco Way • Philadelphia, PA 19104-2210
Phone 215-387-8200 • Fax 215-387-8203

Joan Myers Brown, D.F.A.
Executive/Artistic Director

9.

135
SOUTH
18TH
STREET
PHILADELPHIA
PENNSYLVANIA
19103
TELEPHONE
215
569-8587
FAX
215
569-9497

ANTHONY P. CHECCHIA,
MUSIC DIRECTOR

PHILADELPHIA
CHAMBER MUSIC SOCIETY

10.

. . . . ping!

Cheryl Ping
Typist

1687 Briarcliff Rd. NE
Apartment 5
Atlanta, GA. 30306
(404) 876-1910

11.

(1-11)
Design Firm **Randi Wolf Design**

1.
Client   Garden Court Physical Therapy
Designer   Randi Wolf
2.
Client   Aquatic Therapy International
Designer   Randi Wolf
3.
Client   Babbling Brook
Designer   Randi Wolf
4.
Client   Children's Miracle Network
            of Greater Philadelphia
Designer   Randi Wolf
5.
Client   Deployment Solutions, Inc.
Designer   Randi Wolf

6.
Client   Keystone Eye Associates
Designer   Randi Wolf
7.
Client   Glassboro Center for the Arts
Designer   Randi Wolf
8.
Client   Liz Shapiro Legal Search
Designer   Randi Wolf
9.
Client   Philadanco (The Philadelphia
            Dance Company)
Designer   Randi Wolf
10.
Client   Philadelphia Chamber
            Music Society
Designer   Randi Wolf
11.
Client   ...Ping!
Designer   Randi Wolf

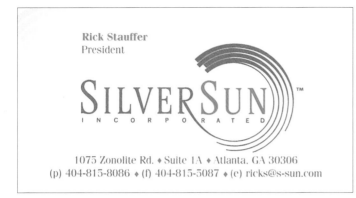

Rick Stauffer
President

SILVERSUN™
INCORPORATED

1075 Zonolite Rd. ◆ Suite 1A ◆ Atlanta, GA 30306
(p) 404-815-8086 ◆ (f) 404-815-5087 ◆ (e) ricks@s-sun.com

1.

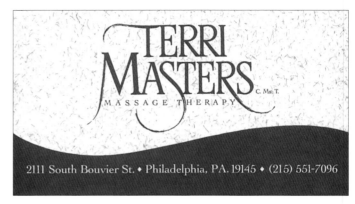

TERRI MASTERS
MASSAGE THERAPY C. Ms. T.

2111 South Bouvier St. ◆ Philadelphia, PA. 19145 ◆ (215) 551-7096

2.

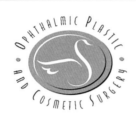

OPHTHALMIC PLASTIC
AND COSMETIC SURGERY

Marc S. Cohen, MD
Nancy G. Swartz, MS, MD

Philadelphia • Bala Cynwyd • Voorhees • Northfield

ph: (888) 478-3535   fax: (856) 772-1946   www.cosmetic-eyes.com

3.

Wills Eye Hospital
840 Walnut St.
Philadelphia, PA 19107
215.772.0900

───────

40 Monument Road, Fifth Floor
Bala Cynwyd, PA 19004
610.660.0662

───────

The Pavilions of Voorhees
2301 Evesham Road, Suite 101
Voorhees, NJ 08043
856.772.2552

───────

1500 Tilton Road
Northfield, NJ 08225
609.646.5200

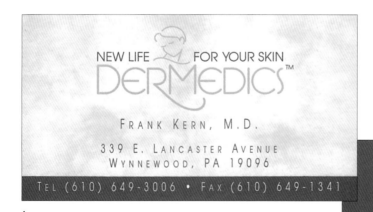

NEW LIFE   FOR YOUR SKIN
DERMEDICS™

FRANK KERN, M.D.

339 E. LANCASTER AVENUE
WYNNEWOOD, PA 19096

TEL (610) 649-3006 • FAX (610) 649-1341

4.

NEW LIFE   FOR YOUR SKIN
DERMEDICS™

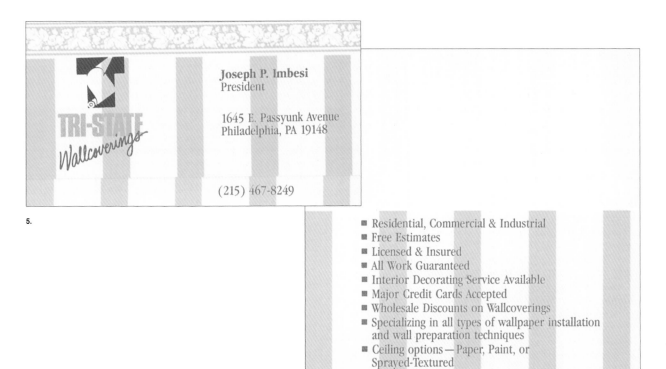

5.

Joseph P. Imbesi
President

1645 E. Passyunk Avenue
Philadelphia, PA 19148

(215) 467-8249

■ Residential, Commercial & Industrial
■ Free Estimates
■ Licensed & Insured
■ All Work Guaranteed
■ Interior Decorating Service Available
■ Major Credit Cards Accepted
■ Wholesale Discounts on Wallcoverings
■ Specializing in all types of wallpaper installation and wall preparation techniques
■ Ceiling options — Paper, Paint, or Sprayed-Textured

(215) 467-8249

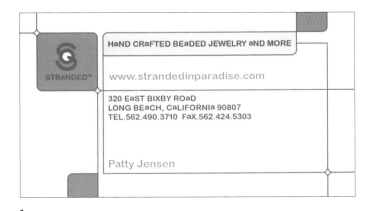

HaND CRaFTED BEaDED JEWELRY aND MORE

www.strandedinparadise.com

320 EaST BIXBY ROaD
LONG BEaCH, CaLIFORNIa 90807
TEL.562.490.3710 FaX.562.424.5303

Patty Jensen

6.

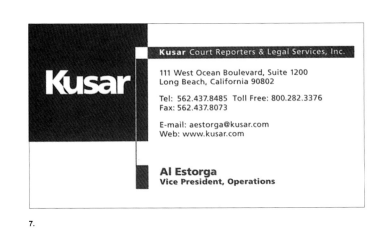

Kusar Court Reporters & Legal Services, Inc.

111 West Ocean Boulevard, Suite 1200
Long Beach, California 90802

Tel: 562.437.8485 Toll Free: 800.282.3376
Fax: 562.437.8073

E-mail: aestorga@kusar.com
Web: www.kusar.com

Al Estorga
Vice President, Operations

7.

b@dinger group

internet and
e-business solutions

president: **Mikel Bedinger**
address: 1071 Sixth Ave., Suite 261, San Diego, CA 92101
phone: 619-233-7550
fax: 619-233-7531
e-mail: mikel@bedinger.com
internet: www.bedinger.com

8.

(1-5)
Design Firm **Randi Wolf Design**
(6-8)
Design Firm **Jensen Design Associates, Inc.**

1.
Client   SilverSun, Incorporated
Designer   Randi Wolf
2.
Client   Terri Masters, Massage Therapy
Designer   Randi Wolf
3.
Client   Ophthalmic Plastic and
            Cosmetic Surgery
Designer   Randi Wolf
4.
Client   Dermedics
Designer   Randi Wolf

5.
Client   Tri-State Wallcoverings
Designer   Randi Wolf
6.
Client   Stranded in Paradise
Designer   David Jensen
7.
Client   Kusar Court Reporters
Designer   David Jensen
8.
Client   Bedinger Group
Designer   David Jensen

157

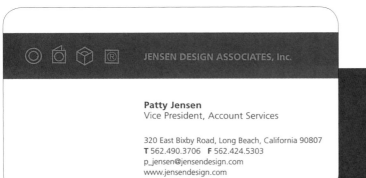

JENSEN DESIGN ASSOCIATES, Inc.

Patty Jensen
Vice President, Account Services

320 East Bixby Road, Long Beach, California 90807
T 562.490.3706 **F** 562.424.5303
p_jensen@jensendesign.com
www.jensendesign.com

1.

Alexander Isley Inc.
DESIGNERS

9 Brookside Place
Redding, CT 06896
f:(203) 544-7189

www.alexanderisley.com

Aline Hilford

aline@alexanderisley.com
t:(203) 544-9692 ext. 15

2.

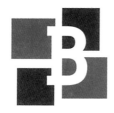 BlueBolt Networks Inc.
3710 University Drive
Suite 160
Durham, NC 27707

p (919) 865-2600
f (919) 865-2601

www.bluebolt.com
info@bluebolt.com

3.

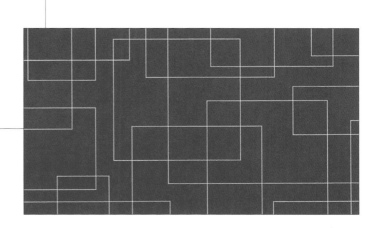

158

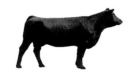

DAN BARBER
Creative Director

TEL: 914 366 6200
FAX: 914 366 7905
danb@stonebarnscenter.org
www.stonebarnscenter.org

STONE BARNS CENTER
FOR FOOD & AGRICULTURE
630 BEDFORD ROAD
POCANTICO HILLS, NEW YORK 10591

4.

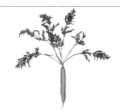

DAN BARBER
Creative Director

TEL: 914 366 6200
FAX: 914 366 7905
danb@stonebarnscenter.org
www.stonebarnscenter.org

STONE BARNS CENTER
FOR FOOD & AGRICULTURE
630 BEDFORD ROAD
POCANTICO HILLS, NEW YORK 10591

DAN BARBER
Creative Director

TEL: 914 366 6200
FAX: 914 366 7905
danb@stonebarnscenter.org
www.stonebarnscenter.org

STONE BARNS CENTER
FOR FOOD & AGRICULTURE
630 BEDFORD ROAD
POCANTICO HILLS, NEW YORK 10591

DAN BARBER
Creative Director

TEL: 914 366 6200
FAX: 914 366 7905
danb@stonebarnscenter.org
www.stonebarnscenter.org

STONE BARNS CENTER
FOR FOOD & AGRICULTURE
630 BEDFORD ROAD
POCANTICO HILLS, NEW YORK 10591

DAVID BARBER

TEL: 914 366 6200
FAX: 914 366 7905
davidb@stonebarnscenter.org
www.stonebarnscenter.org

STONE BARNS CENTER
FOR FOOD & AGRICULTURE
630 BEDFORD ROAD
POCANTICO HILLS, NEW YORK 10591

(1)
Design Firm **Jensen Design Associates, Inc.**
(2-4)
Design Firm **Alexander Isley Inc.**

1.
Client   Jensen Design Associates, Inc.
Designers David Jensen,
      Alyssa Igawa
2.
Client   Alexander Isley Inc.
Designers Alexander Isley,
      Cherith Victorino

3. Client   BlueBolt Networks
Designers Alexander Isley,
      Liesl Kaplan
4.
Client   Stone Barns Center for
      Food & Agriculture
Designers Randi Wolf,
      Alexander Isley,
      Tara Benyei

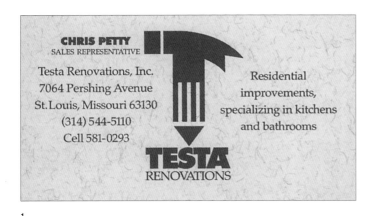

CHRIS PETTY
SALES REPRESENTATIVE

Testa Renovations, Inc.
7064 Pershing Avenue
St. Louis, Missouri 63130
(314) 544-5110
Cell 581-0293

Residential improvements, specializing in kitchens and bathrooms

TESTA RENOVATIONS

1.

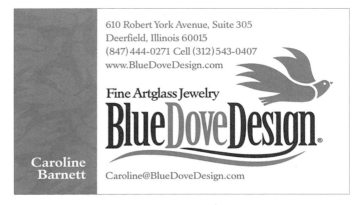

610 Robert York Avenue, Suite 305
Deerfield, Illinois 60015
(847) 444-0271 Cell (312) 543-0407
www.BlueDoveDesign.com

Fine Artglass Jewelry

BlueDoveDesign ®

Caroline Barnett

Caroline@BlueDoveDesign.com

2.

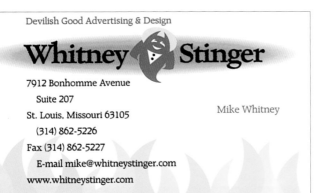

Devilish Good Advertising & Design

Whitney Stinger

7912 Bonhomme Avenue
Suite 207
St. Louis, Missouri 63105
(314) 862-5226
Fax (314) 862-5227
E-mail mike@whitneystinger.com
www.whitneystinger.com

Mike Whitney

3.

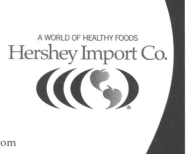

96 Executive Avenue
Edison, NJ 08817
(732) 650-9905 Ext 115
Fax (732) 650-9909

A WORLD OF HEALTHY FOODS

Hershey Import Co.

BRIAN DENMAN
Controller
bdenman@hersheyimport.com

4.

Whitney Design Works, LLC
7066 Pershing Avenue
Suite 300
St. Louis, Missouri 63130
Phone (314) 862-5994
Fax (314) 862-5318
www.whitneydesignworks.com

Mike Whitney
mike@whitneydesignworks.com

Whitney Design Works

Advertising &
Graphic Design

5.

Shropshire Educational
Consulting, LLC

3079½ Royster Road
Lexington, Kentucky 40516
(859) 396-9508

Shropshire
Educational Consulting

Jane Schoenfeld Shropshire
JShrop@att.net

6.

OsmoTech

17295 Chesterfield Airport Road
Suite 200
Chesterfield, Missouri 63005

Toll Free 1 (866) GO-4-OSMO
Phone (636) 733-7570
Fax (636) 733-7571

www.GoOsmo.com

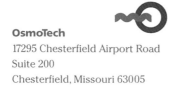

OsmoTech™
OSMOTIC PULSE TECHNOLOGIES

Paul Femmer
Vice President, Sales
pfemmer@GoOsmo.com

FROM DRYTRONIC, INC.

7.

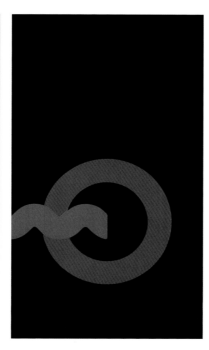

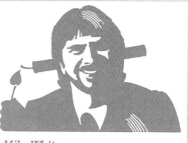

Mike Whitney

7833 Kenridge Lane

St. Louis, Mo. 63119

314.968.1255

Advertising

Design

Sales Promotion

8.

Service Beyond The Call of Duty

Linda Ramin

Linda Ramin
Art Representative
6239 Elizabeth Avenue
Saint Louis, Missouri 63139
(314) 781-8851

9.

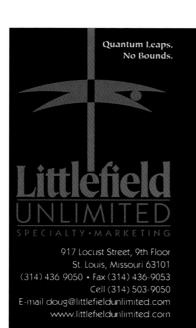

Quantum Leaps.
No Bounds.

Littlefield
UNLIMITED
SPECIALTY · MARKETING

917 Locust Street, 9th Floor
St. Louis, Missouri 63101
(314) 436 9050 • Fax (314) 436-9053
Cell (314) 503-9050
E-mail doug@littlefieldunlimited.com
www.littlefieldunlimited.com

Douglas A. Littlefield

10.

(1,2,5,6,8,9)
  Design Firm **Whitney Design Works, LLC**
(3,4,10)
  Design Firm **Whitney Stinger**
(7)
  Design Firm **Whitney Design Works &**
  Explore Marketing

1.
  Client   Testa Renovations, Inc.
  Designer   Mike Whitney
2.
  Client   Blue Dove Design
  Designer   Mike Whitney
3.
  Client   Whitney Stinger, Inc.
  Designers Mike Whitney,
                   Karl Stinger

4.
  Client   Hershey Imports
  Designers Mike Whitney,
                   Karl Stinger
5.
  Client   Whitney Design Works, LLC
  Designer   Mike Whitney
6.
  Client   Shropshire Educational
                   Consulting
  Designer   Mike Whitney
7.
  Client   Osmotech
  Designer   Mike Whitney
8.
  Client   Mike Whitney
  Designer   Mike Whitney
9.
  Client   Linda Ramin,
                   Art Representative
  Designer   Mike Whitney
10.
  Client   Littlefield Unlimited
  Designers Mike Whitney,
                   Karl Stinger

1056 WEST STREET, LAUREL, MD 20707
TEL 301-776-2812 ▪ FAX 301-953-1196

d

dever designs

JEFFREY L. DEVER
PRESIDENT—CREATIVE DIRECTOR

1.

*the point
where art
and
communication
meet*

1056 WEST STREET, LAUREL, MD 20707
TEL 301-776-2812 ▪ FAX 301-953-1196

dever designs

JEFFREY L. DEVER
PRESIDENT—CREATIVE DIRECTOR

brillhartmedia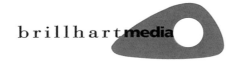

david brillhart
producer/director

9200 RT. 108, SUITE 209 | **T 410-730-5994**
COLUMBIA, MD 21045 | **F 410-730-7496**

2.

We ○ see more...

WWW.BRILLHART.COM

DENNIS
CREWS
PHOTOGRAPHY

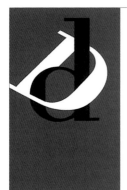

*809-C
E. South
Street,
Frederick,
Maryland
21701*

301-696-9123

3.

CROSSROADS RECORDS INC.
6903 BROOKS ROAD
HIGHLAND, MD 20777
PHONE 301-854-0829

Jerry Rader
Director of Marketing
Phone 301-964-5755

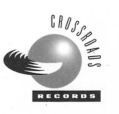

4.

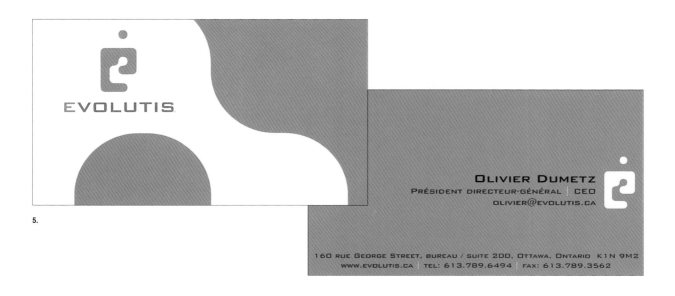

5.

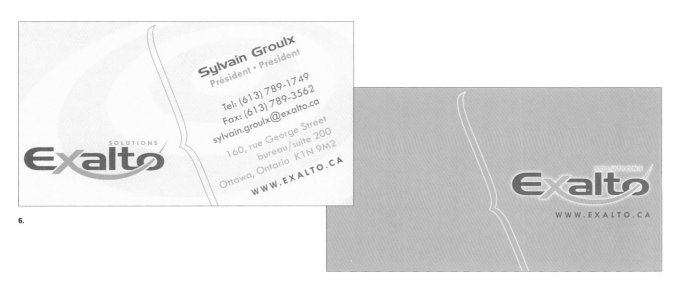

6.

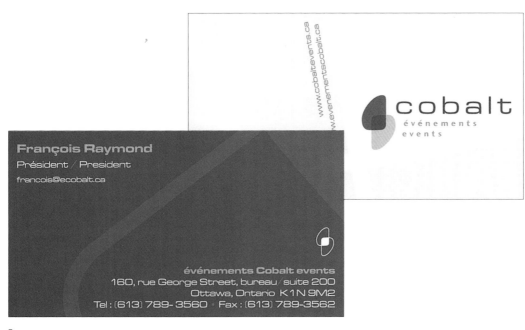

7.

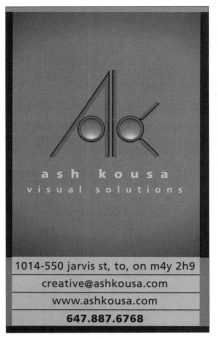

1014-550 jarvis st, to, on m4y 2h9
creative@ashkousa.com
www.ashkousa.com
647.887.6768

1.

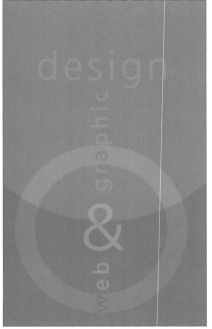

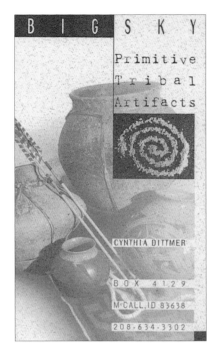

2.

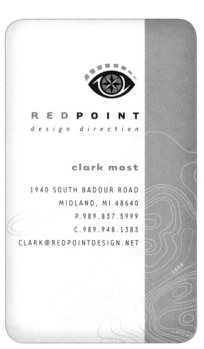

3.

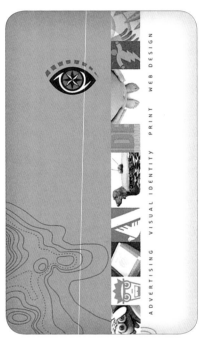

MICHAEL W. CROW
CHAIRMAN

MARQUEE MUSIC, INC.
A SUBSIDIARY OF SPENCER ENTERTAINMENT, INC.

9701 WILSHIRE BOULEVARD, SUITE 1200, BEVERLY HILLS, CA 90212
TEL (310) 786-8877 FAX (310) 786-1701

4.

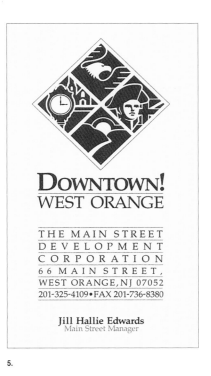

DOWNTOWN!
WEST ORANGE

THE MAIN STREET
DEVELOPMENT
CORPORATION
66 MAIN STREET,
WEST ORANGE, NJ 07052
201-325-4109 • FAX 201-736-8380

Jill Hallie Edwards
Main Street Manager

5.

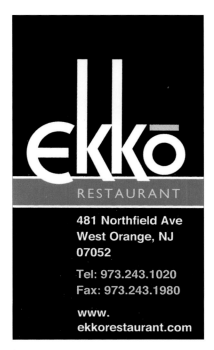

EKKŌ
RESTAURANT

**481 Northfield Ave
West Orange, NJ
07052**

**Tel: 973.243.1020
Fax: 973.243.1980**

**www.
ekkorestaurant.com**

DIRECTIONS

**From New York State and
Northern or Southern New Jersey
via Garden State Parkway
North or South**

- Garden State Parkway
  North or South to Exit 145
- Follow signs for I-280 West
- Take Exit 10 off 280 West
- At the end of exit ramp, turn Left
  at the light onto Northfield Ave.
- After the 6th light, make a Right
  onto Rock Spring Ave.
- Follow to entrance 50 yards on Right

**From Western New Jersey
via I-280 East**

- 280 East to Exit 7
  (Pleasant Valley Way)
- At end of exit ramp, turn Left at the
  traffic light onto Pleasant Valley Way
- Follow Pleasant Valley Way to 2nd
  traffic light and make Left onto
  Northfield Ave./County 508 West
- After the 3rd traffic light, make a Left
  onto Rock Spring Ave. (just before Ekko)
- Follow to entrance 50 yards on Right

6.

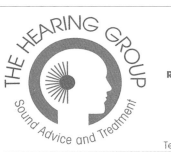

THE HEARING GROUP
Sound Advice and Treatment

Robbi Hershon, Au.D., CCC-A
Doctor of Audiology

Tel 973.243.8860 • Fax 973.243.8863
412 Pleasant Valley Way, West Orange, NJ 07052
www.thehearinggroupusa.com

7.

Stephen Longo

*Package Design, Graphic Design,
Marketing & Corporate Identity*

8 Colony Drive East, West Orange, NJ 07052
973.868.0343

8.

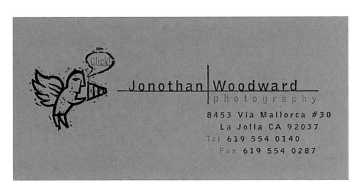

Jonothan | Woodward
p h o t o g r a p h y

8453 Via Mallorca #30
La Jolla CA 92037
Tel 619 554 0140
Fax 619 554 0287

9.

(1)
   Design Firm **Ash Kousa Visual Solutions**
(2,3)
   Design Firm **Redpoint design**
(4-8)
   Design Firm **Stephen Longo**
                Design Associates
(9)
   Design Firm **Visual Asylum**

1.
   Client   Ash Kousa Visual Solutions
   Designer Ash Kousa
2.
   Client   Big Sky Artifacts
   Designer Clark Most
3.
   Client   Redpoint design
   Designer Clark Most

4.
   Client   Marquee Music, Inc.
   Designer Stephen Longo
5.
   Client   The Township of West Orange
   Designer Stephen Longo
6.
   Client   Ekko Restaurant
   Designer Stephen Longo
7.
   Client   The Hearing Group
   Designer Stephen Longo
8.
   Client   Stephen Longo
   Designer Stephen Longo
9.
   Client   Jonothan Woodward
   Designer Joel Sotelo

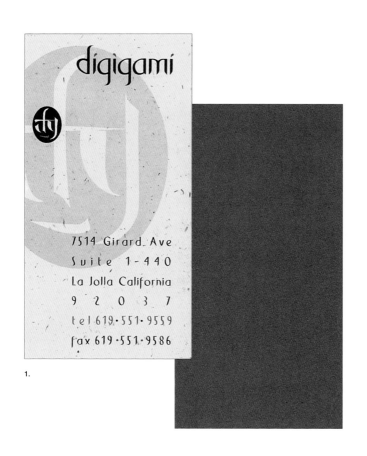

digigami

7514 Girard Ave
Suite 1-440
La Jolla California
9 2 0 3 7
tel 619·551·9559
fax 619·551·9586

1.

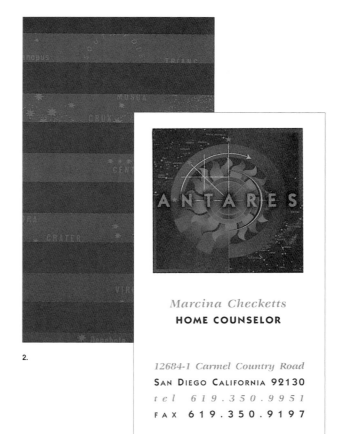

ANTARES

Marcina Checketts
HOME COUNSELOR

12684-1 Carmel Country Road
SAN DIEGO CALIFORNIA 92130
tel 619.350.9951
FAX **619.350.9197**

2.

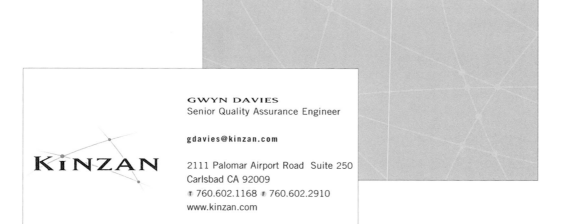

GWYN DAVIES
Senior Quality Assurance Engineer

gdavies@kinzan.com

2111 Palomar Airport Road Suite 250
Carlsbad CA 92009
T 760.602.1168 F 760.602.2910
www.kinzan.com

KINZAN

3.

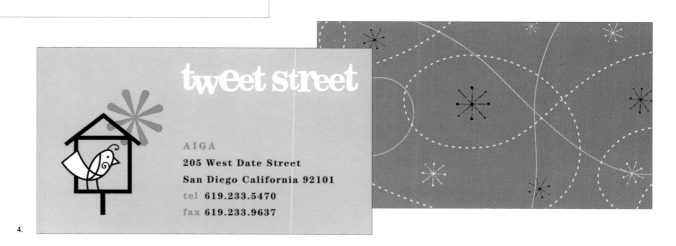

tweet street

AIGA
205 West Date Street
San Diego California 92101
tel **619.233.5470**
fax **619.233.9637**

4.

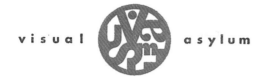

visual asylum

MAELIN LEVINE
partner/designer
maelinl@visualasylum.com

205 WEST DATE SAN DIEGO CA 92101
T 619.233.9633 F 619.233.9637
VISUALASYLUM.COM

5.

SAN DIEGO CITY COLLEGE GRAPHIC DESIGN
1313 PARK BOULEVARD SAN DIEGO CA 92101
TEL (619) 388-3933 FAX (619) 388-3522

ADJUNCT FACULTY

www.sdccgraphicdesign.com

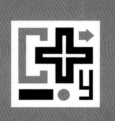

6.

THERESA R. KOSEN
executive director

p.o. box 3836 san diego california 92163
T/F 619.276.0101 sandiegomuseumcouncil.org
tkosen@san.rr.com

 SAN DIEGO MUSEUM COUNCIL

7.

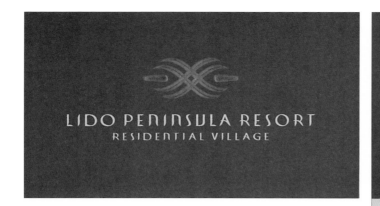

1.

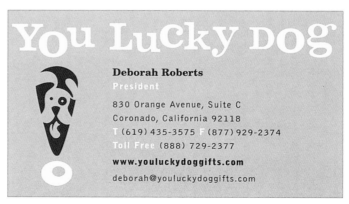

Sherry Coshow

LIDO RESORT HOMES
One Anchorage Way, Newport Beach, CA 92663
TEL 714.673.6623 FAX 714.673.7846

30673 CALLE DE LOS NIÑOS

RANCHO SANTA MARGARITA

ALIFORNIA 92688

AX 714 459-0440

714 459-0707

LOS
ABANICOS
CourtHome
Collection

2.

You Lucky Dog

Deborah Roberts
President

830 Orange Avenue, Suite C
Coronado, California 92118
T (619) 435-3575 F (877) 929-2374
Toll Free (888) 729-2377
www.youluckydoggifts.com
deborah@youluckydoggifts.com

3.

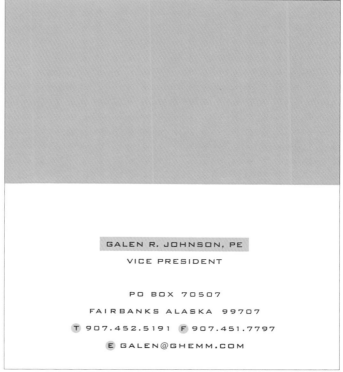

4.

GALEN R. JOHNSON, PE

VICE PRESIDENT

PO BOX 70507
FAIRBANKS ALASKA 99707
T 907.452.5191 F 907.451.7797
E GALEN@GHEMM.COM

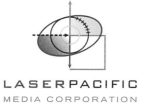

CHITA TUERES

Chief Chemist
Film Laboratory Services

LASERPACIFIC
MEDIA CORPORATION

835 N SEWARD STREET
HOLLYWOOD CA 90038
PHONE 213.462.6266 x4320
FACSIMILE 213.466.5047

5.

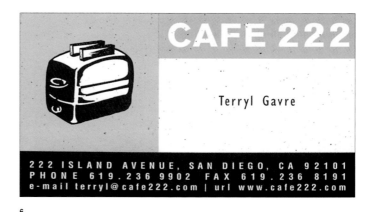

CAFE 222

Terryl Gavre

222 ISLAND AVENUE, SAN DIEGO, CA 92101
PHONE 619.236 9902 FAX 619.236 8191
e-mail terryl@cafe222.com | url www.cafe222.com

6.

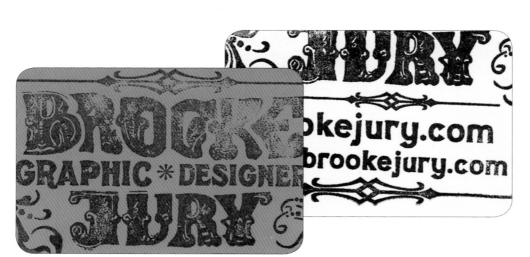

7.

(1-6)
Design Firm **Visual Asylum**
(7)
Design Firm **www.brookejury.com**

1.
Client   Lido Peninsula Resort
Designer   Amy Levine
2.
Client   Los Abanicos
     CourtHome Collection
Designer   Amy Levine
3.
Client   You Lucky Dog
Designer   Joel Sotelo
4.
Client   Ghemm
Designer   Joel Sotelo
5.
Client   LaserPacific
     Media Corporation
Designer   Amy Gingery
6.
Client   Cafe 222
Designer   MaeLin Levine
7.
Client   Brooke Jury Graphic Design
Designer   Brooke Jury

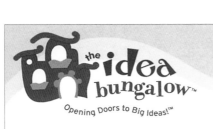

the idea bungalow™

Opening Doors to Big Ideas!™

p 310.823.8742
f 310.823.8743

Lisa Strick
Chief Idea Officer

Lisa@IdeaBungalow.com
4712 Admiralty Way #609 • Marina Del Rey, CA 90292

Branding
Brainstorming
Market Research
Product Innovation
Marketing Strategy
FunVentions™

1.

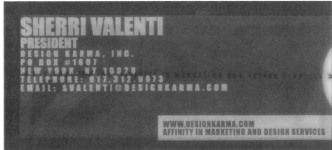

SHERRI VALENTI
PRESIDENT
DESIGN KARMA, INC.
PO BOX #1607
NEW YORK, NY 10028
TELEPHONE: 917.312.9973
EMAIL: SVALENTI@DESIGNKARMA.COM

WWW.DESIGNKARMA.COM
AFFINITY IN MARKETING AND DESIGN SERVICES

2.

SHERRI VALENTI
PRESIDENT
DESIGN KARMA, INC.
PO BOX #1607
NEW YORK, NY 10028
TELEPHONE: 917.312.9973
EMAIL: SVALENTI@DESIGNKARMA.COM

DESIGNKARMA INC.
DESIGN KARMA PROVIDES INTEGRATED
DESIGN SERVICES THAT ENCOMPASS FULL-SCALE
OUR SERVICES RANGE FROM INITIAL
DEVELOPMENT, MESSAGING AND STRATEGY, TO
CREATIVE EXECUTION.

design-karma

WWW.DESIGNKARMA.COM
AFFINITY IN MARKETING AND DESIGN SERVICES

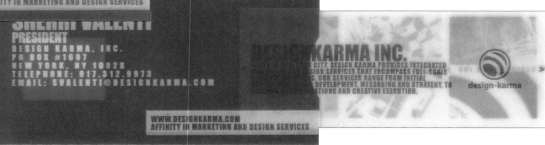

Leslie Lanahan
Board of Directors

Post Office Box 191889
Dallas Texas 75219
TEL 214 821 3112
FAX 214 821 2997
llanahan@gordie.org
www.gordie.org

GORDIE
The Gordie Foundation

Promoting Alcohol Awareness and Education

3.

GORDIE Check   Passing Out

Alcohol Poisoning can
have any of these   Pale Skin   Vomiting
six symptoms.
Not sure? Get help.
Alcohol can kill.   Confusion   Seizures

Irregular Breathing

Jennifer Sailer
Creative Director

jsailer@evokeideagroup.com

902 South Randall Road
Suite 336C
St. Charles, IL 60174

P 630.879.3846
P 866.842.7424
F 630.761.9407

evok

www.evokeideagroup.com

advertising and marketing
with the power to persuade

4.

Flight JOE CAMPAGNA
CHEF

1820 TOWER DRIVE | GLENVIEW, IL 60025

MAIN 847-729-WINE | FAX 847-729-9465

JOE@FLIGHTWINEBAR.COM | FLIGHTWINEBAR.COM

5.

TAKING FOOD, WINE
AND FUN TO NEW HEIGHTS

LIFE IS STRANGE

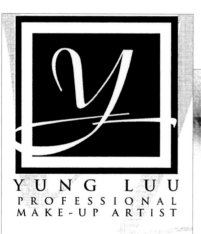

YUNG LUU
PROFESSIONAL
MAKE-UP ARTIST

YUNG LUU
(443) 465-2495
yungbeauty04@yahoo.com

www.geocities.com/yungbeauty04

MARYLAND ★ DC ★ NORTHERN VA

6.

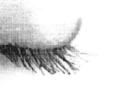

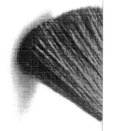

LOOK...

FEEL...

BE...

YUNG

(1)
Design Firm **Otis Design Group**
(2)
Design Firm **DesignKarma Inc.**
(3)
Design Firm **Jowaisas Design**
(4)
Design Firm **Evoke Idea Group, Inc.**
(5)
Design Firm **ZGraphics, Ltd.**
(6)
Design Firm **Trang Dam**

1.
Client   The Idea Bungalow
Designer   Jessica Raddatz
2.
Client   Design Karma Inc.
Designers   Vitaliy Yasch,
            Timofei Youriev

3.
Client   The Gordie Foundation
Designer   Elizabeth Jowaisas
4.
Client   Evoke Idea Group, Inc.
Designers   Jennifer Sailer,
            Jill Roberts
5.
Client   Flight Wine Bar
Designers   Joe Zeller,
            Kris Martinez Farrell
6.
Client   Yung Luu
Designer   Trang Dam

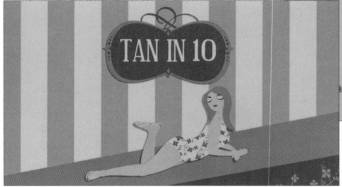

1.

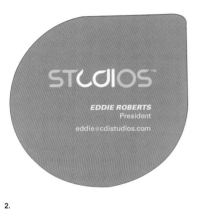

STUDIOS

EDDIE ROBERTS
President
eddie@cdistudios.com

cdi studios // print + interactive

2215a Renaissance Drive
Las Vegas, Nevada 89119
t 702 876+3316 **f** 702 876+3317
cdistudios.com

DAMN GOOD DESIGN

2.

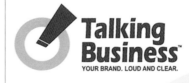

Talking
Business
YOUR BRAND. LOUD AND CLEAR.

Holly M. O'Neill
President

620 Newport Center Drive
Suite 1100
Newport Beach, CA 92660

(949) 721-4160 tel
(949) 209-4946 fax

Holly@TalkingBusiness.net

www.TalkingBusiness.net

3.

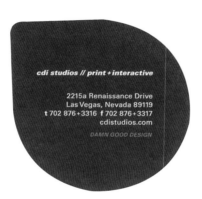

Focus Groups
Branding
Brainstorming

DAVID M. HAHN

GRAPHIC DESIGNER
CORPORATE SERVICES

4111 East 37th Street North
Wichita, Kansas 67220
TEL 316+828.7677
FAX 316+828.5778
CELL 316+214.8954

DAVID.HAHN@KBSLP.COM

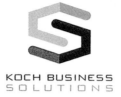

KOCH BUSINESS
SOLUTIONS

4.

VERITAS
INFORMATION AND RISK CONSULTANTS

5.

GABRIEL R. PALAZZI
MANAGING DIRECTOR/TECHNICAL SERVICES

2000 TOWN CENTER - SUITE 2110
SOUTHFIELD MI 48075
PHONE 248 352 5600 FAX 248 352 5671
CELL 248 302 7026
GPALAZZI@VERITAS-GLOBAL.COM

DETROIT | LONDON | NEW YORK | WASHINGTON

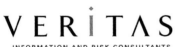
diamantaires

Danya Gerstein
Associate Manager of Sales

The Shops at Columbus Circle
Ten Columbus Circle · New York · NY · 10019
tel 212 823 9511 · fax 212 823 9512 · cel 917 297 2482
dgerstein@lockesdiamonds.com
www.lockesdiamonds.com

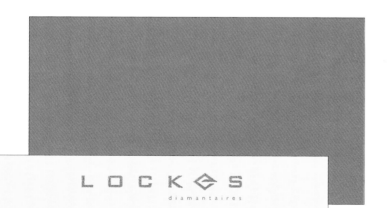

6.

(1)
Design Firm **E-lift Media TM**
(2)
Design Firm **CDI Studios**
(3)
Design Firm **Talking Business**
(4)
Design Firm **KOCH BUSINESS SOLUTIONS**
(5,6)
Design Firm **sterling group**

1.
Client   Tan In 10
Designer   Simone Burdon
2.
Client   CDI Studios
Designers   Michelle Georgilas,
            Victoria Hart

3.
Client   Talking Business
Designers   Holly M. O'Neill
            (Talking Business),
            Suzanne Issa
            (Issa Marketing & Designs)
4.
Client   KOCH BUSINESS
            SOLUTIONS
Designer   David M. Hahn
5.
Client   Veritas
Designers   Marcus Hewitt
6.
Client   Lockes Diamantaires
Designer   Kim Berlin

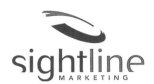

Samantha Guerry
President & CEO

3050 K Street, NW, Suite 400
Washington, DC 20007

PHONE 202.342.8415
FAX 202.342.8546
samantha@sightlinemarketing.com

www.SightlineMarketing.com

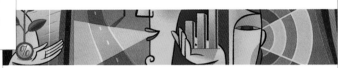

integrated marketing · brand development · advertising · communications

1.

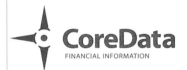
FINANCIAL INFORMATION

Renny Ponvert   7272 Wisconsin Avenue, Suite 3
President   Bethesda, MD 20816

PHONE 301.455.5886
FAX 301.656.0183
rponvert@coredatagroup.com

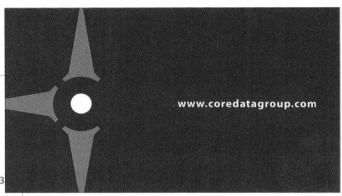

www.coredatagroup.com

2.

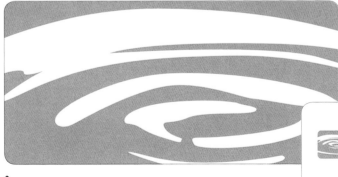

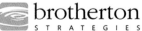

David Brotherton
President

Brotherton Strategies, Inc.
933 11th Avenue East – Suite E
Seattle, WA 98102

206.324.0403 **office**
206.954.8672 **mobile**

www.brothertonstrategies.com   david@brothertonstrategies.com

3.

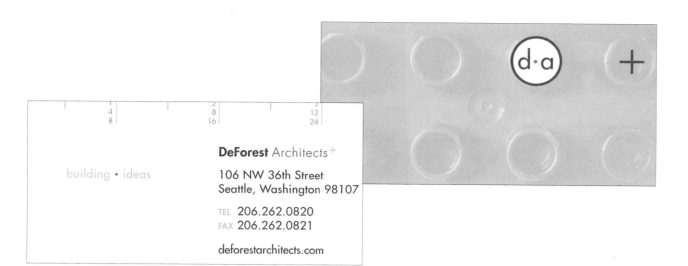

DeForest Architects +

106 NW 36th Street
Seattle, Washington 98107

TEL 206.262.0820
FAX 206.262.0821

deforestarchitects.com

building • ideas

4.

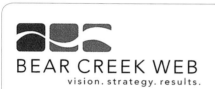

BEAR CREEK WEB
vision. strategy. results.

Tim Riley, President
tim@bearcreekweb.com

206.779.2021 telephone
425.226.5434 facsimile
PO Box 1428
Woodinville, WA 98072

bearcreekweb.com

5.

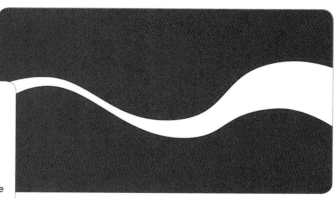

FIRST ONE'S ON ME.
BRING IN THIS CARD FOR ONE FREE RAIL
DRINK OR ICE-COLD TAP BEER. TELL 'EM
ANDREW SENT YOU.

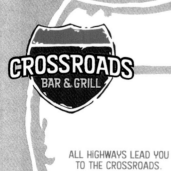

CROSSROADS
BAR & GRILL

ALL HIGHWAYS LEAD YOU
TO THE CROSSROADS.

Andrew Pern
Owner

Just off I-94 and Hwy 10
next to the Red Carpet Inn
12830 Cox Lane
P.O. Box 38
Osseo, WI 54758
Phone (715) 441-9298

6.

(1)
Design Firm **Sightline Marketing**
(2)
Design Firm **CDI Studios**
(3-5)
Design Firm **Monster Design**
(6)
Design Firm **Pernsteiner Creative Group, Inc.**

1.
Client   Sightline Marketing
Designer   Clay Marshall
2.
Client   CoreData
Designer   Clay Marshall

3.
Client   Brotherton Strategies
Designer   Theresa Monica
4.
Client   DeForest Architects
Designer   Hannah Wygal
5.
Client   Bear Creek Web
Designer   Theresa Monica
6.
Client   Crossroads Bar & Grill
Designer   Todd Pernsteiner

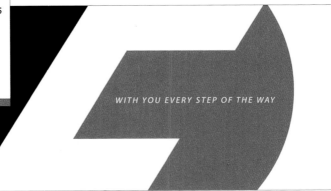

COUNTY
MATERIALS CORPORATION

www.countymaterials.com

205 North St., P.O. Box 100
Marathon, WI 54448-0100
tel (715) 848-1365
toll free (800) 289-2569
fax (715) 443-3691
Rdy Mix Disp. (715) 848-1365

**Marathon Office-Corporate,
Weston & Merrill Offices**

9303 Schofield Ave.
Weston, WI 54476
tel (715) 359-7731
fax (715) 355-5752

496 Brandenburg Ave.
Merrill, WI 54452

WITH YOU EVERY STEP OF THE WAY

1.

PERNSTEINER
CREATIVE GROUP INC

INNOVATIVE MARKETING COMMUNICATIONS THAT DEMAND ATTENTION.

Identity systems > Brand management > Direct mail
Campaign development > Graphic design > Copywriting
Publications > Exhibit design > Advertising

Todd Pernsteiner CREATIVE DIRECTOR

7831 East Bush Lake Rd., Suite 100 > Bloomington, MN 55439

email: info@pernsteiner.com > www.pernsteiner.com

tel [952] 841-1111 > fax [952] 841-3460

2.

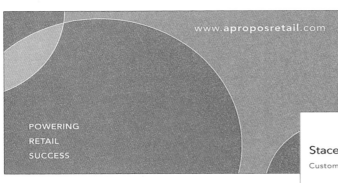

www.aproposretail.com

POWERING
RETAIL
SUCCESS

Stacey Nunn

Customer Account Manager

apropos™

3400 188th St. SW, Ste 185, Lynnwood WA 98037
800 729.4767 ○ 425 672.1304 ○ 425 672.0192 FAX
staceyn@aproposretail.com

3.

fine f eline photography

Kathleen Dudley
PHOTOGRAPHER

3203 13TH Avenue West
Seattle, Washington 98119
206 285 7918

4.

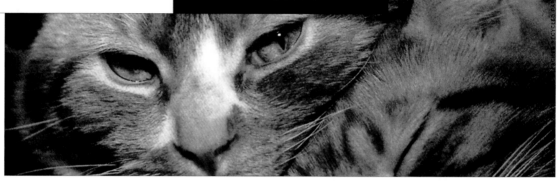

Bill Zuydhoek
INTERNATIONAL SALES MANAGER

425 201 6012 D
425 644 6000 T
425 644 8222 F

15015 Main Street
Suite 200
Bellevue, WA 98007

BILL@ULTRABAC.COM

ULTRABAC
SOFTWARE

www.ultrabac.com
BACKUP AND DISASTER RECOVERY SOFTWARE FOR BUSINESS

5.

Kim Falcon | Principal
kim@graphicasolutions.com
| 611 Eastlake Ave E
            Seattle, WA 98109
            206 652 9646
            206 652 9654 F
            graphicasolutions.com

g
graphica

6.

(1,2)
Design Firm **Pernsteiner Creative Group, Inc.**
(3-6)
Design Firm **Graphica**

1.
Client   County Materials Corporation
Designers   Andy Hauck,
             Todd Pernsteiner
2.
Client   Pernsteiner Creative
             Group, Inc.
Designers   Todd Pernsteiner,
             Kären Larson
3.
Client   Apropos Retail
Designer   Christa Fleming
4.
Client   Fine Feline Photography
Designer   Craig Terrones
5.
Client   Ultrabac
Designer   Robin Walker
6.
Client   Graphica
Designer   Craig Terrones

177

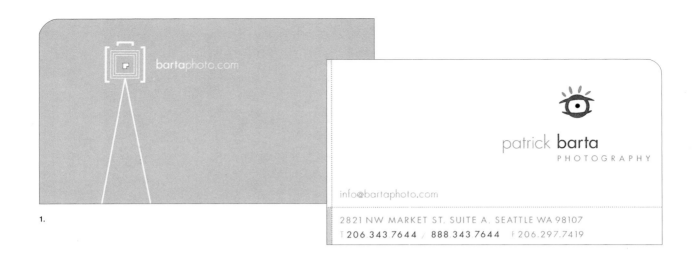

1.

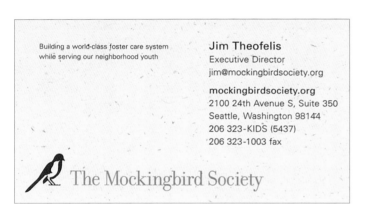

Building a world-class foster care system
while serving our neighborhood youth

Jim Theofelis
Executive Director
jim@mockingbirdsociety.org

mockingbirdsociety.org
2100 24th Avenue S, Suite 350
Seattle, Washington 98144
206 323-KIDS (5437)
206 323-1003 fax

The Mockingbird Society

2.

Margaret Morris
Office Manager
margaretm@sizeti.com

Size Technologies, Inc.
465 10th Street
Suite 101
San Francisco, CA 94103
t: 415.701.0000 x 115
f: 415.701.0293
www.sizeti.com

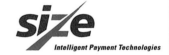

3.

Captive Wild Animal Protection Coalition
P.O. Box 6944 San Carlos, CA 94070
p:650.595.4692 f:650.595.4690
www.cwapc.org

4.

Phone 650-821-6000 • Fax 650-821-6005

San Francisco International Airport, Boarding Area G • San Francisco, CA 94128
Mailing Address • P.O. Box 280417 • San Francisco, CA 94128-0417

5.

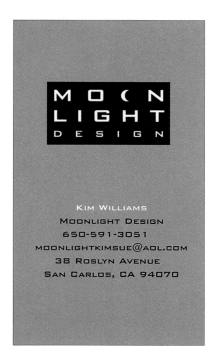

KIM WILLIAMS
MOONLIGHT DESIGN
650-591-3051
MOONLIGHTKIMSUE@AOL.COM
38 ROSLYN AVENUE
SAN CARLOS, CA 94070

6.

Leena
Partner

Hair Loft
1870 South Norfolk Street
San Mateo, CA 94403
650.574.0801

7.

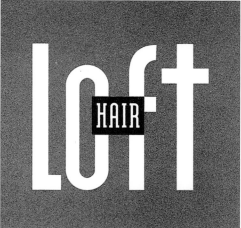

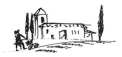

CIAO BAMBINO!

AMIE O'SHAUGHNESSY
FOUNDER
927 SUNNYHILLS ROAD
OAKLAND, CA 94610
510.763.8484 / 866.802.0300
AMIE@CIAOBAMBINO.COM
WWW.CIAOBAMBINO.COM

8.

GLOBAL DESTINATIONS FOR FAMILIES WITH YOUNG CHILDREN

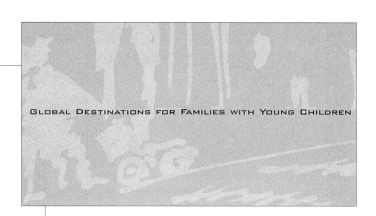

We are focused
We are bright
We are interactive

Appareo

Louis Stone-Collonge
louis@appareointeractive.com
1484 Pollard Rd., Suite 356
Los Gatos, CA 95032
t: 408.348.4026
f: 408.374.9712
www.appareointeractive.com

9.

(1,2)
Design Firm **Graphica**
(3-9)
Design Firm **Look**

1.
Client   Patrick Barta Photography
Designer   Christa Fleming
2.
Client   Mockingbird Society
Designer   Robin Walker
3.
Client   Size
4.
Client   CWAPC
5.
Client   Deli Up
6.
Client   Moonlight Design
7.
Client   Hair Loft
8.
Client   Ciao Bambino!
9.
Client   Appareo

Kurt T. Miyatake
Vice President
Worldwide Sales and Marketing

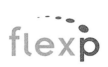

1425 Koll Circle, Suite 106
San Jose, CA 95112
phone (408) 487-9250
direct (408) 487-9251
fax (408) 487-9260
e-mail: Kurt.Miyatake@flex-p.com

www.flex-p.com

1.

Clair de Lune

Bonnie Addario
625 Laurel Street San Carlos, CA 94070
t: 650.593.2073 *f:* 650.593.3313
clrdlune@cs.com

2.

Marcie Adary

Jewelry Designs

3.

Marcie Adary
Marcie Adary Jewelry Designs
p: 650-346-4822
jewelsbymarcie@aol.com
www.jewelsbymarcie.com
500 St. Thomas Lane
Foster City, CA 94404

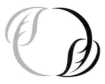

Al Helmersen
MANAGER
PROJECT DEVELOPMENT AND IMPLEMENTATION

Mail - PO Box 8248 Victoria BC V8W 3R9

Courier - 3rd Flr. 808 Douglas St.

Victoria BC V8W 2Z7

Phone 250-356-1675 Fax 250-953-5162

Al.helmersen@gems2.gov.bc.ca

www.iafbc.ca

**Investment
Agriculture
Foundation**
of British Columbia

4.

QV
QUEEN
VICTORIA
HOTEL
AND SUITES

WWW.QVHOTEL.COM
1-800-663-7007

DEBORAH HARMACY
DIRECTOR SALES AND MARKETING

655 DOUGLAS ST
VICTORIA BC
CANADA V8V 2P9

TEL 250-386-1312 EXT.1153
FAX 250-386-0687
DEBORAHH@QVHOTEL.COM

5.

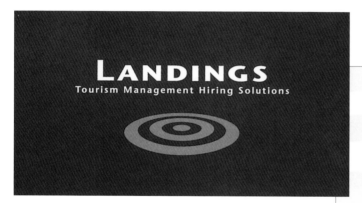

LANDINGS
Tourism Management Hiring Solutions

6.

Carolyn Yeager
Senior Manager – Sales & Marketing

Cell: 250 812-3611
cyeager@grantthornton.ca

3rd Floor   888 Fort Street   Victoria   BC V8W 1H8
Tel: 250 383-4191   Fax: 250 383-4142   www.landings.ca
Landings is operated by GT Hiring Solutions a wholly-owned subsidiary of Grant Thornton LLP

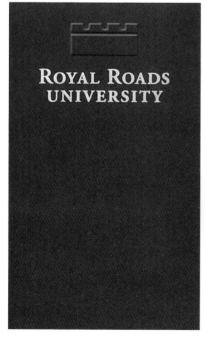

**ROYAL ROADS
UNIVERSITY**

7.

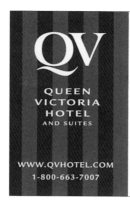

**ROYAL ROADS
UNIVERSITY**

You can get there from here

DR RICHARD A SKINNER
PRESIDENT AND VICE-CHANCELLOR

2005 Sooke Road
Victoria BC Canada V9B 5Y2
Telephone 250-391-2517
Fax 250-391-2538
richard.skinner@royalroads.ca
www.royalroads.ca

(1-3)
Design Firm **Look**
(4-7)
Design Firm **Trapeze Communications Inc.**

1.
   Client   Flex-p
2.
   Client   Clair de Lune
3.
   Client   Marcie Adary
4.
   Client   Investment Agriculture
               Foundation of British Columbia
   Designer Marianne Unger
5.
   Client   QV Hotel & Suites
   Designer Joe Hedges
6.
   Client   Landings
   Designer Joe Hedges
7.
   Client   Royal Roads University
   Designer Joe Hedges

TRAPEZE

Mark Bawden

Trapeze Communications Incorporated
301-852 Fort Street Victoria BC V8W 1H8

Telephone 250-380-0501
Fax 250-382-0501
Email mark@trapeze.ca
www.trapeze.ca

1.

stop.
International for Spa

238 Wellington Street Toronto Ontario M5V 3T5
Telephone 416-596-7723 Fax 416-596-8185

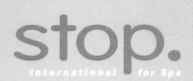

stop.
International for Spa

2.

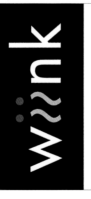

#103 ~ 561 Johnson Street
Victoria, BC V8W 1M2
(Across from Market Square)

250-382-WINK (9465)
Aveda Concept Salon

3.

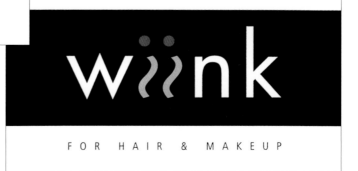

FOR HAIR & MAKEUP

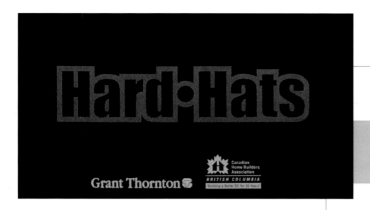

4.

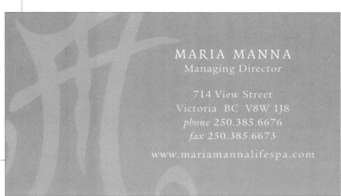

Kim Osborne
Assistant Manager - Lower Mainland

Hard·Hats

Training & Employment for the Construction Industry

100 535 Thurlow Street Vancouver BC V6E 3L2
Toll Free (888) 430-9911 Tel (604) 893-8566 Fax (604) 893-8833 Cell (604) 782-1995
k.osborne@destinations.ca www.hardhats.ca

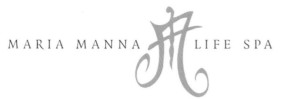

MARIA MANNA LIFE SPA

5.

MARIA MANNA
Managing Director

714 View Street
Victoria BC V8W 1J8
phone 250.385.6676
fax 250.385.6673

www.mariamannalifespa.com

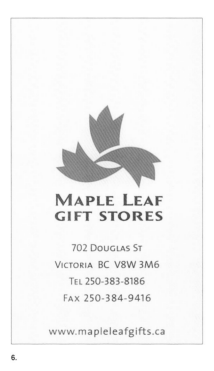

MAPLE LEAF GIFT STORES

702 DOUGLAS ST
VICTORIA BC V8W 3M6
TEL 250-383-8186
FAX 250-384-9416

www.mapleleafgifts.ca

6.

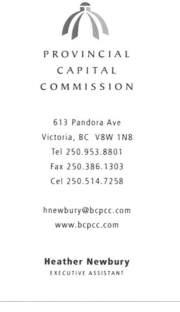

PROVINCIAL
CAPITAL
COMMISSION

613 Pandora Ave
Victoria, BC V8W 1N8
Tel 250.953.8801
Fax 250.386.1303
Cel 250.514.7258

hnewbury@bcpcc.com
www.bcpcc.com

Heather Newbury
EXECUTIVE ASSISTANT

7.

(1-7)
Design Firm **Trapeze Communications Inc.**

1.
Client   Trapeze Communications Inc.
Designer   Mark Bawden
2.
Client   Stop. International for Spa
Designers   Mark Bawden,
             Marianne Unger
3.
Client   Wink
Designers   Marianne Unger,
             Joe Hedges
4.
Client   Hard Hats
Designer   Neil Tran
5.
Client   Maria Manna Life Spa
Designer   Neil Tran
6.
Client   Maple Leaf Gift Stores
Designer   Joe Hedges
7.
Client   Provincial Capital Commission
Designer   Joe Hedges

Su Everts
Solution Centre Agent

GT Hiring Solutions Inc.
764 Fort Street
Victoria, BC V8W 1H2

Tel: 1-866-388-4323 or 250-388-0858
Fax: 1-866-388-0814 or 250-388-0814
s.everts@gthiringsolutions.ca

A wholly-owned subsidiary of Grant Thornton LLP

GT Hiring Solutions

www.gthiringsolutions.ca

Destinations | HardHats | Destinations Aboriginal | Landings

1.

LONE STAR NUCLE

2.

Richard Bassett
Chairman

Cell: (604) 505-8870
rbassett@lonestarnuclear.com

1330 Post Oak Boulevard
Suite 1600
Houston, TX USA 77056
Tel: (713) 963-3643
Fax: (832) 201-7589
www.lonestarnuclear.com

2 2 c

TWENTY TWO C PARTNERS INC

JOHN O'CONNOR
PARTNER

DIRECT TEL: 416-491-3120
DIRECT FAX: 416-491-8692
CELL: 416-258-2032
E-MAIL: johno@22cpartners.com

TORONTO

THE EXCHANGE TOWER
SUITE 1800
130 KING STREET WEST
PO BOX 427
TORONTO ON CANADA
M5X 1E3
TEL 416-410-6380
FAX 416-410-3822

VANCOUVER

SUITE 2300
1066 WEST HASTINGS ST
VANCOUVER BC CANADA
V6E 3X2
TEL 604-681-0990

www.22cpartners.com

3.

VICTORIA
FOUNDATION

CONNECTING PEOPLE
WHO CARE WITH CAUSES
THAT MATTER

Sandra Richardson
Executive Director / CEO

418-645 Fort Street
Victoria BC V8W 1G2
Phone [250] 381-5532
Fax [250] 480-1129

www.victoriafoundation.bc.ca
sandra@victoriafoundation.bc.ca

4.

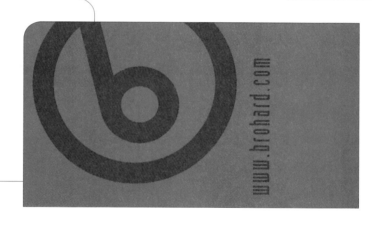

VICTORIA
CONFERENCE
CENTRE

720 Douglas Street
Victoria BC
Canada V8W 3M7

Phone 250-361-1000
Fax 250-361-1099
Toll Free 1-866-572-1151

www.victoriaconference.com

5.

**VICTORIA
CONFERENCE
CENTRE**

Lorraine Brewster
Senior Account Executive

Direct Line 250-361-1015
lorrainebr@victoriaconference.com

brohard design

16045 jonella farm drive
purcellville. va 20132

bill brohard

6.

www.brohard.com

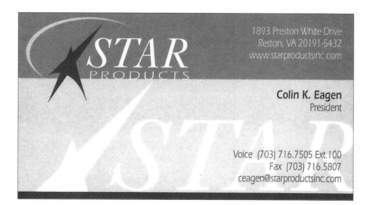

STAR
PRODUCTS

1893 Preston White Drive
Reston, VA 20191-5432
www.starproductsinc.com

Colin K. Eagen
President

Voice (703) 716.7505 Ext.100
Fax (703) 716.5807
ceagen@starproductsinc.com

7.

(1-5)
Design Firm **Trapeze Communications Inc.**
(6,7)
Design Firm **Brohard Design Inc.**

1.
Client   GT Hiring Solutions
Designer   Joe Hedges
2.
Client   Lone Star Nuclear
Designers   Joe Hedges
3.
Client   Twenty Two C Partners Inc.
Designer   Joe Hedges
4.
Client   Victoria Foundation
Designer   Joe Hedges
5.
Client   Victoria Conference Centre
Designers   Mark Bawden,
              Joe Hedges
6.
Client   Brohard Design Inc.
Designer   William Brohard
7.
Client   STAR Products
Designers   Michael Drake,
              William Brohard

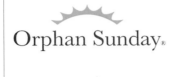

one day - one voice - one purpose

Orphan Sunday®

● Janna L. Bowman
International Director

T 866.776.6573
T 540.338.1694
F 540.338.1695
E janna@orphansunday.org

PO Box 20263 • Washington, D.C. 20041 • www.orphansunday.org

1.

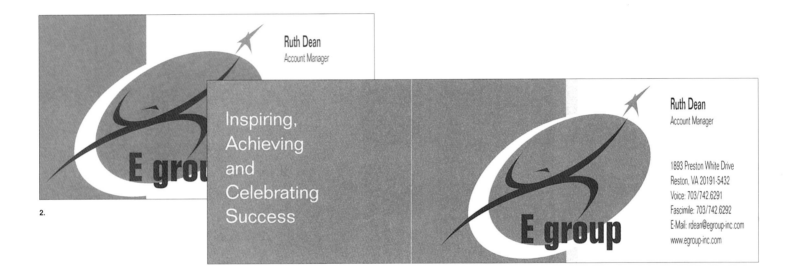

Ruth Dean
Account Manager

Inspiring,
Achieving
and
Celebrating
Success

Ruth Dean
Account Manager

1893 Preston White Drive
Reston, VA 20191-5432
Voice: 703/742.6291
Fascimile: 703/742.6292
E-Mail: rdean@egroup-inc.com
www.egroup-inc.com

E group

2.

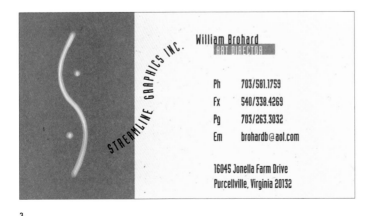

STREAMLINE GRAPHICS INC.

William Brohard
ART DIRECTOR

Ph 703/581.1759
Fx 540/338.4269
Pg 703/263.3032
Em brohardb@aol.com

16045 Jonella Farm Drive
Purcellville, Virginia 20132

3.

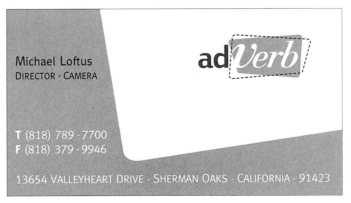

Michael Loftus
DIRECTOR · CAMERA

ad Verb

T (818) 789 · 7700
F (818) 379 · 9946

13654 VALLEYHEART DRIVE · SHERMAN OAKS · CALIFORNIA · 91423

4.

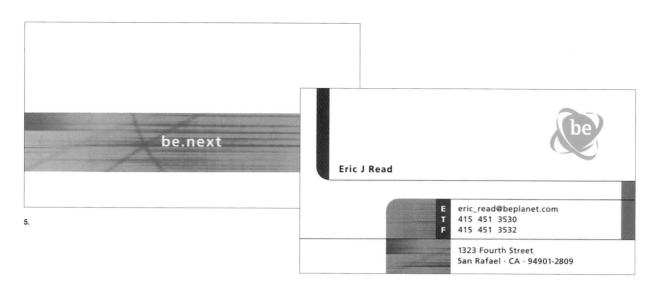

be.next

Eric J Read

eric_read@beplanet.com
E 415 451 3530
T
F 415 451 3532

1323 Fourth Street
San Rafael · CA · 94901-2809

5.

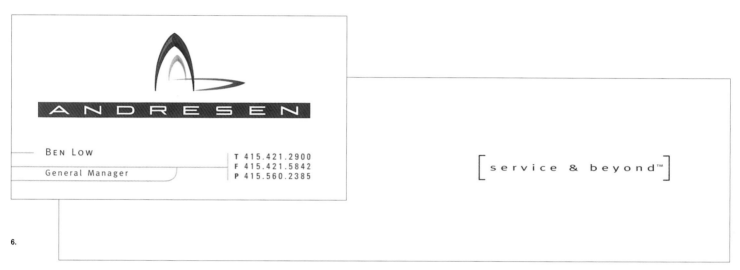

BEN LOW

General Manager

T 415.421.2900
F 415.421.5842
P 415.560.2385

[service & beyond™]

6.

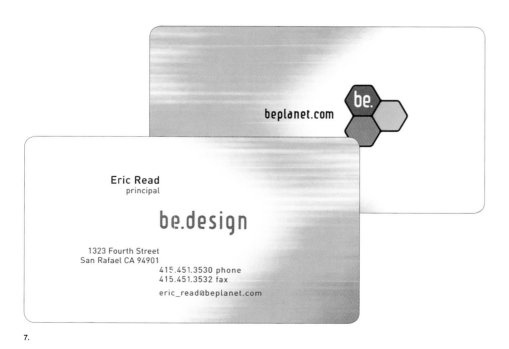

beplanet.com

Eric Read
principal

be.design

1323 Fourth Street
San Rafael CA 94901

415.451.3530 phone
415.451.3532 fax

eric_read@beplanet.com

7.

(1-3)
Design Firm **Brohard Design Inc.**
(4-7)
Design Firm **Be Design**

1.
Client   Orphan Sunday
Designer   William Brohard
2.
Client   E group
Designers   Michael Drake,
             William Brohard
3.
Client   Streamline Graphics, Inc.
Designer   William Brohard
4.
Client   Adverb
Designers   Eric Read,
             Yusuke Asaka
5.
Client   Be Design
Designer   Yusuke Asaka
6.
Client   Andresen
Designers   Eric Read, Rick Gaston,
             Coralie Russo
7.
Client   Be Design
Designers   Eric Read, Coralie Russo

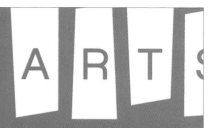

North Second Street • Suite 210 • San Jose • CA • 95113

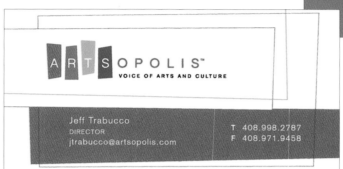

ARTSOPOLIS™
VOICE OF ARTS AND CULTURE

Jeff Trabucco
DIRECTOR
jtrabucco@artsopolis.com

T 408.998.2787
F 408.971.9458

1.

BUILDING SUCCESSFUL BRANDS

2.

GEORGIA MORF THUNES
project manager
georgia_thunes@bedesign.net
T 415.451.3530
F 415.451.3532

1306
Third Street
San Rafael
CA 94901

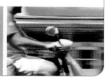

be.design

www.bedesign.net

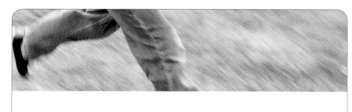

BUILDING SUCCESSFUL BRANDS

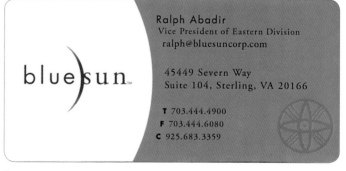

blue)sun™

Ralph Abadir
Vice President of Eastern Division
ralph@bluesuncorp.com

45449 Severn Way
Suite 104, Sterling, VA 20166

T 703.444.4900
F 703.444.6080
C 925.683.3359

3.

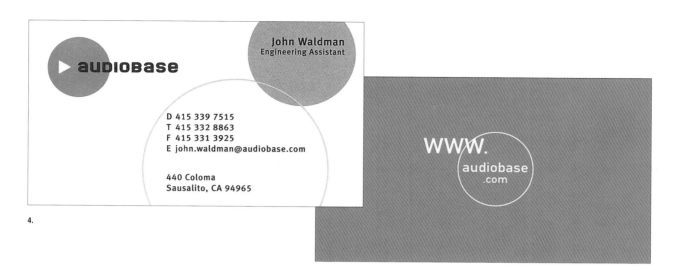

audiobase

John Waldman
Engineering Assistant

D 415 339 7515
T 415 332 8863
F 415 331 3925
E john.waldman@audiobase.com

440 Coloma
Sausalito, CA 94965

WWW.
audiobase
.com

4.

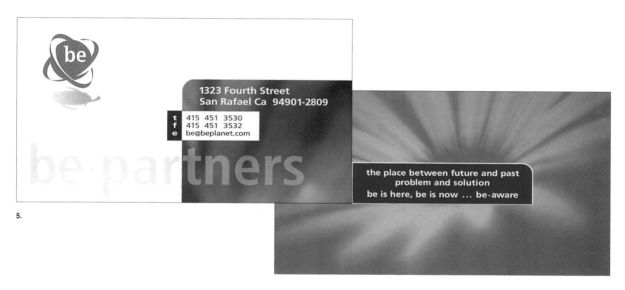

be

1323 Fourth Street
San Rafael Ca 94901-2809

t 415 451 3530
f 415 451 3532
e be@beplanet.com

be·partners

the place between future and past
problem and solution

be is here, be is now ... be·aware

5.

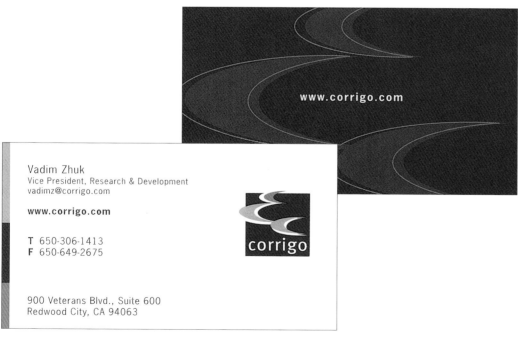

www.corrigo.com

Vadim Zhuk
Vice President, Research & Development
vadimz@corrigo.com

www.corrigo.com

T 650-306-1413
F 650-649-2675

900 Veterans Blvd., Suite 600
Redwood City, CA 94063

corrigo

6.

(1-6)
Design Firm **Be.Design**

1.
Client   Artsopolis
Designers Yusuke Asaka,
           Monica Schlaug
2.
Client   Be.Design
Designers Yusake Asaka,
           Yoko Carley
3.
Client   Blue Sun
Designers Eric Read,
           Kimberly Bell
4.
Client   AudioBase
Designers Will Burke, Eric Read,
           Yusuke Asaka
5.
Client   Be.Design
Designers Eric Read
6.
Client   Corrigo
Designers Eric Read,
           Yusuke Asaka

Georgette Marshall
PROPERTY MANAGER

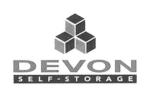
DEVON
SELF-STORAGE

10101 Martin Luther King Jr. Hwy.
Lanham, MD 20706

T 301 918 9000
F 301 918 4796
E dln@devonselfstorage.com

1.

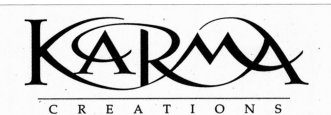
KARMA
C R E A T I O N S

101 Main Street, Annapolis, MD 21401 • 410.268.6677
52B Rehoboth Ave., Rehoboth, DE 19971 • 302.227.3544
fax 410.268.4014
www.karmacreations.com

2.

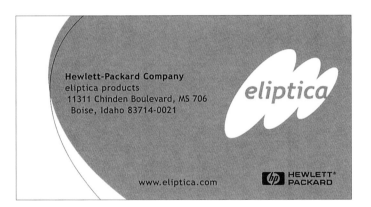

Hewlett-Packard Company
eliptica products
11311 Chinden Boulevard, MS 706
Boise, Idaho 83714-0021

eliptica

www.eliptica.com

hp HEWLETT*
PACKARD

3.

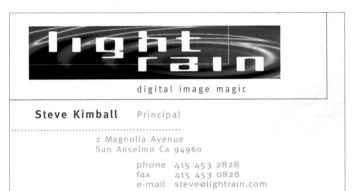
light rain
digital image magic

Steve Kimball   Principal

2 Magnolia Avenue
San Anselmo Ca 94960

phone   415 453 2828
fax   415 453 0828
e-mail steve@lightrain.com

4.

TEL 415·482·9324

digital

RON BEDNAR Principal

hothouse

FAX 415·482·9314

EMAIL ron@dahothouse.com

1323 Fourth Street · San Rafael · CA · 94901

5.

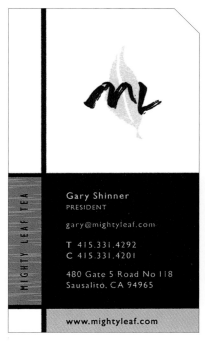

MIGHTY LEAF TEA

Gary Shinner
PRESIDENT

gary@mightyleaf.com

T 415.331.4292
C 415.331.4201

480 Gate 5 Road No 118
Sausalito, CA 94965

www.mightyleaf.com

PURE INDULGENCE

6.

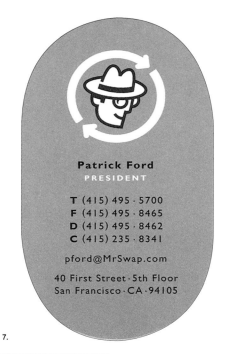

Patrick Ford
PRESIDENT

T (415) 495 · 5700
F (415) 495 · 8465
D (415) 495 · 8462
C (415) 235 · 8341

pford@MrSwap.com

40 First Street · 5th Floor
San Francisco · CA · 94105

7.

Women's Challenge, Inc.
P.O. Box 299, Boise, ID 83701
314 South Sixth, Boise, ID 83702

Annie Tucher
Director of Marketing
and Development
atucher@micron.net

208.345.RACE (7223)
fax 208.345.5325

www.hplwc.com

8.

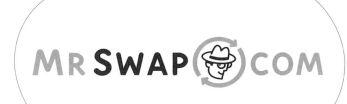

MR SWAP COM

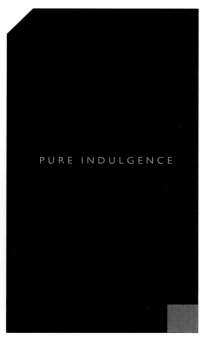

MISSION

Interpret the desires of our clients
To solve the seemingly unsolvable
Beautifully

JAMES PHILLIP WRIGHT ARCHITECTS

ADDRESS 5221 Cochrane Avenue
Oakland, California
USA 94618

STUDIO VENICE ATELIER

CONTACT James P. Wright
Architect/Principal

510 653 5555 : T
510 653 5550 : F
JPW archit@aol.com

9.

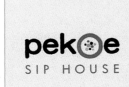

pekoe
SIP HOUSE

MONICA SCHLAUG
designer

monicas@pekoe.com
1325b Pine Street
Boulder, CO 54678
℗456.273.3234
℗456.273.3247

1.

SIP. RELAX. ENJOY.

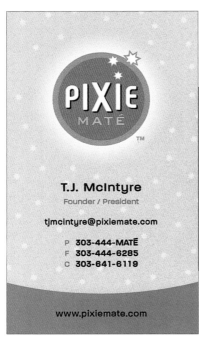

PIXIE
MATÉ
™

T.J. McIntyre
Founder / President

tjmcintyre@pixiemate.com

P **303-444-MATÉ**
F **303-444-6285**
C **303-641-6119**

www.pixiemate.com

2.

✳ DRINK DEEP. TAKE FLIGHT. ✳

Gordon Antonello
Board Member
Chair, 2-11GHz Technical
Working Group

Wi-LAN Inc.
2891 Sunridge Way NE
Calgary, Alberta T1Y 7K7
Canada

403 207 6477
403 273 5100 fax
gantonello@wi-lan.com

3.

WiMAX
FORUM

www.wimaxforum.org

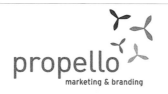

propello
marketing & branding

| MAYA BABISH | Principal | 18217 NE 179th ST Woodinville WA 98072 |
| maya.propello@comcast.net | T 425.844.8306 | F 425.788.5773 |

4.

THE NEW SOURCE OF CORPORATE ENERGY

SKYLAR
+
HALEY

Ralph Abadir
Account Executive

ralph@skylarhaley.com

T 925.600.9397
F 925.600.9357
C 925.683.3359

6601 Koll Center Parkway, Suite 205
Pleasanton, CA 94566
(866) SKYLARH

5.

innovative products

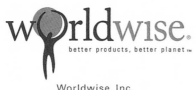

worldwise.
better products, better planet ™

Amy Fullerton
Operations Manager

Worldwise, Inc.
Ⓐ 851 Irwin Street, Suite 200
San Rafael, CA USA 94901-3343
Ⓣ 800 967 5394
Ⓓ 415 721 7400 ext.258
Ⓕ 415 721 7418
Ⓔ afullerton@worldwise.com
Ⓦ worldwise.com

6.

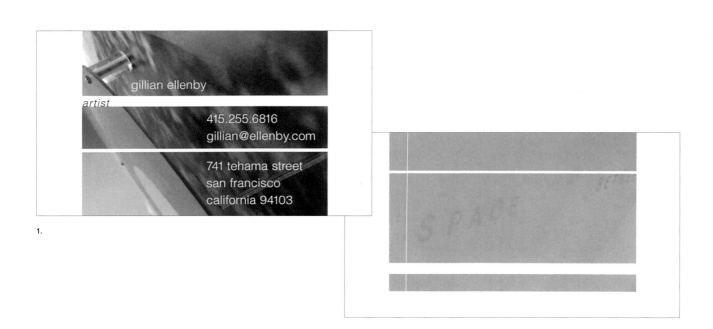

1.

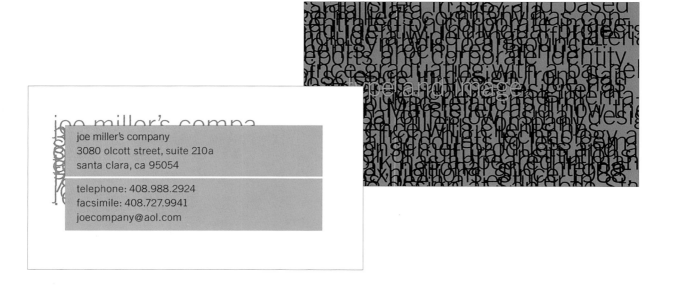

2.

Willow Technology

Gary Clueit *President & CEO*

Willow Technology, Inc.
469 El Camino Real, Suite 220
Santa Clara, CA 95050-4372
tel +1.408.296.7400, fax +1.408.296.7700
mobile +1.408.966.9025
clueit@willowtech.com

www.willowtech.com

3.

194

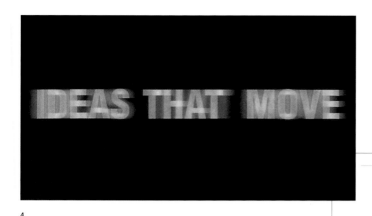

4.

compass
rose media

105 Locust Street
Santa Cruz, California 95060
408.457.3533
facsimile 408.457.0614
stevew@crosemedia.com

Steve Weisser
executive producer

Businesses United in Investing, Lending, and Development
www.build.org

5.

Suzanne McKechnie Klahr, Esq.
ceo and president

1600 Adams Drive
Menlo Park, CA 94025
tel 650.688.5846
fax 650.688.5847
suzanne@build.org

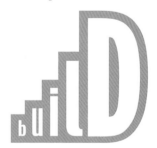

contemporary
art and
performance

www.workssanjose.org
408.295.8378
works_sj@yahoo.com

6.

(1-6)
Design Firm **Joe Miller's Company**

1.
Client   Gillian Ellenby
Designer   Joe Miller
2.
Client   Joe Miller's Company
Designer   Joe Miller
3.
Client   Willow Technology
Designer   Joe Miller
4.
Client   Compass Rose Media
Designer   Joe Miller

5.
Client   BUILD
Designer   Joe Miller
6.
Client   Works/San José
Designer   Joe Miller

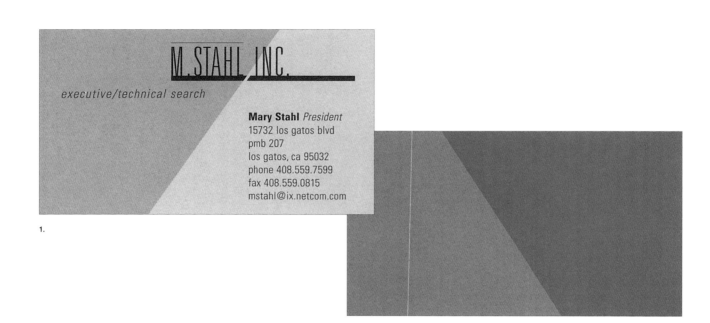

M.STAHL INC.

executive/technical search

Mary Stahl *President*
15732 los gatos blvd
pmb 207
los gatos, ca 95032
phone 408.559.7599
fax 408.559.0815
mstahl@ix.netcom.com

1.

Rebecca Davis
46691 mission blvd
pmb 105
fremont ca 94539
phone 510.490.6027
fax 510.226.8315
aspire2@home.com

Mary Stahl
15732 los gatos blvd
pmb 207
los gatos, ca 95032
phone 408.559.7599
fax 408.559.0815
mstahl@ix.netcom.com

stahldavis

2.

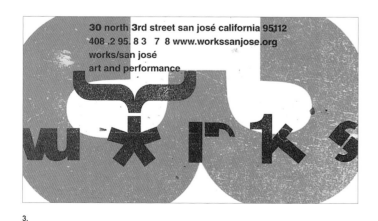

30 north 3rd street san josé california 95112
408 .2 95. 8 3   7 8 www.workssanjose.org
works/san josé
art and performance

3.

works/san josé
30 north 3rd street
san josé, california 95112

408 . 295.8   3   7   8
www.workssanjose.org

gallery hours:
tuesday through saturday,
noon to 4
thursday, noon to 7

4.

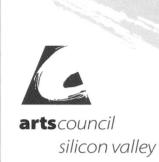

Lisa A. Cole
director of development

4 North Second Street, Suite 210
San José, CA 95113-1305
phone 408-998-2787 ext. 204
facsimile 408-971-9458
lcole@artscouncil.org
www.artscouncil.org

artscouncil
silicon valley

5.

CAMP collaborative
arts marketing partnership

Ed Sengstack
director

4 North Second Street, Suite 275, San José, CA 95113
phone 408-998-2787 ext. 220, fax 408-998-4299
esengstack@artscouncil.org
www.artscouncil.org/camp

a program of Arts Council Silicon Valley

6.

Renee Vaughn
Director, Women's Residential Program

1796 Bay Road
East Palo Alto, California 94303
phone 650.462.6999
fax 650.462.1055
www.freeatlast.org

7.

Danyelle Phillips office manager
ksjs 90.5fm, hgh 121a, san josé state university
san josé, califorhia. 95192-0094
phone: 408-924-5762
fax: 408-924-4583
e-mail: prog@ksjs.org

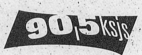

8.

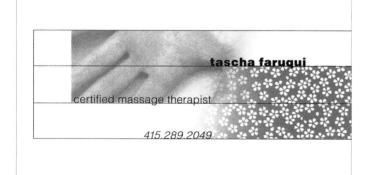

tascha faruqui

certified massage therapist

415.289.2049

9.

(1-9)
   Design Firm **Joe Miller's Company**

1.
   Client   M. Stahl, Inc.
   Designer   Joe Miller
2.
   Client   Stahl/Davis
   Designer   Joe Miller
3,4.
   Client   Works/San José
   Designer   Joe Miller
5.
   Client   Arts Council Silicon Valley
   Designer   Joe Miller
6.
   Client   Camp/Arts Council
              Silicon Valley
   Designer   Joe Miller

7.
   Client   Free At Last
   Designer   Joe Miller
8.
   Client   KSJS Radio
   Designer   Joe Miller
9.
   Client   Tascha Faruqui
   Designer   Joe Miller

197

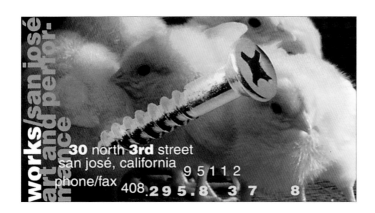

1.

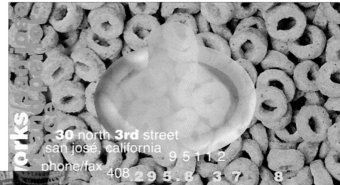

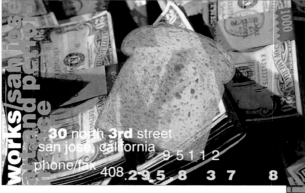

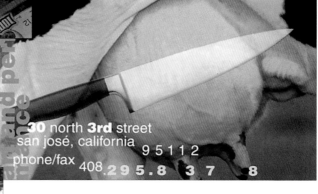

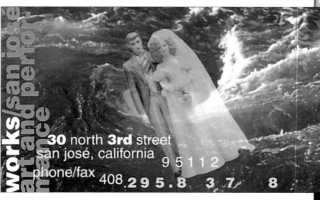

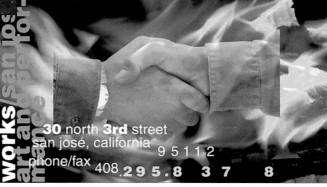

The Good Shepherd Fund

Linda Fast Office Manager

1641 North First Street, Suite 155

San José, California 95112

408-573-9606 phone, 408-573-9609 fax

lfast@goodshepherdfund.org

2.

NORGLOBE

Shariff Elsheikh
MANAGING DIRECTOR

6041 Woodmont Road
Alexandria, VA 22307-1159
USA

T 01.703.851.4313
F 01.703.317.0782
E selsheikh@norglobe.com

www.norglobe.com

3.

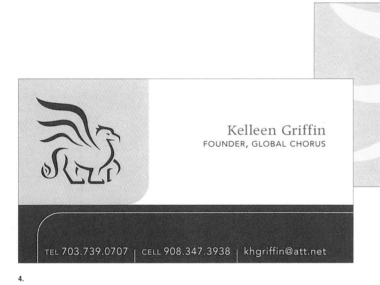

Kelleen Griffin
FOUNDER, GLOBAL CHORUS

TEL 703.739.0707 | CELL 908.347.3938 | khgriffin@att.net

4.

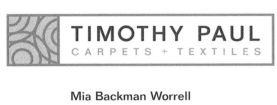

TIMOTHY PAUL
C A R P E T S + T E X T I L E S

Mia Backman Worrell

1404 14th Street NW • Washington DC 20005
TEL 202.319.1100 FAX 202.319.1110
EMAIL mia@timothypaulcarpets.com
www.timothypaulcarpets.com

5.

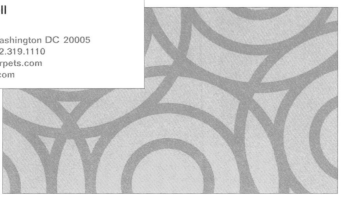

(1,2)
Design Firm **Joe Miller's Company**
(3-5)
Design Firm **Design Nut**

1.
Client   Works/San José
Designer   Joe Miller
2.
Client   The Good Shepherd Fund
Designer   Joe Miller
3.
Client   NorGlobe
Designer   Brent M. Almond
4.
Client   Kelleen Griffin
Designer   Brent M. Almond
5.
Client   Timothy Paul
              Carpets + Textiles
Designer   Brent M. Almond

1.

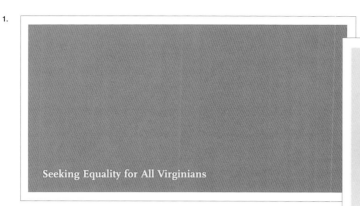

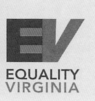

Joseph R. Price, Esq.
CHAIR, BOARD OF DIRECTORS

T 202.775.5769
E price.joseph@arentfox.com

6 North Sixth Street, LL3
Richmond, Virginia 23219

T 804.643.4816
F 804.643.2050
E info@equalityvirginia.org

EqualityVirginia.org

EV
EQUALITY
VIRGINIA

Seeking Equality for All Virginians

2.

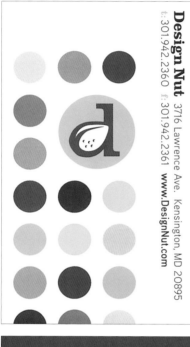

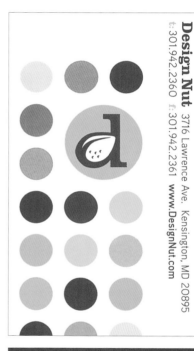

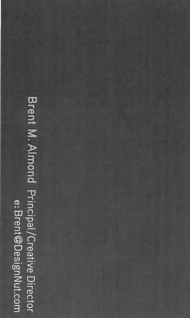

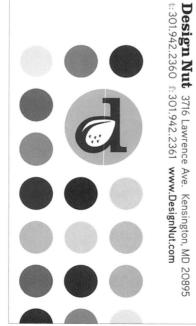

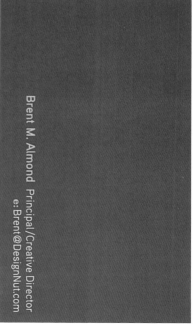

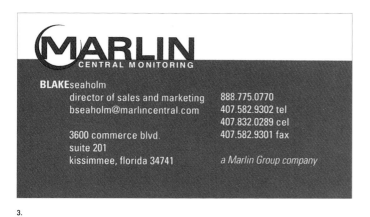

3.

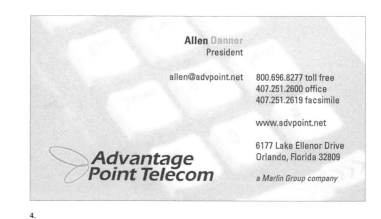

Allen Danner
President

allen@advpoint.net

800.696.8277 toll free
407.251.2600 office
407.251.2619 facsimile

www.advpoint.net

6177 Lake Ellenor Drive
Orlando, Florida 32809

a Marlin Group company

4.

WHITEHALL
P R O P E R T I E S

401 Whitehall Rd. • Chattanooga, TN 37405
jay@whproperty.com • www.whproperty.com
(323) 646-8982 O • (423) 757-4969 F

Jay Floyd

5.

brianmay
v.p. media services
v.p. marketing services
bmay@st3.com

pob 5414
1516 riverside drive
chattanooga, tn 37406

423.242.6000 o
423.622.4392 f

6.

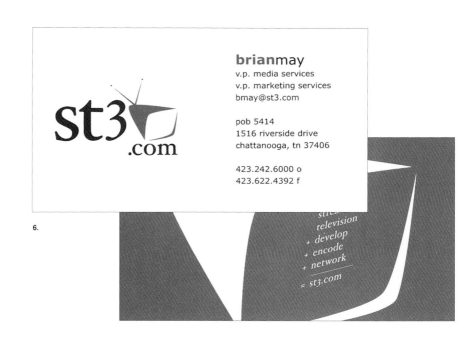

stream
television
+ develop
+ encode
+ network
= st3.com

MegTillia
president

mtillia@marlinpayments.com

toll free: 888.705.2055

www.marlinpayments.com

6177 Lake Ellenor Drive
Orlando, Florida 32809

tel: 407.816.5251
cel: 727.224.3099
fax: 407.816.5257

MARLIN
payment solutions

Payment Processing Partner

marlinpayments.com

7.

(1,2)
Design Firm **Design Nut**
(3-7)
Design Firm **Maycreate**

1.
Client   Equality Virginia
Designer   Brent M. Almond
2.
Client   Design Nut
Designer   Brent M. Almond
3.
Client   Marlin Central Monitoring
Designer   Grant Little
4.
Client   Advantage Point Telecom
Designer   Brian May
5.
Client   Whitehall Properties
Designer   Brian May
6.
Client   st3
Designer   Brian May
7.
Client   Marlin Payment Solutions
Designer   Brian May

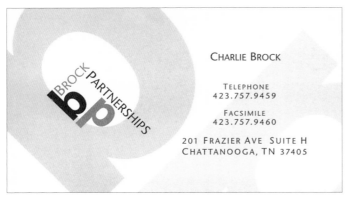

CHARLIE BROCK

TELEPHONE
423.757.9459

FACSIMILE
423.757.9460

201 FRAZIER AVE SUITE H
CHATTANOOGA, TN 37405

1.

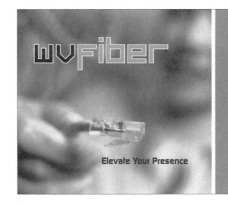

Brian May
VP Mktg. & Advertising
bmay@wvfiber.com

404 488 2572 : mobile
404 222 9911 : office
404 581 9911 : fax

4501 Circle 75 Pkwy.
Suite E-5210
Atlanta, GA 30339

www.wvfiber.com

Elevate Your Presence

2.

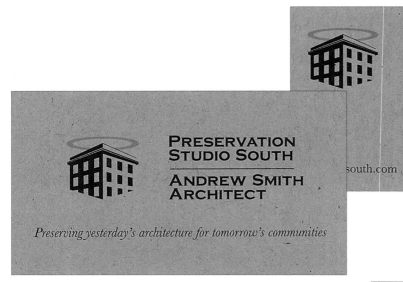

PRESERVATION
STUDIO SOUTH

ANDREW SMITH
ARCHITECT

Preserving yesterday's architecture for tomorrow's communities

Erin May
erin@pssouth.com

(423) 752 4018 tel
(423) 752 7859 fax
(423) 605 6764 cell

737 Market Street
Suite 719
Chattanooga, TN 37402

3.

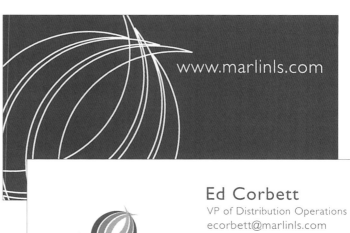

www.marlinls.com

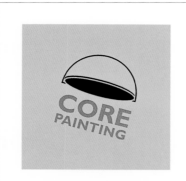

Al Victoria

alvaro@core-ltd.com

p.o. box 80723
chattanooga, tn 37414

423.504.6278 t
423.624.0345 f

4.

MARLIN
LOGISTICS

Ed Corbett
VP of Distribution Operations
ecorbett@marlinls.com

3600 Commerce Blvd.
Kissimmee, FL 34741
407.251.2076 Tel
407.251.2021 Fax
www.marlinls.com

5.

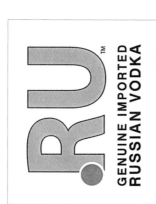

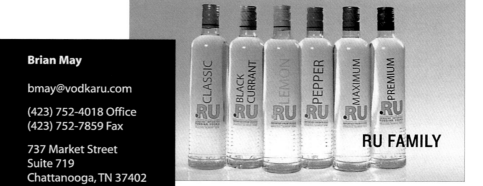

RU FAMILY

6.

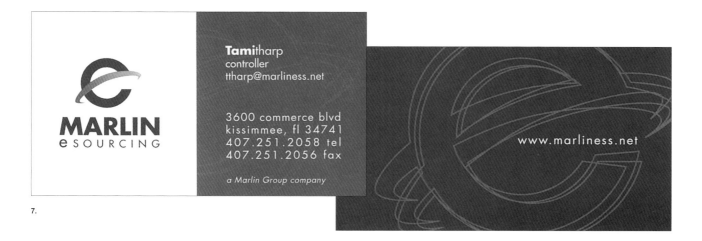

Brian May

bmay@vodkaru.com

(423) 752-4018 Office
(423) 752-7859 Fax

737 Market Street
Suite 719
Chattanooga, TN 37402

www.vodkaru.com

Tamitharp
controller
ttharp@marliness.net

3600 commerce blvd
kissimmee, fl 34741
407.251.2058 tel
407.251.2056 fax

a Marlin Group company

www.marliness.net

7.

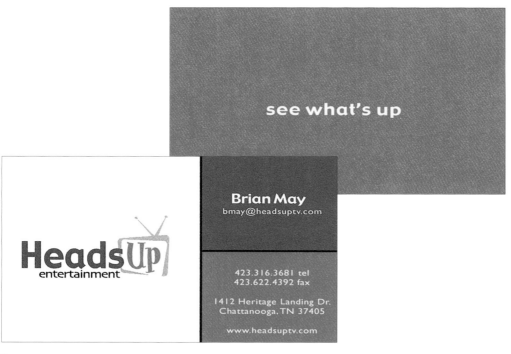

see what's up

Brian May
bmay@headsuptv.com

423.316.3681 tel
423.622.4392 fax

1412 Heritage Landing Dr.
Chattanooga, TN 37405

www.headsuptv.com

8.

(1-8)
Design Firm **Maycreate**

1.
Client   Brock Partnerships
Designer   Brian May
2.
Client   WVFiber
Designer   Brian May
3.
Client   Preservation Studio South
Designer   Brian May
4.
Client   Core Painting
Designer   Brian May
5.
Client   Marlin Logistics
Designer   Brian May
6.
Client   RU Vodka
Designer   Brian May
7.
Client   Marlin eSourcing
Designer   Brian May
8.
Client   HeadsUp Entertainment
Designer   Brian May

www.maycreate.com

Brian May
bmay@maycreate.com   423 752 4018 t   423 752 7859 f
737 Market Street   Suite 719   Chattanooga, TN 37402

1.

Scott Sentell
President & CEO

ssentell@marliness.net

3600 Commerce Blvd
Kissimmee, Fl 34741
T (407) 582-9422
F (407) 582-9421

a Marlin Group company

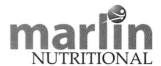

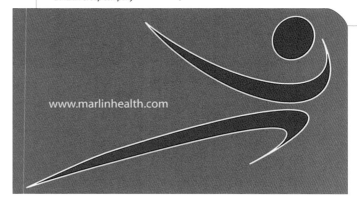
www.marlinhealth.com

2.

themāvicgroup

Brian May
Managing Partner

bmay@mavicgroup.com

423 752 4018 office • 423 752 7859 fax • www.mavicgroup.com
737 Market Street • Suite 719 • Chattanooga, TN 37402

3.

themāvicgroup
driving market growth

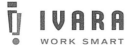
IVARA
WORK SMART   www.ivara.com

Peter Neo
DATABASE SPECIALIST
peter.neo@ivara.com

935 Sheldon Court
Burlington, ON, Canada L7L
TEL   905 632.8000   x 254
FAX   905 632.5129

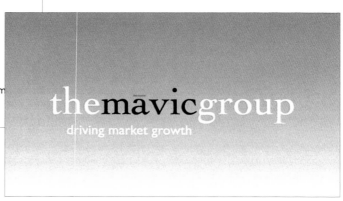
WORK SMART
Optimize asset reliability
to drive business results

4.

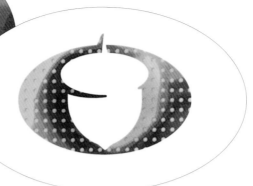

OAK CLOSET
FASHION FOREWARD GOLF

Jim Theaker PRESIDENT
sales@oakcloset.com

80 Park Lawn Rd, Suite 208, Toronto, ON, Canada M?
T 416.999.9623   C 416.738.5917   F 416.252.08

WWW.OAKCLOSET.COM

5.

EXPLORE · IMAGINE

ISLAND QUEEN CRUISE

RON ANDERSON
ron@islandqueencruise.com
CELL 705.774.3300

30,000 ISLAND CRUISE LINES INC.
9 BAY STREET, PARRY SOUND
ONTARIO, CANADA P2A 1S4
TEL 705.746.2311   FAX 705.746.9696
TOLL FREE 1.800.506.2628
WWW.ISLANDQUEENCRUISE.COM

6.

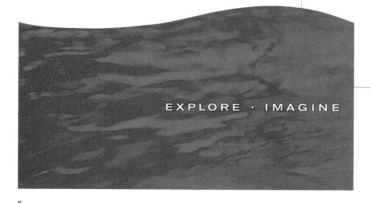

riordondesign

Oakville, ON L6J 3B9

TEL 905.339.0750
FAX 905.339.0753
group@riordondesign.com

7.

(1-3)
Design Firm **Maycreate**
(4-7)
Design Firm **Riordon Design**

1.
Client   Maycreate
Designer   Brian May
2.
Client   Marlin Nutritional
Designer   Brian May
3.
Client   The Mavic Group
Designer   Brian May
4.
Client   Ivara Corporation
Designers   Dan Wheaton, Alan Krpan
5.
Client   Oak Closet
Designers   Ric Riordon, Alan Krpan
6.
Client   Island Queen Cruise
Designers   Ric Riordon, Alan Krpan
7.
Client   Riordon Design
Designers   Dan Wheaton, Alan Krpan

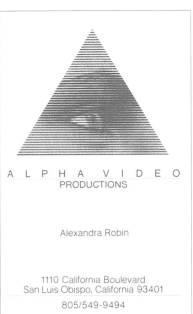

A L P H A   V I D E O
PRODUCTIONS

Alexandra Robin

1110 California Boulevard
San Luis Obispo, California 93401

805/549-9494

1.

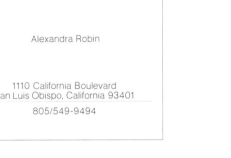

Robert J. Holzhauer, M.D.
Diplomate, American Board of Allergy and Immunology

Robert J. Holzhauer, M.D., A Medical Corporation
1551 Bishop Street, Suite 510
San Luis Obispo, CA 93401   (805) 541-5525

2.

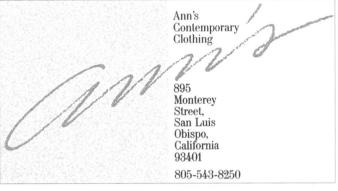

Ann's
Contemporary
Clothing

895
Monterey
Street,
San Luis
Obispo,
California
93401

805-543-8250

3.

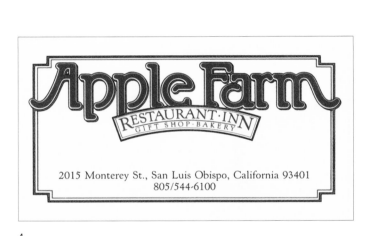

2015 Monterey St., San Luis Obispo, California 93401
805/544-6100

4.

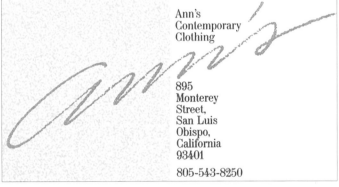

·674·
HIGUERA STREET
SAN LUIS OBISPO, CALIFORNIA 93401
805·544·8988

5.

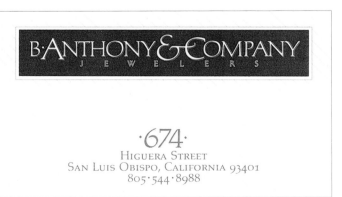

BLAKE PRINTERY

A Graphic Center Company

TOM DAVEY

805/543-6843 · FAX 805/543-2982 · 800/234-3320
2222 Beebee Street, San Luis Obispo, California 93401

6.

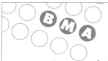

Brummel, Myrick & Associates, mechanical engineering

3562 Empleo St., Suite A
San Luis Obispo, CA 93401
805 544-4269 fax 805 544-4335

Keith D. Brummel, P.E.
Principal

7.

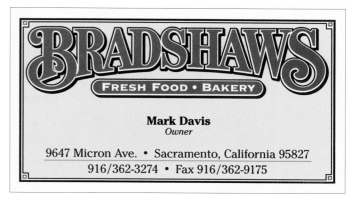

Mark Davis
Owner

9647 Micron Ave. • Sacramento, California 95827
916/362-3274 • Fax 916/362-9175

8.

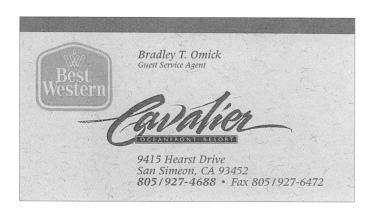

Bradley T. Omick
Guest Service Agent

9415 Hearst Drive
San Simeon, CA 93452
805/927-4688 • Fax 805/927-6472

9.

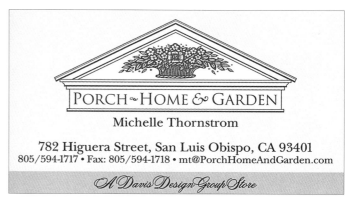

Michelle Thornstrom

782 Higuera Street, San Luis Obispo, CA 93401
805/594-1717 • Fax: 805/594-1718 • mt@PorchHomeAndGarden.com

A Davis Design Group Store

10.

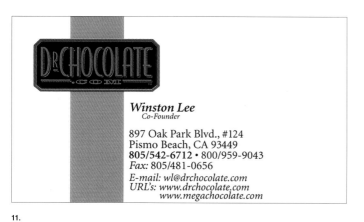

Winston Lee
Co-Founder

897 Oak Park Blvd., #124
Pismo Beach, CA 93449
805/542-6712 • **800/959-9043**
Fax: 805/481-0656
E-mail: wl@drchocolate.com
URL's: www.drchocolate.com
www.megachocolate.com

11.

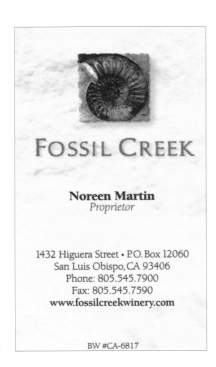

FOSSIL CREEK

Noreen Martin
Proprietor

1432 Higuera Street • P.O. Box 12060
San Luis Obispo, CA 93406
Phone: 805.545.7900
Fax: 805.545.7590
www.fossilcreekwinery.com

BW #CA-6817

1.

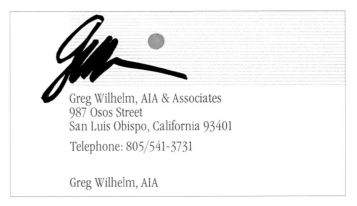

Greg Wilhelm, AIA & Associates
987 Osos Street
San Luis Obispo, California 93401

Telephone: 805/541-3731

Greg Wilhelm, AIA

2.

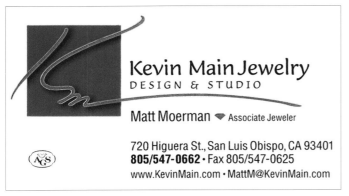

Kevin Main Jewelry
DESIGN & STUDIO

Matt Moerman ❤ Associate Jeweler

720 Higuera St., San Luis Obispo, CA 93401
805/547-0662 • Fax 805/547-0625
www.KevinMain.com • MattM@KevinMain.com

3.

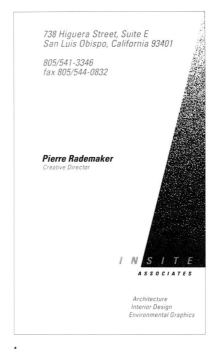

738 Higuera Street, Suite E
San Luis Obispo, California 93401

805/541-3346
fax 805/544-0832

Pierre Rademaker
Creative Director

I N S I T E
ASSOCIATES

Architecture
Interior Design
Environmental Graphics

4.

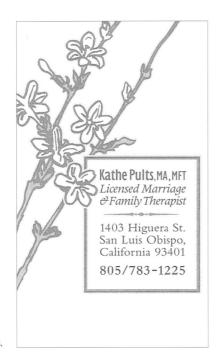

Kathe Pults,MA,MFT
Licensed Marriage
& Family Therapist

1403 Higuera St.
San Luis Obispo,
California 93401

805/783-1225

5.

MID-STATE
BANK & TRUST

P.O. Box 580, Arroyo Grande, CA 93421-0580

HEIDY MANGIARDI
Marketing Officer

991 Bennett Avenue • Arroyo Grande, CA 93420
805/473-6834 • Fax 805/473-7767
hmangiardi@midstatebank.com

WWW.MIDSTATEBANK.COM

6.

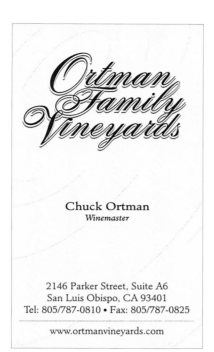

Chuck Ortman
Winemaster

2146 Parker Street, Suite A6
San Luis Obispo, CA 93401
Tel: 805/787-0810 • Fax: 805/787-0825

www.ortmanvineyards.com

7.

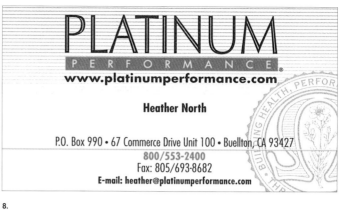

PLATINUM
PERFORMANCE
www.platinumperformance.com

Heather North

P.O. Box 990 • 67 Commerce Drive Unit 100 • Buellton, CA 93427
800/553-2400
Fax: 805/693-8682
E-mail: heather@platinumperformance.com

8.

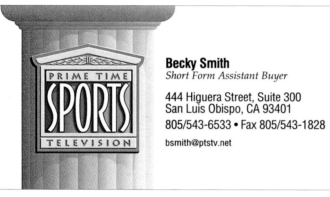

Becky Smith
Short Form Assistant Buyer

444 Higuera Street, Suite 300
San Luis Obispo, CA 93401

805/543-6533 • Fax 805/543-1828

bsmith@ptstv.net

9.

Petit Soleil
BED & BREAKFAST

John and Dianne Conner
Hôteliers

A Touch of European Charm
1473 Monterey Street
San Luis Obispo, CA 93401
www.PetitSoleilSLO.com
805.549.0321

10.

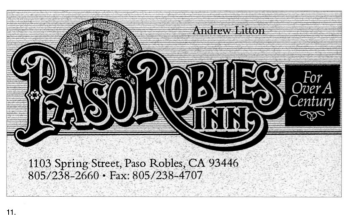

1103 Spring Street, Paso Robles, CA 93446
805/238-2660 • Fax: 805/238-4707

11.

(1-11)
Design Firm **Pierre Rademaker Design**

1.
Client   Fossil Creek
Designers   Anne Bussone, Pierre Rademaker
2.
Client   Greg Wilhelm
Designers   Jeff Austin, Pierre Rademaker
3.
Client   Kevin Main Jewelry
Designers   Debbie Shibata, Pierre Rademaker
4.
Client   Insite Associates
Designer   Pierre Rademaker
5.
Client   Kathe Pults
Designers   Debbie Shibata, Pierre Rademaker
6.
Client   Mid-State Bank & Trust
Designers   Debbie Shibata, Pierre Rademaker
7.
Client   Ortman Family Vineyards
Designers   Elisa York, Pierre Rademaker

8.
Client   Platinum Performance
Designers   Debbie Shibata, Kenny Swete,
              Pierre Rademaker
9.
Client   Prime Time Sports TV
Designers   Debbie Shibata, Pierre Rademaker
10.
Client   Petit Soleil
Designers   Anne Bussone, Pierre Rademaker
11.
Client   Paso Robles Inn
Designers   Marci Russo, Pierre Rademaker

PRESSURE TEK

Teflon® & Engineered Plastics

John Rademaker
Production Manager

580 Linne Rd., Unit 140
Paso Robles, CA 93446
800/987-3257 fax: 805/238-9203

1.

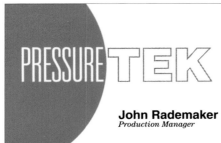

Santa Ynez Inn
VICTORIAN ELEGANCE *in the* WINE COUNTRY

John Martino, *General Manager*
3627 Sagunto Street, Box 628, Santa Ynez, CA 93460
TEL: 805-688-5588   FAX: 805-686-4294
info@santaynezinn.com

2.

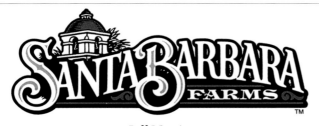

SANTA BARBARA FARMS ™

Jeff Martin
Plant Manager
1200 Union Sugar Avenue • Lompoc, California 93436
805/737-3233
A Limited Liability Company

3.

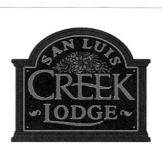

SAN LUIS CREEK LODGE

PATTY OXFORD
Proprietor

1941 MONTEREY STREET
SAN LUIS OBISPO, CA 93401

RESERVATIONS: **(800)593-0333**
(805)541-1122
FAX (805)541-2475

www.SanLuisCreekLodge.com

4.

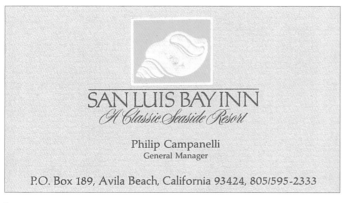

SAN LUIS BAY INN
A Classic Seaside Resort

Philip Campanelli
General Manager

P.O. Box 189, Avila Beach, California 93424, 805/595-2333

5.

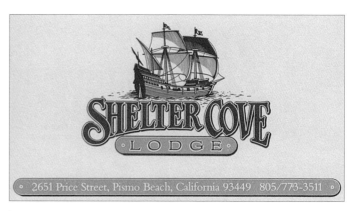

SHELTER COVE LODGE

2651 Price Street, Pismo Beach, California 93449   805/773-3511

6.

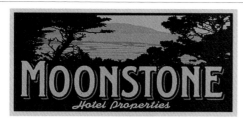

Lauren Winter
Owner / Buyer

2905 Burton Drive, Cambria, California 93428
(805) 927-6113 • (805) 927-4747 • Fax (805) 927-6289

7.

Lisa Cameron
Sales Manager
lisac@moonstonehotels.com
2905 Burton Drive, Cambria, California 93428
(805) 927-6114 Ext. 203 • Fax (805) 927-1610

8.

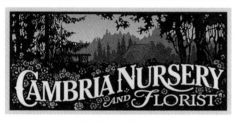

Deborah Gran
Floral Designer
deborah@cambrianursery.com
2801 Eton Road, Cambria, California 93428
(805) 927-4747 • (800) 414-6915 • Fax (805) 927-0437

9.

Robert L. Hunt
General Manager
roberth@moonstonehotels.com
725 Row River Road, Cottage Grove, Oregon 97424
(541) 942-2491 • (800) 343-7666 • Fax (541) 942-2386

10.

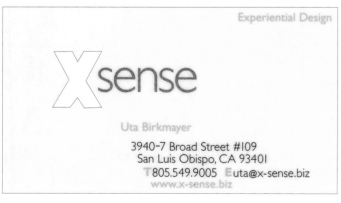

11.

(1-11)
Design Firm **Pierre Rademaker Design**

1.
Client   Pressure Tek
Designers   Elisa York, Pierre Rademaker

2.
Client   Santa Ynez Inn
Designers   Debbie Shibata, Pierre Rademaker

3.
Client   Santa Barbara Farms
Designers   Debbie Shibata, Pierre Rademaker

4.
Client   San Luis Creek Lodge
Designers   Debbie Shibata, Pierre Rademaker

5.
Client   San Luis Bay Inn
Designers   Pierre Rademaker, Mary Brucken

6.
Client   Shelter Cove Lodge
Designer   Pierre Rademaker

7.
Client   Moonstone Hotel Properties
Designers   Debbie Shibata, Pierre Rademaker

8.
Client   Moonstone Hotel Properties
            Cambria Pines Lodge
Designers   Debbie Shibata, Pierre Rademaker

9.
Client   Moonstone Hotel Properties
            Cambria Nursery & Florist
Designers   Debbie Shibata, Pierre Rademaker

10.
Client   Moonstone Hotel Properties
            Village Green
Designers   Debbie Shibata, Pierre Rademaker

11.
Client   Xsense
Designers   Debbie Shibata, Pierre Rademaker

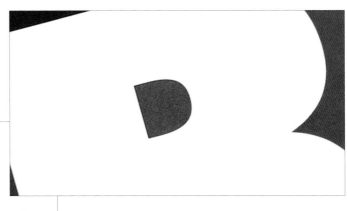

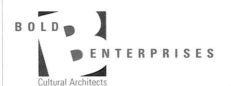

BOLD **B** **ENTERPRISES**

Cultural Architects

Karl D. Edwards

2623 Veteran Avenue
Los Angeles, CA 90064

P 310/234-0148   **F** 310/234-0149
W www.boldenterprises.com   **E** karledw@boldenterprises.com

1.

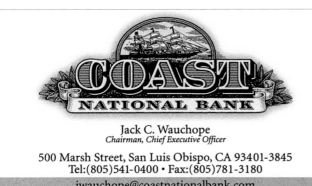

Jack C. Wauchope
Chairman, Chief Executive Officer

500 Marsh Street, San Luis Obispo, CA 93401-3845
Tel:(805)541-0400 • Fax:(805)781-3180

jwauchope@coastnationalbank.com

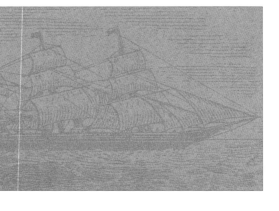

2.

COURTNEY ARCHITECTS

Carolyn Courtney

656 Santa Rosa Street, Suite 3A   805/541-3150
San Luis Obispo, CA 93401   805/541-3173 FAX

3.

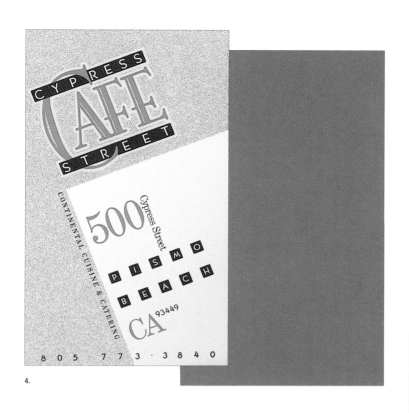

4.

5.

OceanParkHotels

Jerry A. Harris
Operations Manager

28005 N. Smyth Drive, Suite 121

Valencia, CA 91355

T 805.896.8788 **F** 661.295.4649

E jharris@ophot.com

6.

(1-6)
Design Firm **Pierre Rademaker Design**

1.
Client   Bold Enterprises
Designers Debbie Shibata,
          Pierre Rademaker

2.
Client   Coast National Bank
Designers Debbie Shibata,
          Pierre Rademaker

3.
Client   Courtney Architects
Designers Pierre Rademaker,
          Jeff Austin

4.
Client   Cypress Cafe Street
Designer Pierre Rademaker

5.
Client   Madonna Inn
Designers Debbie Shibata,
          Pierre Rademaker

6.
Client   Ocean Park Hotels
Designers Anne Bussone,
          Pierre Rademaker

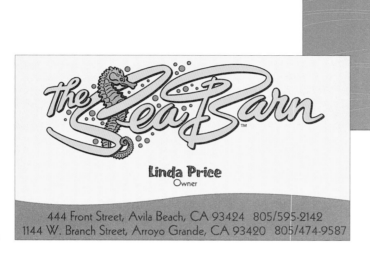

1.

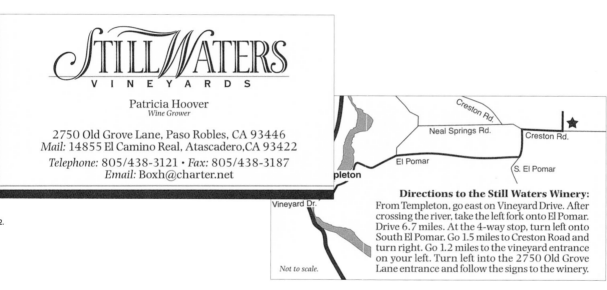

Directions to the Still Waters Winery:
From Templeton, go east on Vineyard Drive. After crossing the river, take the left fork onto El Pomar. Drive 6.7 miles. At the 4-way stop, turn left onto South El Pomar. Go 1.5 miles to Creston Road and turn right. Go 1.2 miles to the vineyard entrance on your left. Turn left into the 2750 Old Grove Lane entrance and follow the signs to the winery.

2.

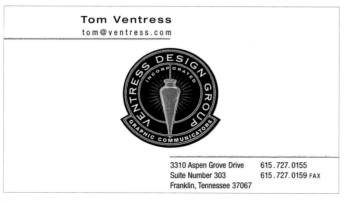

3.

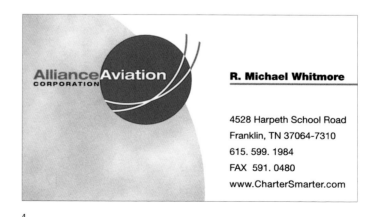

4.

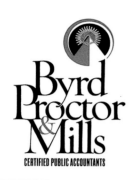

Alice Crafts CPA
PARTNER

111 Westwood Place, Suite 400
Brentwood, Tennessee 37027
acrafts@bpmcpas.com
615.467.7306 DIRECT
615.467.7300 MAIN
615.467.7301 FAX

5.

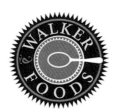

RICHARD J. MAGER
President

8541 BASH STREET, SUITE 102
INDIANAPOLIS, INDIANA 46250
317.585.9538 ✆ FAX 317.585.9647
r mager@walkerfoodsinc.com

6.

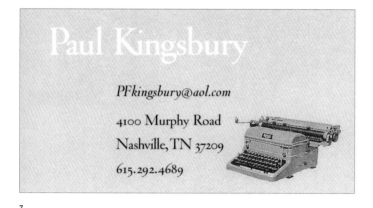

Paul Kingsbury

PFkingsbury@aol.com

4100 Murphy Road

Nashville, TN 37209

615.292.4689

7.

Holly Tashian
FENG SHUI CONSULTATIONS
Creating Solutions for Homes and Businesses

615.383.1875

615.292.6722 FAX

holly@tashian.com

www.tashian.com/fengshui

8.

emsi ENVIRONMENTAL MANAGEMENT SERVICES, INC.

William Ney Hansard
CET, CHMM, REA

5655 Valley View Road
Brentwood, Tennessee 37027
615.370.0907 Fax 370.0908
hansard@emsi-solutions.com
www.emsi-solutions.com

9.

(1,2)
Design Firm **Pierre Rademaker Design**
(3-9)
Design Firm **Ventress Design Group**

1.
Client   The Sea Barn
Designers   Elisa York, Pierre Rademaker
2.
Client   StillWaters Vineyards
Designers   Debbie Shibata, Pierre Rademaker
3.
Client   Ventress Design Group
Designer   Tom Ventress
4.
Client   Alliance Aviation
Designer   Tom Ventress
5.
Client   Byrd, Proctor and Mills
Designer   Tom Ventress
6.
Client   Walker Foods
Designer   Tom Ventress

7.
Client   Paul Kingsbury
Designer   Tom Ventress
8.
Client   Holly Tashian
Designer   Tom Ventress
9.
Client   Environmental Management
             Services, Inc.
Designer   Tom Ventress

1.

T TOMPKINS SQUARE Middle School

Patricia Macken | **GUIDANCE COUNSELOR**
600 East 6th Street | New York, NY 10009
phone 212.995.1430 | fax 212.602.9671

2.

LA TECHNIQUE™
Personal Fitness Studio

Spread Eagle Village • 503 West Lancaster Avenue • Wayne, PA 19087 • 610.687.2040

3.

Stephen Bemis
PRESIDENT

P.O. Box 1233
Canton, CT 06019

PHONE:
860-693-8179
FAX:
860-693-0856
EMAIL:
steve@newenglandreunions.com
WEB:
www.newenglandreunions.com

New England Reunions LLC

4.

Michael Seifert
Partner

One Dock Street
Suite 310
Stamford, CT 06902

203|973|1220...Phone
203|973|1251...Direct
203|973|1221...Fax

Concept
INFORMATION SYSTEMS

5.

Mitch Margolis
Principal

mitch@yohay.com
718.857.4514 tel

60 grand avenue
brooklyn, ny 11205
718.230.0759 fax

www.yohay.com

since 1948
yohay
BAKING CO.

6.

nsc
NUTRACEUTICAL SOLUTIONS CONSULTING

WILLIAM P. ARTHUR

1830 Meridian Avenue, Suite 1504
Miami Beach, FL 33139

646.271.2103 phone 305.538.2630 fax
warthur@nscnyc.com

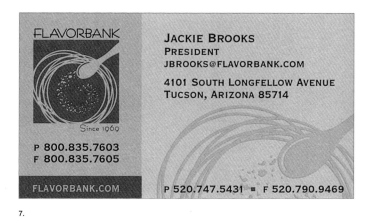

JACKIE BROOKS
PRESIDENT
JBROOKS@FLAVORBANK.COM

4101 SOUTH LONGFELLOW AVENUE
TUCSON, ARIZONA 85714

P 800.835.7603
F 800.835.7605

FLAVORBANK.COM
P 520.747.5431 ■ F 520.790.9469

7.

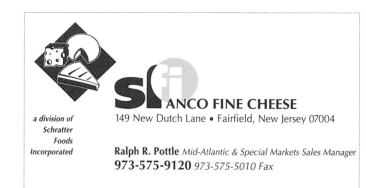

a division of
Schratter
Foods
Incorporated

ANCO FINE CHEESE
149 New Dutch Lane • Fairfield, New Jersey 07004

Ralph R. Pottle *Mid-Atlantic & Special Markets Sales Manager*
973-575-9120 *973-575-5010 Fax*

8.

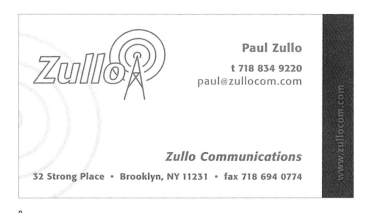

Paul Zullo

t 718 834 9220

paul@zullocom.com

www.zullocom.com

Zullo Communications

32 Strong Place • Brooklyn, NY 11231 • fax 718 694 0774

9.

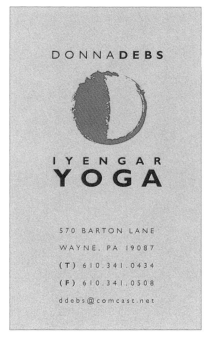

DONNADEBS

IYENGAR
YOGA

570 BARTON LANE

WAYNE, PA 19087

(T) 610.341.0434

(F) 610.341.0508

ddebs@comcast.net

10.

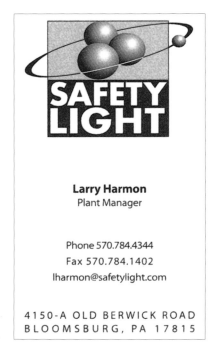

Larry Harmon
Plant Manager

Phone 570.784.4344

Fax 570.784.1402

lharmon@safetylight.com

4150-A OLD BERWICK ROAD
BLOOMSBURG, PA 17815

11.

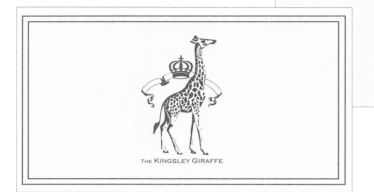

THE KINGSLEY GIRAFFE

212.260.7224 *phone*
212.533.8002 *fax*
New York, New York

sales@kingsleygiraffe.com
www.kingsleygiraffe.com

1.

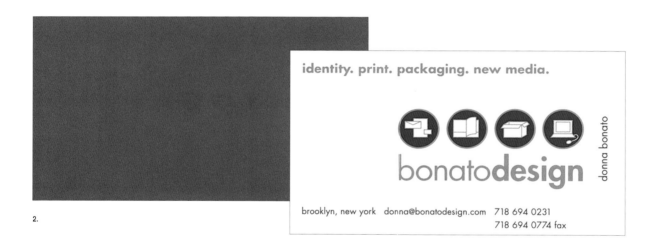

identity. print. packaging. new media.

bonato**design**

donna bonato

brooklyn, new york   donna@bonatodesign.com   718 694 0231
718 694 0774 fax

2.

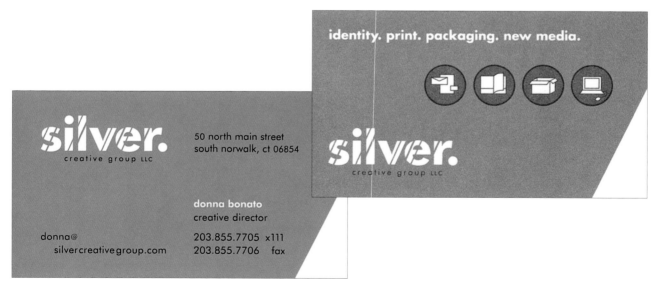

silver.
creative group LLC

50 north main street
south norwalk, ct 06854

donna bonato
creative director

donna@
silvercreativegroup.com

203.855.7705 x111
203.855.7706   fax

identity. print. packaging. new media.

silver.
creative group LLC

3.

218

Fuvurological
strategies

Matias Zadicoff   Animation
mzadicoff@futurological.com

45 MAIN STREET, SUITE 707
BROOKLYN, NY 11201

P 866.4.FUTURO x217
F 708.260.9593

www.futurological.com

- Voice & Data Networking
- Hardware & Software Sales
- Multimedia & Web
- Email & Web Hosting

...perienced • Responsible • Ethical

4.

zenergy

HEALTH   AND
FITNESS   CLUB

3197 Beaver Vu Drive   Beavercreek, OH 45434-6366
937.320.0599   937.320.0665 fax

5.

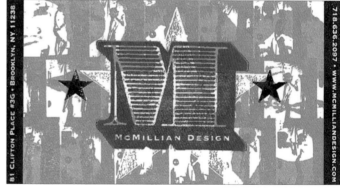

6.

Marea Fowler
COSTUMIER

98 Brooklyn Road Brooklyn NSW 2083
ph 02 9985 7609 fax 02 9985 7000
mobile 0413 808 989 email MAREAC@CIA.COM.AU

7.

(1-4)
Design Firm **Silver Creative Group**
(5)
Design Firm **VMA, Inc.**
(6)
Design Firm **McMillian Design**
(7)
Design Firm **Jennifer Shanley**

1.
| Client | Kingsley Giraffe |
| Designer | Robin Bonato |

2.
| Client | Bonato Design |
| Designer | Donna Bonato |

3.
| Client | Silver Creative Group |
| Designer | Donna Bonato |

4.
| Client | Futurological |
| Designer | Donna Bonato |

5.
Client	Zenergy
Designers	Al Hidalgo,
	Kenneth Botts

6.
Client	McMillian Design
Designers	Bill McDevitt,
	William McMillian

7.
| Client | Marea Fowler |
| Designer | Jennifer Shanley |

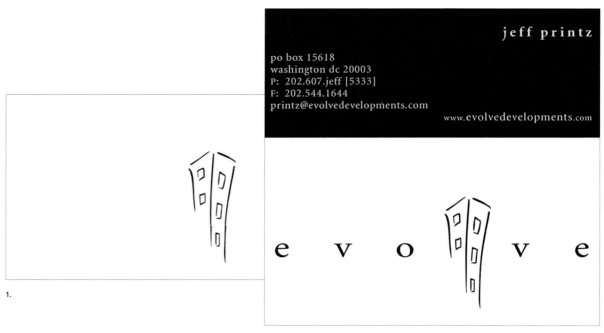

jeff printz

po box 15618
washington dc 20003
P: 202.607.jeff [5333]
F: 202.544.1644
printz@evolvedevelopments.com

www.evolvedevelopments.com

e v o v e

1.

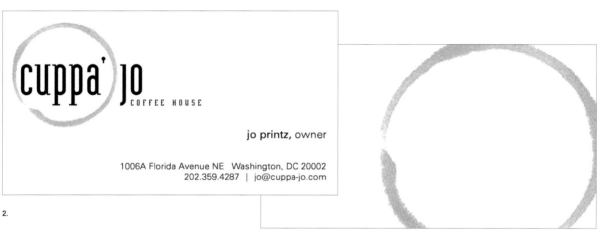

cuppa' jo
COFFEE HOUSE

jo printz, owner

1006A Florida Avenue NE   Washington, DC 20002
202.359.4287 | jo@cuppa-jo.com

2.

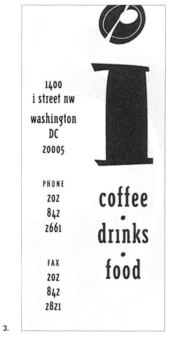

1400
i street nw

washington
DC
20005

PHONE
202
842
2661

FAX
202
842
2821

coffee
·
drinks
·
food

[open early]

[open late]

3.

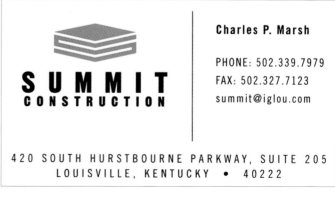

Charles P. Marsh

SUMMIT
CONSTRUCTION

PHONE: 502.339.7979
FAX: 502.327.7123
summit@iglou.com

420 SOUTH HURSTBOURNE PARKWAY, SUITE 205
LOUISVILLE, KENTUCKY   •   40222

4.

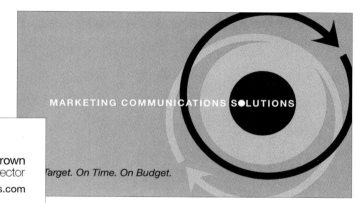

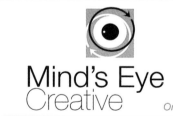

Mind's Eye
Creative

Stephen Brown
Art Director

steve@earthlygoods.com

On Target. On Time. On Budget.

Mind's Eye Creative	Ⓟ 812 944 3283
620 East Main Street	Ⓒ 502 338 4285
New Albany, IN 47150	Ⓕ 812 944 2903

5.

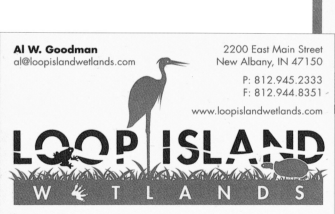

Al W. Goodman
al@loopislandwetlands.com

2200 East Main Street
New Albany, IN 47150

P: 812.945.2333
F: 812.944.8351

www.loopislandwetlands.com

LOOP ISLAND
W E T L A N D S

The Loop Island Wetlands is located at the corner of
East Main and Silver Streets in New Albany, Indiana.
For more information visit: www.loopislandwetlands.com

6.

Chesapeake PERL

Nathan DeCarolis
Research Associate

Chesapeake PERL, Inc. Protein Expression and Recovery Labs
8510A Corridor Road, Savage, MD 20763
301.317.9300 x107 Fax: 301.317.9343
ndecarolis@c-perl.com   www.c-perl.com

7.

(1-3)
  Design Firm **Pensaré Design Group**
(4-6)
  Design Firm **Mind's Eye Creative**
(7)
  Design Firm **Martin-Schaffer, Inc.**

1.
  Client   Evolve Developments
  Designer Kundia D. Wood
2.
  Client   cuppa' jo
  Designer Kundia D. Wood
3.
  Client   i
  Designer Amy E. Billingham
4.
  Client   Summit Construction
  Designer Stephen Brown
5.
  Client   Mind's Eye Creative
  Designer Stephen Brown

6.
  Client   Loop Island Wetlands
  Designer Stephen Bowman
7.
  Client   Chesapeake PERL, Inc.
  Designers Steve Cohn,
            Tina Martin

ACME COMMUNICATIONS, INC.
200 PARK AVENUE SOUTH
NEW YORK, NEW YORK 10003
☎ 212 505-0048
Fax: 212 202-4412
Email: kboucher@acmeny.com
Portfolio: www.acmeny.com
KIKI BOUCHER

1.

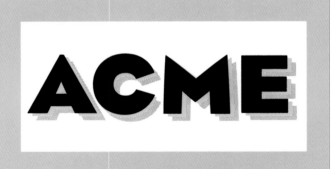

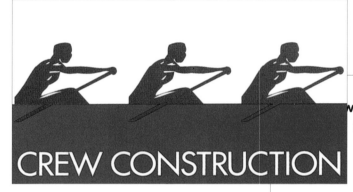

CREW CONSTRUCTION

2.

W CONSTRUCTION CORP.
FRANK WISNIESKI

200 Park Avenue South
New York, NY 10003
⌀ 212.505.3190
fax 212.505.0904
fawizz1@verizon.net

WE WOULD LIKE TO TALK TO YOU, IF YOU ARE:
• a self-starter with a positive attitude,
• looking for a rewarding career,
• seeking above average earnings potential,
• and is someone who likes working with people

CALL the number on this card for furth

WE WILL PROVIDE:
• professional training,
• ongoing supervisory support,
• an established client base,
• benefits, include:
    annual seminars
    hospitalization insurance
    group ter
    401K pla
• and an opp
    successful f

3.

SECURITY PLAN

LIFE INSURANCE CO. | **FIRE INSURANCE CO.**
914 East 70th Street   Shreveport, Louisiana 71106

Ronald E. Smith
District Manager

318.868.2768
Fax 318.868.2796
dst51em@securityplan.com

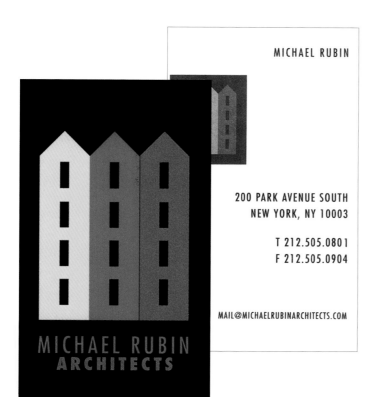

MICHAEL RUBIN

200 PARK AVENUE SOUTH
NEW YORK, NY 10003

T 212.505.0801
F 212.505.0904

MAIL@MICHAELRUBINARCHITECTS.COM

MICHAEL RUBIN
ARCHITECTS

4.

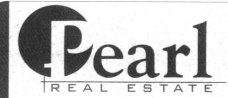

DIRTWORKS, PC
LANDSCAPE ARCHITECTURE

200 PARK AVENUE SOUTH
NEW YORK, NEW YORK 10003
TEL 212-529-2263
FAX 212-505-0904
DKAMP@DIRTWORKS.US

DAVID KAMP, ASLA, LF
PRESIDENT

5.

Pearl
REAL ESTATE

Lea Turner-Betts
Broker

DIRECT: 503.803.7969
LTURNERBETTS@PEARLREALESTATE.COM

1001 NW 14th Avenue
Portland, Oregon 97209
Phone: 503.223.2255
Fax: 503.224.2255
www.pearlrealestate.com

6.

JEFF FISHER
Lego
MOTIVES

JEFF FISHER
Engineer of Creative Identity

Fax: 503.283.8995 • Phone: 503.283.8673

Email address: jeff@jfisherlogomotives.com

Web site URL: www.jfisherlogomotives.com

P.O. Box 17155 • Portland, OR 97217-0155

Helping businesses and organizations stay on
track through creative, innovative, affordable and
award-winning identity design.

7.

JB SCOTT SEARCH

Brady V. Hoag
Principal

Direct 612.381.8942
Cell 612.384.2755

2501 Wayzata B␣
Minneapolis, MN␣
bhoag@jbscottse␣
www.jbscottsear␣

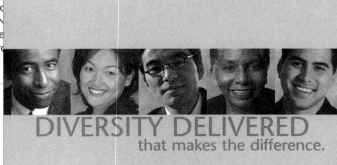

DIVERSITY DELIVERED
that makes the difference.

1.

horizon college

Chris Olson, Minister of Divinity
Academic Dean
[e]colson@horizoncollege.org

P.O. Box 17480
San Diego, CA 92177
[P]858.277.4991
[f]858.277.1365

[www.horizoncollege.org]

2.

Design North

BRANDING FOR THE
RETAIL ENVIRONMENT

GWEN GRANZOW
Vice President/Creative Director
Principal

Design North, Inc.
8007 Douglas Avenue
Racine, Wisconsin 53402
www.designnorth.com

Phone 262.639.2080
Toll Free 800.247.8494
Fax 262.639.5230

gwen@designnorth.com

3.

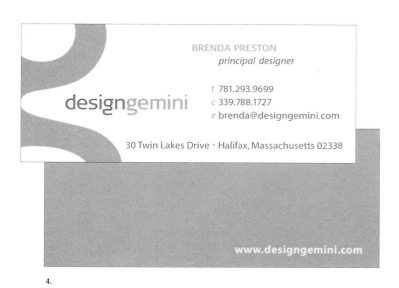

BRENDA PRESTON
principal designer

designgemini

t 781.293.9699
c 339.788.1727
e brenda@designgemini.com

30 Twin Lakes Drive • Halifax, Massachusetts 02338

www.designgemini.com

4.

MAX GRAPHICS

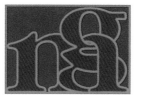

BOB SCHONFISCH
Creative Director

1820 POPLAR AVENUE   REDWOOD CITY, CA 94061-2102
PHONE: 650. 568. 3238   E-MAIL: MAXGRAPHICS@RCN.COM

5.

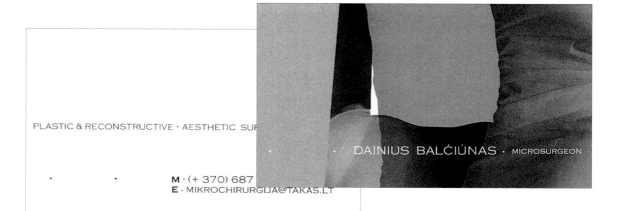

PLASTIC & RECONSTRUCTIVE · AESTHETIC SUR

M · (+ 370) 687
E · MIKROCHIRURGIJA@TAKAS.LT

DAINIUS BALĆIŪNAS · MICROSURGEON

6.

www.kriste.lt

GRaPHic dESigner
kriste@stx.lt | mobile: +

+ 370 699 80482

LGDA
LITHUANIAN ASSOCIATION OF GRAPHIC DESIGNERS
KRISTINA ŽALNIERUKYNAITĖ

7.

(1)
Design Firm **Franke + Fiorella**
(2)
Design Firm **Wheeler Design**
(3)
Design Firm **Design North, Inc.**
(4)
Design Firm **Design Gemini**
(5)
Design Firm **Max Graphics**
(6,7)
Design Firm **Kristina Zalnierukynaite**

1.
Client   J.B. Scott
Designers   Craig Franke,
             Rich Ketelsen

2.
Client   Horizon College
Designer   Stephanie Wheeler
3.
Client   Design North, Inc.
Designers   Gwen Granzow,
             Design North, Inc.
4.
Client   Design Gemini
Designer   Brenda Preston
5.
Client   Max Graphics
Designer   Bob Schonfisch
6.
Client   Dainius Balčiūnas
Designer   Kristina Zalnierukynaite
7.
Client   Kristina Zalnierukynaite
Designer   Kristina Zalnierukynaite

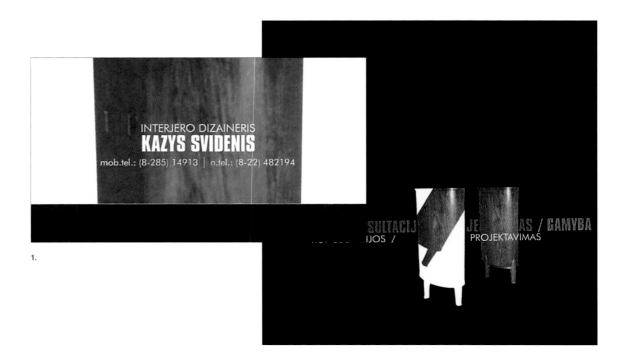

INTERJERO DIZAINERIS
KAZYS SVIDENIS
mob.tel.: (8-285) 14913 | n.tel.: (8-22) 482194

SULTACIJ   JE...AS / GAMYBA
IJOS /   PROJEKTAVIMAS

1.

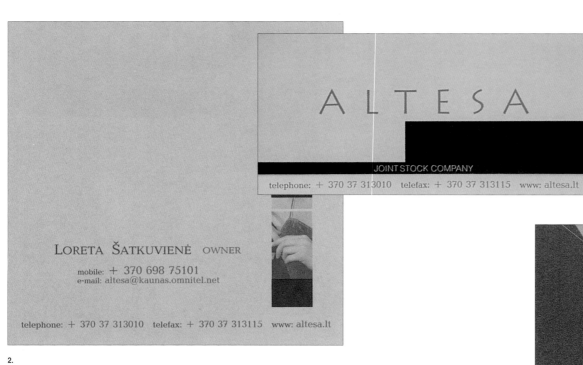

A L T E S A

JOINT STOCK COMPANY

telephone: + 370 37 313010   telefax: + 370 37 313115   www: altesa.lt

LORETA ŠATKUVIENĖ OWNER

mobile: + 370 698 75101
e-mail: altesa@kaunas.omnitel.net

telephone: + 370 37 313010   telefax: + 370 37 313115   www: altesa.lt

2.

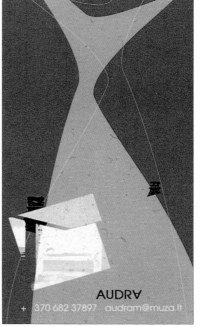

AUDRA
+ 370 682 37897   audram@muza.lt

3.

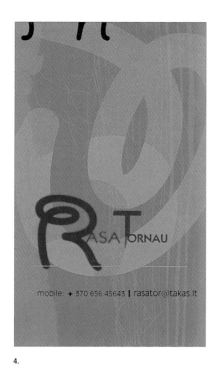

RASA TORNAU

mobile: + 370 656 45643 | rasator@takas.lt

4.

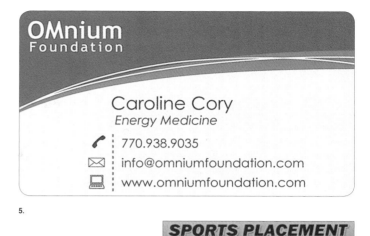

OMnium
Foundation

Caroline Cory
Energy Medicine

☎ 770.938.9035
✉ info@omniumfoundation.com
🖥 www.omniumfoundation.com

5.

**SPORTS PLACEMENT
SERVICE, INC.**
REPRESENTING ATHLETES WORLDWIDE

Harlan J. Werner
harlan@sportsplacement.com
Phone (323)938-6444   Fax (323)938-6677
www.sportsplacement.com
5458 Wilshire Blvd. Los Angeles, CA 90036

6.

Mike Takas
Regional Sales Manager
miket@cmpaper.com

Main 616 676-9203
Toll Free 800 632-4910
Direct 616 676-3965 ext. 209
Mobile 616 318-4135
Fax 616 676-2637

CMP
6194 E. Fulton Rd.
Ada, MI 49301
www.cmpaper.com

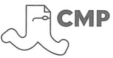 **CMP**

John W. Garrison
Regional Sales Manager

Main 616 676-9203
Toll Free 800 632-4910
Mobile 616 490-2819
Home Office 231 266-5362
Home Fax 231 266-8720
Fax 616 676-2637

CMP
6194 E. Fulton Rd.
Ada, MI 49301
www.cmpaper.com

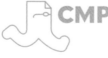 **CMP**

Liz Zezulk
Sample D
lizz@cmp

Main 616
Toll Free 8
Direct 616
Fax 616 67

CMP
6194 E. Ful
Ada, MI 4
www.cmp

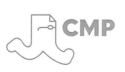 **CMP**

7.

Your next appointment is:

_____

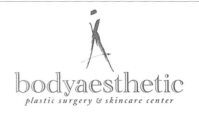

bodyaesthetic
plastic surgery & skincare center

Mary R. Pfitzinger, B.S.N., R.N.F.A.

969 North Mason Road, Suite 170 ▪ **St. Louis, Missouri 63141**
314-628-8200 phone ▪ 314-628-9504 fax
mpfitzinger@bodyaesthetic.com ▪ www.bodyaesthetic.com

1.

The **Great Rivers Greenway** District

Jennifer Olmstead, AICP
Project Manager
jolmstead@greatrivers.info

1000 St. Louis Union Station
Suite 102
St. Louis, MO 63103
Phone: 314.436.7009
Fax: 314.436.8004

www.greatrivers.info
109

for a clean, green, connected St. Louis region

www.greatrivers.info

2.

Anne Ainslie
Vice President of Operations

Love it LLC
1123 BROADWAY
SUITE 1211
NEW YORK, NY 10010
www.loveitretail.com

T 212.367.3727
F 212.367.3726
aainslie@loveitretail.com

Smart retail

Love it LLC

3.

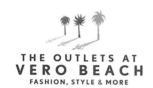

THE OUTLETS AT
VERO BEACH
FASHION, STYLE & MORE

Owned, leased and managed by

🔲 STOLTZ

Susan Belgam Hunt
General Manager
772.770.6097
fax 772.770.5787
shunt@stoltzusa.com

The Outlets at Vero Beach
1824 94th Drive
Vero Beach, FL 32966
www.verobeachoutlets.com
www.stoltzusa.com

4.

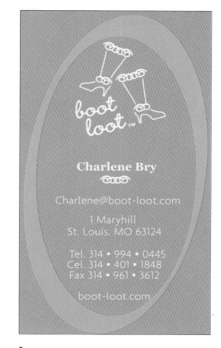

Charlene Bry

Charlene@boot-loot.com

1 Maryhill
St. Louis, MO 63124

Tel. 314 • 994 • 0445
Cel. 314 • 401 • 1848
Fax 314 • 961 • 3612

boot-loot.com

5.

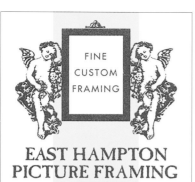

FINE
CUSTOM
FRAMING

EAST HAMPTON
PICTURE FRAMING

374 Montauk Hwy.
PO Box 560
Wainscott
New York
11975

631 537-0012

Nina Bataller, GCF, CPF

6.

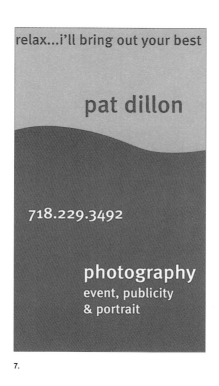

relax...i'll bring out your best

pat dillon

718.229.3492

photography
event, publicity
& portrait

7.

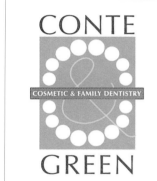

CONTE
COSMETIC & FAMILY DENTISTRY
GREEN

Gabriel Conte, DDS
David J. Green, DDS

877 Stewart Avenue, Suite 26
Garden City, NY 11530

(516) 222-1717 Phone
(516) 222-1867 Fax

www.contegreen.com

8.

(1-5)
Design Firm **Kiku Obata & Company**
(6-8)
Design Firm **Fleury Design**

1.
Client   Body Aesthetic
Designer   Amy Knopf
2.
Client   Great Rivers Greenway
Designers   Troy Guzman,
            Teresa Norton-Young
3.
Client   Love it
Designer   Eleanor Safe
4.
Client   Stoltz/The Outlets at Vero Beach
Designer   Amy Knopf
5.
Client   Boot Loot
Designer   Jennifer McBath
6.
Client   East Hampton Picture Framing
Designer   Ellen Fleury

7.
Client   Pat Dillon Photography
Designer   Ellen Fleury
8.
Client   Conte & Green
Designer   Ellen Fleury

229

1.

Mary English, PT DPT
Dave Hynds, PT MA
Dave Fontana, PTA

232 East Main Street
Huntington, NY 11743

Tel **(631) 427-7807**
Fax (631) 427-7887

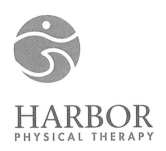

HARBOR
PHYSICAL THERAPY

2.

Win Thin, Ph.D.
President

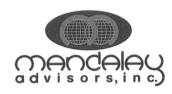

223 Wall Street
Huntington, NY 11743-2060

Tel: 631-425-1955
Fax: 631-425-1975

wthin@mandalayadvisors.com

3.

Tangram Strategic Design

Enrico Sempi
Partner

Tangram Strategic Design s.r.l.
viale Michelangelo Buonarroti 10/C
28100 Novara, Italia
032 135 662 / 0321 392 232
f. 0321 390 914
esempi@tangramsd.it

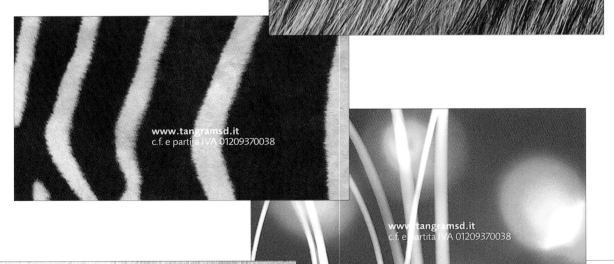

www.tangramsd.it
c.f. e partita IVA 01209370038

Tangram Strategic Design

Antonella Trevisan
Senior designer

Tangram Strategic Design s.r.l.
viale Michelangelo Buonarroti 10/C
28100 Novara, Italia
032 135 662 / 0321 392 232
f. 0321 390 914
atrevisan@tangramsd.it

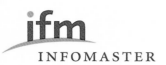

Emilio Barlocco
President

IFM Infomaster S.r.l.
Sede Legale:
Via V Maggio 81
16147 Genova, Italy
Tel. +39 0103 747 811 (r.a.)
Fax +39 0103 747 861
E-mail: emilio.barlocco@ifminfomaster.com

4.

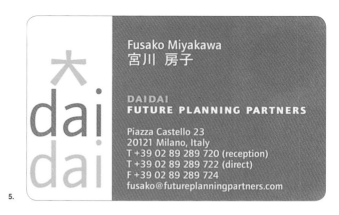

Fusako Miyakawa
宮川 房子

DAIDAI
FUTURE PLANNING PARTNERS

Piazza Castello 23
20121 Milano, Italy
T +39 02 89 289 720 (reception)
T +39 02 89 289 722 (direct)
F +39 02 89 289 724
fusako@futureplanningpartners.com

5.

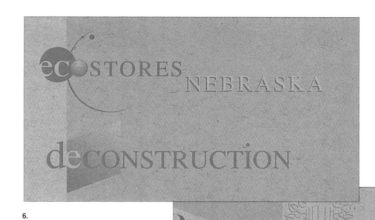

ecoSTORES NEBRASKA

deCONSTRUCTION

6.

NCSC

402 477•3606 voice
402 477•3607 FAX

ron bartels
@sustainabledesign.org

www.ecospheres.com

Nebraska Center
for Sustainable
Construction

530 West P Street
Lincoln,
Nebraska 68528•1542

STEVE WOODS PRINTING COMPANY
2205 EAST UNIVERSITY PHOENIX ARIZONA 85034
MAIN 602 484 8888 DIRECT 602 625 2222 FAX 602 484 8899
TOLL FREE 888 484 2448 STEVE@STEVEWOODSPRINTING.COM

STEVE WOODS
RELATIONSHIP GUY

7.

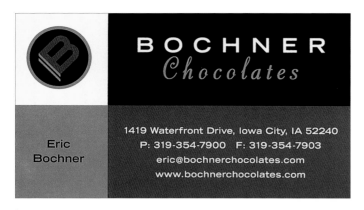

1.

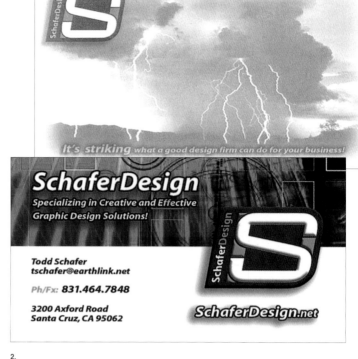

2.

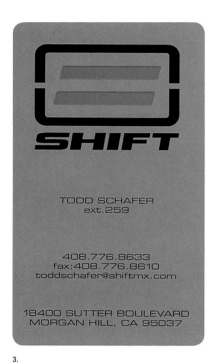

3.

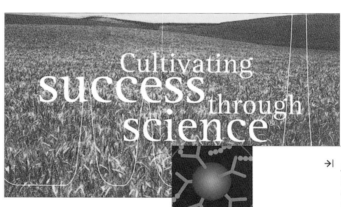

4.

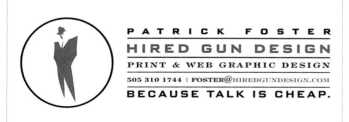

5.

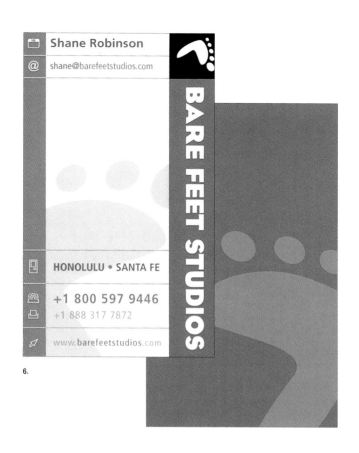

Shane Robinson

shane@barefeetstudios.com

BARE FEET STUDIOS

HONOLULU • SANTA FE

+1 800 597 9446

+1 888 317 7872

www.barefeetstudios.com

6.

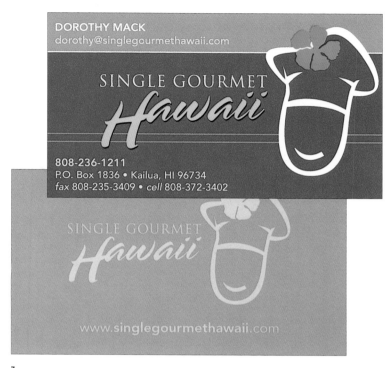

DOROTHY MACK
dorothy@singlegourmethawaii.com

SINGLE GOURMET
Hawaii

808-236-1211
P.O. Box 1836 • Kailua, HI 96734
fax 808-235-3409 • cell 808-372-3402

SINGLE GOURMET
Hawaii

www.singlegourmethawaii.com

7.

1656 WASHINGTON, SUITE 210
KANSAS CITY, MO 64108
℗ 816/283.8480   ℗ 816/283.8475
© 816/807.2539

THE
**BUCKLEY
GROUP**

HELEN E. MILLER
SENIOR MANAGEMENT CONSULTANT

HEALTHCARE CONSULTING
& MANAGEMENT SERVICES

hmiller@thebuckleygroupllc.com

8.

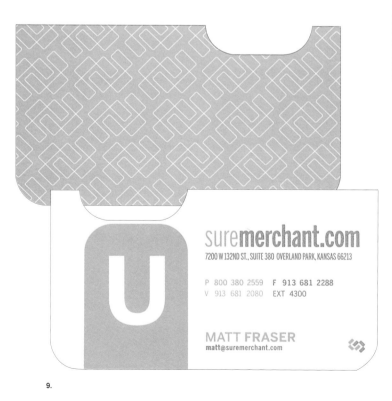

suremerchant.com
7200 W 132ND ST., SUITE 380 OVERLAND PARK, KANSAS 66213

P 800 380 2559   F 913 681 2288
V 913 681 2080   EXT 4300

MATT FRASER
matt@suremerchant.com

9.

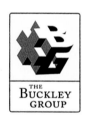

(1)
    Design Firm **Mires**
(2,3)
    Design Firm **Schafer Design**
(4)
    Design Firm **VICAM**
(5-7)
    Design Firm **Hired Gun Design**
(8,9)
    Design Firm **Indicia Design, Inc.**

1.
    Client Bochner Chocolates
    Designers José Serrano,
      Miguel Perez
2.
    Client Schafer Design
    Designer Todd Schafer
3.
    Client Shift
    Designer Todd Schafer
4.
    Client VICAM
    Designers Jennifer Smith/VICAM,
      Dave Phoenix/
      TRIAD Communications
5.
    Client Hired Gun Design
    Designer Patrick Foster

6.
    Client Bare Feet Studios
    Designers Patrick Foster,
      Roxanne Darling
7.
    Client Single Gourmet Hawaii
    Designer Patrick Foster
8.
    Client The Buckley Group, LLC
    Designers Ryan Hembree,
      Ryan Glendening
9.
    Client SureMerchant, LLC
    Designers Ryan Hembree,
      Hunter Eshelman

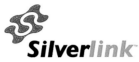

Silverlink™

The Trusted Voice in Client Communications

Gareth Taube
Marketing
gtaube@silverlink.com

PH (781) 272 3080 × 286
FAX (781) 272 7417

15 New England Executive Park, Suite 135
Burlington, MA 01803

www.silverlink.com

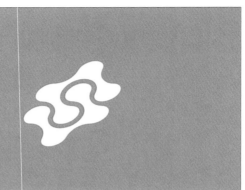

1.

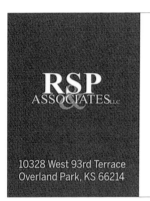

RSP
ASSOCIATESLLC

10328 West 93rd Terrace
Overland Park, KS 66214

Robert S. Schwarz, A

rob@RSP-Associates.co
www.RSP-Associates.co

PH 913.963.5967
FX 913.438.1984

RSP
ASSOCIATESLLC

2.

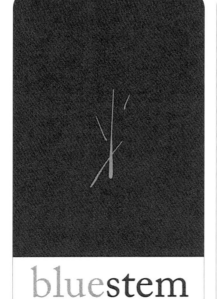

bluestem
RESTAURANT

colby garrelts
megan garrelts

CHEFS/OWNERS

900 WESTPORT ROAD
KANSAS CITY, MO 64111
P 816 561 1101

3.

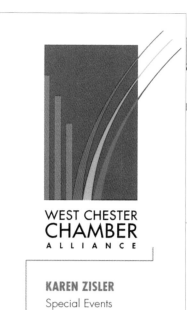

WEST CHESTER
CHAMBER
ALLIANCE

KAREN ZISLER
Special Events

ST CHESTER CHAMBER ALLIANCE
...connecting people and possibilities

7 Voice of America Centre Drive • West Chester, OH 45069
513.777.3600 P • 513.777.0188 F • 877.WCHESTER

• www.westchesterchamberalliance.com
• **kzisler@westchesterchamberalliance.com**

4.

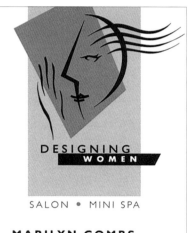

DESIGNING
WOMEN

SALON • MINI SPA

MARILYN COMBS
513.398.9722

1072 READING ROAD
MASON, OHIO 45040

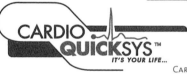

Master Designer

Advanced Color Specia

7.

Bill Walsh Agency
BUSINESS MANAGEMENT SOLUTIONS

7723 TYLERS PLACE BLVD. SUITE 129
WEST CHESTER, OHIO 45069
DIRECT: 513 608.6005
FAX: 513 779.1668
E-MAIL: MANAGE1@FUSE.NET

5.

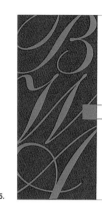

CARDIO
QUICKSYS™
IT'S YOUR LIFE...

MICHAEL HOSKINS
SALES SPECIALIST

CELL **773 383.8678**

CARDIOQUICKSYS, LLC.
6215 CENTRE PARK DRIVE
WEST CHESTER, OH 45069 USA

P 513 759.4333 EXT. 138
F 513 759.3312
TOLL FREE 888 387.8425
MHOSKINS@CARDIOQUICKSYS.COM
WWW.CARDIOQUICKSYS.COM

6.

(1-3)
Design Firm **Indicia Design, Inc.**
(4-7)
Design Firm **Five Visual Communication
& Design**

1.
Client   Silverlink Communications
Designers   Ryan Hembree,
                   Ryan Glendening

2.
Client   RSP & Associates
Designers   Ryan Hembree,
                   Hunter Eshelman

3.
Client   BlueStem Restaurant
Designers   Ryan Hembree,
                   Ryan Glendening

4.
Client   West Chester Chamber Alliance
Designer   Rondi Tschopp

5.
Client   Bill Walsh Agency
Designer   Rondi Tschopp

6.
Client   CardioQuickSys, LLC
Designer   Rondi Tschopp

7.
Client   Designing Women
Designer   Rondi Tschopp

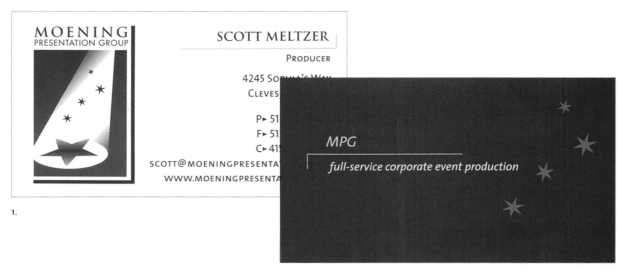

MOENING
PRESENTATION GROUP

SCOTT MELTZER

PRODUCER

4245 SOPHIA'S WAY

CLEVES

P► 51

F► 51

C► 419

SCOTT@MOENINGPRESENTA

WWW.MOENINGPRESENTA

MPG

full-service corporate event production

1.

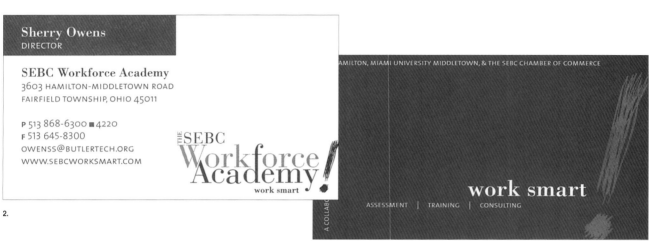

Sherry Owens
DIRECTOR

SEBC Workforce Academy
3603 HAMILTON-MIDDLETOWN ROAD
FAIRFIELD TOWNSHIP, OHIO 45011

P 513 868-6300 ■ 4220
F 513 645-8300
OWENSS@BUTLERTECH.ORG
WWW.SEBCWORKSMART.COM

THE SEBC
Workforce
Academy!
work smart

HAMILTON, MIAMI UNIVERSITY MIDDLETOWN, & THE SEBC CHAMBER OF COMMERCE

work smart

ASSESSMENT | TRAINING | CONSULTING

A COLLAB

2.

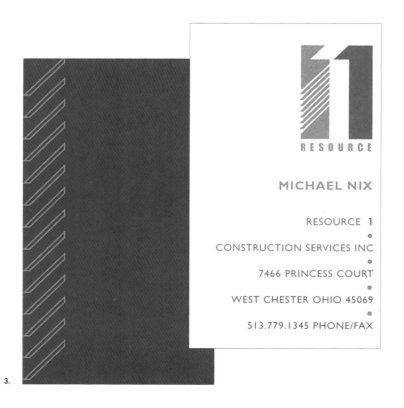

RESOURCE

MICHAEL NIX

RESOURCE 1
·
CONSTRUCTION SERVICES INC
·
7466 PRINCESS COURT
·
WEST CHESTER OHIO 45069
·
513.779.1345 PHONE/FAX

3.

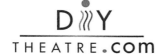

DIY THEATRE.com

Richard S. Burrows, Ph.D.
Director, Product Development
rburrows@diytheatre.com

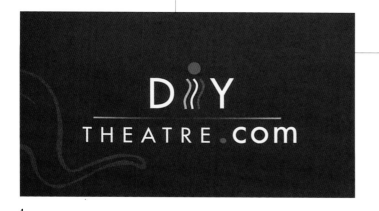

DIY THEATRE.com

4.

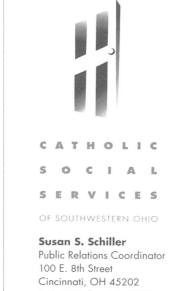

CATHOLIC SOCIAL SERVICES
OF SOUTHWESTERN OHIO

Susan S. Schiller
Public Relations Coordinator
100 E. 8th Street
Cincinnati, OH 45202
241-7745 Fax 241-4333

5.

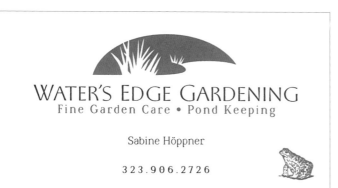

WATER'S EDGE GARDENING
Fine Garden Care • Pond Keeping

Sabine Höppner

323.906.2726

6.

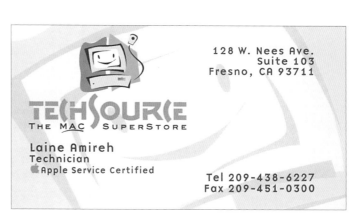

TECHSOURCE
THE MAC SUPERSTORE

Laine Amireh
Technician
 Apple Service Certified

128 W. Nees Ave.
Suite 103
Fresno, CA 93711

Tel 209-438-6227
Fax 209-451-0300

7.

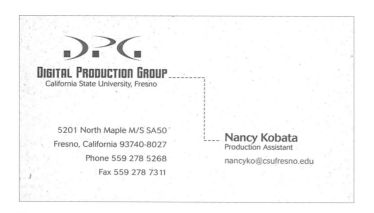

DPG
DIGITAL PRODUCTION GROUP
California State University, Fresno

5201 North Maple M/S SA50
Fresno, California 93740-8027
Phone 559 278 5268
Fax 559 278 7311

Nancy Kobata
Production Assistant
nancyko@csufresno.edu

8.

(1-5)
Design Firm **Five Visual Communication & Design**
(6-8)
Design Firm **Shields Design**

1.
Client   Moening Presentation Group
Designer   Rondi Tschopp
2.
Client   SEBC Workforce Academy
Designer   Rondi Tschopp
3.
Client   Resource 1
Designer   Rondi Tschopp
4.
Client   DIY Theater.com
Designer   Rondi Tschopp
5.
Client   Catholic Social Services
Designer   Rondi Tschopp

6.
Client   Water's Edge Gardening
Designer   Charles Shields
7.
Client   TechSource
Designers Charles Shields,
                 Juan Vega
8.
Client   Digital Production Group
Designers Charles Shields,
                 Tom Kimmelman

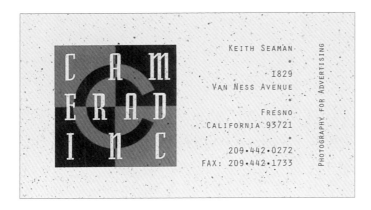

1.

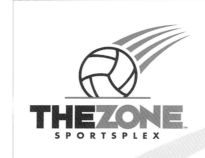

Christopher Johnson

THE ZONE
SPORTSPLEX

2037 W. Bullard Ave.
Suite 186
Fresno, CA 93711
T (209) 2 SPORTS
F (209) 431-4934

2.

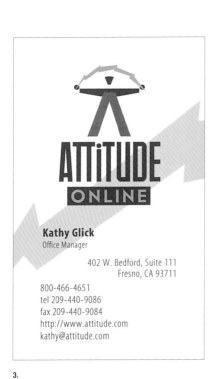

ATTITUDE
ONLINE

Kathy Glick
Office Manager

402 W. Bedford, Suite 111
Fresno, CA 93711

800-466-4651
tel 209-440-9086
fax 209-440-9084
http://www.attitude.com
kathy@attitude.com

3.

SEE YOUR PROOFS ONLINE!

Ojo Photography

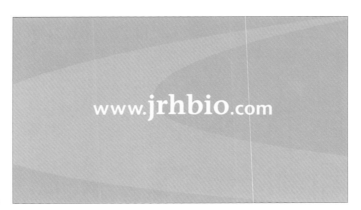

415.640.5990 PHONE
shawn@ojophotography.com

www.ojophotography.com

4.

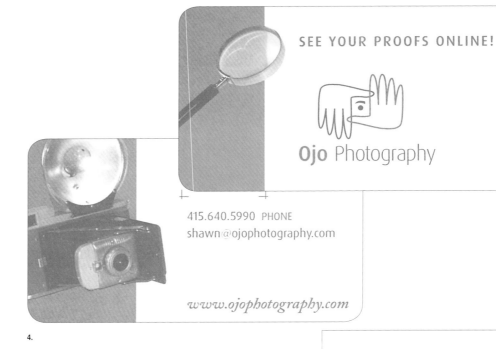

www.jrhbio.com

5.

JRH BIOSCIENCES™
Accelerate Success

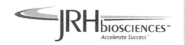

Susan A. Bridges
Marketing Communications Manager
susan.bridges@jrhbio.com

JRH Phone 913-469-5580 Ext. 6796
Toll free-USA 800-255-6032 Ext. 6796
JRH Fax 913-469-5584

JRH Biosciences, Inc.
11296 Renner Blvd.
Lenexa, Kansas 66219 USA
www.jrhbio.com

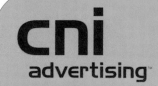

Jake Lord
Director of Visual Interface Design
jake@cniadvertising.com

913.341.6090 phone/ext. 209
913.341.6095 fax

10261 W. 87th St., Suite 200
Overland Park, KS 66212

creating new ideas   cniadvertising.com

6.

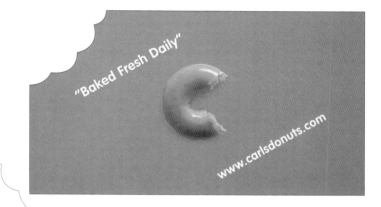

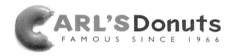

ARL'SDonuts
FAMOUS SINCE 1966

Keith Sanders

6350 Sunset Corporate Drive   702.382.6138 TEL
Las Vegas, Nevada 89120   702.382.6183 FAX
www.carlsdonuts.com   702.338.3899 CELL

7.

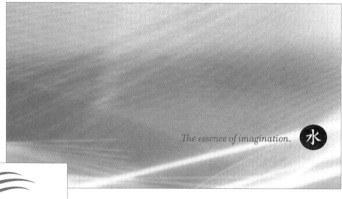

The essence of imagination.

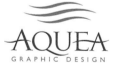

AQUEA
GRAPHIC DESIGN

TRISTA PEREZ
Marketing/PR Coordinator
trista@aqueadesign.com

4933 West Craig Road #377 Las Vegas, Nevada 89130
TEL **702.646.9067** FAX 702.646.9087 www.aqueadesign.com

8.

(1-3)
Design Firm **Shields Design**
(4)
Design Firm **Jenny Kolcun Design**
(5,6)
Design Firm **CNI Advertising**
(7,8)
Design Firm **Aquea Design**

1.
Client   Camerad, Inc.
Designer   Charles Shields
2.
Client   The Zone
Designer   Charles Shields
3.
Client   Attitude Online
Designers   Charles Shields,
            Juan Vega
4.
Client   Ojo Photography
Designer   Jenny Kolcun

5.
Client   JRH Biosciences
Designers   Tim McNamara,
            Corey Shulda,
            Jake Lord,
            Abby Bock
6.
Client   CNI Advertising
Designers   Tim McNamara,
            Corey Shulda,
            Jake Lord
7.
Client   Carl's Donuts
Designer   Raymond Perez
8.
Client   Aquea Design
Designer   Raymond Perez

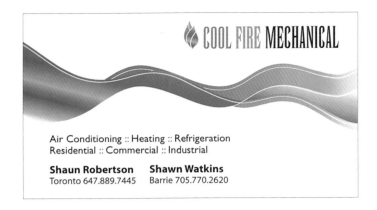

Air Conditioning :: Heating :: Refrigeration
Residential :: Commercial :: Industrial

Shaun Robertson
Toronto 647.889.7445

Shawn Watkins
Barrie 705.770.2620

1.

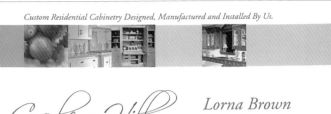

2.

Mark Hallis
PRESIDENT

Ice Life Canada Inc.
6174 Yonge Street Suite 200
Toronto ON Canada M2M 3X1

Toll Free: 1.800.477.0628
T. 416.590.1919
C. 416.278.0093
F. 416.225.3071
E. mark@icelife.com

:: skate the world ::
www.icelife.com

3.

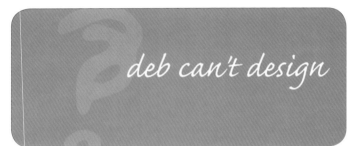

unless you hire her.

deb von sychowski
e. debsfreelance@yahoo.ca
c. 416.892.5874

4.

240

1376 BAYVIEW AVENUE

TORONTO, ON M4G 3A1

T: 416.481.1175

F: 416.481.0774

www.iQinc.ca

iQ inc

PATRICE BANTON   patrice@iQinc.ca

5.

1376 BAYVIEW AVENUE

TORONTO, ON M4G 3A1

T: 416.481.1175

F: 416.481.0774

www.iQinc.ca

iQ inc

[keep an open mind]

PATRICE BANTON   patrice@iQinc.ca

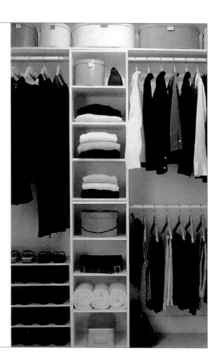

Patti-Anne Fitzpatrick

Design Consultant

CALEDON ▯ CLOSETS

e: 905.584.0617
e: 416.409.5464

CALEDON ▯ CLOSETS

6.

(1-4)
Design Firm **Deb's Freelance**
(5,6)
Design Firm **iQ inc**

1.
Client   Cool Fire Mechanical
Designer   Deb Von Sychowski
2.
Client   Cranberry Hill
                   Kitchens
Designer   Deb Von Sychowski
3.
Client   Ice Life Canada Inc.
Designer   Deb Von Sychowski
4.
Client   Deb's Freelance
Designer   Deb Von Sychowski
5.
Client   iQ inc
Designers   Patrice Banton,
                   Samantha Murray,
                   Michelle Allard,
                   Julie Cairns
6.
Client   Caledon Closets
Designers   Patrice Banton,
                   David Banton

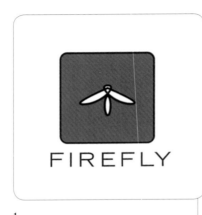

FIREFLY

1.

CHRIS WASS
cwass@fireflyliving.com

8525 E Pinnacle Peak Rd
Scottsdale, Arizona 85255

FIND ME ANYWHERE // VOICE & FAX
800.704.1263

enlightened living
fireflyliving.com

Proud member of *Keller Williams*
High Desert Realty

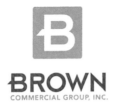

BROWN

COMMERCIAL GROUP, INC.

DANIEL R. BROWN
President/CEO
dbrown@browncommercialgroup.com

1550 Higgins Road, Suite 118 // Elk Grove Village, Illinois 60007
T 847.758.9200   F 847.758.9292

2.

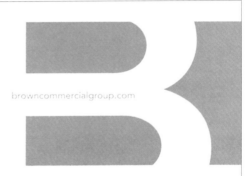

browncommercialgroup.com

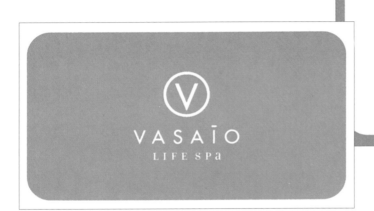

VASAIO
LIFE SPA

THE ART OF BEAUTY

RUTH MIRZA
ruth.mirza@vasaiolifespa.com

1100 East Paris Ave. SE | Grand Rapids, MI 49546

616-942-2966 | vasaiolifespa.com

3.

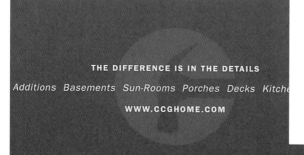

THE DIFFERENCE IS IN THE DETAILS

Additions Basements Sun-Rooms Porches Decks Kitche...

WWW.CCGHOME.COM

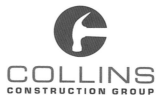

COLLINS
CONSTRUCTION GROUP

DAN COLLINS
GENERAL CONTRACTOR & BUILDER
dan@ccghome.com

1224 NARY COURT
BATAVIA, IL 60510
TEL 630.406.8434
FAX 630.406.0528
CELL 630.561.3511

4.

jimcraig™

P.O. BOX 2740
GLEN ELLYN, IL 60138-2740
jimcraigcartoons.com

jim@jimcraigcartoons.com

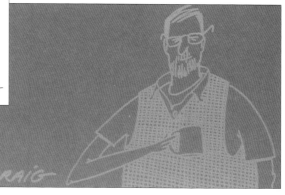

5.

Kristina S. Garcia
407 South 3rd Street · Geneva · IL 60134
tel 630 · 232 · 9780
fax 630 · 232 · 4096

Cradles & All

Distinctive furnishings from infant to t...
Baby registry & custom orders available

6.

prams   moses baskets   cribs

bassinets   bed linens   carriages

www.cradlesandall.com

changing tables   furniture   rocking chairs

strollers   crib bedding   cradles

(1-6)
Design Firm **Rule 29**

1.
Client Firefly
Designers Justin Ahrens,
Kerri Herner
2.
Client Brown Commercial
Group, Inc.
Designer Justin Ahrens
3.
Client Vasaio
Designer Justin Ahrens
4.
Client Collins Construction
Group
Designer Justin Ahrens
5.
Client Jim Craig
Designer Justin Ahrens
6.
Client Cradles and All
Designers Justin Ahrens,
Kerri Herner

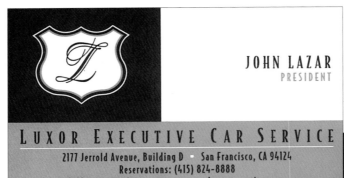

1.

Luxor Executive Car Service
Elite Transportation for Business or Pleasure
Reservations: (415) 824-8888

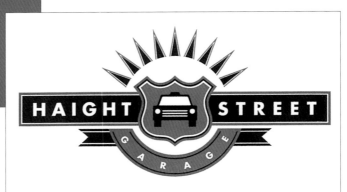

2.

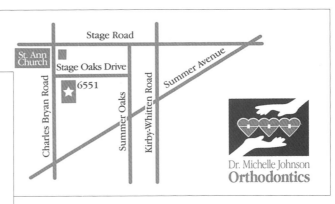

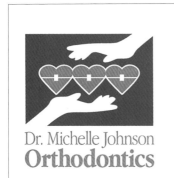

3.

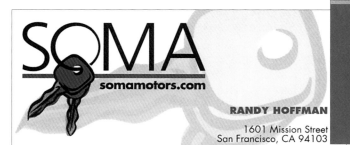

somamotors.com

1.888.425.SOMA

RANDY HOFFMAN

1601 Mission Street
San Francisco, CA 94103

p: 415.701.7662   f: 415.701.7606

randy@somamotors.com

4.

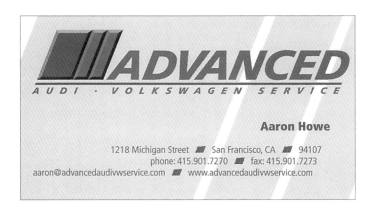

ADVANCED

A U D I · V O L K S W A G E N   S E R V I C E

Aaron Howe

1218 Michigan Street ▦ San Francisco, CA ▦ 94107
phone: 415.901.7270 ▦ fax: 415.901.7273
aaron@advancedaudivwservice.com ▦ www.advancedaudivwservice.com

5.

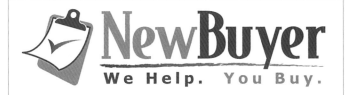

NewBuyer

We Help.   You Buy.

Andrew Dennis
PRESIDENT & CEO

NewBuyer.com, LLC
Phone: (203) 262-6266 • Fax: (203) 264-6579
andrewdennis@newbuyer.com • www.newbuyer.com
9 Union Square #250 • Southbury, CT 06488

6.

corporate identity

package design

publications

advertising

illustration

consulting

education

marketing

copywriting

7.

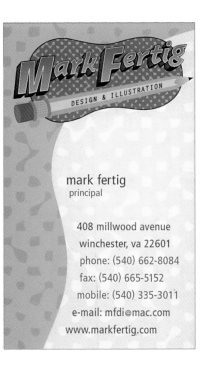

Mark Fertig
DESIGN & ILLUSTRATION

mark fertig
principal

408 millwood avenue

winchester, va 22601

phone: (540) 662-8084

fax: (540) 665-5152

mobile: (540) 335-3011

e-mail: mfdi@mac.com

www.markfertig.com

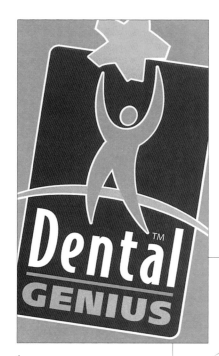

1.

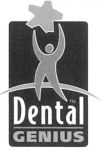

Teresa Blanton

1227 Tara Ridge Drive
Collierville, TN 38017

toll free: (866) 332–6224
phone: (901) 210–3039
fax: (800) 404–3895

teresa@dentalgenius.com
www.dentalgenius.com

Your Genius At Work

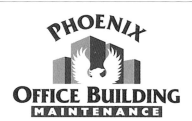

ROD M. EGNASH

13040 N. 48th Place • Scottsdale AZ 85254-3517
voice: (602) 826-9147 • fax: (602) 953-7325
e-mail: phxofficemaint@aol.com • www.phxofficemaint.com

2.

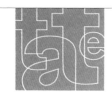

Kurt Winters
Partner
kwinters@tatecapital.com

TATE CAPITAL PARTNERS

PO Box 24499
Minneapolis, Minnesota 55424

T 612 210 1940

3.

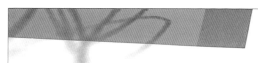

Joe Culligan
President
jculligan@cva.edu

COLLEGE of VISUAL ARTS
344 Summit Ave, St Paul, Minnesota 55102
T 651.224.3416 F 651.224.8854 www.cva.edu

4.

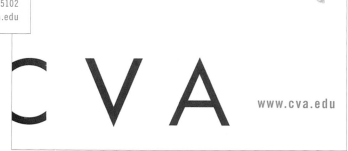

www.cva.edu

John Farrell
john@johnfarrell.biz

John Farrell, LLC
18050 Langford Blvd
Jordan, MN 55352

TEL 651 690 10
CELL 651 331 99
FAX 888 522 29
www.johnfarrell

5.

work relationships that _____

mesh　　click　　win　　rock　　work

p s y m a r k
COMMUNICATIONS

33 MAIN STREET

OLD SAYBROOK CT 06475

phone 860.395.0512　　fax 860.395.0514

THOMAS G. FOWLER
PARTNER

tom@psymark.com

6.

**I N U A
G A L L E R Y**

NORTHERN INDIGENOUS ART
AND ANTIQUITIES

THOMAS G. FOWLER
NINE WEBBS HILL ROAD
STAMFORD, CT 06903 USA

P 203-329-1105
F 203-847-1138
E TGF@INUAGALLERY.COM
W WWW.INUAGALLERY.COM

7.

TOM FOWLER, INC.
Graphic Communicators

ELIZABETH P. BALL
VICE PRESIDENT

111 WESTPORT AVENUE
NORWALK, CONNECTICUT 06851
T: 203·845·0700 EXT: 11
F: 203·846·6682
E: LIZ@TOMFOWLERINC.COM
W: TOMFOWLERINC.COM

8.

(1,2)
Design Firm **MFDI**
(3-5)
Design Firm **Larsen**
(6-8)
Design Firm **Tom Fowler, Inc.**

1.
　Client　　Dental Genius
　Designer　Mark Fertig
2.
　Client　　Phoenix Office
　　　　　　Building Maintenance
　Designer　Mark Fertig
3.
　Client　　Tate Capital
　Designers　Jo Davison,
　　　　　　Bill Pflipsen,
　　　　　　Jules Miller
4.
　Client　　College of Visual Arts
　Designers　Nancy Whittlesey,
　　　　　　Nick Zdon,
　　　　　　Liina Koukkari
5.
　Client　　Farrell
　Designers　Jo Davison,
　　　　　　Mark Saunders,
　　　　　　Trish Adams

6.
　Client　　Psymark Communications
　Designers　Thomas G. Fowler,
　　　　　　Brien O'Reilly
7.
　Client　　Inua Gallery
　Designer　Thomas G. Fowler
8.
　Client　　Tom Fowler, Inc.
　Designer　Thomas G. Fowler

1.

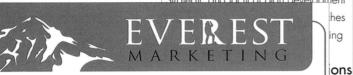

EVEREST
MARKETING

Mike Aistrup

957 Ashland Avenue
St. Paul, MN 55104-7019
651-222-2660
Mobile 612-581-1333

2.

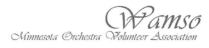

Wamso
Minnesota Orchestra Volunteer Association

Karen Walkowski
Executive Director

1111 Nicollet Mall
Minneapolis, MN
55403-2477
p. 612.371.5694
f. 612.371.7176
email. kwalkows@mnorch.org

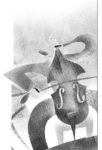

3.

jeff kaphingst
designer/webmaster

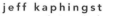

SPANGLERDESIGNTEAM

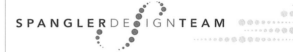

P: 952-927-5425 F: 952-927-7034
415 BLAKE ROAD NORTH HOPKINS, MINNESOTA 55343
E: JEFF@SPANGLERDESIGN.COM
WWW.SPANGLERDESIGN.COM

4.

make the city your home

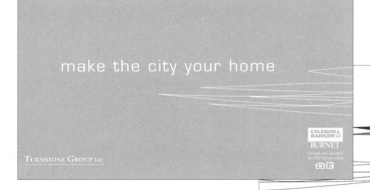

TURNSTONE GROUP llc

COLDWELL BANKER
BURNET
Owned and operated by NRT Incorporated

RIVERWEST

make the city your home

e: info@riverwestliving.com
401 south first street, minneapolis, minnesota 55401
p: 612.436.7600 **f:** 612.436.7601 **w:** riverwestliving.com

5.

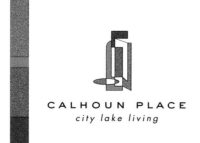

CALHOUN PLACE
city lake living

DREW PALMER

3131 excelsior boulevard
minneapolis, minnesota 55416
ph: (612) 922.3111
f: (612) 922.3115
e: djpalmer@cbburnet.com
www.calhounplace.com

COLDWELL BANKER
BURNET
Owned and Operated By NRT Incorporated

www.calhounplace.com

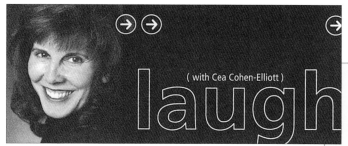

(with Cea Cohen-Elliott)

laugh

To schedule a presentation with Cea, please contact her at the following numbers:

☎ 937.429.9201

✉ 2370 Clubside Drive Dayton, Ohio 45431

more

(laughter is Cea's prescription for life!)

6.

| cerebral solutions |

design

[cheryl roder-quill

angryporcupine_design
1720 creekside lane
park city utah 84098
435 655 0645 tel
435 604 6970 fax
angryporcupine.com

angryporcupine

7.

breathe 408 **921 2307**

315½ University Avenue
Los Gatos, CA 95032

Your next appointment is

Date _____

Time _____

Please give 24 hours notice for cancellations.

breathe
healing, skin & body treatments

Kimberly Kutler
licensed esthetician
certified Reiki &
massage practitioner

8.

1.

STREAMWORKS
CONSULTING

Brent Ramsby | President / CEO

4096 Piedmont Avenue   877.919.6700 ext. 501
Suite 206   510.919.6700 mobile
Oakland, CA 94611   877.919.6700 fax

www.streamworksconsulting.com
brent@streamworksconsulting.com

2.

the
organization
it pays to be organized.

Cindy Gunderson
Professional Organizer

3548 Eagle Beach Circle
Port Clinton Ohio 43452

419 732 1560
shadgun@infinet.com

3.

TANDLÆGE
PETER JERLANG

Lipkesgade 14
2100 København Ø
tel: 35-26-04-14

4.

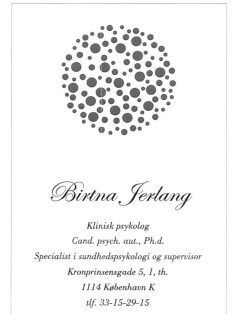

Birtna Jerlang

Klinisk psykolog
Cand. psych. aut., Ph.d.
Specialist i sundhedspsykologi og supervisor
Kronprinsensgade 5, 1, th.
1114 København K
tlf. 33-15-29-15

5.

communications

[BBC]

JØNSTERUDVEIEN 32
FIEMYR, NORWAY
00410   F. 66 80 04 11
YCE@BRYCE.NO

t, art director

SPIKE SAYS

THERE'S NO BUSINESS LIKE DOG BUSINESS.

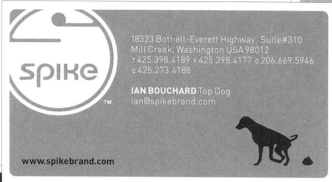

6.

SPIKE SAYS

IT'S RAINING CATS AND DOGS AND I JUST STEPPED IN A POODLE. THANK YOU, GOODNIGHT.

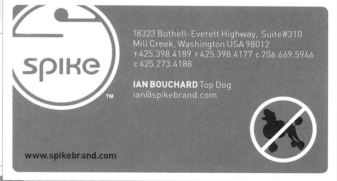

SPIKE SAYS

JUST SAY "NO" TO BIG HAIR.

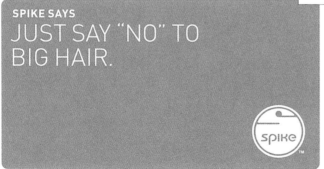

(1,2)
Design Firm **angryporcupine_design**
(3,4)
Design Firm **AD WORKS**
(5)
Design Firm **Bryce Bennett Communications**
(6)
Design Firm **Karacters Design Group**

1.
Client   StreamWorks Consulting
Designer Cheryl Roder-Quill
2.
Client   the organization
Designer Cheryl Roder-Quill
3.
Client   Peter Jerlang, Tandlaege
Designer Anna Björnsdóttir

4.
Client   Birtna Jerlang,
           Klinisk Psykolog
Designer Anna Björnsdóttir
5.
Client   Bryce Bennett Communications
6.
Client   Spike
Designer Jeff Harrison

251

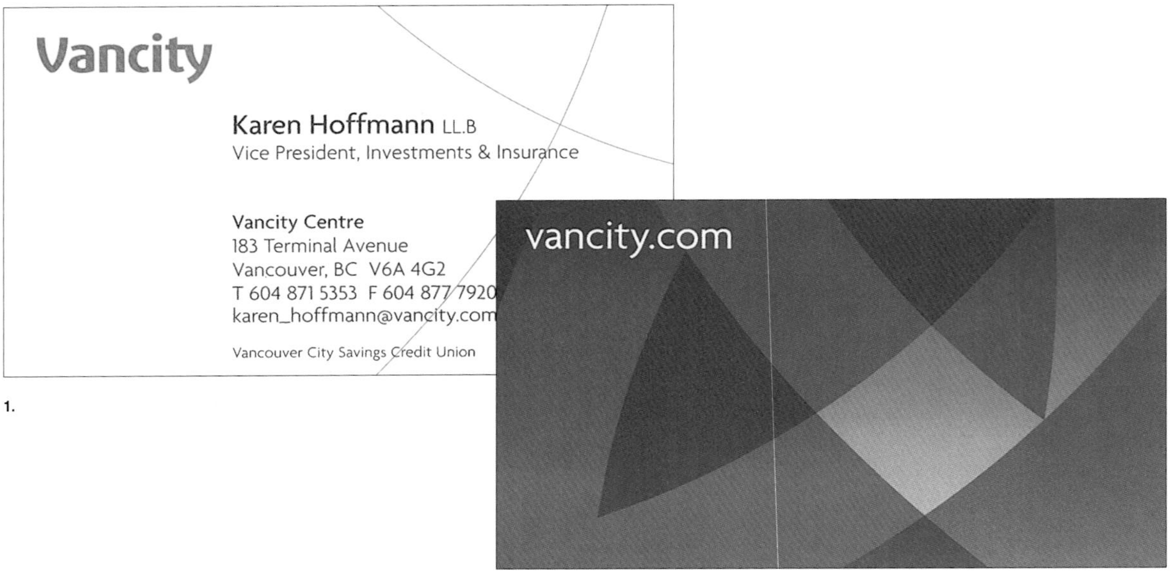

Vancity

Karen Hoffmann LL.B
Vice President, Investments & Insurance

Vancity Centre
183 Terminal Avenue
Vancouver, BC V6A 4G2
T 604 871 5353 F 604 877 7920
karen_hoffmann@vancity.com

Vancouver City Savings Credit Union

vancity.com

1.

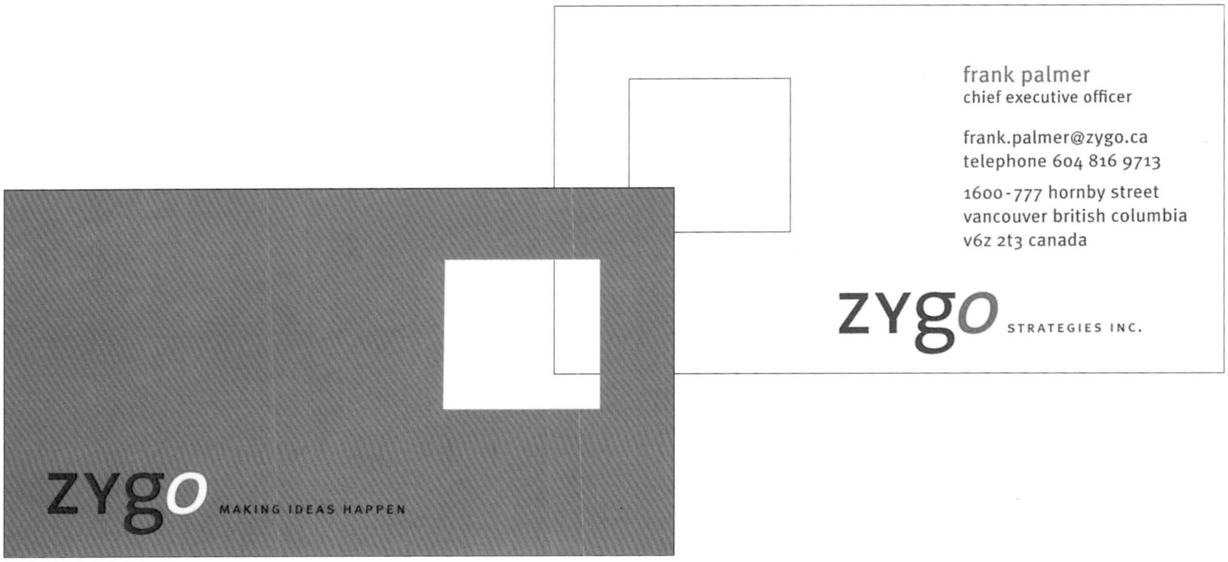

frank palmer
chief executive officer

frank.palmer@zygo.ca
telephone 604 816 9713

1600-777 hornby street
vancouver british columbia
v6z 2t3 canada

ZYGO STRATEGIES INC.

ZYGO MAKING IDEAS HAPPEN

2.

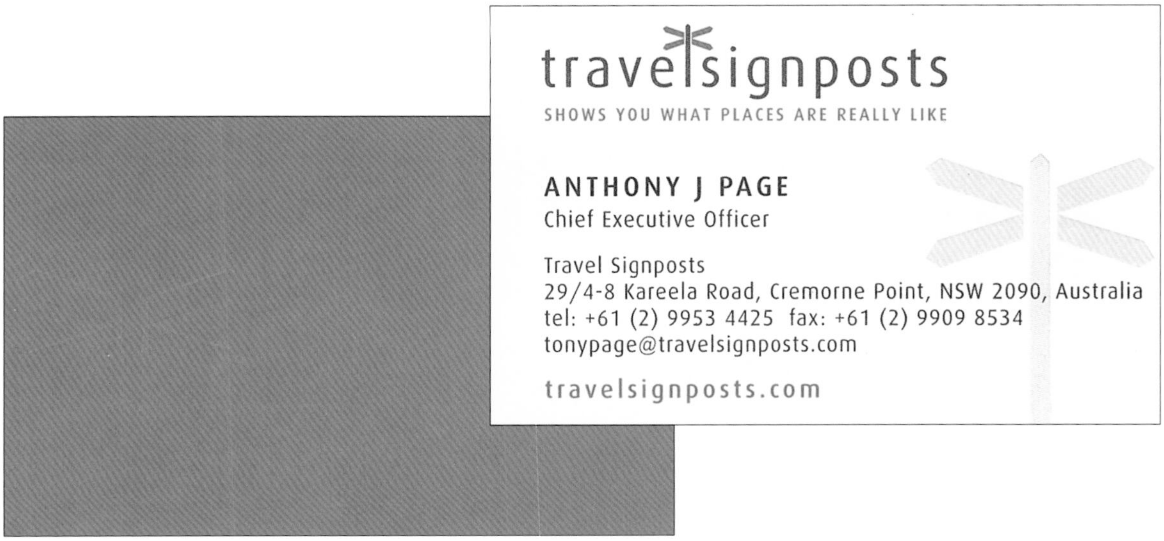

travelsignposts
SHOWS YOU WHAT PLACES ARE REALLY LIKE

ANTHONY J PAGE
Chief Executive Officer

Travel Signposts
29/4-8 Kareela Road, Cremorne Point, NSW 2090, Australia
tel: +61 (2) 9953 4425 fax: +61 (2) 9909 8534
tonypage@travelsignposts.com

travelsignposts.com

3.

MALMSTROM
ASSOCIATES
ORIENT

KARIN MALMSTROM
CEO

Hong Kong tel +852 9135 5435
Beijing tel +86 1360 125 0297
karin@malmstrom.biz

4.

毛 東 行

董
事
長

毛
凱
琳

...M ASSOCIATES ORIENT CO. LTD.
Communications Consultancy
毛東行有限公司—市場策劃顧問

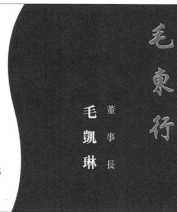

MICHAEL TANG
DIRECTOR

CORPORATE ID
ASSET MANAGEMENT LIMITED

SUITE 701, BARTLOCK CENTRE
3 YIU WA STREET
CAUSEWAY BAY
HONG KONG

TELEPHONE 2831 9902
FACSIMILE   2831 9907

5.

CORPORATE ID

鄧 子 豪
董事

高達物資管理有限公司

香港銅鑼灣耀華街3號百樂中心701室
電話 2831 9902
傳真 2831 9907

KODIT
Means you keep it!

AUTHORISED DISTRIBUTORS OF
KODIT SECURITY TAGGING AND
ASSET IDENTIFICATION SYSTEMS

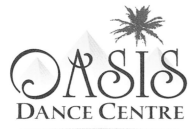

OASIS
DANCE CENTRE

MEY JEN STAGE PRODUCTIONS

BELLY DANCE ◆ FLAMENCO ◆ HAWAIIAN
CLASSES ◆ COSTUMES ◆ SHOWS ◆ STUDIO HIRE

6.

珍

(OPPOSITE PACIFIC PLACE 3)
1 Anton Street
Wanchai
Hong Kong

tel/fax 2522 6698
oasisdance_hk@yahoo.com.hk
www.oasis-dance-centre.com

MEY JEN TILLYER
ARTISTIC DIRECTOR

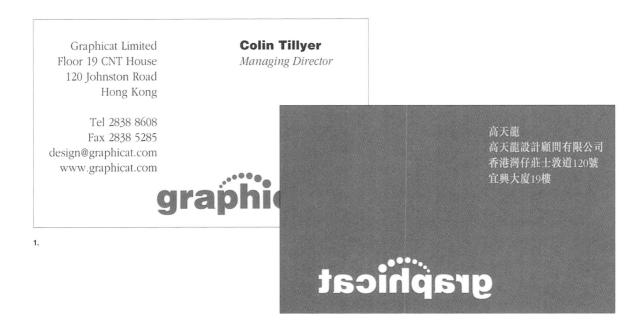

Graphicat Limited
Floor 19 CNT House
120 Johnston Road
Hong Kong

Tel 2838 8608
Fax 2838 5285
design@graphicat.com
www.graphicat.com

Colin Tillyer
Managing Director

高天龍
高天龍設計顧問有限公司
香港灣仔莊士敦道120號
宜興大廈19樓

1.

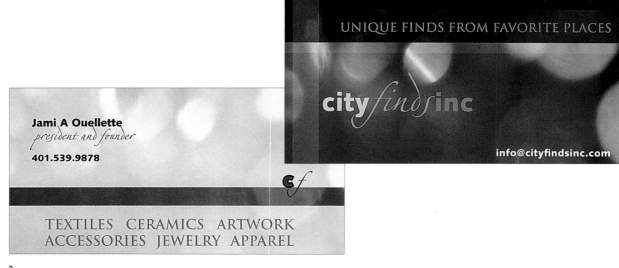

UNIQUE FINDS FROM FAVORITE PLACES

Jami A Ouellette
president and founder
401.539.9878

city*finds*inc

info@cityfindsinc.com

TEXTILES   CERAMICS   ARTWORK
ACCESSORIES   JEWELRY   APPAREL

2.

3.

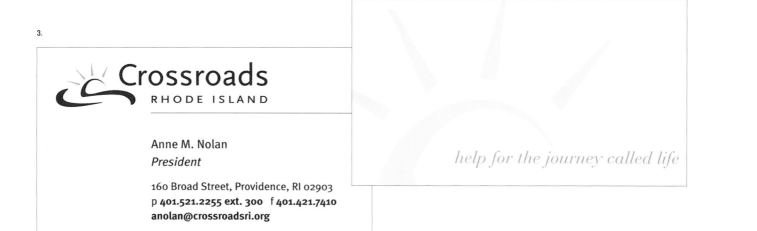

Crossroads
RHODE ISLAND

Anne M. Nolan
President

160 Broad Street, Providence, RI 02903
p **401.521.2255 ext. 300**   f **401.421.7410**
anolan@crossroadsri.org

help for the journey called life

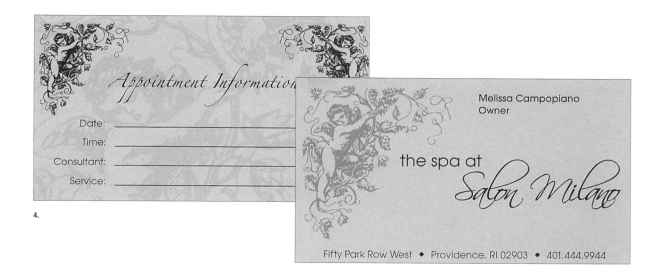

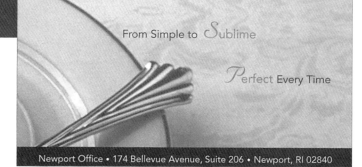

4.

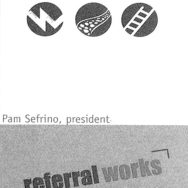

5.

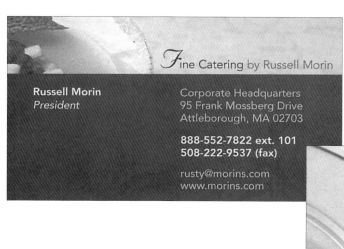

Pre-screened professionals for jobs large and small, inside and out...residential and commercial. All contractors are stringently pre-qualified, licensed and insured.

We match your project or task with the contractors who meet your specific needs.

Builders, Painters, Electricians, Landscapers, Plumbers, Decorators and much more.

Won't cost a dime... just saves you time!

www.referralworksinc.com
referralworks@comcast.net

6.

(1)		
Design Firm	**Graphicat Limited**	
(2–6)		
Design Firm	**Im-aj Communications &** **Design, Inc.**	

1.		
Client	Graphicat Limited
Designer	Colin Tillyer
2.		
Client	City Finds, Inc.
Designer	Jami Ouellette
3.		
Client	Crossroads
Designers	Jami Ouellette, Amy Medina, Katie Wetherby

4.		
Client	The Spa at Salon Milano
Designers	Jami Ouellette, Amy Medina, Katie Wetherby
5.		
Client	Fine Catering by Russell Morin
Designers	Jami Ouellette, Mark Bevington, Lee Kosa
6.		
Client	Referral Works
Designer	Jami Ouellette

rhode island children's crusade

Mary Sylvia Harrison
president and CEO

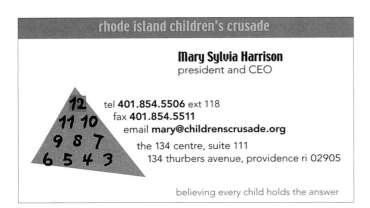

tel **401.854.5506** ext 118
fax **401.854.5511**
email **mary@childrenscrusade.org**

the 134 centre, suite 111
134 thurbers avenue, providence ri 02905

believing every child holds the answer

1.

im-aj communications & design, inc.

Jami A. Ouellette
President and
Creative Director

11 william reynolds farm road
west kingston - rhode island 02892
t **401.539.9886** f **401.539.9879**
email jami@imajcommunications.com

2.

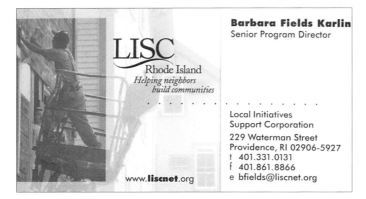

Barbara Fields Karlin
Senior Program Director

LISC
Rhode Island
Helping neighbors
build communities

Local Initiatives
Support Corporation
229 Waterman Street
Providence, RI 02906-5927
t 401.331.0131
f 401.861.8866
e bfields@liscnet.org
www.**liscnet**.org

3.

PETE'S
LADIES
& MENS
ALTERATIONS

6309 Roswell Road
Suite 2F
Atlanta, Georgia 30328
404-256-3653

4.

5.

THE TAPESTRY GROUP

SUSAN JONES MILLER
GENERAL CONTRACTOR
404.787.7499
FAX: 770.594.8983

ERIC DATRY
Owner

SELIQUEY PLANTATION
814 MCMATH MILL ROAD
AMERICUS, GEORGIA 31719
T: 229.924.5470
C: 404.931.2698

SOUTHERN UPLANDS, LLC

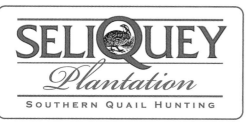

SOUTHERN QUAIL HUNTING

6.

PRESCHOOL

M I N I S T R Y

Linda Pirkle
Assistant

Wieuca Road
Baptist Church
3626 Peachtree Rd, NE
Atlanta, GA 30326
(404) 261-4220

7.

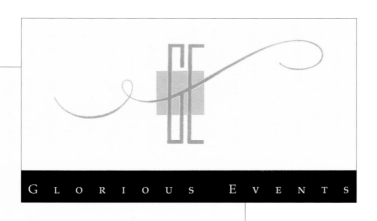

G L O R I O U S   E V E N T S

DIANA HARRIS
PRESIDENT

GLORIOUS EVENTS, INC.
4048 FLOWERS ROAD, SUITE 200
ATLANTA, GA 30360
(404) 455-6600
FAX: (404) 455-6744

8.

(1-3)
Design Firm **Im-aj Communications & Design, Inc.**

(4-8)
Design Firm **Young & Martin Design**

1.
Client   Rhode Island Children's Crusade
Designers   Jami Ouellette,
             Robin Gerardi-Sarro

2.
Client   Im-aj Communications &
             Design, Inc.
Designer   Jami Ouellette

3.
Client   LISC Rhode Island
Designers   Jami Ouellette,
             Robin Gerardi-Sarro

4.
Client   Pete's Ladies &
             Mens Alterations
Designer   Young & Martin Design

5.
Client   The Tapestry Group
Designer   Young & Martin Design

6.
Client   Seliquey Plantation
Designer   Young & Martin Design

7.
Client   Wieuca Road Baptist
             Church
Designer   Young & Martin Design

8.
Client   Glorious Events
Designer   Young & Martin Design

257

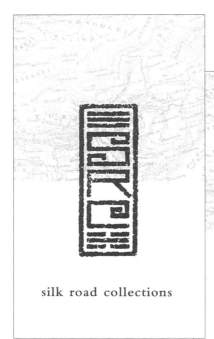

Marcia Shawler

Silk Road Collections, Inc.
411 Pembrooke Circle
Alpharetta, Georgia 30004

770.569.1256 fax
770.569.8133

silk road collections

1.

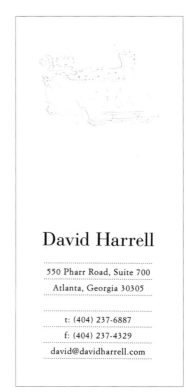

David Harrell

550 Pharr Road, Suite 700
Atlanta, Georgia 30305

t: (404) 237-6887

f: (404) 237-4329

david@davidharrell.com

2.

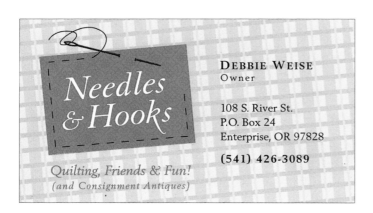

Needles & Hooks

Quilting, Friends & Fun!
(and Consignment Antiques)

DEBBIE WEISE
Owner

108 S. River St.
P.O. Box 24
Enterprise, OR 97828

(541) 426-3089

3.

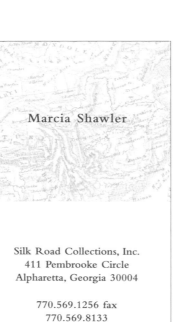

Mad Mary & Company

Everything
Fun & Fattening!

Mary Burns
Owner

5 S. Main Street
P.O. Box 199
Joseph, Oregon 97846

(541) 432-0547
1-866-432-0547
fax: (541) 432-0549

www.madmaryandcompany.com

4.

RED BARN
VETERINARY

Comprehensive Medicine & Surgery
Farm & Companion Animals

Karl D. Zwanziger, DVM
65254 Pine Tree Road · Enterprise, Oregon 97828
Office: (541) 426-3832 **Cell:** (541) 398-1217 **Fax:** (541) 426-3836
E-mail: drkarl@gocougs.wsu.edu

5.

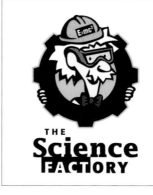

THE
Science
FACTORY

• 2300 Leo Harris Parkway
• P.O. Box 1518
• Eugene, OR 97440
   (541) 682-7888 •
fax: (541) 484-9027 •
sciencefactory.org

6.

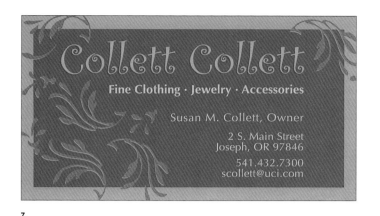

7.

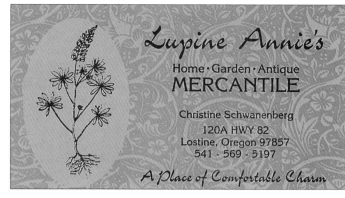

8.

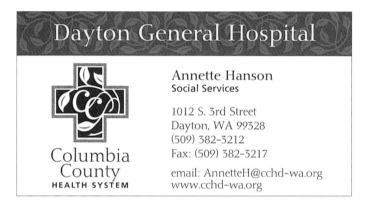

9.

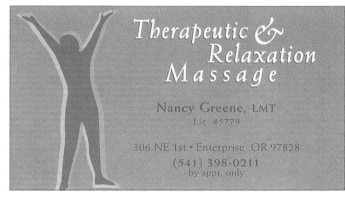

10.

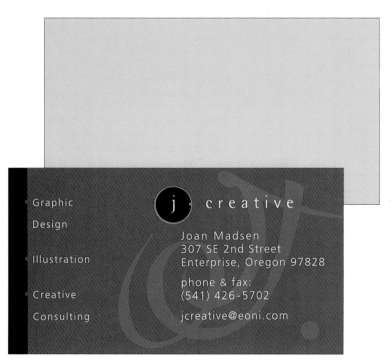

11.

(1,2)		
Design Firm	**Young & Martin Design**	
(3-11)		
Design Firm	**j. creative**	

1.
Client	Silk Road Collections, Inc.
Designer	Young & Martin Design

2.
Client	David Harrell
Designer	Young & Martin Design

3.
Client	Needles & Hooks
Designer	Joan Madsen

4.
Client	Mad Mary & Company
Designer	Joan Madsen

5.
Client	Red Barn Veterinary
Designer	Joan Madsen

6.
Client	The Science Factory
Designer	Joan Madsen

7.
Client	Collett Collett
Designer	Joan Madsen

8.
Client	Lupine Annie's
Designer	Joan Madsen

9.
Client	Dayton General Hospital
Designer	Joan Madsen

10.
Client	Therapeutic & Relaxation Massage
Designer	Joan Madsen

11.
Client	j. creative
Designer	Joan Madsen

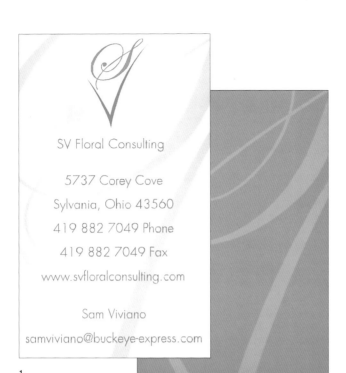

SV Floral Consulting

5737 Corey Cove

Sylvania, Ohio 43560

419 882 7049 Phone

419 882 7049 Fax

www.svfloralconsulting.com

Sam Viviano

samviviano@buckeye-express.com

1.

Lawrence P. Schmakel, DDS
Oral Surgeon

General and Cosmetic Dentistry

709 Madison Avenue
315 Bell Building
Toledo, Ohio 43624
419.241.3757

2.

Racing for Recovery
A non-profit organization

6936 Clare Court
Sylvania, Ohio 43560
419-824-8462 phone
419-824-8473 fax
www.racingforrecovery.com

Todd Crandell
racing4recovery@aol.com

3.

Racing for Recovery™

Rob Pettrey
President

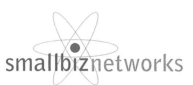

728 W Samaria Rd
Temperance, MI 48182
419.466.0248 phone
rob@smallbiznetworks.biz
www.smallbiznetworks.biz

network solutions for small businesses

4.

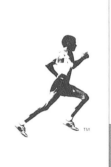

www.smallbiznetworks.biz

260

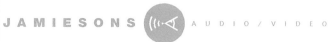

Ric Clark

Vice President

JAMIESONS AUDIO / VIDEO

5421 Monroe Street   **419 882 2571**

Toledo, Ohio 43623   c 419 351 5420

ric@jamiesonsaudiovideo.com   f 419 841 8303

5.

Hear. See. Believe.

www.jamiesonsaudiovideo.com

Of Learning

The Power

tps.org

Toledo Public Schools

420 E. Manhattan Blvd.
Toledo, Ohio 43608-1267
419.729.8281
419.729.8392 Fax

Eugene T. W. Sanders, Ph.D.
Superintendent and CEO

6.

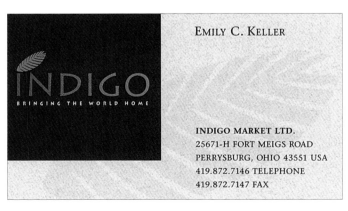

EMILY C. KELLER

INDIGO
BRINGING THE WORLD HOME

INDIGO MARKET LTD.
25671-H FORT MEIGS ROAD
PERRYSBURG, OHIO 43551 USA
419.872.7146 TELEPHONE
419.872.7147 FAX

7.

(1-7)
Design Firm **Lesniewicz Associates**

1.
Client   SV Floral Consulting
Designer   Amy Lesniewicz
2.
Client   Schmakel Dentistry
Designer   Les Adams
3.
Client   Racing for Recovery
Designer   Amy Lesniewicz
4.
Client   Small Biz Networks
Designer   Jack Bollingers
5.
Client   Jamiesons Audio/Video
Designer   Jack Bollingers
6.
Client   Toledo Public Schools
Designer   Les Adams
7.
Client   Indigo
Designer   Jack Bollingers

1.

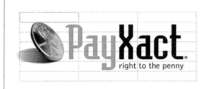

right to the penny

5535 Greenridge Drive
Toledo, Ohio 43615
p 419.343.0776
f 419.868.1736
tyost@payxact.com
www.payxact.com

Todd W. Yost
President

2.

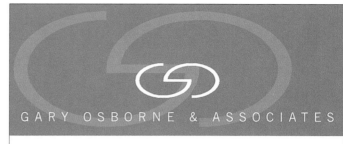

GARY OSBORNE & ASSOCIATES

Medical Malpractice Attorneys
7150 Granite Circle
Toledo, Ohio 43617

Gary W. Osborne
go@garyosbornelaw.com
419.842.8200

3.

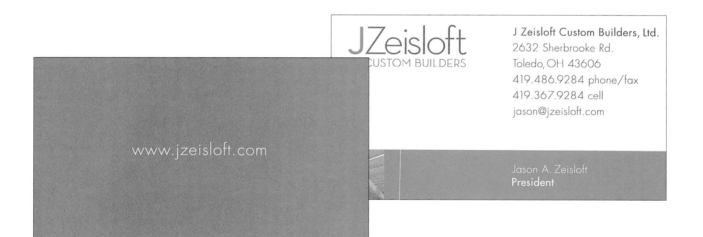

www.jzeisloft.com

JZeisloft
CUSTOM BUILDERS

J Zeisloft Custom Builders, Ltd.
2632 Sherbrooke Rd.
Toledo, OH 43606
419.486.9284 phone/fax
419.367.9284 cell
jason@jzeisloft.com

Jason A. Zeisloft
President

4.

Alliance Venture Mortgage, LLC
3600 Briarfield Blvd. Suite 100
Maumee, Ohio 43537
MB#1888
419.930.5656 phone
419.930.5627 fax
419.704.5656 mobile

 Alliance Venture Mortgage

Gregory L. Cepek
Partner/Lending Consultant
gcepek@AVMHomeLoan.com

www.avmhomeloan.com

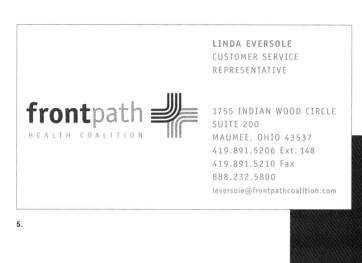

frontpath
HEALTH COALITION

LINDA EVERSOLE
CUSTOMER SERVICE
REPRESENTATIVE

1755 INDIAN WOOD CIRCLE
SUITE 200
MAUMEE, OHIO 43537
419.891.5206 Ext. 148
419.891.5210 Fax
888.232.5800
leversole@frontpathcoalition.com

5.

www.frontpathcoalition.com

WWW.GRROM.COM

GRROM
P.O. Box 250583
Franklin, MI 48025
Hotline 248.988.0154
www.grrom.com

GOLDEN RETRIEVER RESCUE OF MICHIGAN

Laura Culp

6.

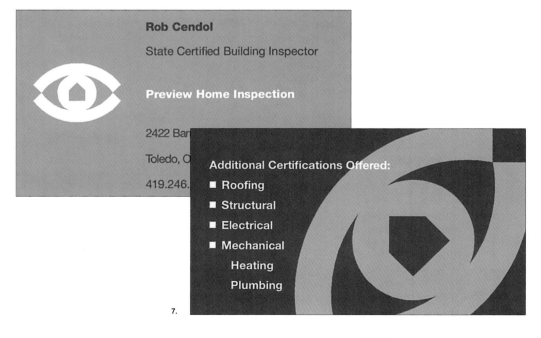

Rob Cendol

State Certified Building Inspector

Preview Home Inspection

2422 Bar

Toledo, O

419.246.

Additional Certifications Offered:

■ Roofing
■ Structural
■ Electrical
■ Mechanical
　Heating
　Plumbing

7.

(1-7)
Design Firm **Lesniewicz Associates**

1.
Client　PayXact
Designer　Jack Bollingers
2.
Client　Gary Osborne & Associates
Designer　Jack Bollingers
3.
Client　J Zeisloft Custom Builders
Designer　Amy Lesniewicz
4.
Client　Alliance Venture Mortgage
Designer　Amy Lesniewicz
5.
Client　Frontpath
Designer　Jack Bollingers
6.
Client　Golden Retriever Rescue
　　　　of Michigan
Designer　Amy Lesniewicz
7.
Client　Preview Home Inspection
Designer　Amy Lesniewicz

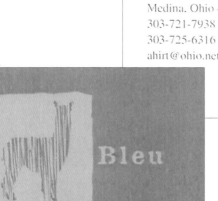

Erie Bleu
AlpacaFarm
1020 Gentry
Medina, Ohio 44256
303-721-7938 phone
303-725-6316 fax
ahirt@ohio.net

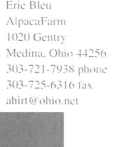

1.

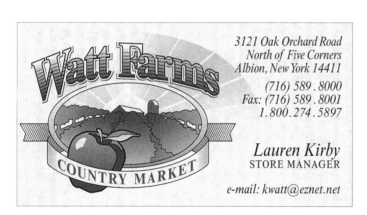

3121 Oak Orchard Road
North of Five Corners
Albion, New York 14411

(716) 589.8000
Fax: (716) 589.8001
1.800.274.5897

Lauren Kirby
STORE MANAGER

e-mail: kwatt@eznet.net

3.

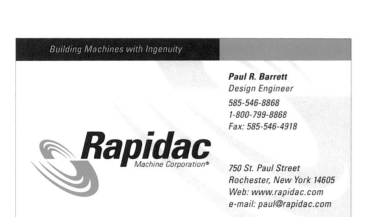

Building Machines with Ingenuity

Paul R. Barrett
Design Engineer

585-546-8868
1-800-799-8868
Fax: 585-546-4918

750 St. Paul Street
Rochester, New York 14605
Web: www.rapidac.com
e-mail: paul@rapidac.com

5.

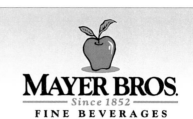

MAYER BROS.
Since 1852
FINE BEVERAGES

KENT WAKEFIELD
PLANT SUPERINTENDENT-SOMERSET DIVISION

P.O. Box 277, 7389 Lake Road, Barker, New York 14012
716.795.9930 ext.1   Fax 716.795.3901
www.mayerbrothers.com

2.

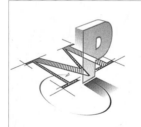

McElveney & Palozzi
DESIGN GROUP INC.

1255 University Avenue - Suite 200
Rochester, New York 14607
(585) 473-7630   fax (585) 473-9506

Gloria Kreitzberg

gloriak@mandpdesign.com   **ACCOUNT**EXECUTIVE

4.

Quality Vision Services, Inc.
1175 North Street
Rochester, New York 14621 USA
716-555-1212 Fax: 716-555-1313
www.qvsmeasurement.com

Frederick Mason
Marketing Communications Manager

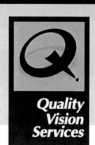

6.

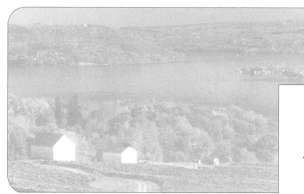

7.

Beulah Decker
Marketing

NEW YORK'S *Finger Lakes*

Finger Lakes Tourism
309 Lake Street
Penn Yan, New York 14527
Phone: 315.536.7488 ext. 16
800.530.7488
Fax: 315.536.1237
www.fingerlakes.org   beulahd@fingerlakes.org

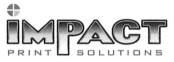

PAT.DUGGAN@IMPACTPRINTSOLUTIONS.COM

iMPACT
PRINT SOLUTIONS

PATRICK J. DUGGAN
PRESIDENT

306 STAFFORD WAY
ROCHESTER, NY 14626
PHONE: (585) 227-6850 FAX: (585) 227-6939

FORMS
LABELS
INDUSTRIAL SILK SCREENING
APPAREL

8.

WORLD CLASS PINOT NOIR FROM THE NIAGARA ESCARPMENT

Warm Lake Estate V
3868 Lower Mountain R
www.WarmL

9.

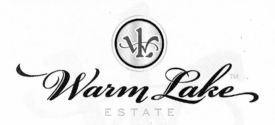

Warm Lake ™
ESTATE

Michael J. VonHeckler
Certified Wine Judge · Diploma in Wine
office 716.731.5900 cell 716.471.5108
fax 716.731.2926

(1)
Design Firm **Lesniewicz Associates**
(2-9)
Design Firm **McElveney & Palozzi**
Design Group, Inc.

1.
Client — Erie Bleu Alpaca Farm
Designer — Amy Lesniewicz
2.
Client — Mayer Bros.
Designers — Lisa Parenti, Bill McElveney
3.
Client — Watt Farms
Designer — Steve Palozzi
4.
Client — McElveney & Palozzi Design
Group, Inc.
Designers — Bill McElveney, Steve Palozzi
5.
Client — Rapidac Machine Corporation
Designers — Matt Nowicki, Lisa Gates
6.
Client — Quality Vision Services, Inc.
Designer — Matt Nowicki
7.
Client — Finger Lakes Tourism
Designer — Matt Nowicki
8.
Client — Impact Print Solutions
Designer — Matt Nowicki
9.
Client — Warm Lake Estate
Designer — Mike Johnson

OUR MISSION

To maintain our stature as a first-class resort and
conference center dedicated to consistently providing
our guests with outstanding personal service
and exceptional quality

THE LODGE AT
Woodcliff

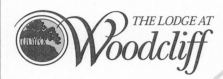

199 Woodcliff Drive
Box 22850
Rochester, NY 14692
Ph. (716) 381-4000
Fax (716) 381-2673

Peter R. McCrossen, C.H.A.
General Manager
(716) 248-4820

e-Mail:pmccrossen@woodclifflodge.com
Visit us at: www.woodclifflodge.com

1.

RIVEREDGE
RESORT

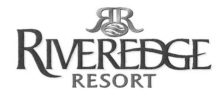

John J. Doe ◆ Director of Sales

17 Holland Street ◆ Alexandria Bay, New York 13607
Phone: 1-800-ENJOY-US ◆ Fax: (315) 482-5010
www.riveredge.com ◆ e-mail: Enjoyus@Riveredge.com

2.

DOCUMENT SECURITY
SYSTEMS | INC.

AMERICAN
STOCK EXCHANGE®
LISTED
DMC™

PATRICK WHITE | PRESIDENT/CEO
PATRICK.WHITE@DOCUMENTSECURITY.COM

WWW.DOCUMENTSECURITY.COM

28 MAIN STREET EAST, SUITE 1525 | ROCHESTER, NY 14614
PH: 585.325.3610 | 1.877.276.0293 | FAX: 585.325.2977

3.

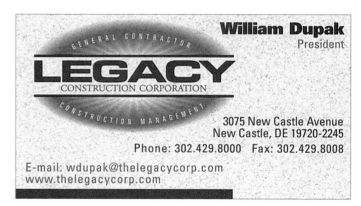

William Dupak
President

LEGACY
CONSTRUCTION CORPORATION

3075 New Castle Avenue
New Castle, DE 19720-2245
Phone: 302.429.8000 Fax: 302.429.8008

E-mail: wdupak@thelegacycorp.com
www.thelegacycorp.com

4.

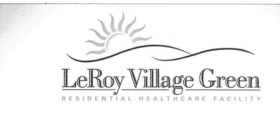

LeRoy Village Green
RESIDENTIAL HEALTHCARE FACILITY

10 Munson Street
LeRoy, New York 14482
(716) 768-2561
Fax (716) 768-4335

Catherine M. Caito
Admissions Coordinator

5.

CPI
BUSINESS GROUPS

Jeff Bruce
MANAGER
MATERIAL CONTROL
Injection Molding

2278 WESTSIDE DRIVE ROCHESTER, NEW YORK 14624-1996
716 . 594 . 9422 Fax: 716 . 594 . 9486

6.

266

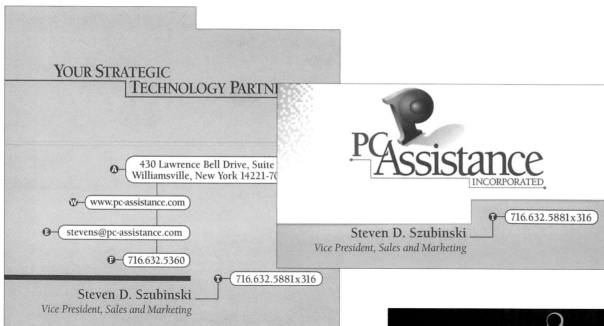

YOUR STRATEGIC
TECHNOLOGY PARTN[...]

Ⓐ 430 Lawrence Bell Drive, Suite
Williamsville, New York 14221-7[...]

Ⓦ www.pc-assistance.com

Ⓔ stevens@pc-assistance.com

Ⓕ 716.632.5360

Ⓣ 716.632.5881x316

Steven D. Szubinski
Vice President, Sales and Marketing

PCAssistance
INCORPORATED.

Ⓣ 716.632.5881x316

Steven D. Szubinski
Vice President, Sales and Marketing

7.

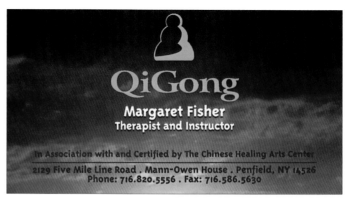

QiGong

Margaret Fisher
Therapist and Instructor

In Association with and Certified by The Chinese Healing Arts Center

2129 Five Mile Line Road . Mann-Owen House . Penfield, NY 14526
Phone: 716.820.5556 . Fax: 716.586.5630

9.

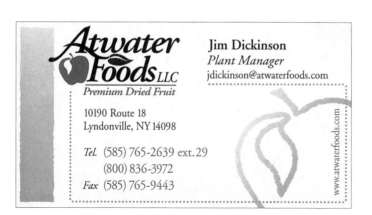

Atwater Foods LLC
Premium Dried Fruit

Jim Dickinson
Plant Manager
jdickinson@atwaterfoods.com

www.atwaterfoods.com

10190 Route 18
Lyndonville, NY 14098

Tel. (585) 765-2639 ext.29
(800) 836-3972
Fax (585) 765-9443

8.

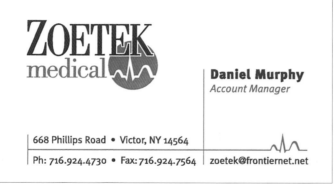

ZOETEK
medical

Daniel Murphy
Account Manager

668 Phillips Road • Victor, NY 14564

Ph: 716.924.4730 • Fax: 716.924.7564 | zoetek@frontiernet.net

10.

(1-10)
Design Firm **McElveney & Palozzi**
Design Group, Inc.

1.
Client   The Lodge at Woodcliff
Designers   Ellen Johnson, Bill McElveney
2.
Client   Riveredge Resort
Designer   Lisa Gates
3.
Client   Document Security Systems, Inc.
Designer   Lisa Gates
4.
Client   Legacy Construction Corporation
Designers   Jon Westfall, Matthew Dundon
5.
Client   LeRoy Village Green
Designers   Lisa Parenti, Jan Marie Gallagher
6.
Client   CPI Business Groups
Designer   Jon Westfall
7.
Client   PC Assistance, Inc.
Designer   Lisa Gates
8.
Client   Atwater Foods LLC
Designer   Lisa Gates
9.
Client   Margaret Fisher-QiGong
Designer   Lisa Parenti
10.
Client   Zoetek Medical
Designer   Lisa Gates

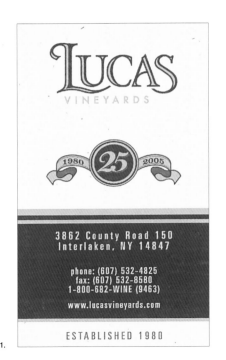

1.

2.

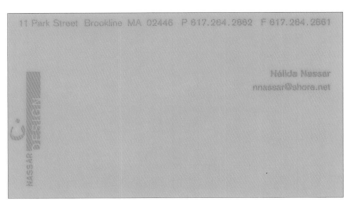

Erica Fawell, Ph.D.
V. P. Business Development

82 West Cedar Street, Suite 8
Boston, Massachusetts 02114
Telephone 617 803.9563

Strand Farm House
Currabinny, County Cork, Ireland
Telephone +353 21 378.117

e-mail ericafawell@westgate.ie

Westgate Biological Ltd.
Mucosal Health

3.

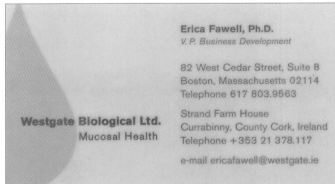

Lisa T. Buyuk

177 Newbury Street
Boston, MA 02116
617 262 · 0780

4.

LINDA CHRISTIAN-HEROT
TREASURER AND CLERK

ARCHIVES FOR
HISTORICAL
DOCUMENTATION

25 ARLINGTON STREET
BRIGHTON, MA 02135-2197
TELEPHONE 617.562.0754
TELEFAX 617.562.0832

5.

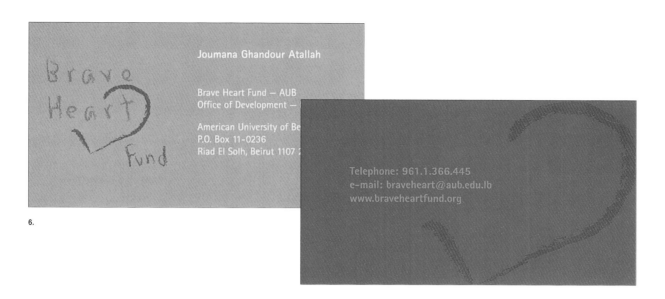

6.

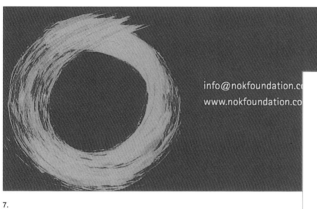

7.

Paula Tursi Executive Director

NOK Foundation Inc
c/o Quest Partners LLC
126 East 56th Street
19th Floor
New York NY 10022

Telephone 212 838.7222
Telefax 212 838.4440

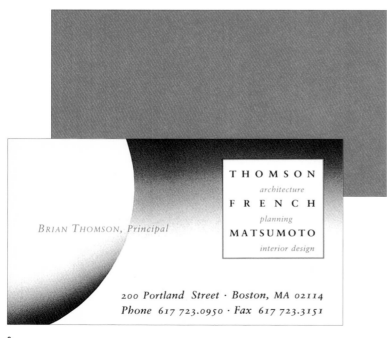

THOMSON
architecture
FRENCH
planning
MATSUMOTO
interior design

BRIAN THOMSON, *Principal*

200 Portland Street · Boston, MA 02114
Phone 617 723.0950 · Fax 617 723.3151

8.

(1)
Design Firm **McElveney & Palozzi Design Group, Inc.**
(2-8)
Design Firm **Nassar Design**

1.
| Client | Lucas Vineyards |
| Designer | Mike Johnson |

2.
| Client | Nassar Design |
| Designers | Nélida Nassar, Margarita Encomienda |

3.
| Client | Westgate Biological Ltd. |
| Designers | Nélida Nassar, Margarita Encomienda |

4.
| Client | Marcoz Antiques · Decorations |
| Designer | Nélida Nassar |

5.
| Client | Archives for Historical Documentation |
| Designer | Nélida Nassar |

6.
| Client | Brave Heart Fund |
| Designers | Nélida Nassar, Margarita Encomienda |

7.
| Client | NOK Foundation Inc. |
| Designers | Nélida Nassar, Jon Walters |

8.
| Client | Thomson French Matsumoto |
| Designer | Nélida Nassar |

FEVZI GANDUR DENIZCILIK A.Ş.

Ali Fuad Gandur

Eski Büyükdere Caddesi Ayazaga Yolu
Iz Giz Plaza   34398   Maslak   Istanbul

P +90 (212) 290 6565   **F** +90 (212) 290 6555
fgm@seahorsenet.com

A Member of
Multiport
Ship Agencies Network

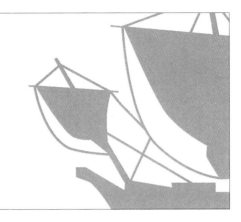

1.

Chris Leary, AIA
Vice President . LEED™ 2.0 Accredited Professional
Architecture

THE
STUBBINS
ASSOCIATES

Architecture | Planning | Interior Design

T 617 491.6450
F 617 491.7104
Direct 617 250.4910

1030 Massachusetts Avenue
Cambridge
Massachusetts 02138-5388

www.stubbins.us
cleary@stubbins.us

The Stubbins Associates, Inc.

2.

CONSULTING

N2

NADINE NASSAR
N2_consulting@yahoo.com

MARKETING STRATEGY . VISUAL DESIGN
231 West 26th Street Suite 6 New York NY 10001 **T** 917 992.8376

3.

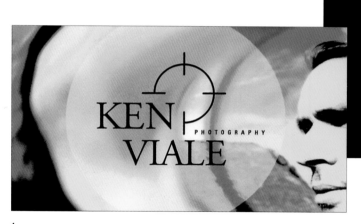

KEN VIALE PHOTOGRAPHY

415 497 1995
photos@kenviale.com

www.kenviale.com

4.

R J MUNA

PICTURES

AMY AUERBA

225 INDUSTRIAL STREET
SAN FRANCISCO, CALIFORNIA
ZIP 94124-8975

415.468.8225 TEL
415.468.8295 FAX
pictures@rjmuna.com NET

5.

still | moving | pictures

Shamrock Ranch
Kennels & Stables

Peter Voskes

Pacifica, CA 94044-4099 t.650.359.1627 f. 650.359.1670

6.

Beach House

BEACH HOUSE
INN & CONFERENCE CENTER

4100 NORTH CABRILLO HIGHWAY
HALF MOON BAY, CALIFORNIA 94019

TEL 415.712.0220
FAX 415.712.0693
800.315.9366

VIEW@BEACH-HOUSE.COM

7.

ach House

ocean lofts

CARRIE FLYNN

OR OF SALES & MARKETING

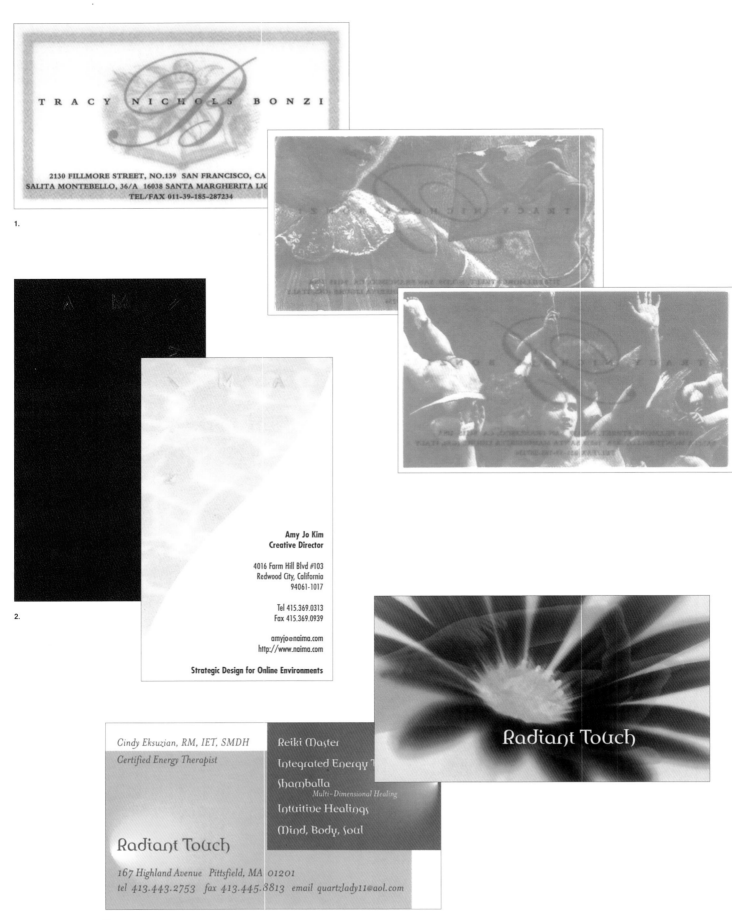

1.

T R A C Y N I C H O L S B O N Z I

2130 FILLMORE STREET, NO.139 SAN FRANCISCO, CA
SALITA MONTEBELLO, 36/A 16038 SANTA MARGHERITA LIG
TEL/FAX 011-39-185-287234

2.

Amy Jo Kim
Creative Director

4016 Farm Hill Blvd #103
Redwood City, California
94061-1017

Tel 415.369.0313
Fax 415.369.0939

amyjo@naima.com
http://www.naima.com

Strategic Design for Online Environments

3.

Cindy Eksuzian, RM, IET, SMDH

Certified Energy Therapist

Reiki Master

Integrated Energy T

Shamballa
Multi-Dimensional Healing

Intuitive Healings

Mind, Body, Soul

Radiant Touch

167 Highland Avenue Pittsfield, MA 01201
tel 413.443.2753 fax 413.445.8813 email quartzlady11@aol.com

Radiant Touch

VINEYARD CREEK HOTEL
Spa & Conference Center

SANDY L. GIBBONS
DIRECTOR OF SALES, MPI

170 Railroad Street
Santa Rosa CA 95401

tel 707.528.4542
fax 707.528.1554
toll free reservations 888.920.000
sgibbons@vineyardcreek.com

4.

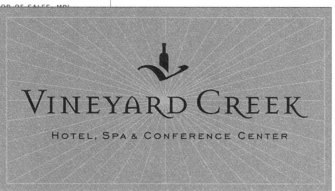

VINEYARD CREEK
HOTEL, SPA & CONFERENCE CENTER

lenox

1278 third ave.
new york 10021
t 212 772 0404
f 212 772 3229
lenoxrestaurant.com

eat.drink.lounge.lenox.

5.

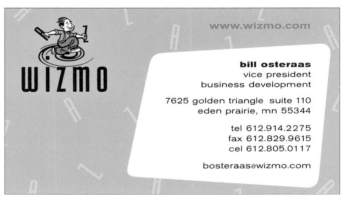

WIZMO

www.wizmo.com

bill osteraas
vice president
business development

7625 golden triangle suite 110
eden prairie, mn 55344

tel 612.914.2275
fax 612.829.9615
cel 612.805.0117

bosteraas@wizmo.com

7.

dog days
Marin Dog Walking Services

Raquel Barrios › Alpha Dog

415-518-4761 raquel@dogdaysmarin.com
{ Insured › Licensed › Bonded }

Ken Viale

6.

(1-7)
Design Firm **Studio Moon**

1.
Client   Tracy Nichols
Designer   Tracy Moon
2.
Client   Amy Jo Kim, NAIMA
Designer   Tracy Moon
3.
Client   Cindy Eksuzian
Designer   Tracy Moon
4.
Client   Vineyard Creek Hotel & Spa
Designers   Tracy Moon,
            Justine Descollonges

5.
Client   Tony Fortuna, Lenox NY
Designers   Tracy Moon,
            Justine Descollonges
6.
Client   Raquel Barrios, Dog Days
Designer   Tracy Moon
7.
Client   Wizmo, Inc.
Designer   Tracy Moon

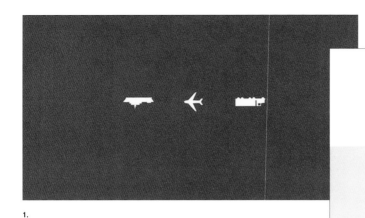

1.

FAB|LOGISTICS
GLOBAL LOGISTICS | AND
TRANSPORTATION SERVICES

THOMAS H. MOON President

437 Rozzi Place N° 112, S. San Francisco, CA 94080
tel 650 827 1050   fax 650 827 1049   cel 415 999 3127
email tmoon@fablogistics.com   www.fablogistics.com

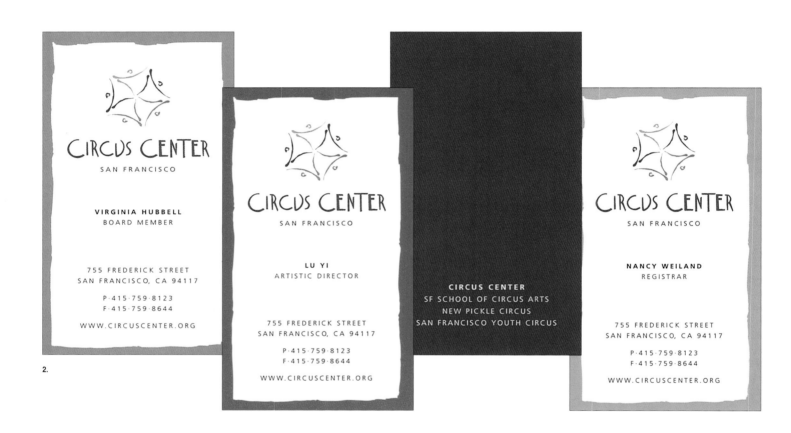

CIRCUS CENTER
SAN FRANCISCO

VIRGINIA HUBBELL
BOARD MEMBER

755 FREDERICK STREET
SAN FRANCISCO, CA 94117

P·415·759·8123
F·415·759·8644

WWW.CIRCUSCENTER.ORG

2.

CIRCUS CENTER
SAN FRANCISCO

LU YI
ARTISTIC DIRECTOR

755 FREDERICK STREET
SAN FRANCISCO, CA 94117

P·415·759·8123
F·415·759·8644

WWW.CIRCUSCENTER.ORG

CIRCUS CENTER
SF SCHOOL OF CIRCUS ARTS
NEW PICKLE CIRCUS
SAN FRANCISCO YOUTH CIRCUS

CIRCUS CENTER
SAN FRANCISCO

NANCY WEILAND
REGISTRAR

755 FREDERICK STREET
SAN FRANCISCO, CA 94117

P·415·759·8123
F·415·759·8644

WWW.CIRCUSCENTER.ORG

FORMIKA FILMS

JACOB ROSENBERG

7245 HILLSIDE AVE. #211
LOS ANGELES, CALIFORNIA 90046-2360
VOICE 888.414.0387 EMAIL jacob@formikafilms.com
WEB www.formikafilms.com

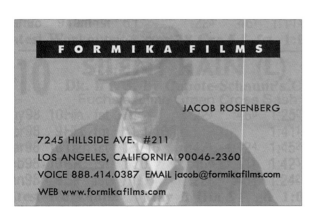

3.

GERALD A. EMANUEL
L A W   O F F I C E S

97 East St. James Street Suite 102   San Jose, Ca 95112
Tel 408.286.3710   Fax 408.292.4436

4.

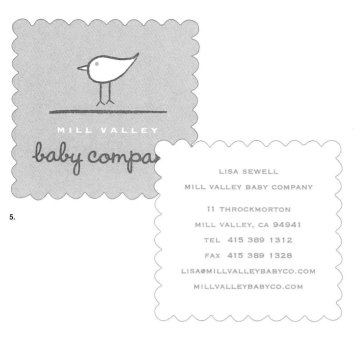

5.

LISA SEWELL

MILL VALLEY BABY COMPANY

11 THROCKMORTON

MILL VALLEY, CA 94941

TEL 415 389 1312

FAX 415 389 1328

LISA@MILLVALLEYBABYCO.COM

MILLVALLEYBABYCO.COM

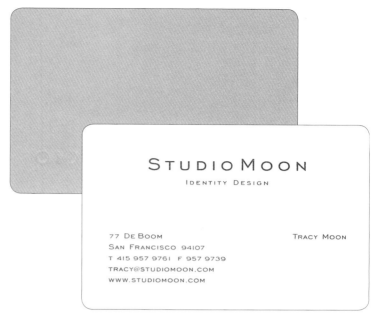

STUDIO MOON
IDENTITY DESIGN

77 DE BOOM   TRACY MOON
SAN FRANCISCO 94107
T 415 957 9761 F 957 9739
TRACY@STUDIOMOON.COM
WWW.STUDIOMOON.COM

6.

Al Chang
VP, Engineering

7 heron street
san francisco 9410

tel 415.503.3600
fax 415.503.3630

al@violet.com
direct 415.503.361

violet™

7.

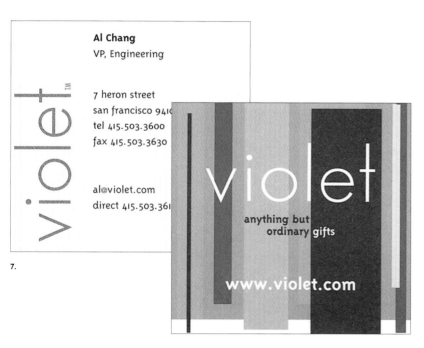

MILL VALLEY KIDS COMPANY

12 MILLER AVENUE

MILL VALLEY, CA 94941

TEL 415 389 1312

FAX 415 389 1328

STORE@MVBABYANDKIDS.COM

...KIDS.COM

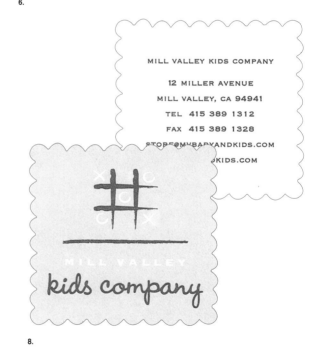

8.

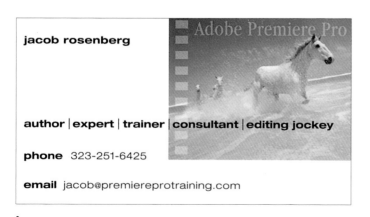

9.

You Have an Appointment With Lisa

Name: _____

Time: _____

Date: _____

t. 650.359.1627   f. 650.359.4
www.shamrockranchkennels.

1.

Shamrock Ranch
Dog Training

Lisa Rhodes
Director of Training

Pacifica, CA 94044-4099   650.359.1627   ext. 308

Calypso
IMAGING

DOUGLAS MADELEY
GENERAL MANAGER

CALYPSO IMAGING, INC.
2000 MARTIN AVENUE
SANTA CLARA, CALIFORNIA
ZIP 95050.2700

VOICE MAIL 408.450.2136

TEL 408.727.2318
TOLL FREE 800.794.2755
FAX 408.727.1705

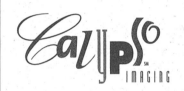

IMAGES/EVERYTHING℠

2.

Peter Douglas
President and CEO

salus media
14529 Dickens Street • Sherman Oaks • California 91403
tel 818.990.0607 • fax 818.990.4408
pdouglas@salus.net

salus media

3.

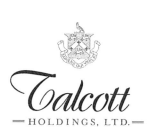

Talcott
═ HOLDINGS, LTD. ═

4.

EPHRAIM GREENWALL

51 FEDERAL STREET SUITE 303 SAN FRANCISCO CA 94107
telephone 415.357.1005 *facsimile* 415.357.1006
egreenwall@talcottholdings.com

C2 team Communication · Coaching · Training

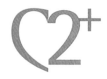

Karin Dölla-Höhfeld

Am Römerberg 38   Fon 0 61 36/95 34 80
D-55270 Essenheim/Mainz   Fax 0 61 36/95 34 84

info@C2team.de · www.C2team.de

5.

Sei, der Du bist und werde,
der Du sein kannst.

Ziegeler
Home & Garden

Andreas Ziegeler
Geschäftsführer

Am Hang 2
27711 Osterholz-Scharmbeck
Fon 0 47 91.96 62-44
Fax 0 47 91.96 62-77
www.ziegeler-web.com
a.ziegeler@ziegeler-web.com

6.

Unsere Filiale im
Haven Höövt Center
in Bremen-Vegesack
www.leichtsinn.com

Leicht*sinn*
Schöner schenken

(1-4)
Design Firm **Studio Moon**
(5,6)
Design Firm **Buttgereit und Heidenreich GmbH**

1.
Client   Lisa Rhodes, Shamrock Ranch
           Dog Training
Designers Tracy Moon,
           Kevin Bonner
2.
Client   Joseph Levine
Designer   Tracy Moon
3.
Client   Peter Douglas
Designers Tracy Moon,
           Justine Descollonges
4.
Client   Talcott Holdings
Designer   Tracy Moon

5.
Client   C2 Team
6.
Client   Ziegeler Home
           & Garden

1.

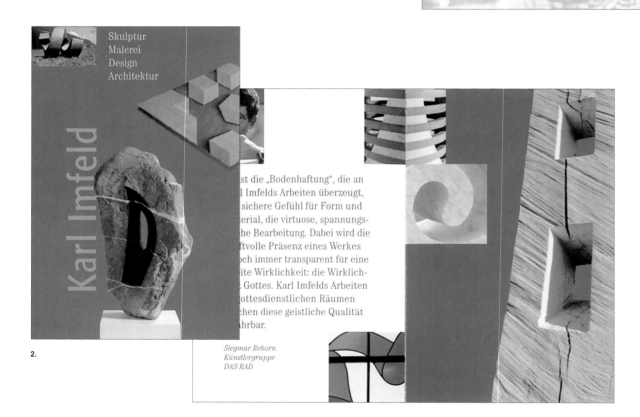

Skulptur
Malerei
Design
Architektur

Karl Imfeld

st die „Bodenhaftung", die an
l Imfelds Arbeiten überzeugt,
sichere Gefühl für Form und
erial, die virtuose, spannungs-
he Bearbeitung. Dabei wird die
ftvolle Präsenz eines Werkes
ch immer transparent für eine
ite Wirklichkeit: die Wirklich-
Gottes. Karl Imfelds Arbeiten
ottesdienstlichen Räumen
chen diese geistliche Qualität
hrbar.

*Siegmar Rehorn
Künstlergruppe
DAS RAD*

2.

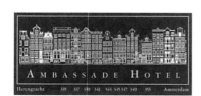
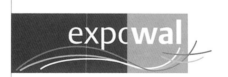
3.

4.

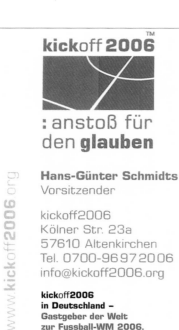

kickoff 2006™

: anstoß für
den **glauben**

Hans-Günter Schmidts
Vorsitzender

kickoff2006
Kölner Str. 23a
57610 Altenkirchen
Tel. 0700-96 97 20 06
info@kickoff2006.org

kickoff2006
in Deutschland –
Gastgeber der Welt
zur Fussball-WM 2006.

www.kickoff2006.org

5.

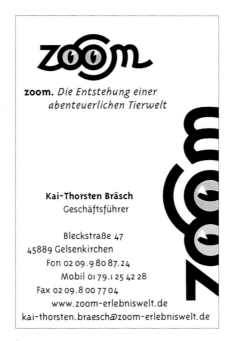

zoom. Die Entstehung einer
abenteuerlichen Tierwelt

Kai-Thorsten Bräsch
Geschäftsführer

Bleckstraße 47
45889 Gelsenkirchen
Fon 02 09. 9 80 87. 24
Mobil 01 79. 1 25 42 28
Fax 02 09. 8 00 77 04
www.zoom-erlebniswelt.de
kai-thorsten. braesch@zoom-erlebniswelt.de

6.

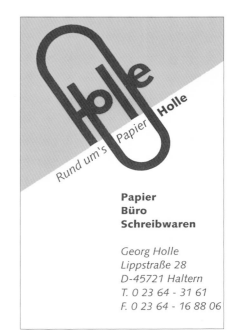

Rund um's Papier Holle

Papier
Büro
Schreibwaren

Georg Holle
Lippstraße 28
D-45721 Haltern
T. 0 23 64 - 31 61
F. 0 23 64 - 16 88 06

7.

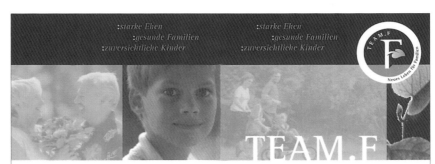

:starke Ehen
:gesunde Familien
:zuversichtliche Kinder

TEAM.F

Christliche Ehe- und
Familienseminare

TEAM.F
Neues Leben für Familien e. V.
Christliche Ehe- und Familienseminare
Honseler Bruch 30 · 58511 Lüdenscheid
Fon 0 23 51. 8 16 86 · Fax 0 23 51. 8 06 64
info@team-f.de · www.team-f.de

Wir sind
für Sie da!

8.

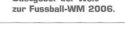

simplify
your life

Michaela Lück
Produktmanagement

Einfacher und glücklicher Leben

VNR Verlag für die
Deutsche Wirtschaft AG
Theodor-Heuss-Str. 2-4
53177 Bonn
Tel.: (02 28) 82 05-73 54
Fax: (02 28) 36 67 07
mlue@vnr.de

9.

(1-9)
Design Firm **Buttgereit und Heidenreich GmbH**

1.
Client Wort und Tat
2.
Client Karl Imfeld
3.
Client Ambassade Hotel
4.
Client expowal
5.
Client Kick Off 2006 TM
6.
Client Zoom
7.
Client Holle
8.
Client Team.F
9.
Client Simplify your life

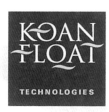

Wouter Schopman
directeur

Koan Float Technologies b.v.
Oude Spiegelstraat 7
1016 BM Amsterdam
Telefoon +31 (0) 20 5 55 03 00
Fax +31 (0) 20 5 55 03 77
info@koan-float.com
www.koan-float.com

1.

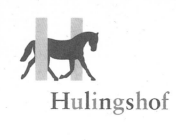

Hulingshof

Andreas Baumann
Pferdewirtschaftsmeister

Klixdorf 51
D-47906 Kempen
Tel.: 0 21 52/5 13 36
Fax: 0 21 52/51 88 82

mail@hulingshof.de
www.hulingshof.de

**Der Ausbildungsstall
für Vielseitigkeits-Pferde.**

2.

Hotel Rössli
Lungern · Zentralschweiz

Hotel Rössli
Familie B. und D. Caluori-Imfeld
CH-6078 Lungern am See
Telefon 041/69 11 71
Fax 041/69 11 81

3.

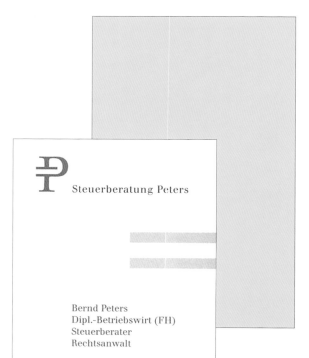

Steuerberatung Peters

Bernd Peters
Dipl.-Betriebswirt (FH)
Steuerberater
Rechtsanwalt

Chemnitzer Straße 11
45699 Herten
Fon 0 23 66/18 07 44
Fax 0 23 66/18 07 45
info@beratung-peters.de
www.beratung-peters.de

4.

Helping companies obtain eye-opening recognition through
creative visual communication and strategic design

www.cognitocreative.com

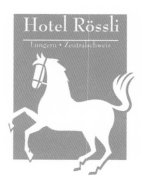

Is your
company
incognito?

Dave Gilman
President

Phone 781 891 4162
Fax   781 891 4557
Mobile 617 947 5661

dgilman@cognitocreative.com
www.cognitocreative.com

99-B Charlesbank Way
Waltham, MA 02453

5.

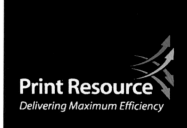

Print Resource
Delivering Maximum Efficiency

Chris McCann
chris@print-resource.com

Ph 508-424-1177
Cell 508-400-4411
Fax 508-424-118

965 Concord Stree
Framingham, MA

6.

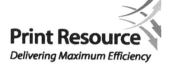
Delivering Maximum Efficiency

Chris McCann
chris@print-resource.com

Ph 508-424-1177
Cell 508-400-4411
Fax 508-424-1188

965 Concord Street
Framingham, MA 01701

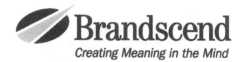
Creating Meaning in the Mind

Heidi Mercer
Principal

8 Notre Dame Road
Bedford, MA 01730
781.276.7993

hmercer@brandscendconsulting.com
www.brandscendconsulting.com

7.

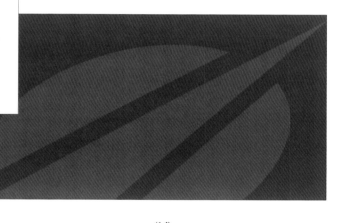

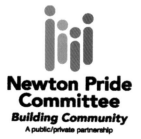

Newton Pride Committee
Building Community
A public/private partnership

Linda R. Plaut
Consultant

70 Crescent Street
Newton, MA 02466
617.527.8283 Phone
617.552.7133 Facsimile
www.ci.newton.ma.us

8.

(1-4)
Design Firm **Buttgereit und Heidenreich GmbH**
(5-8)
Design Firm **Cognito**

1.
Client   Koan Float Technologies
2.
Client   Hulingshof
3.
Client   Hotel Rössli
4.
Client   Haus der Beratung
5.
Client   Cognito
Designer   Dave Gilman
6.
Client   Print Resource
Designer   Dave Gilman
7.
Client   Brandscend
Designer   Dave Gilman
8.
Client   Newton Pride Committee
Designer   Dave Gilman

1.

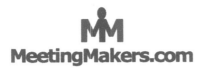

MeetingMakers.com

Robyn Andelman
Event Planner

100 Commerce Way, Woburn, MA 01801
1-888-MAK-MEET(ings) 781-994-1200

r.andelman@meetingmakers.com • www.meetingmakers.com

2.

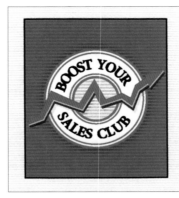

Steve Lentini
President

Phone 781-592-9129
Mobile 978-257-0610

129 Lynn Shore Drive
Lynn, MA 01902

3.

ALPINE GLASS

1-800-320-2213
1-978-692-5655

Stephen R. Shane
owner

369 Littleton Road
Westford, MA 01886

Hours:
Mon. – Fri. 8:00–5:00
Saturday   9:00–2:00

Evening Appointments Available

4.

" L I N K I N G
P E O P L E
A N D   I D E A S ,
F I N D I N G
C O N T E M P O R A R Y
S O L U T I O N S . "

960 W. Hedding
Suite 164
San Jose
CA   95126
Tel: 408.452.4700
Fax: 408.452.4636

Community Partnership
of Santa Clara County

5.

NOTES

CASTILE VENTURES

Maria Lewis Kussmaul
GENERAL PARTNER
maria@castileventures.com

890 Winter Street
SUITE 140
Waltham, MA 0 2 4 5 1

TEL 781.890.0060
FAX 781.890.0065

www.castileventures.com

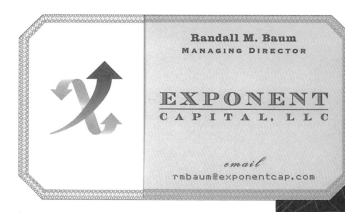

Randall M. Baum
MANAGING DIRECTOR

EXPONENT
CAPITAL, LLC

email

rmbaum@exponentcap.com

www.exponentcap.com

6.

ROLAND A. VAN DER MEER
rvandermeer@comven.com

COMVENTURES

T 650.325.9600
F 650.325.9608

SUITE 305
505 HAMILTON AVENUE
PALO ALTO, CA 94301

www.comven.com

www.
comven.com

Seeing It First

Taking the Lead

Staying Committed

7.

JONGHYUN KAHNG
STAFF ENGINEER

JKAHNG@NANOCOSM.COM

NANOCOSM TECHNOLOGIES, INC.
1291 E. HILLSDALE BLVD., SUITE 210
FOSTER CITY, CA 94404
TEL: 650.345.7400   FAX: 650.345.7497

WWW.NANOCOSM.COM

NANOCOSM
TECHNOLOGIES, INC.

8.

(1-3)
Design Firm **Cognito**
(4-8)
Design Firm **Gee + Chung Design**

1.
Client	MeetingMakers.com
Designer	Dave Gilman

2.
Client	Boost Your Sales Club
Designer	Dave Gilman

3.
Client	Alpine Glass
Designer	Dave Gilman

4.
Client	Community Partnership of Santa Clara County
Designer	Fani Chung

5.
Client	Castile Ventures
Designers	Earl Gee, Fani Chung

6.
Client	Exponent Capital, LLC
Designer	Earl Gee

7.
Client	Comventures
Designers	Earl Gee, Fani Chung

8.
Client	Nanocosm Technologies, Inc.
Designers	Earl Gee, Fani Chung

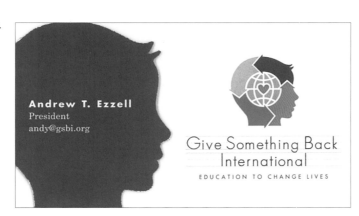

1.

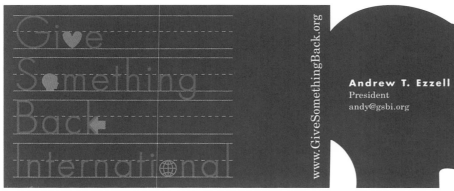

Andrew T. Ezzell
President
andy@gsbi.org

Give Something Back
International
EDUCATION TO CHANGE LIVES

Andrew T. Ezzell
President
andy@gsbi.org

www.GiveSomethingBack.org

GIVE SOMETHING BACK
INTERNATIONAL
FOUNDATION, INC.

2015 S. Tuttle Avenue
Sarasota, Florida 34239 USA
TEL: 941.924.0025
FAX: 941.921.8133
www.gsbi.org

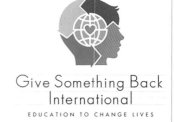

Give Something Back
International
EDUCATION TO CHANGE LIVES

GIVE SOMETHING BACK
INTERNATIONAL
FOUNDATION, INC.

2015 S. Tuttle Avenue
Sarasota, Florida 34239 USA
TEL: 941.924.0025
FAX: 941.921.8133
www.gsbi.org

Give Something Back
Inte
EDUCATIO

JoAnn Patrick-Ezzell
Chairman
joann@gsbi.org

Give Something Back
International
EDUCATION TO CHANGE LIVES

284

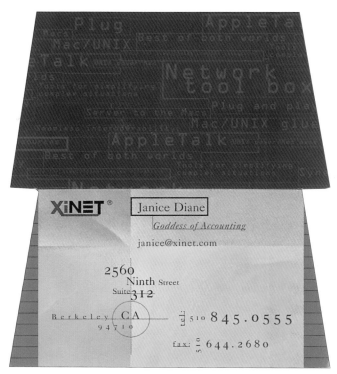

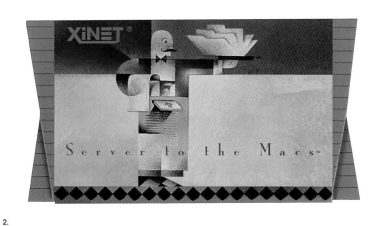

2.

eldersupport
SERVICES, INC.

Christy Stangler, MA, NHA
Geriatric Consultant

777 S. New Ballas Rd.
Suite 301E
St. Louis, MO 63141

(p) **314.989.1000**
(f) 314.989.1133
(e) eldsupservinc@aol.com

3.

F I R S T & M A I N
PROPERTIES

Richard M. Robinson
PRESIDENT

3405 Hawthorne Blvd.
St. Louis, MO 63104

t **314.405.2664**
f *314.732.4199*

rmr@firstandmainproperties.com

4.

Charlie Smith
Building Engineer

tel: 314.241.1175

701 Market Street
Suite 1230
Saint Louis, MO 63101

realty advisors, inc.

fax: 314.241.4867
web: evsra.com
e-mail: charlie.smith@evsra.com

5.

(1,2)
Design Firm **Gee + Chung Design**
(3-5)
Design Firm **Paradowski Creative**

1.
Client   Give Something Back International
Designer   Earl Gee
2.
Client   Xinet, Inc.
Designer   Earl Gee
3.
Client   Eldersupport Services, Inc.
Designer   Steve Cox

4.
Client   First & Main Properties
Designer   Shawn Cornell
5.
Client   EVS Realty Advisors, Inc.
Designer   Steve Cox

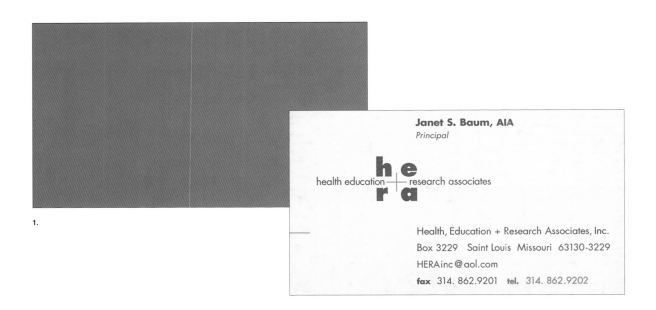

Janet S. Baum, AIA
Principal

he
r a
health education —|— research associates

Health, Education + Research Associates, Inc.
Box 3229   Saint Louis Missouri 63130-3229
HERAinc@aol.com
fax 314. 862.9201 **tel.** 314. 862.9202

1.

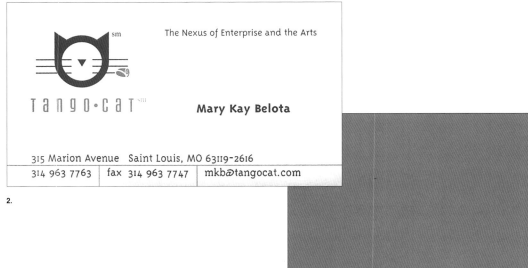

The Nexus of Enterprise and the Arts

tango•cat ^{sm}

Mary Kay Belota

315 Marion Avenue   Saint Louis, MO 63119-2616

| 314 963 7763 | fax 314 963 7747 | mkb@tangocat.com |

2.

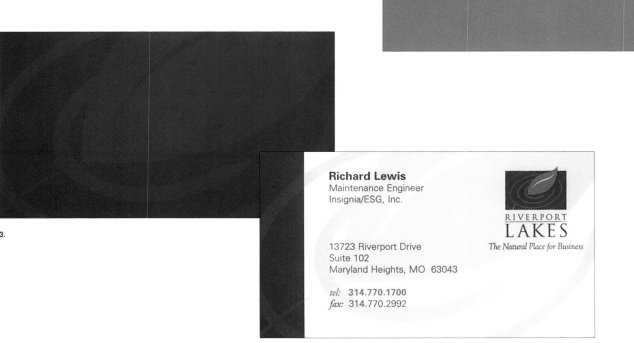

Richard Lewis
Maintenance Engineer
Insignia/ESG, Inc.

RIVERPORT
LAKES
The Natural Place for Business

13723 Riverport Drive
Suite 102
Maryland Heights, MO 63043

tel: **314.770.1700**
fax: 314.770.2992

3.

standing
partnership

public relations
strategic communications
issues management

WORLDCOM
Public Relations Group

LAURA MCALLISTER
vice president

540 maryville centre drive
suite 100
st. louis, missouri 63141

314.469.3500
314.469.3512 [fax]
lmcallister@standingpr.c
www.standingpr.com

4.

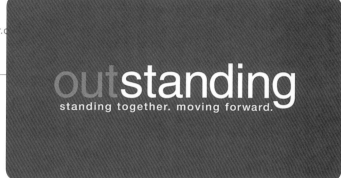
outstanding
standing together. moving forward.

www.DrErinScottGardner.com

paradowskicreative

account manager heather m. wolfe

303 north broadway
saint louis, missouri 63102
www.paradowski.com
(email) heather@paradowski.com
(fax) 314.241.0241
(phone) 314.241.2150

5.

exceeding everyone's expectations but our own.

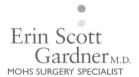

Erin Scott
Gardner M.D.
MOHS SURGERY SPECIALIST

skin cancer & cutaneous surgery

5000
Cedar Plaza Parkway
Suite 240
Saint Louis,
Missouri 63128

314/849-7546

(f) 314/849-7558

6.

(1-6)
Design Firm **Paradowski Creative**

1.
Client   HERA
Designer   Joy Marcus

2.
Client   Tango Cat
Designer   Shawn Cornell

3.
Client   Riverport Lakes
Designer   Shawn Cornell

4.
Client   Standing Partnership
Designers   Alex Paradowski,
      Steve Cox

5.
Client   Paradowski Creative
Designers   Alex Paradowski,
      Steve Cox

6.
Client   Erin Scott Gardner, M.D.
Designer   Steve Cox

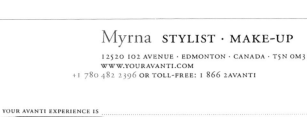

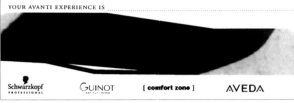

YOUR AVANTI EXPERIENCE IS ....

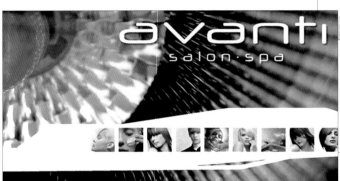

1.

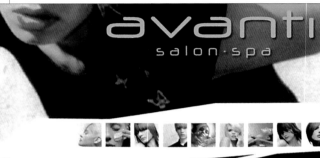

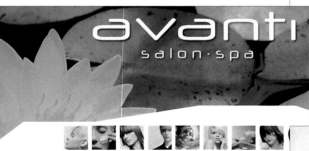

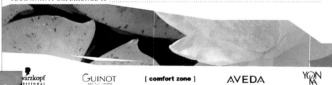

YOUR AVANTI EXPERIENCE IS ....

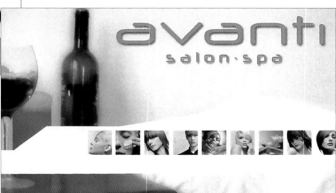

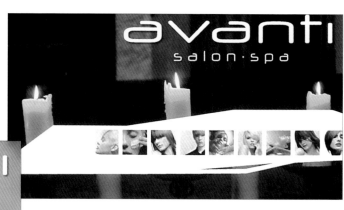

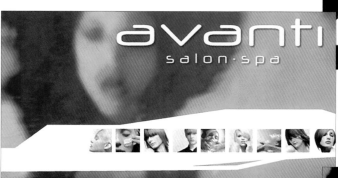

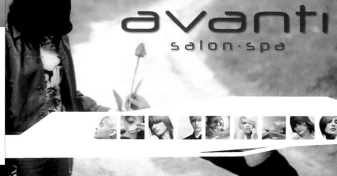

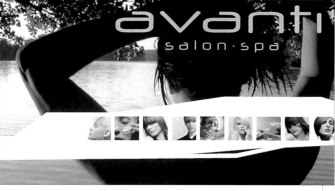

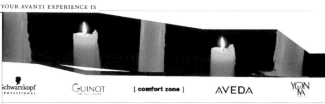

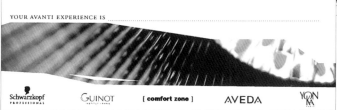

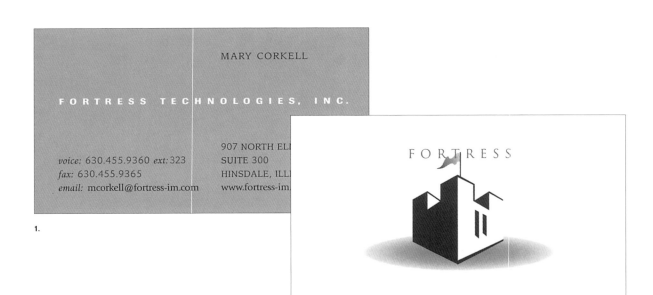

1.

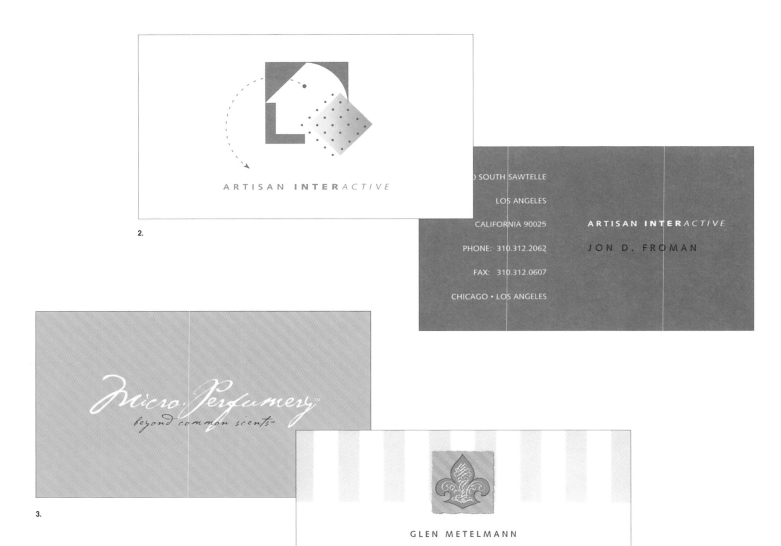

2.

3.

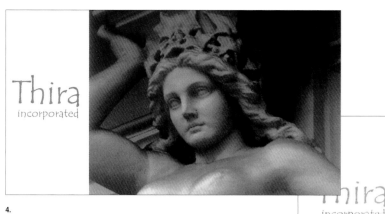

Thira
incorporated

4.

Cynthia Pougiales, AIA
ARCHITECTURE :: DESIGN/BUILD

Thira
incorporated

350 Old Y Road · Golden, Colorado 80401
tel > 303·526·9128   fax > 303·526·9131
cell > 720·581·9128   email > pougiales@msn.com

HALSA
BY ALLHANDS

...rd means health,
...s beauty.

...PARTMENT TOWER
...KE SHORE DRIVE

...OIS 60611

DORINDA ALLHANDS
ESTHETICIAN/REFLEXOLOGIST

5.

ROMAN
DESIGN

LISA ROMANOWSKI
23486 CURRANT DRIVE
GOLDEN, COLOR...
www.studioRoman...
lisa@studioRoman...

303 | 526...
FAX | 526...

6.

ROMAN
DESIGN

(1-6)
Design Firm **Roman Design**

1.
Client   Fortress Technologies
Designer   Lisa Romanowski

2.
Client   Artisan Interactive
Designer   Lisa Romanowski

3.
Client   The Micro-Perfumery, Inc.
Designer   Lisa Romanowski

4.
Client   Thira, Incorporated
Designer   Lisa Romanowski

5.
Client   Halsa
Designer   Lisa Romanowski

6.
Client   Roman Design
Designer   Lisa Romanowski

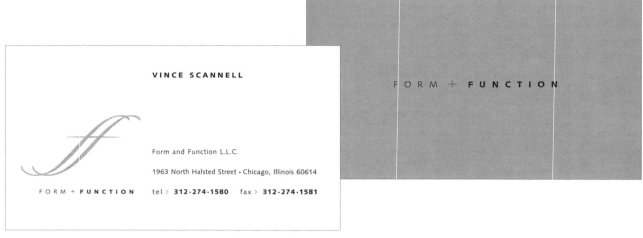

VINCE SCANNELL

Form and Function L.L.C.

1963 North Halsted Street · Chicago, Illinois 60614

FORM + FUNCTION   tel > **312·274·1580**   fax > **312·274·1581**

FORM + FUNCTION

1.

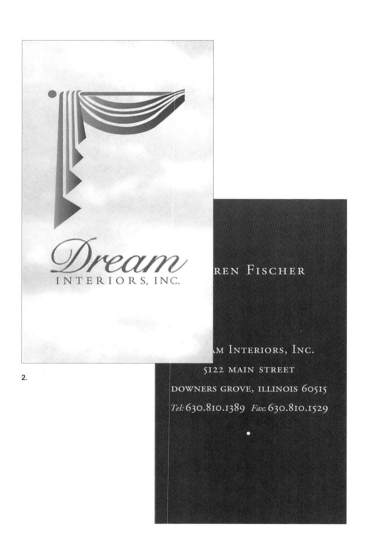

Dream
INTERIORS, INC.

REN FISCHER

AM INTERIORS, INC.

5122 MAIN STREET

DOWNERS GROVE, ILLINOIS 60515

Tel: 630.810.1389 *Fax:* 630.810.1529

2.

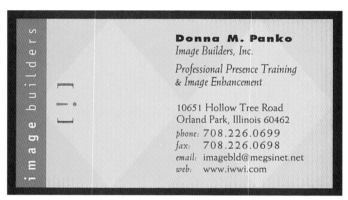

image builders

Donna M. Panko
Image Builders, Inc.

Professional Presence Training
& Image Enhancement

10651 Hollow Tree Road
Orland Park, Illinois 60462
phone: 708.226.0699
fax: 708.226.0698
email: imagebld@megsinet.net
web: www.iwwi.com

3.

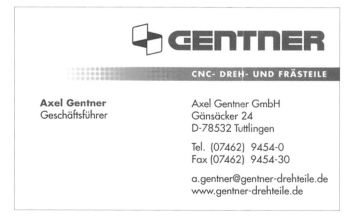

GENTNER

CNC- DREH- UND FRÄSTEILE

Axel Gentner
Geschäftsführer

Axel Gentner GmbH
Gänsäcker 24
D-78532 Tuttlingen

Tel. (07462) 9454-0
Fax (07462) 9454-30

a.gentner@gentner-drehteile.de
www.gentner-drehteile.de

4.

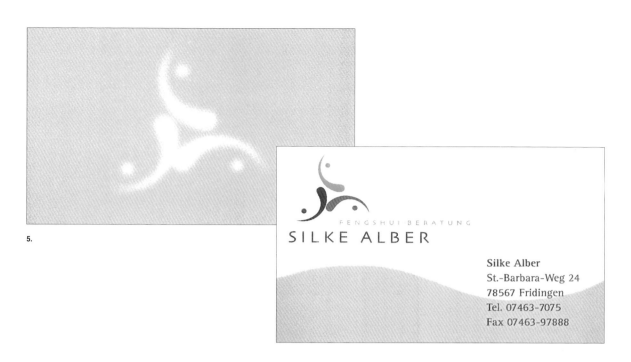

5.

SILKE ALBER

FENGSHUI BERATUNG

Silke Alber
St.-Barbara-Weg 24
78567 Fridingen
Tel. 07463-7075
Fax 07463-97888

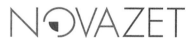

NOVAZET GmbH   Tel. 07424 5275
Zerspanungstechnik   Fax 07424 5306
Max-Planck-Str. 5/1A info@novazet.com
D-78549 Spaichingen   www.novazet.com

6.

INNOVATION
PRÄZISION
SERVICE

www.novazet.com

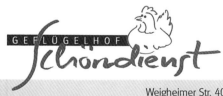

GEFLÜGELHOF

Weigheimer Str. 40
78647 Trossingen-Schura

Tel. 07425 1788 Fax 1739
mobil 0170 5617304

JAN SCHÖNDIENST

7.

(1-3)
Design Firm **Roman Design**
(4-7)
Design Firm **revoLUZion, advertising
              and design**

1.
Client   Form + Function
Designer   Lisa Romanowski
2.
Client   Dream Interiors, Inc.
Designer   Lisa Romanowski
3.
Client   Image Builders, Inc.
Designer   Lisa Romanowski
4.
Client   Gentner, Tuttlingen
Designer   Bernd Luz

5.
Client   Silke Alber, Fridingen
Designer   Bernd Luz
6.
Client   Novazet GmbH, Spaichingen
Designer   Bernd Luz
7.
Client   Geflügelhof Schöndienst
Designer   Bernd Luz

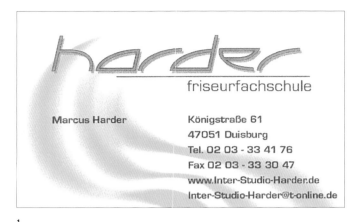

Marcus Harder

Königstraße 61
47051 Duisburg
Tel. 02 03 - 33 41 76
Fax 02 03 - 33 30 47
www.Inter-Studio-Harder.de
Inter-Studio-Harder@t-online.de

1.

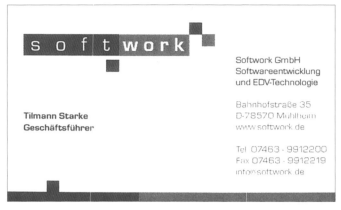

Tilmann Starke
Geschäftsführer

Softwork GmbH
Softwareentwicklung
und EDV-Technologie

Bahnhofstraße 35
D-78570 Mühlheim
www.softwork.de

Tel 07463 - 9912200
Fax 07463 - 9912219
info@software.de

2.

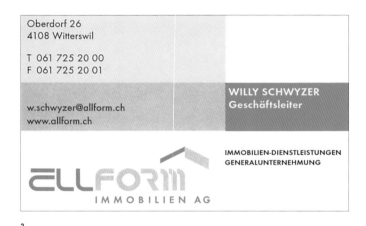

Oberdorf 26
4108 Witterswil

T 061 725 20 00
F 061 725 20 01

w.schwyzer@allform.ch
www.allform.ch

WILLY SCHWYZER
Geschäftsleiter

IMMOBILIEN-DIENSTLEISTUNGEN
GENERALUNTERNEHMUNG

3.

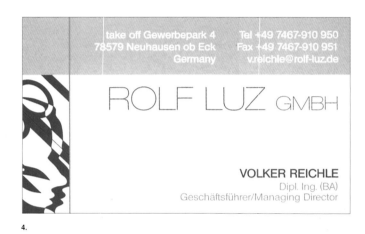

take off Gewerbepark 4   Tel +49 7467-910 950
78579 Neuhausen ob Eck   Fax +49 7467-910 951
Germany   v.reichle@rolf-luz.de

ROLF LUZ GMBH

VOLKER REICHLE
Dipl. Ing. (BA)
Geschäftsführer/Managing Director

4.

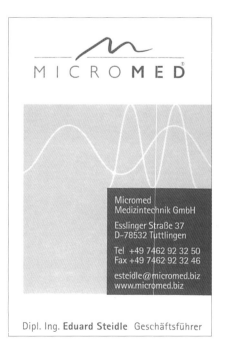

Dipl. Ing. **Eduard Steidle**   Geschäftsführer

5.

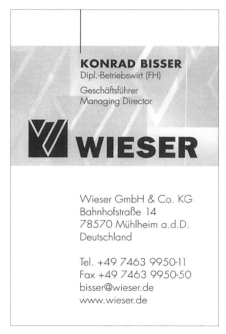

KONRAD BISSER
Dipl.-Betriebswirt (FH)

Geschäftsführer
Managing Director

Wieser GmbH & Co. KG
Bahnhofstraße 14
78570 Mühlheim a.d.D.
Deutschland

Tel. +49 7463 9950-11
Fax +49 7463 9950-50
bisser@wieser.de
www.wieser.de

6.

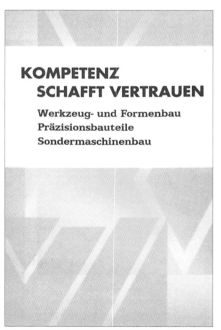

bw PROPERTY
consultants

Brad Wheatley
Principal & L.R.E.A

96A Glenhaven Road
Glenhaven NSW 2156

M **0408 414 070**
T/F 02 9894 5787
E enquiries@bwproperty.com.au
W www.bwproperty.com.au

7.

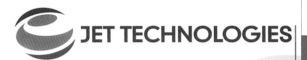
JET TECHNOLOGIES

119 McEvoy Street
Locked Bag 5010
Alexandria NSW 2015 Australia

Jason Garrett
Product Development
Manager

Tel (61 2) 8399 4999
Mobile 0403 857 542
Fax (61 2) 8399 2277
jgarrett@jet-technologies.com.au

8.

www.jet-technologies.com.au

experience+ideas+skill=**profits**

Patrick Gallagher
MANAGING DIRECTOR

Suite 1, 271 Pacific Highway
North Sydney 2060
T: 02 9922 2177
F: 02 9922 5944

M: 0405 100 751
E: patrick@ghm.net.au

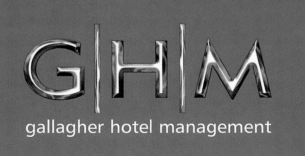
G|H|M
gallagher hotel management

9.

(1-6)
Design Firm **revoLUZion, advertising and design**
(7-9)
Design Firm **Aslan Design & Graphics**

1.
Client   Harder Friseurfachschule
Designer Bernd Luz
2.
Client   Softwork GmbH, Mühlheim
Designer Bernd Luz
3.
Client   Allform Immobilien AG
Designer Bernd Luz
4.
Client   Rolf Luz GmbH, Neuhausen
Designer Bernd Luz

5.
Client   Micromed Medizintechnik GmbH
Designer Bernd Luz
6.
Client   Wieser, Mühlheim
Designer Bernd Luz
7.
Client   bw property
Designer Charlene Walker
8.
Client   Jet Technologies
Designer Charlene Walker
9.
Client   Gallagher Hotel Management
Designer Charlene Walker

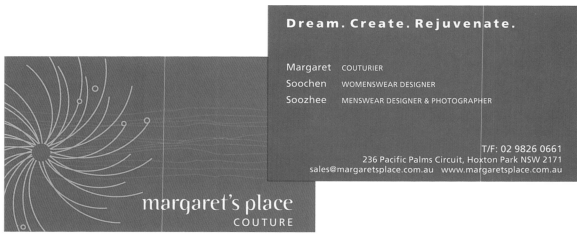

Dream. Create. Rejuvenate.

Margaret   COUTURIER
Soochen   WOMENSWEAR DESIGNER
Soozhee   MENSWEAR DESIGNER & PHOTOGRAPHER

T/F: 02 9826 0661
236 Pacific Palms Circuit, Hoxton Park NSW 2171
sales@margaretsplace.com.au   www.margaretsplace.com.au

margaret's place
COUTURE

1.

Tim Coughlan
Director

17a Pirrama Road
Pyrmont NSW 2009

PO Box 403
Neutral Bay NSW 2089

T: +61 (0)2 9571 6900
M: +61 (0)409 990 333
F: +61 (0)2 9571 6899
E: tim@incognitoevents.
W: www.incognitoevents

vision is...   ...the do-able ...the conceivable ...and the previously unthi

incognito
events

2.

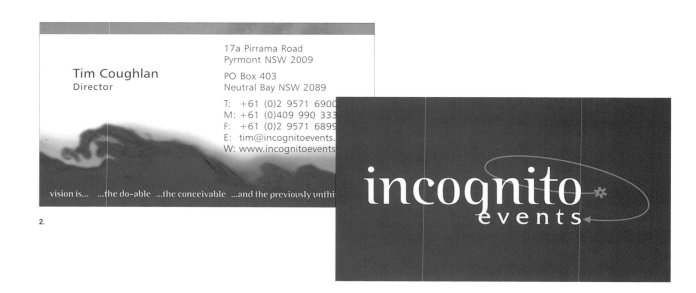

LATIN RESTAURANT • BAR & CI

laCita

9 Lime Street
King Street Wharf
Sydney 2000

T: **02 9299 9100**
F: 02 9299 2522
E: info@lacita.com.au
W: **lacita.com.au**

3.

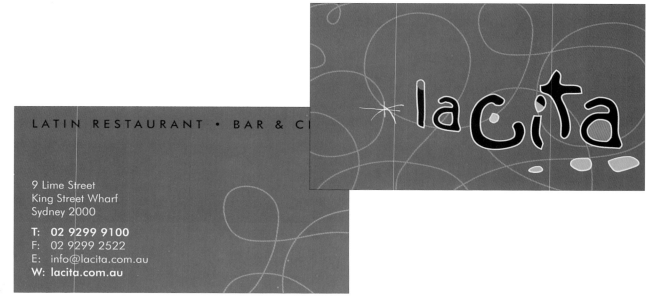

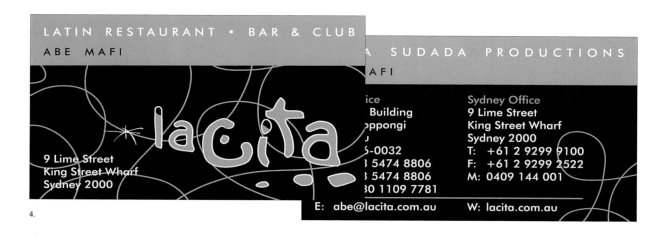

4.

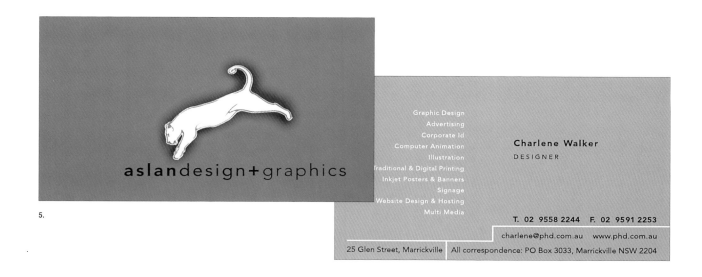

5.

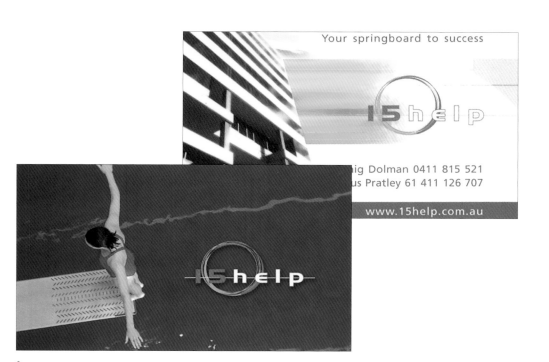

6.

Your springboard to success

15help

Craig Dolman 0411 815 521
Angus Pratley 61 411 126 707

www.15help.com.au

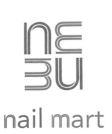

ne
ЗU

nail mart

Christina Farrugia
Director

Unit 1, 2 Endeavour Road
Caringbah NSW 2229

T: 02 9526 2457
F: 02 9526 145
M: 0418 388 86

christina@nailma
nailmart.com.au

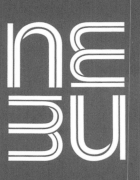

1.

 citrus group

Citrus Group Pty Ltd
PO Box 380 Vaucluse NSW 2030

T: 1800 097 957
F: + 61 2 9388 8894
E: sales@dibi.com.au
W: www.dibi.com.au

2.

 citrus group

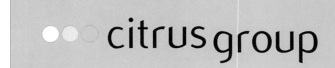

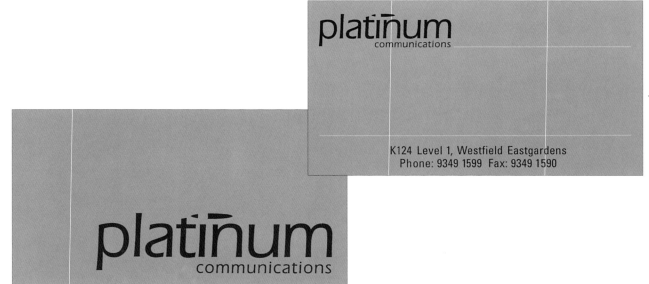

platinum
communications

K124 Level 1, Westfield Eastgardens
Phone: 9349 1599 Fax: 9349 1590

platinum
communications

3.

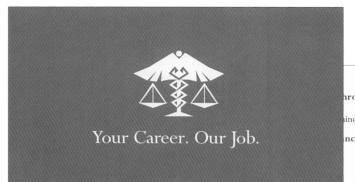

Your Career. Our Job.

4.

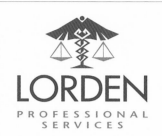

...hroader, Sr.

...inc.com

...inc.com

LORDEN
PROFESSIONAL SERVICES

T . 253.460.9261   F . 253.566.9901   C . 253.861.8845
4618 Alameda Avenue West . University Place, WA 98466

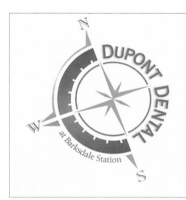

Sukhui Rodgers, RDH, BS

1100 Station Drive, Suite 221

DuPont, Washington 98327

Tel 253.912.4443

Fax 253.912.4426

WebSite www.dupontdental.com

5.

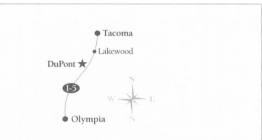

● Tacoma

● Lakewood

DuPont ★

I-5

● Olympia

Take exit 119 off I-5, head west to Wilmington Dr., turn right.
Barksdale Station is on the right, we are on the second floor above Starbucks.

www.jndprinting.com

Jim Vitzthum

jim@jndprinting.com

253.272.2600 ex.211
253.572.1464 fax
253.606.8088 cell

815 South 28th Street,
Tacoma, Washington 98409

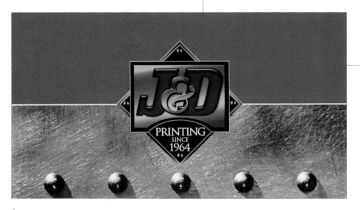

6.

(1-3)
Design Firm **Aslan Design & Graphics**
(4-6)
Design Firm **Colin Magnuson Creative**

1.
Client   Nail Mart Australia
Designer   Charlene Walker
2.
Client   Citrus Group
Designer   Charlene Walker
3.
Client   Platinum
Designer   Charlene Walker
4.
Client   Lorden Professional Services
Designer   Colin Magnuson
5.
Client   DuPont Dental
Designer   Colin Magnuson
6.
Client   J&D Printing
Designer   Colin Magnuson

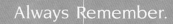

Always Remember.

1.

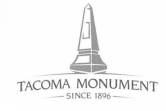

TACOMA MONUMENT
— SINCE 1896 —

Robb J. Stilnovich President
robb.stilnovich@tacomamonument.com

2309 South Tacoma Way . Tacoma, WA 98409
Tel | **800.426.5973** . Fax | 253.472.4832

www.tacomamonument.com

GARRETT T. ZUMINI | Financial Officer
gtz@creationdental.com

7727 40TH STREET WEST
UNIVERSITY PLACE, WA 98466

p   253 565 1035
f   253 565 4801
tf 800 694 1035

www.creationdental.com

CREATION **DENTAL** ARTS

C D A

2.

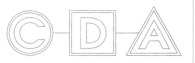

3.

R U E P P E L L . C O M

Rueppell
Home Design

Darin Rueppell President

2605 Jahn Ave. NW . Suite D-7
Gig Harbor, Washington 98335

1.877.RUEPPELL (783.7735)
Fax . 1.877.257.5127

info@rueppell.com

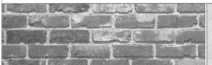

Susan K. Boiter
Principal

www.crestbuilders.com

5516 75th Street, West . Suite A . Lakewood, Washington 98499

253.475.6300 tel
253.475.1060 fax
sue@crestbuilders.com eMail
CR-ES-TB*334NG

4.

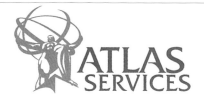

Craig E. Goebbel
President
cgoebbel@loantek.com

5812 67th Avenue West
University Place, WA 98467
tel 1.888.LOANTEK
local 253.565.4495
fax 253.565.4542
www.loantek.com

WISHES WELCOME. DREAMS APPROVED.

5.

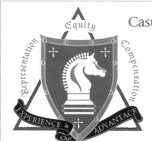

Casualty Loss Consultants, Inc.

Roger W. Maib
Licensed Public Adjuster

800.457.2054 . Toll Free
360.446.7770 . Residence
253.377.3546 . Cellular

Serving the Northwest Since 1981

WASHINGTON   OREGON   ALASKA

6.

ATLAS SERVICES

Building Maintenance
Landscape Maintenance
Janitorial Services
New Construction Cleanup
Interior Demolition
Remodels
Commercial/Residential

2522 North Proctor Street (PMB #304)
Tacoma, Washington 98406
T. 206.817.0844
F. 253.212.2695

Erik Kepler
Business Development
e. ekepler@wamail.net

WWW.ATLASCOMPANIES.NET

7.

CHASE
Chiropractic
Center

ROBERT E. WAGNER, D.C.

10415 Canyon Road E   Puyallup, WA 98373
Tel 253 537 6000   Fax 253 536 5544

8.

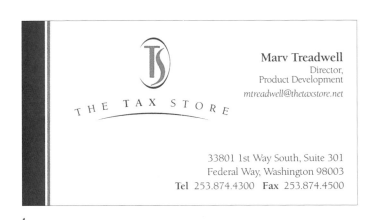

TS

THE TAX STORE

Marv Treadwell
Director,
Product Development
mtreadwell@thetaxstore.net

33801 1st Way South, Suite 301
Federal Way, Washington 98003
Tel 253.874.4300 **Fax** 253.874.4500

1.

WWW.QUALITYPAINTINGINC.COM

15111 105th Avenue Court East Puyallup, Washington 98374	253	tel 848 8153 fax 845 6898
	253	cell 405 5333

Specializing in commercial painting,
special coatings, wall coverings,
and water repellents for the
Northwest's environment

QUALITY
PAINTING
INCORPORATED

Marlene Anglemyer
CEO
marlene@qualitypaintinginc.com

2.

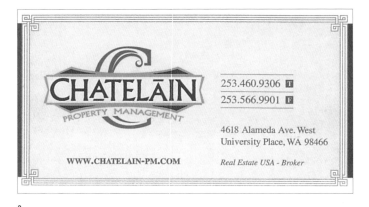

CHATELAIN
PROPERTY MANAGEMENT

253.460.9306 T
253.566.9901 F

4618 Alameda Ave. West
University Place, WA 98466

WWW.CHATELAIN-PM.COM

Real Estate USA - Broker

3.

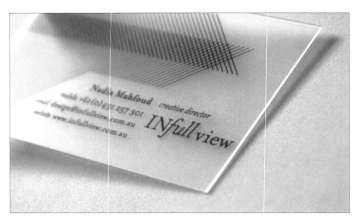

4.

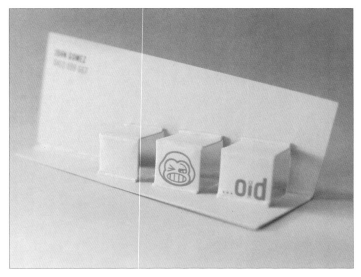

5.

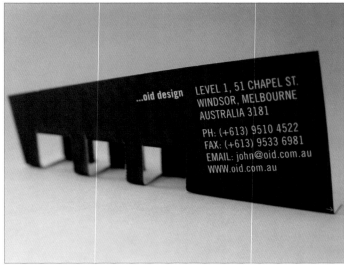

Scott E. Parker
principal
scott@fuellounge.com

fuellounge.com
348 south main st.
akron, oh 44311
tel 330.434.FUEL
/3835/
fax 330.761.9795

6.

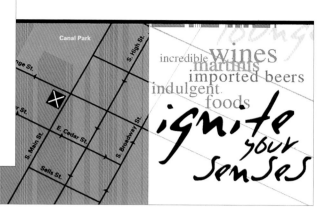

Leslie R. Letner
EVENTS COORDINATOR

546 Grant Street
Akron, OH 44311-1158
p: 330 535 6900 x237
f: 330 996 5337

leslie@akroncantonfoodbank.org
www.akroncantonfoodbank.org

7.

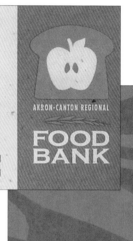

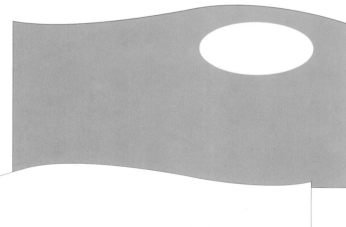

Keeven White
keeven@whitespace-creative.com

WhiteSpace Creative
24 North High Street, Suite 200
Akron, OH 44308

330.762.9320 // Fx: 330.762.9323
www.whitespace-creative.com

8.

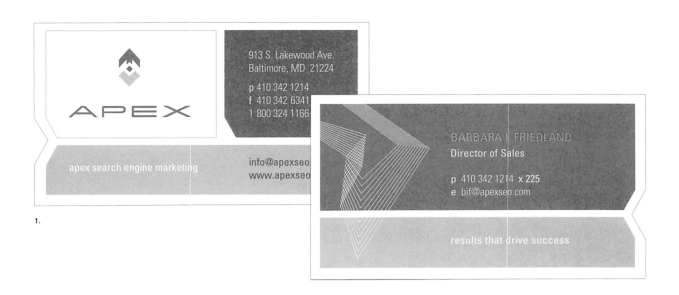

1.

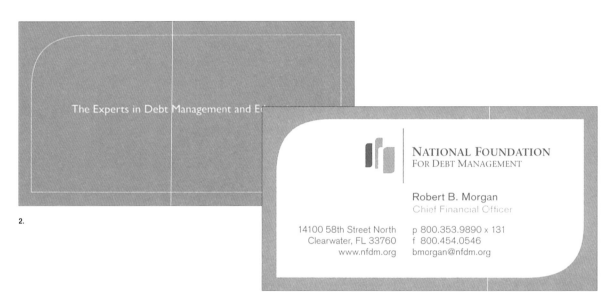

2.

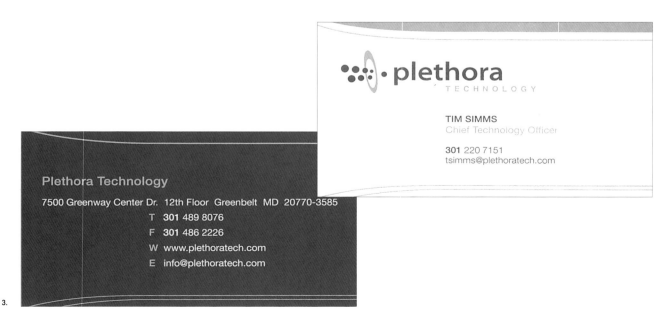

3.

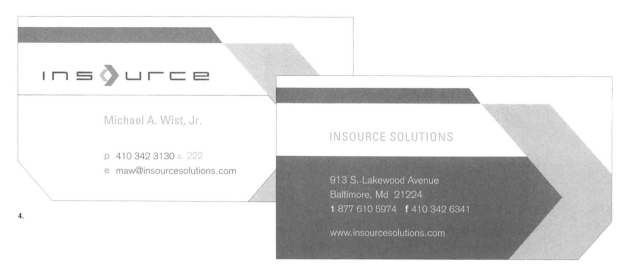

Michael A. Wist, Jr.

p 410 342 3130 x. 222
e maw@insourcesolutions.com

4.

INSOURCE SOLUTIONS

913 S. Lakewood Avenue
Baltimore, Md 21224
1 877 610 5974 f 410 342 6341

www.insourcesolutions.com

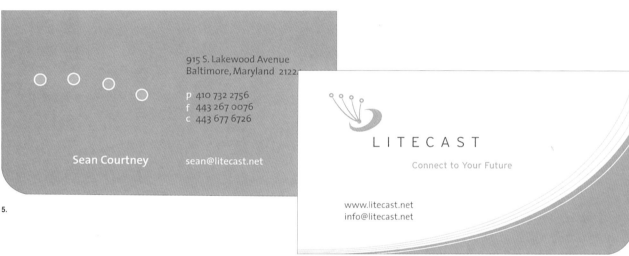

915 S. Lakewood Avenue
Baltimore, Maryland 2122...

p 410 732 2756
f 443 267 0076
c 443 677 6726

Sean Courtney   sean@litecast.net

5.

LITECAST

Connect to Your Future

www.litecast.net
info@litecast.net

IDA CHEINMAN CREATIVE DIRECTOR
2304 East Baltimore Street Baltimore Maryland 21224
410 732 8379 f. 1 425 940 7800 ida.cheinman@verizon.net
www.substance151.com

6.

(1-6)
Design Firm **Substance151**

1.
  Client   Apex SEO
  Designers   Ida Cheinman,
              Rick Salzman
2.
  Client   National Foundation for
              Debt Management
  Designers   Ida Cheinman,
              Rick Salzman
3.
  Client   Plethora Technology
  Designers   Ida Cheinman,
              Rick Salzman
4.
  Client   InSource
  Designers   Ida Cheinman,
              Rick Salzman
5.
  Client   Litecast
  Designers   Ida Cheinman,
              Rick Salzman
6.
  Client   Substance151
  Designers   Ida Cheinman,
              Rick Salzman

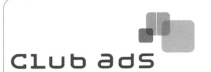

cLub adS

Gregory J. Sarno
President & CEO

gsarno@clubads.tv

542 Westport Avenue
Norwalk CT 06851

203 840-0020 Office
203 840-1310 Fax
203 919-2005 Cell

Get Noticed™

www.clubads.tv

1.

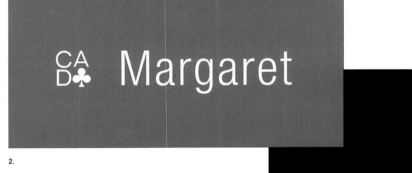

CA
D♣ Margaret

Margaret Tobelman
executive director

send
PO Box 921, Killingworth, CT 06419

surf
www.cadc.org

talk
860.663.1264

fax
860.663.2018

write
m_tobelman@cadc.org

2.

**Alli Ugosoli
Photography**

123 rivington st #9
new york ny 10002

917 566 2536

alliuphotography
@yahoo.com

Alli Ugosoli

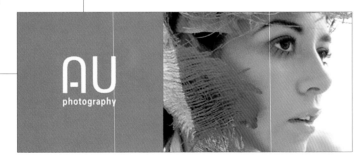

AU
photography

3.

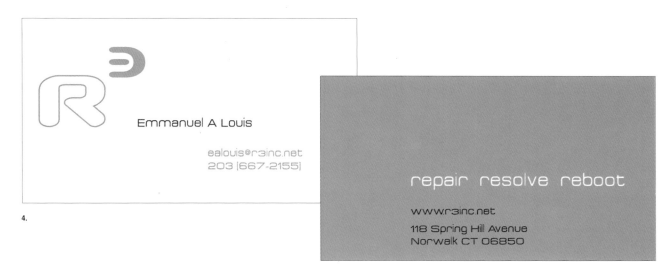

4.

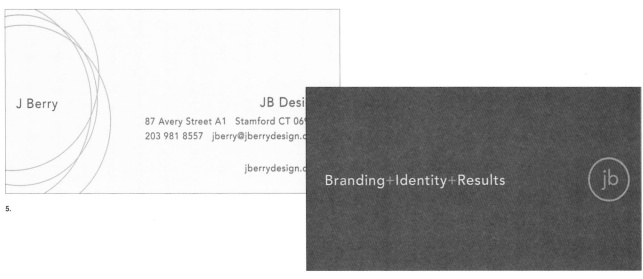

5.

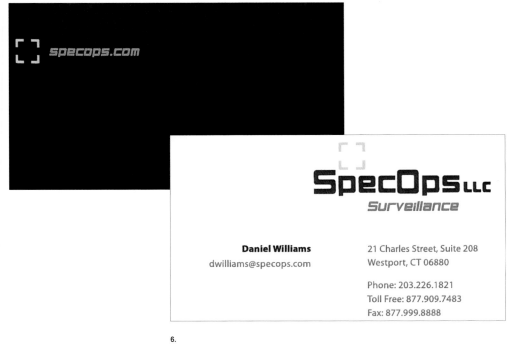

6.

(1-6)
Design Firm **JB Design**

1.
Client	ClubAds
Designer	J. Berry

2.
Client	CADC
Designer	J. Berry

3.
Client	AU Photography
Designer	J. Berry

4.
Client	R3
Designer	J. Berry

5.
Client	JB Design
Designer	J. Berry

6.
Client	Spec Ops
Designer	J. Berry

1.

Berry's
Emerald
pub

894 Bank Street
Waterbury
CT 06708

203.574.4229

2.

the gourmet Café

125 Bantam Lake Road
Bantam, Connecticut 06750
860.567.7786

3.

tonic

live jazz & blues

15 N Main Street
South Norwalk, CT

203. 838. 3531

4.

BUNDESRAT I.R.

Manfred Mautner Markhof

PROF. DR. H.C. GESCHÄFTSFÜHRENDER GESELLSCHAFTER

MAUTNER MARKHOF
INDUSTRIEBETEILIGUNGS G.M.B.H.
SIMMERINGER HAUPTSTRASSE 101
A - 1 1 1 0   W I E N

TELEFON (43) 1 740 44-121
TELEFAX (43) 1 740 44-228
EMAIL profmmm@mmag.at

5.

werbe
3

AGENTUR / KONZEPT / GESTALTUNG

BEATE HEMMERLEIN

WERBE 3 / FLIEDERWEG 3 / A 2380 PERCHTOLDSDORF
TELEFON +43 1 86 53 400 / FAX +43 1 596 82 24
MOBIL +43 676 311 56 00 / EMAIL beate@trias.at

6.

Ton ab!
AKUSTISCHE MASSARBEITEN

Kupelwiesergasse 14/3
A 1130 Wien
t + 43 1 877 15 75
m + 43 664 761 54 99
e tonab@inode.at

Don H.M. Reetz

Ton ab!
AKUSTISCHE MASSARBEITEN

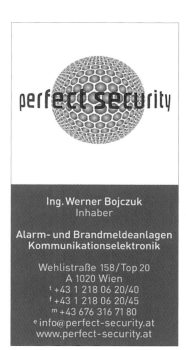

perfect security

Ing. Werner Bojczuk
Inhaber

**Alarm- und Brandmeldeanlagen
Kommunikationselektronik**

Wehlistraße 158/Top 20
A 1020 Wien
t +43 1 218 06 20/40
f +43 1 218 06 20/45
m +43 676 316 71 80
e info@perfect-security.at
www.perfect-security.at

7.

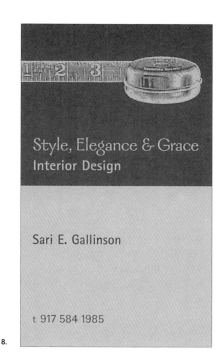

Style, Elegance & Grace
Interior Design

Sari E. Gallinson

t 917 584 1985

8.

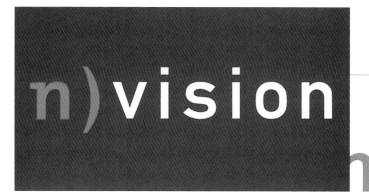

n)vision

9.

maxim m. rivkin president

n)vision

128 wheeler road, burlington, ma 01803   781.505.8360
fax 781.998.5656 max@nvisionoptics.com www.nvisionoptics.com

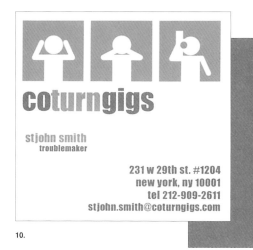

coturngigs

stjohn smith
troublemaker

231 w 29th st. #1204
new york, ny 10001
tel 212-909-2611
stjohn.smith@coturngigs.com

10.

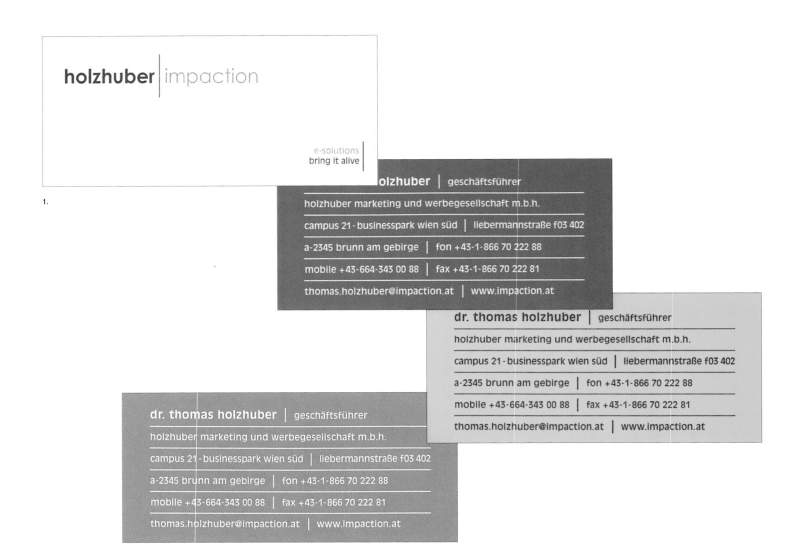

holzhuber | impaction

e-solutions |
bring it alive

1.

...olzhuber | geschäftsführer

holzhuber marketing und werbegesellschaft m.b.h.

campus 21 - businesspark wien süd | liebermannstraße f03 402

a-2345 brunn am gebirge | fon +43-1-866 70 222 88

mobile +43-664-343 00 88 | fax +43-1-866 70 222 81

thomas.holzhuber@impaction.at | www.impaction.at

dr. thomas holzhuber | geschäftsführer

holzhuber marketing und werbegesellschaft m.b.h.

campus 21 - businesspark wien süd | liebermannstraße f03 402

a-2345 brunn am gebirge | fon +43-1-866 70 222 88

mobile +43-664-343 00 88 | fax +43-1-866 70 222 81

thomas.holzhuber@impaction.at | www.impaction.at

dr. thomas holzhuber | geschäftsführer

holzhuber marketing und werbegesellschaft m.b.h.

campus 21 - businesspark wien süd | liebermannstraße f03 402

a-2345 brunn am gebirge | fon +43-1-866 70 222 88

mobile +43-664-343 00 88 | fax +43-1-866 70 222 81

thomas.holzhuber@impaction.at | www.impaction.at

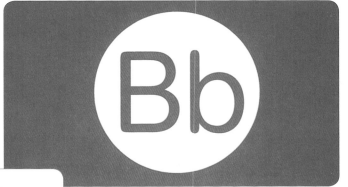

2.

belly **Bb** basics®

Juliana Alvim Brand Director

Juliana@BellyBasics.com

55 W 39th St, 17th Fl. NY, NY 10018 T 212.685.6825 F 212.768.3470

www.blueribbonprostateinitiative.org
www.brprostate.org

250 West 57ᵗʰ St, Suite 716 New York, NY 10107 212.489.0
1616 Walnut St, Ste 1520 Philadelphia, PA 19103 215.732.2

3.

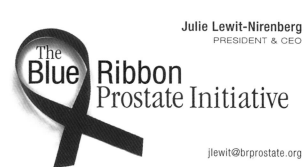

Julie Lewit-Nirenberg
PRESIDENT & CEO

The
Blue Ribbon
Prostate Initiative

jlewit@brprostate.org

4.

über, inc.

tanya pramongkit
senior designer

231 w 29ᵗʰ st, #1204
new york, ny 10001
tel 212.643.1135
fax 212.643.1205
tanya@uber-inc.com

Preventive · Restorative · Esthetic · Implant
Dentistry For The Family

5.

Dr. Howard Ehrenkranz

201 S. Livingston Ave.
Livingston · NJ 07039
tel 973 994 4200
fax 973 994 3933

lynn knoepfler
r.d.h
dental hygienist

(1-5)
Design Firm **über, inc.**

1.
Client   Holzhuber Impaction
Designer   Jimmy Ng
2.
Client   Belly Basics
Designer   Herta Knegner
3.
Client   Blue Ribbon Prostate Initiative
Designer   Herta Kriegner
4.
Client   über, inc.
Designers Herta Kriegner,
           Suzanne Jennerich
5.
Client   Dr. Ehrenkranz
Designers David Wolf,
           Jimmy Ng

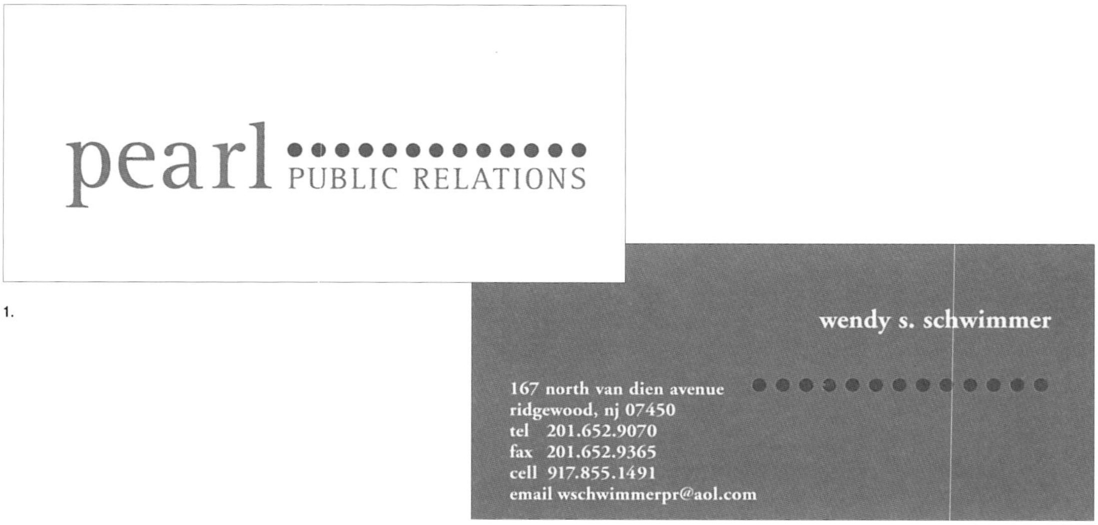

pearl •••••••••••••• PUBLIC RELATIONS

1.

wendy s. schwimmer

167 north van dien avenue
ridgewood, nj 07450
tel   201.652.9070
fax   201.652.9365
cell 917.855.1491
email wschwimmerpr@aol.com

•••••••••••••

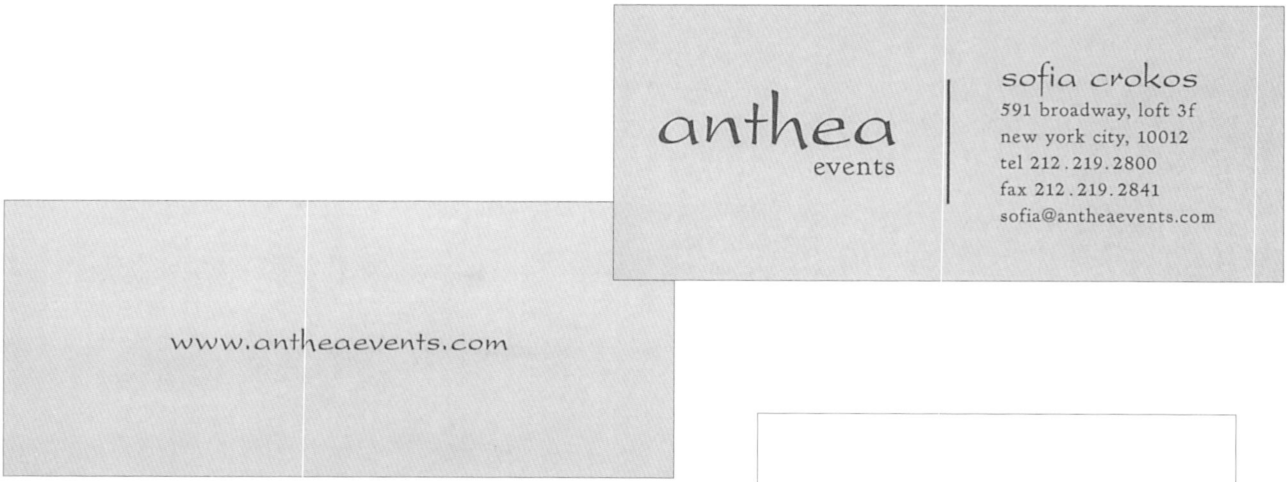

anthea
events

sofia crokos
591 broadway, loft 3f
new york city, 10012
tel 212.219.2800
fax 212.219.2841
sofia@antheaevents.com

www.antheaevents.com

2.

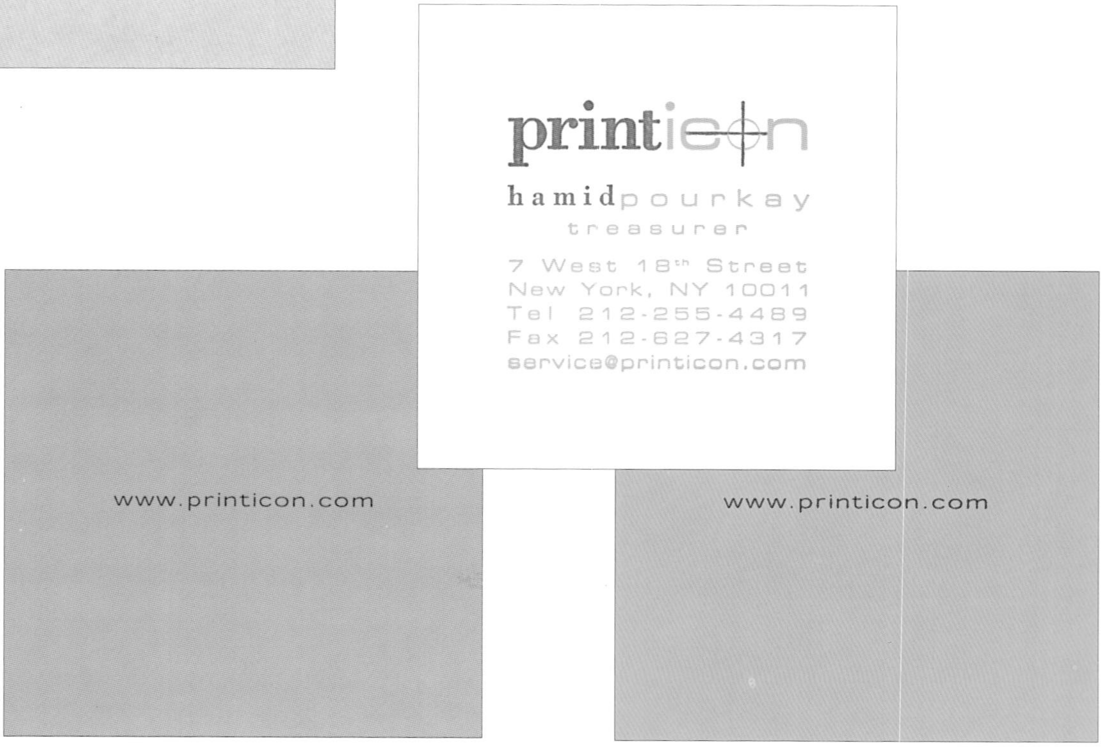

printic•n

hamid pourkay
treasurer

7 West 18ᵗʰ Street
New York, NY 10011
Tel 212-255-4489
Fax 212-627-4317
service@printicon.com

www.printicon.com

www.printicon.com

3.

PO Box 10848
Scottsdale AZ 85271-0848
480 945 0846
480 945 6596 fx
infodesign2@cox.net
sanft@infodesign2.com
infodesign2.com

4.

Alfred C Sanft | **InfoDesign Management Inc**

480 946 0846

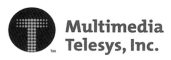

**Multimedia
Telesys, Inc.**

Richard J. Ozga
Director of Operations

1205 South Park Lane
Suite 5
Tempe, AZ 85281

v 602 894 9225
f 602 894 9231

5.

J Q C D E V E L O P M E N T C O M P A N Y, L L C

Robert A. Campbell   PO Box 1549   602 568 0850
Managing Member   Scottsdale, AZ 85252   480 949 8150 fx

6.

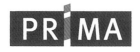

COMMERCIAL LEASING

Robb Horlacher
Executive VP   8350 McDonald Dr. Ste C   480 951.8989
Operations   Scottsdale AZ 85250   480 951.8995 fx

7.

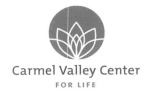

Carmel Valley Center
FOR LIFE

Dr. Tony Miszlevitz
President

114 Carmel Valley Rd   831 951.2244
Carmel Valley, CA 93924   831 219.0128 F

1.

Taylor Homes

Jonathan Taylor
President
55 East Harvard Road
Phoenix AZ 85002
602 568 0900

2.

Property One Management

James W. Scott
CFO

8350 McDonald Dr. Ste C
Scottsdale AZ 85250

480 951.8989
480 951.8995 fx

3.

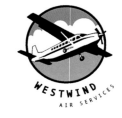
WESTWIND
AIR SERVICES

Ron Strong
General Manager

732 West Deer Valley Rd.
Phoenix, AZ 85027

480 991.5557
623 587.9198 fx

4.

UALTE

USER ADAPTABLE
LEARNING &   DARREN PETRUCCI
TEACHING   SCHOOL OF ARCHITECTURE, ASU
ENVIRONMENTS   480 329 1888
                         DARREN.PETRUCCI@ASU.EDU

5.

ALL POINTS MEDIA

VALERIE HOYT
vhoyt@allpointsco.com
503-626-0669

9950 ARCTIC DR. BEAVERTON OR, 97140
WWW.ALLPOINTSCO.COM

ALL POINTS MEDIA

6.

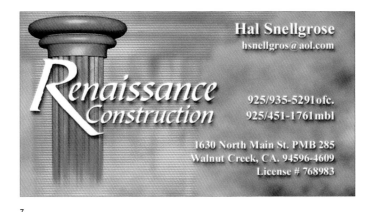

7.

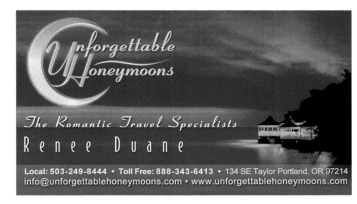

8.

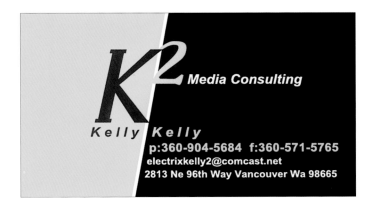

9.

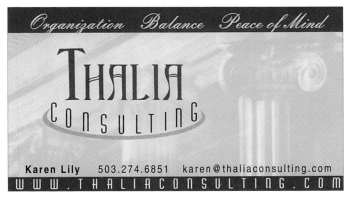

10.

We take care of the details...
So you can
Live your dreams.

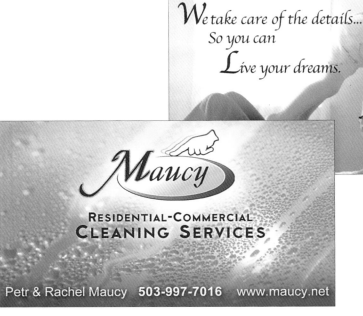

11.

(1-5)
Design Firm **InfoDesign Management Inc.**
(6-11)
Design Firm **Panghansen Creative Group**

1.
  Client   Carmel Valley Center for Life
  Designer Alfred C. Sanft
2.
  Client   Taylor Homes
  Designer Alfred C. Sanft
3.
  Client   Property One Management
  Designer Alfred C. Sanft
4.
  Client   Westwind Air Services
  Designer Alfred C. Sanft
5.
  Client   uALTe, Arizona State University
  Designer Alfred C. Sanft
6.
  Client   All Points Media
  Designer Lili Pang
7.
  Client   Renaissance Construction
  Designer Chris Hansen
8.
  Client   Unforgettable Honeymoons
  Designer Lili Pang
9.
  Client   K2 Media Consulting
  Designer Lili Pang
10.
  Client   Thalia Consulting
  Designer Lili Pang
11.
  Client   Maucy Cleaning Services
  Designer Lili Pang

1.

HEALTH BENEFITS THAT WORK FOR Y...

- AFFORDABLE dental, vision, prescription pac...
- DISCOUNTS for ALTERNATIVE MEDICAL nee...
- ESSENTIAL NUTRIENTS - the way foods used...
- Provide cost savings to meet HIGH DEDUCTIE...
- All PRE-EXISTING CONDITIONS accepted

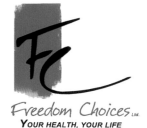

Sondra Hampe

503.618.8133

Freedom Choices Ltd.
YOUR HEALTH, YOUR LIFE

1121 SE 214th Avenue
Gresham, OR 97030-3444
www.yourfreedomchoices.com

2.

Kobe Austin
Assistant Program Director
On Air 3 - 7 PM

*Z100 - KKRZ - Portland
Clear Channel Radio*

ph: 503.323.6495
fx: 503.323.6677

kobeaustin@z100portland.com
4949 SW Macadam, Portland, Oregon 97239

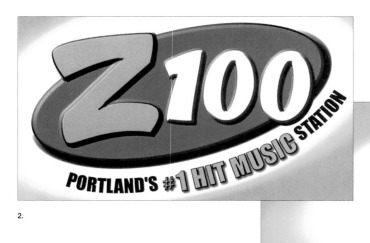

CREATE**CREDIBILITY**

3.

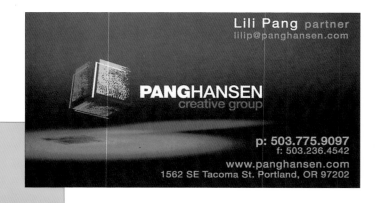

Lili Pang partner
lilip@panghansen.com

PANGHANSEN
creative group

p: **503.775.9097**
f: 503.236.4542
www.panghansen.com
1562 SE Tacoma St. Portland, OR 97202

THE CIMARRON GROUP

THE MOUNTAIN WILL TRANSFORM YOU

605 County Road 23, Ridgway, Colorado 814
p. 970-626-3438 f. 970-325-0384
www.cimarronleadership.com

MICHAEL O'DONNELL, PRINCIPAL

970-325-4597 modonnell@cimarronleadership

4.

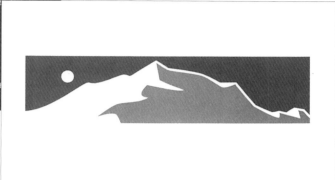

Tom Caprel
CEO
tcaprel@itlighthouse.com

7560 Quincy Street
Willowbrook, IL 60527
630 789.3880 *main*
630 918.0757 *cell*
630 789.3556 *facsimile*
www.itlighthouse.com

IT LIGHTHOUSE™
The way small business manages information technology ™

5.

GEOFFREY C. FENNER, M.D.

Chief of Plastic Surgery

1000 Central Street, Suite 840
Evanston, IL 60201

www.fennerplasticsurgery.com

T · 847.570.1300

F · 847.570.1352

FENNER
PLASTIC SURGERY

6.

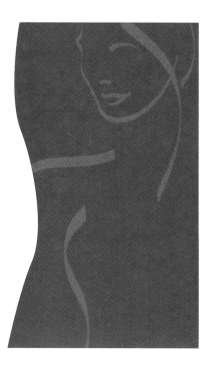

(1-3)
Design Firm **Panghansen Creative Group**
(4-6)
Design Firm **Torque Ltd.**

1.
Client Freedom Choices Ltd.
Designer Lili Pang
2.
Client Clear Channel–Z100
 KKRZ-Portland
Designers Chris Hansen,
 Lili Pang
3.
Client Panghansen Creative Group
Designers Chris Hansen,
 Lili Pang
4.
Client The Cimarron Group
Designer Tim Hogan
5.
Client IT Lighthouse
Designers Dexter Cura,
 Adam Lilly
6.
Client Fenner Plastic Surgery
Designer Ian Law

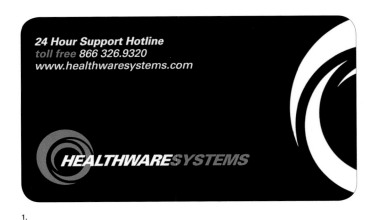

24 Hour Support Hotline
toll free 866 326.9320
www.healthwaresystems.com

HEALTHWARESYSTEMS

1.

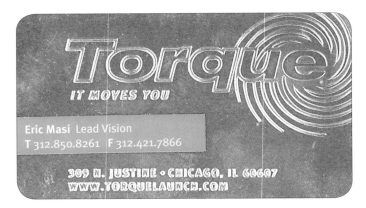

Torque

IT MOVES YOU

Eric Masi Lead Vision
T 312.850.8261 F 312.421.7866

309 N. JUSTINE • CHICAGO, IL 60607
WWW.TORQUELAUNCH.COM

2.

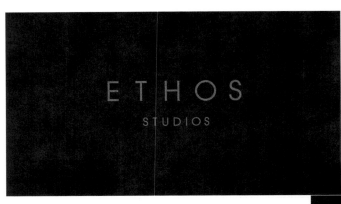

E T H O S
STUDIOS

3.

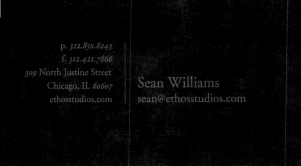

p. 312.850.8243
f. 312.421.7866
309 North Justine Street
Chicago, IL 60607
ethosstudios.com

Sean Williams
sean@ethosstudios.com

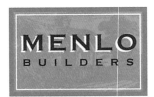

MENLO
BUILDERS

Sherwood Anderson

P.O.Box 367
Menlo Park, CA 94026-0367
c 650 804 1395
t 650 330 1892
f 650 330 1792
sherwood@menlobuilders.com
www.menlobuilders.com

CA License #732412

4.

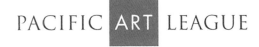

Patricia O'Brien, Development Director
patricia.obrien@ pacificartleague.org

PACIFIC ART LEAGUE

668 Ramona Street, Palo Alto, California 94301
t 650 321 3891 x 14   f 650 321 3617   www.pacificartleague.org

5.

Cliff F. Kilb
Senior Technical Education Specialist
ckilb@convera.com

CONVERA™

1921 Gallows Road, Suite 200 Vienna VA 22182
T 703 761 3700 F 703 761 1984
www.convera.com

6.

David M. Licurse, Sr., CFO & VP Operations

@pos.com™

www.atpos.com | 500 Oakmead Parkway, Sunnyvale, California 94086 U.S.A.
T 408.524.4212 F 408.524.4299 E dlicurse@atpos.com

7.

WEALTHCYCLE™

900 ISLAND DRIVE, SUITE 102 | REDWOOD CITY, CA 94065

Joe Welsh *Director, Strategic Accounts*

T 650 413 5854   C 281 382 5291
F 650 413 5761
E jwelsh@wealthcycle.com

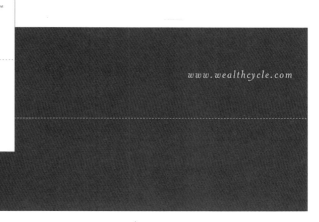

www.wealthcycle.com

8.

SAND HILL SH
A D V I S O R S

Enrique Figueroa, CFA
Senior Research Analyst

3000 Sand Hill Road
Building 3, Suite 150
Menlo Park . CA 94025-7116
T 650 854 9150
F 650 854 2941
efigueroa@shadv.com

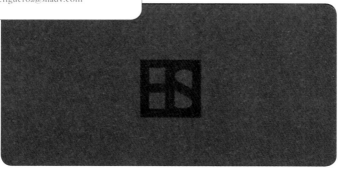

9.

(1-3)
Design Firm **Torque Ltd.**
(4-9)
Design Firm **Michael Patrick Partners, Inc.**

1.
Client   Healthware Systems
Designer   Adam Lilly
2.
Client   Torque
Designer   Rich Smith
3.
Client   Ethos Studio
Designer   Hellbox Design
4.
Client   Menlo Builders
Designer   Dan O'Brien
5.
Client   Pacific Art League
Designer   Dan O'Brien
6.
Client   Convera
Designer   Eko Tjoek
7.
Client   @POS.com
Designer   Eko Tjoek
8.
Client   WealthCycle
Designer   Dan O'Brien
9.
Client   Sand Hill Advisors
Designer   Eko Tjoek

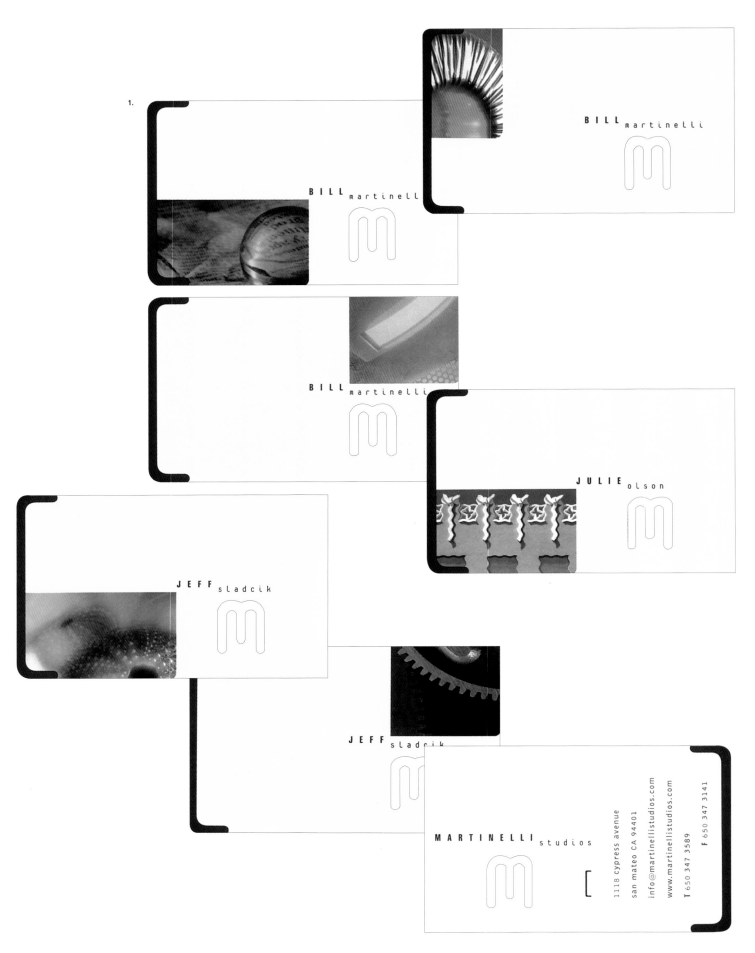

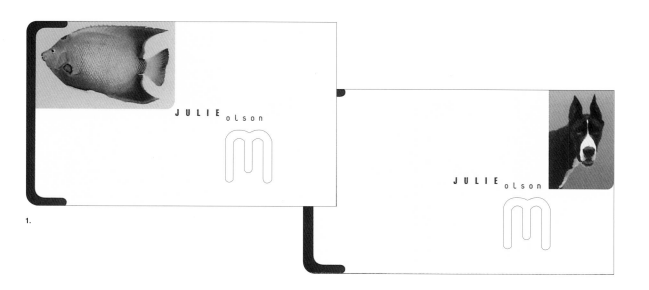

JULIE olson

JULIE olson

1.

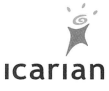

||| financialprinter|com ||.™

Randy Churchill | client development
rchurchill@financialprinter.com
10100 santa monica boulevard suite 600
los angeles ca 90067
main 310 407 1200 fax 310 407 1300
direct 310 407 1215 mobile 310 770 2068

a conscium business

2.

icarian

Tim O'Bryan
Principal Consultant
eServices

555 North Mathilda Avenue
Sunnyvale, CA 94086
tel/fax 408.743.5700
cell 415.999.8249
main fax 408.743.5701
tobryan@icarian.com

3.

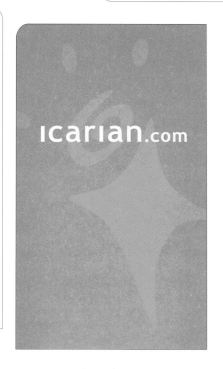

icarian.com

(1-3)
Design Firm **Michael Patrick Partners, Inc.**

1.
Client Martinelli Studios
Designer Dan O'Brien
2.
Client financialprinter.com
Designer Duane Maidens
3.
Client Icarian
Designer Eko Tjoek

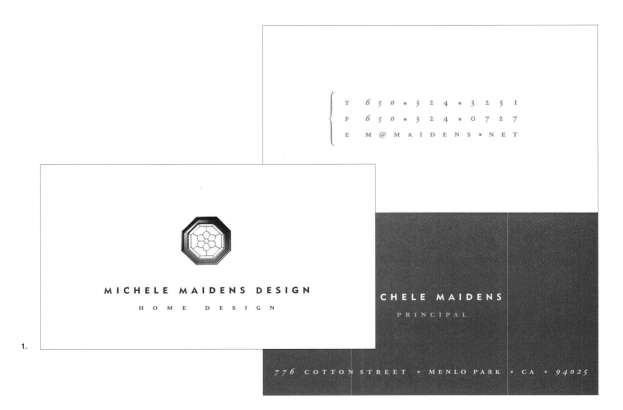

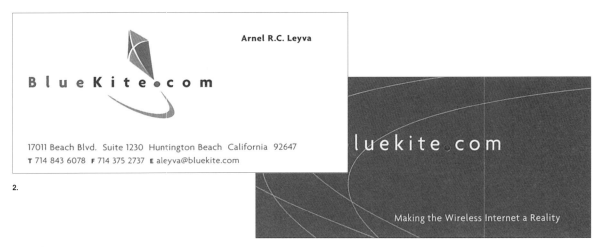

1.

MICHELE MAIDENS DESIGN

HOME   DESIGN

T   6 5 0 • 3 2 4 • 3 2 5 1
F   6 5 0 • 3 2 4 • 0 7 2 7
E   M @ M A I D E N S • N E T

CHELE MAIDENS

PRINCIPAL

7 7 6   C O T T O N   S T R E E T   •   M E N L O   P A R K   •   C A   •   9 4 0 2 5

BlueKite.com

Arnel R.C. Leyva

17011 Beach Blvd. Suite 1230 Huntington Beach California 92647
T 714 843 6078 F 714 375 2737 E aleyva@bluekite.com

2.

luekite.com

Making the Wireless Internet a Reality

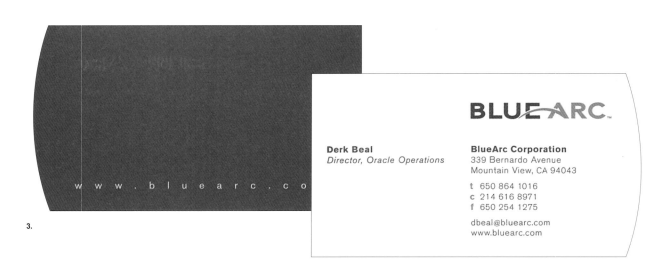

www.bluearc.co

3.

BLUE ARC.™

Derk Beal
Director, Oracle Operations

BlueArc Corporation
339 Bernardo Avenue
Mountain View, CA 94043

t 650 864 1016
c 214 616 8971
f 650 254 1275

dbeal@bluearc.com
www.bluearc.com

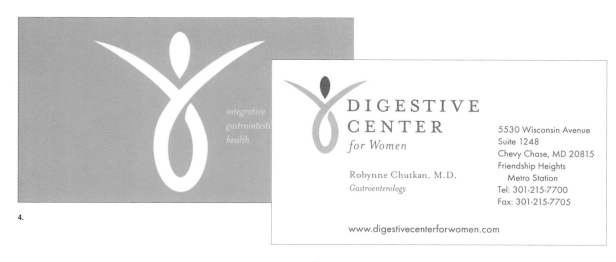

integrative
gastrointestinal
health

4.

DIGESTIVE CENTER
for Women

Robynne Chutkan, M.D.

Gastroenterology

5530 Wisconsin Avenue
Suite 1248
Chevy Chase, MD 20815
Friendship Heights
 Metro Station
Tel: 301-215-7700
Fax: 301-215-7705

www.digestivecenterforwomen.com

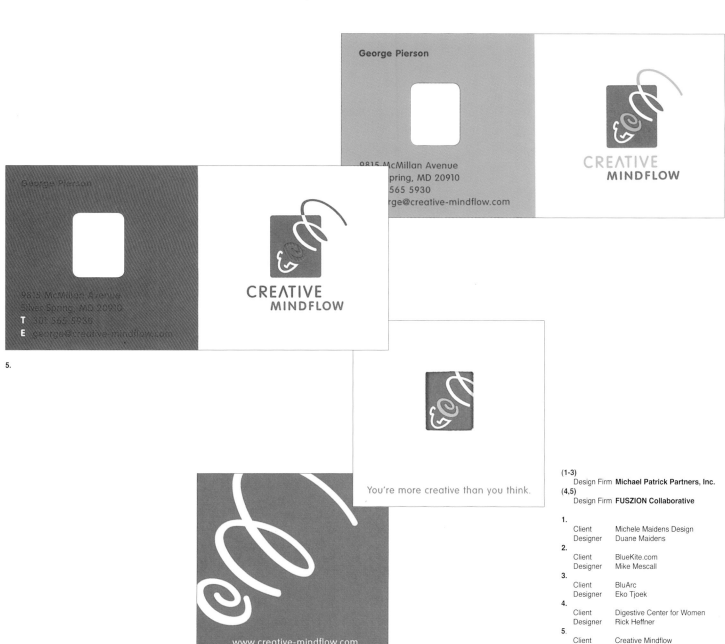

George Pierson

9815 McMillan Avenue
 pring, MD 20910
 565 5930
 rge@creative-mindflow.com

**CREATIVE
MINDFLOW**

George Pierson

9815 McMillan Avenue
Silver Spring, MD 20910
T 301 565 5930
E george@creative-mindflow.com

**CREATIVE
MINDFLOW**

5.

You're more creative than you think.

www.creative-mindflow.com

(1-3)
Design Firm **Michael Patrick Partners, Inc.**
(4,5)
Design Firm **FUSZION Collaborative**

1.
 Client   Michele Maidens Design
 Designer   Duane Maidens
2.
 Client   BlueKite.com
 Designer   Mike Mescall
3.
 Client   BluArc
 Designer   Eko Tjoek
4.
 Client   Digestive Center for Women
 Designer   Rick Heffner
5.
 Client   Creative Mindflow
 Designer   Christian Baldo

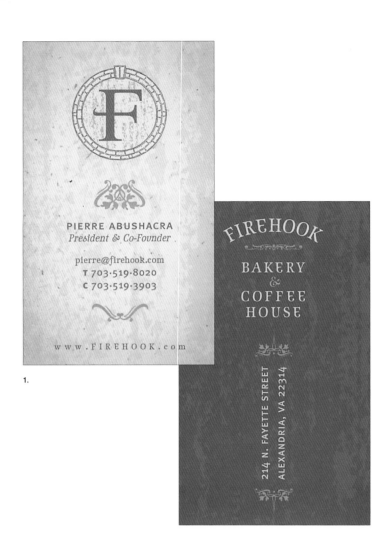

1.

PIERRE ABUSHACRA
President & Co-Founder

pierre@firehook.com
T 703·519·8020
C 703·519·3903

w w w . F I R E H O O K . c o m

FIREHOOK

BAKERY
&
COFFEE
HOUSE

214 N. FAYETTE STREET
ALEXANDRIA, VA 22314

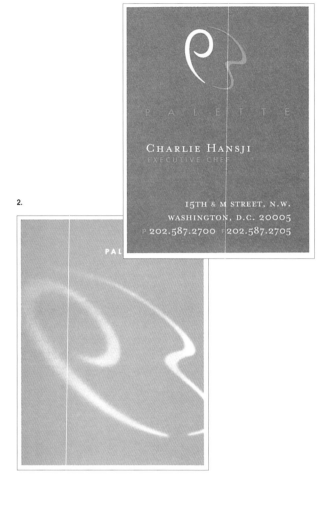

2.

PALETTE

CHARLIE HANSJI
EXECUTIVE CHEF

15TH & M STREET, N.W.
WASHINGTON, D.C. 20005
P 202.587.2700 F 202.587.2705

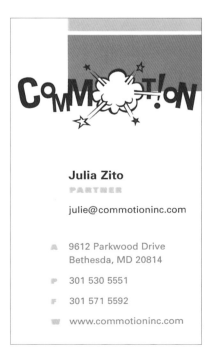

COMMOT!ON

Julia Zito
PARTNER

julie@commotioninc.com

🏠 9612 Parkwood Drive
Bethesda, MD 20814

📞 301 530 5551

📠 301 571 5592

🌐 www.commotioninc.com

3.

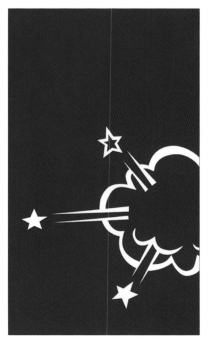

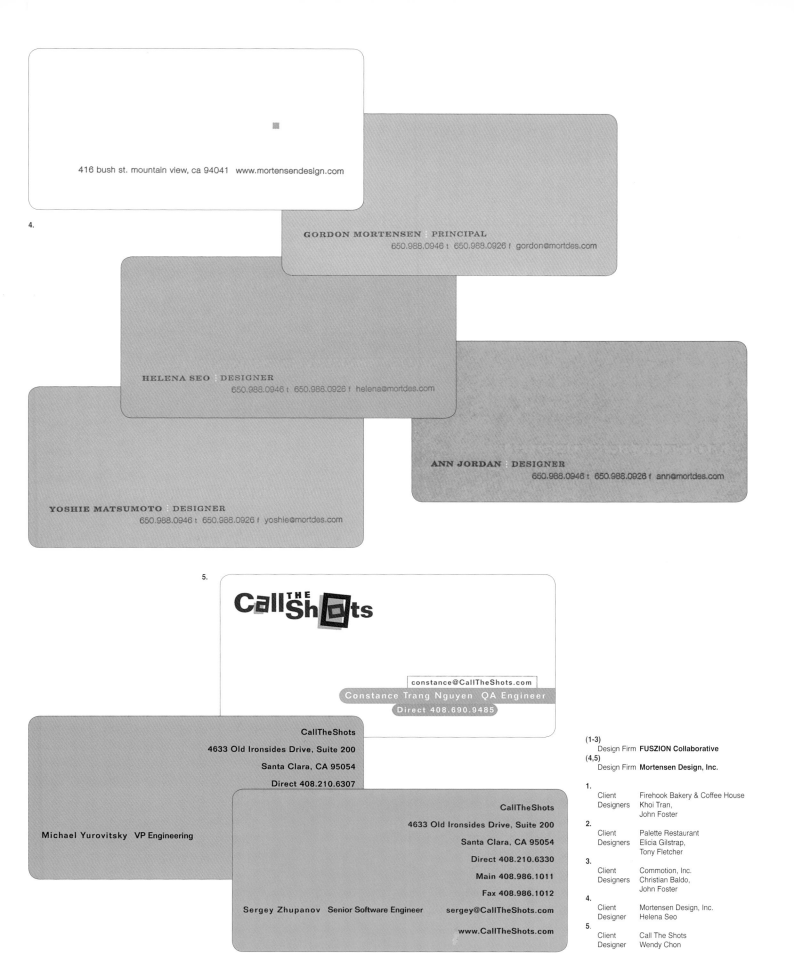

416 bush st. mountain view, ca 94041   www.mortensendesign.com

4.

GORDON MORTENSEN : PRINCIPAL
650.988.0946 t 650.988.0926 f gordon@mortdes.com

HELENA SEO : DESIGNER
650.988.0946 t 650.988.0926 f helena@mortdes.com

ANN JORDAN : DESIGNER
650.988.0946 t 650.988.0926 f ann@mortdes.com

YOSHIE MATSUMOTO : DESIGNER
650.988.0946 t 650.988.0926 f yoshie@mortdes.com

5.

CallTHEShots

constance@CallTheShots.com
Constance Trang Nguyen   QA Engineer
Direct 408.690.9485

CallTheShots
4633 Old Ironsides Drive, Suite 200
Santa Clara, CA 95054
Direct 408.210.6307

Michael Yurovitsky   VP Engineering

CallTheShots
4633 Old Ironsides Drive, Suite 200
Santa Clara, CA 95054
Direct 408.210.6330
Main 408.986.1011
Fax 408.986.1012
Sergey Zhupanov   Senior Software Engineer   sergey@CallTheShots.com
www.CallTheShots.com

(1-3)
Design Firm **FUSZION Collaborative**
(4,5)
Design Firm **Mortensen Design, Inc.**

1.
Client   Firehook Bakery & Coffee House
Designers   Khoi Tran,
            John Foster
2.
Client   Palette Restaurant
Designers   Elicia Gilstrap,
            Tony Fletcher
3.
Client   Commotion, Inc.
Designers   Christian Baldo,
            John Foster
4.
Client   Mortensen Design, Inc.
Designer   Helena Seo
5.
Client   Call The Shots
Designer   Wendy Chon

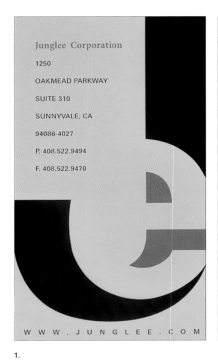

Junglee Corporation

1250

OAKMEAD PARKWAY

SUITE 310

SUNNYVALE, CA

94086-4027

P. 408.522.9494

F. 408.522.9470

W W W . J U N G L E E . C O M

1.

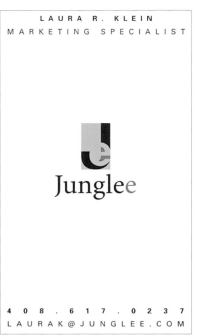

LAURA R. KLEIN
MARKETING SPECIALIST

Junglee

4 0 8 . 6 1 7 . 0 2 3 7
L A U R A K @ J U N G L E E . C O M

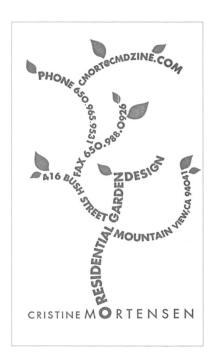

PHONE 650.965.9531
CMORT@CMDZINE.COM
FAX 650.988.0926
416 BUSH STREET
RESIDENTIAL GARDEN DESIGN
MOUNTAIN VIEW, CA 94041

CRISTINE MORTENSEN

2.

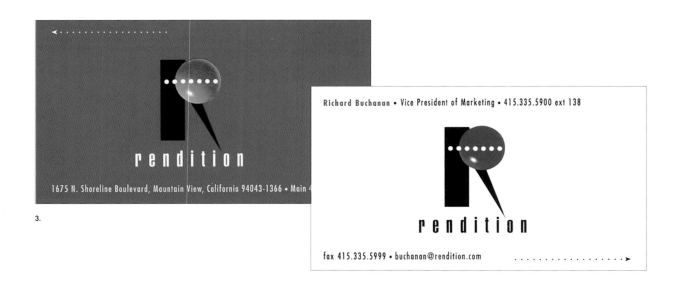

rendition

1675 N. Shoreline Boulevard, Mountain View, California 94043-1366 • Main 4

3.

Richard Buchanan • Vice President of Marketing • 415.335.5900 ext 138

rendition

fax 415.335.5999 • buchanan@rendition.com

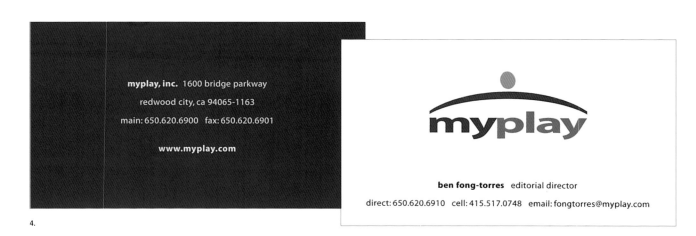

myplay, inc. 1600 bridge parkway

redwood city, ca 94065-1163

main: 650.620.6900 fax: 650.620.6901

www.myplay.com

myplay

ben fong-torres editorial director

direct: 650.620.6910 cell: 415.517.0748 email: fongtorres@myplay.com

4.

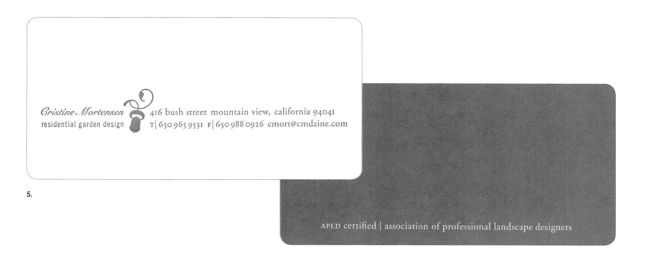

5.

APLD certified | association of professional landscape designers

6.

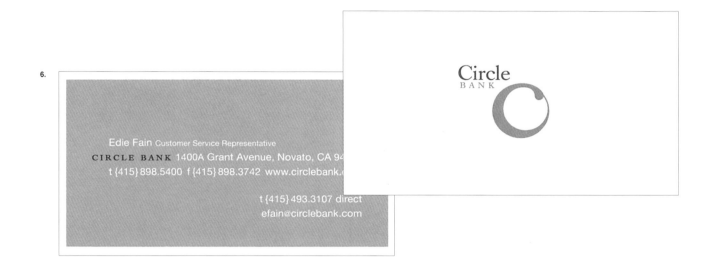

Edie Fain Customer Service Representative
CIRCLE BANK 1400A Grant Avenue, Novato, CA 94
t {415} 898.5400 f {415} 898.3742 www.circlebank.
t {415} 493.3107 direct
efain@circlebank.com

Circle
BANK

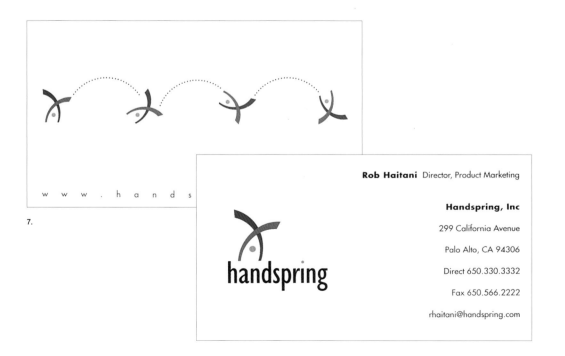

w w w . h a n d s

7.

Rob Haitani Director, Product Marketing

Handspring, Inc

299 California Avenue

Palo Alto, CA 94306

Direct 650.330.3332

Fax 650.566.2222

rhaitani@handspring.com

handspring

Ambric

IAN GETREU | director of partnership development
ian@ambric.com

direct 503 601 6505 cell 503 888 2372

1.

AMBRIC, INC. | 15655 sw greystone court, suite 150. beaverton, or 97006
main
503.601.6500 fax **503.601.6596**

Barbara Gibson [*freelance writing*] bga@earthlink.net ▪ 251 Loucks Los Altos CA 94022
(P) 650-941-2300 (F) 650-949-3038

2.

Edward T. Colligan

Director, Customer Marketing

Radius Inc.

1710 Fortune Drive

San Jose, CA 95131

(408) 434-1010

FAX: (408) 434-0127

Direct Line:

(408) 954-6831

radius

3.

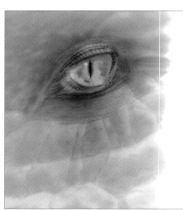

G&HS

Geoff Spring DIRECTOR

Spring Consulting
Services PTY LTD

Ph 02 9999 0552
Int +61 2 9999 0552
Mob 0418 831 206
Email gspring@bigpond.com

155 McCarrs Creek Road Church Point
PO Box 1251 Mona Vale 1660

4.

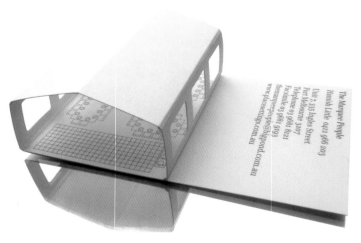

The Marquee People
Hamish Little 0412 966 203
Unit 7, 335 Ingles Street
Port Melbourne 3207
Telephone 03 9681 8121
Facsimile 03 9681 9191
themarqueepeople@bigpond.com.au
www.placesettings.com.au

5.

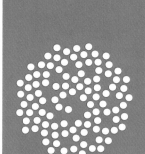

Professor Tony Guttmann

ARC Centre of Excellence for Mathematics
and Statistics of Complex Systems

139 Barry Street
The University of Melbourne
Parkville Victoria 3010 Australia

T +61 3 8344 1618
F +61 3 9347 8165

director@complex.org.au
www.ms.unimelb.edu.au/~tonyg

6.

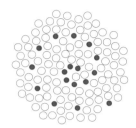

Centre of Excellence for Mathematics
and Statistics of Complex Systems

Reinout Quispel

Professor of Mathematics
La Trobe University

Chief Investigator

www.complex.org.au

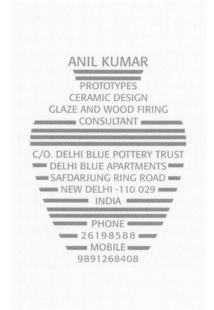

ANIL KUMAR

PROTOTYPES
CERAMIC DESIGN
GLAZE AND WOOD FIRING
CONSULTANT

C/O. DELHI BLUE POTTERY TRUST
DELHI BLUE APARTMENTS
SAFDARJUNG RING ROAD
NEW DELHI -110 029
INDIA

PHONE
26198588
MOBILE
9891268408

7.

əxtɾəmə spəcial cɐɾ̆əmᵢcₛ

Tanuja Jain

mobile : 98101 69090
e-mail : tanuja.jain@rediffmail.com

8.

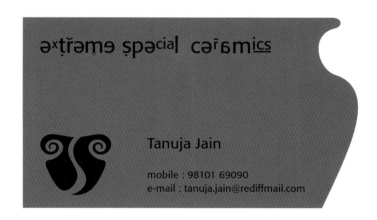

DATA-FACTORY DESIGNS . LOOK . IDENTIFY . FEEL .
multidiscipline design and marketing consultation

br/designer
10.3777 CELL

1331 40th street | suite 315 | emeryville | california | 94608
510.547.7777 TEL | www.data-factory.com

9.

(1-3)
Design Firm **Mortensen Design, Inc.**
(4)
Design Firm **Designoz**
(5,6)
Design Firm **GollingsPidgeon**
(7,8)
Design Firm **Surinder Singh**
(9)
Design Firm **Data-Factory Designs**

1.
Client   Ambric, Inc.
Designer   Patricia Margaret
2.
Client   Barbara Gibson
Designer   Sabiha Basrai
3.
Client   Radius, Inc.
Designer   Gordon Mortensen
4.
Client   Geoff Spring
Designers   Greg Campbell,
            Medium Greg
5.
Client   Hamish Little, The Marquee People
Designer   David Pidgeon
6.
Client   Tony Guttman, ARC Centre of
            Excellence for Mathematics &
            Statistics of Complex Systems
Designer   John Calabro
7.
Client   Anil Kumar
Designer   Surinder Singh
8.
Client   Extreme Special Ceramics
Designer   Surinder Singh
9.
Client   Data Factory
Designer   Adam Gross

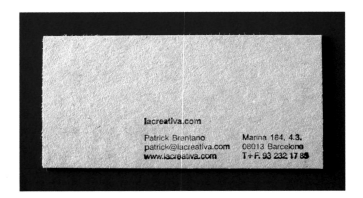

1.

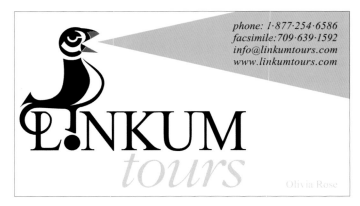

lacreativa.com

Patrick Brentano
patrick@lacreativa.com
www.lacreativa.com

Marina 164, 4.3.
08013 Barcelona
T + F. 93 232 17 85

L!NKUM
tours

Olivia Rose

2.

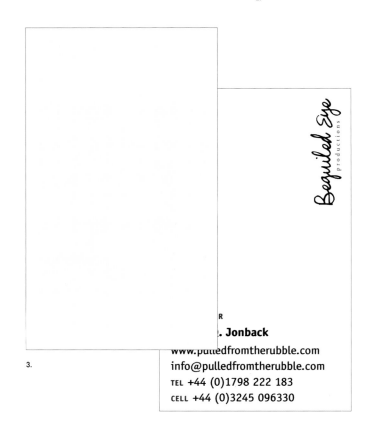

3.

Beguiled Eye
productions

R

. Jonback

www.pulledfromtherubble.com
info@pulledfromtherubble.com
TEL +44 (0)1798 222 183
CELL +44 (0)3245 096330

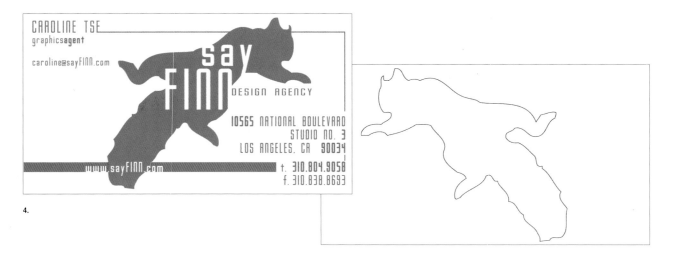

CAROLINE TSE
graphics**agent**

caroline@sayFINN.com

say
FINN
DESIGN AGENCY

10565 NATIONAL BOULEVARD
STUDIO NO. 3
LOS ANGELES, CA 90034

www.sayFINN.com

t. 310.804.9058
f. 310.838.8693

4.

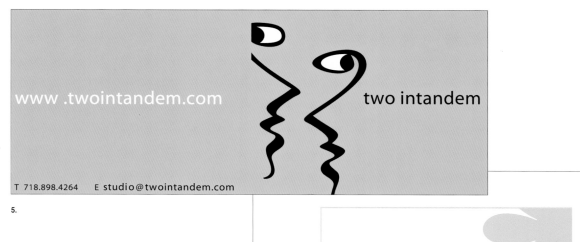

www .twointandem.com

two intandem

T 718.898.4264   E studio@twointandem.com

5.

design   freshen up your look

PROMOTIONALS

IDENTITY/LOGO

COLL ATERAL

WEB/INTE RACTIV E

PACK AGING

ILLUST RATION

CONTIGLI

LUCIANO CONTIGLI *DIRECTOR CREATIVO*
luciano@contigli.com

CONTIGLI ESTUDIO DE DISEÑO

Campichuelo 279 (c1405boa)
Capital Federal Buenos Aires Argentina
Tel: +(5411) 4903-6610
Fax: +(5411) 4901-4737
www.contigli.com

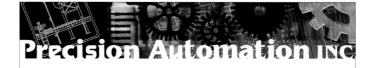

Precision Automation INC

David E. Koetsch
Technical Consultant

Tel: 604.240.5384
Fax: 604.857.0409
techshop@telus.ca

#104-5498 267 St.
Langley , BC
V4W 3S8 ,Canada

Automation Equiptment , Design Manufacturing & Service

7.

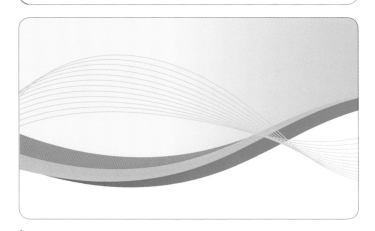

6.

(1)
Design Firm **La Creativa**
(2)
Design Firm **Sequent Mktg. & Comm.**
(3)
Design Firm **La Chispa**
(4)
Design Firm **Say Finn**
(5)
Design Firm **Twointandem Design**
(6)
Design Firm **Greenhouse PhotoGraphix**
(7)
Design Firm **Contigli**

1.
Client   Brentano
Designer   Patrick Brentano
2.
Client   Linkum Tours
Designer   Andrew Metz
3.
Client   beguiled
Designer   Emma Arnold

4.
Client   Say Finn
Designer   Caroline Tse
5.
Client   Two in Tandem Design
Designer   Elena Ruano Kanidinc
6.
Client   Contigli
Designer   Luciano Contigli
7.
Client   Precision Automation
Designer   Byron A. Smith

1.

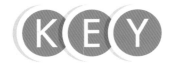

KNOWLEDGE ENERGY YIELD

KEES MENSCH | MANAGING DIRECTOR
Mob: 06 54 20 81 38   kees.mensch@keyonline.nl

Geelvinckstraat 18 1901 AH Castricum
Tel: 0251 67 20 88 Fax: 0251 67 20 85
www.keyonline.nl

2.

Bradley J. Kabanuk   President
brad@kabanuk.com

content enablers

Content Enablers Inc.
9803 Thunderhill Court
Great Falls, VA 22066

P 703-757-8088
F 703-757-9894
M 202-247-7101

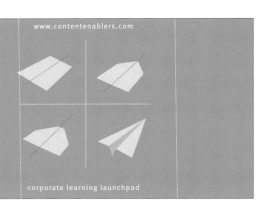

www.contentenablers.com

corporate learning launchpad

3.

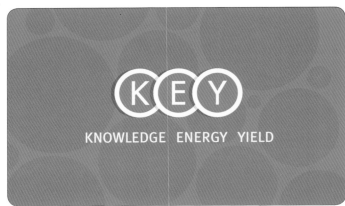

exceptional people • extraordinary results

Jack E. Handy   Director, Network
jehandy@esymmetrix.com

eSymmetrix

13808 Holly Crest Lane, Dayton, Maryland 21036
443-535-9368x302   443-535-9369   410-627-2820
www.esymmetrix.com

4.

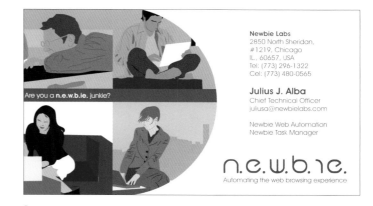

Newbie Labs
2850 North Sheridan,
#1219, Chicago
IL, 60657, USA
Tel: (773) 296-1322
Cel: (773) 480-0565

Julius J. Alba
Chief Technical Officer
juliusa@newbielabs.com

Newbie Web Automation
Newbie Task Manager

n.e.w.b.ie.
Automating the web browsing experience

5.

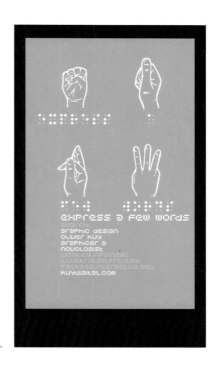

6.

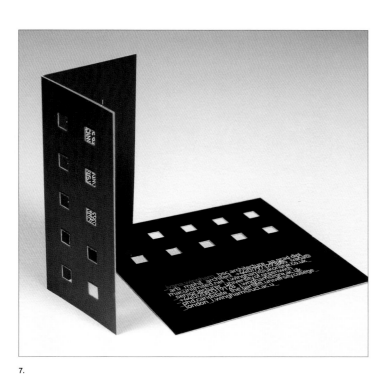

7.

(1)
Design Firm **Contigli**
(2,3)
Design Firm **Apparatus Media Lab**
(4)
Design Firm **Thinking Cap Design**
(5,6)
Design Firm **Kuy Digital**
(7)
Design Firm **Eduard Cehovin**

1.
Client — Key
Designer — Luciano Contigli
2.
Client — Content Enablers
Designer — Sharad Nayak
3.
Client — esymmetrix
Designer — Sharad Nayak
4.
Client — Thinking Cap Design
Designer — Kelly D. Lawrence

5.
Client — Newbie
Designer — Oliver Kuy
6.
Client — Express A Few Words
Designer — Oliver Kuy
7.
Client — Ivana Wingham
Designer — Eduard Cehovin

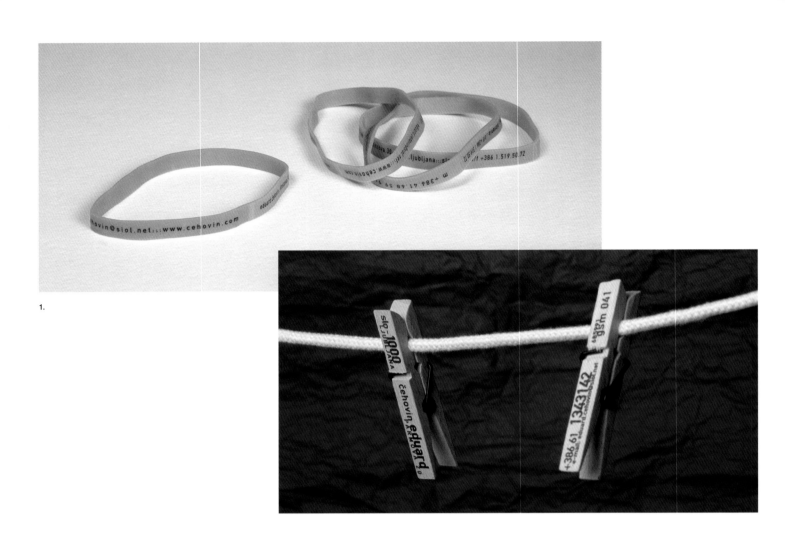

1.

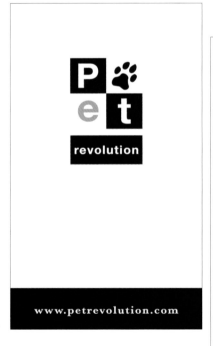

P e t
revolution

www.petrevolution.com

2.

Pet Revolution Inc.
#2-6344 Kingsway
Burnaby, BC. V5E 1C5

Jae-Won Sim
Co-Founder & Industrial Designer

tel : 604.451.0321
fax : 604.451.0322
cel : 604.780.9984

jaewon@petrevolution.com

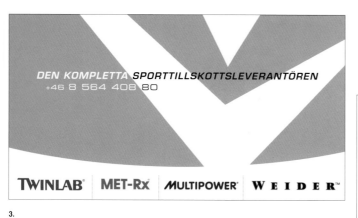

DEN KOMPLETTA SPORTTILLSKOTTSLEVERANTÖREN
+46 8 564 408 80

TWINLAB® | **MET-Rx**® | **MULTIPOWER**® | **W E I D E R**™

3.

Florin Suhoschi
ART DIRECTOR

Direkt: +46 8 **564 408 89**
Fax: +46 8 **38 51 08**
Mobil: +46 **734 31 43 30**
E-mail: **florin@sppab.se**

Finspångsgatan 51, 163 53 Spånga, Sverige

SCANDINAVIAN
PRO PRODUCTS

www.**sppab.se**

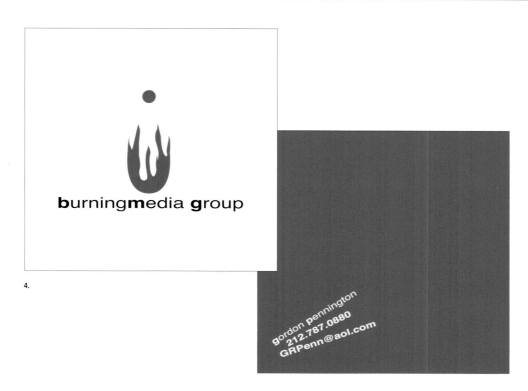

burningmedia group

gordon pennington
212.787.0880
GRPenn@aol.com

4.

Darby Automation Inc.

359 East 50th Street, #3
New York, New York 10022

Kevin Darby

kdarby@darbyautomation.com

tlf . 212 . 758 . 1614
fax . 212 . 758 . 1614
cell . 917 . 680 . 1443

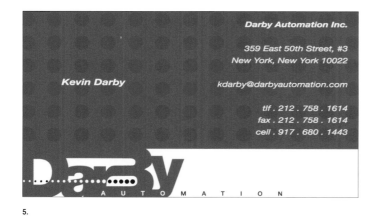

5.

(1)
 Design Firm **Eduard Cehovin**
(2)
 Design Firm **Pet Revolution**
(3)
 Design Firm **Florin Suhoschi**
(4,5)
 Design Firm **Mónica Torrejón Kelly**

1.
 Client   Cehovin
 Designer   Eduard Cehovin
2.
 Client   Pet Revolution
 Designer   Jae-Won Sim
3.
 Client   Scandanavian Pro Products
 Designer   Florin Suhoschi
4.
 Client   Burning Media
 Designer   Mónica Torrejón Kelly
5.
 Client   Darby Automation
 Designer   Mónica Torrejón Kelly

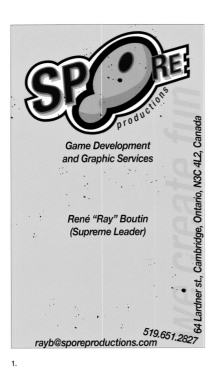

1.

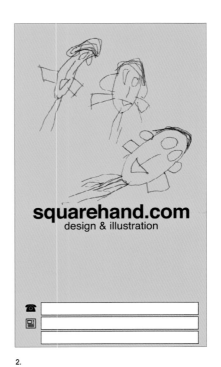

2.

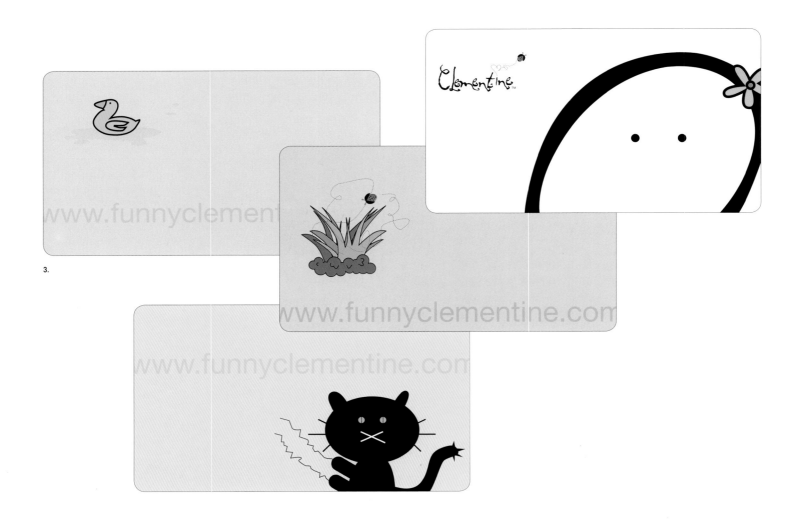

3.

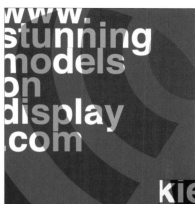

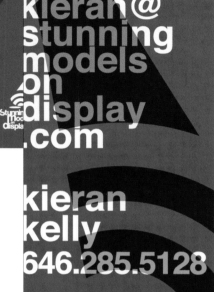

kieran@
stunning
models
on
display
.com

kieran
kelly
646.285.5128

4.

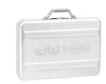

360 Fillmore St. #3   San Francisco, CA   94117
www.DWORKZ.com

STAS UDOTOV
Senior Art Director

stas@DWORKZ.com
email

415 378 7840
phone

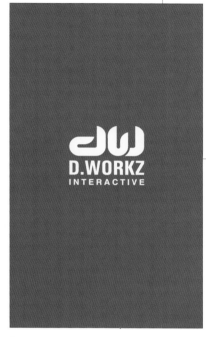

D.WORKZ
INTERACTIVE

5.

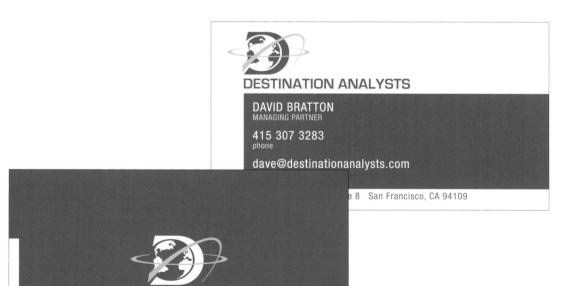

DESTINATION ANALYSTS

DAVID BRATTON
MANAGING PARTNER

415 307 3283
phone

dave@destinationanalysts.com

e 8   San Francisco, CA 94109

DESTINATION ANALYSTS
A MARKETING AND RESEARCH COMPANY

6.

(1-4)
Design Firm **Mónica Torrejón Kelly**
(5,6)
Design Firm **D.Workz Interactive**

1.
Client   Spore
Designer   Mónica Torrejón Kelly
2.
Client   Squarehand
Designer   Mónica Torrejón Kelly
3.
Client   Funny Clementine
Designer   Mónica Torrejón Kelly
4.
Client   SMOD
Designer   Mónica Torrejón Kelly
5.
Client   dWorkz
Designer   Stas Udotov
6.
Client   DestinationAnalysts
Designer   Stas Udotov

ELIE NAKAMURA
fashion designer

415.216.7386
phone

elie.xcuseme@gmail.com
email

www.2shin.net/xcuseme
website

XCUSEME
life design

1.

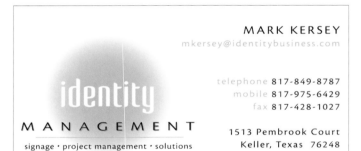

LOGO DESIGN

BUSINESS COLLATERAL

POSTCARDS & FLYERS

BROCHURES & CATALOGS

NEWSLETTER DESIGN

SIGNAGE DESIGN & WAYFINDING

CADENCE
studio

Jill P. Beck

3411 South Beverly Place
Chandler, AZ 85248-3822

480.219.3380 p
480.219.3382 f
jbeck@cadencestudio.com

2.

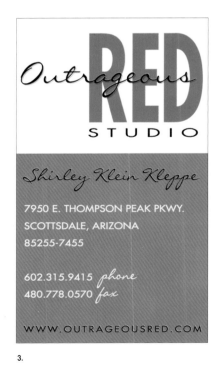

Outrageous RED
STUDIO

Shirley Klein Kleppe

7950 E. THOMPSON PEAK PKWY.
SCOTTSDALE, ARIZONA
85255-7455

602.315.9415 phone
480.778.0570 fax

WWW.OUTRAGEOUSRED.COM

3.

MARK KERSEY
mkersey@identitybusiness.com

identity
MANAGEMENT
signage · project management · solutions

telephone 817-849-8787
mobile 817-975-6429
fax 817-428-1027

1513 Pembrook Court
Keller, Texas 76248

www.identitybusiness.com

4.

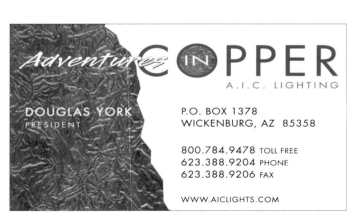

Adventures IN COPPER
A.I.C. LIGHTING

DOUGLAS YORK
PRESIDENT

P.O. BOX 1378
WICKENBURG, AZ 85358

800.784.9478 TOLL FREE
623.388.9204 PHONE
623.388.9206 FAX

WWW.AICLIGHTS.COM

5.

338

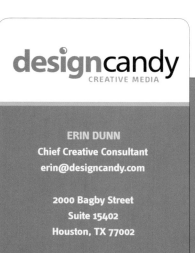

ERIN DUNN

Chief Creative Consultant
erin@designcandy.com

2000 Bagby Street
Suite 15402
Houston, TX 77002

ph 832.651.5384
fax 713.523.5582

www.designcandy.com

6.

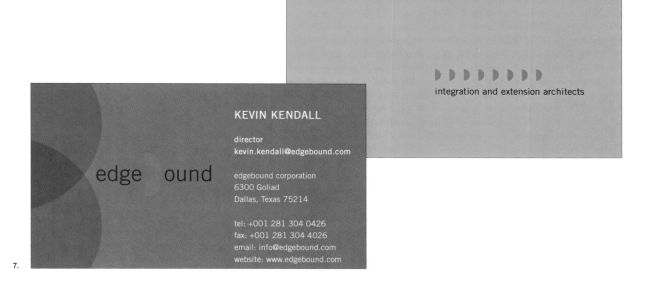

designcandy
CREATIVE MEDIA

integration and extension architects

KEVIN KENDALL

director
kevin.kendall@edgebound.com

edge bound

edgebound corporation
6300 Goliad
Dallas, Texas 75214

tel: +001 281 304 0426
fax: +001 281 304 4026
email: info@edgebound.com
website: www.edgebound.com

7.

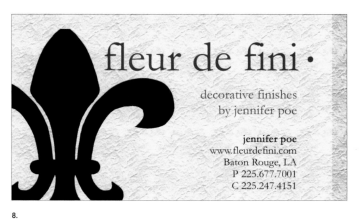

fleur de fini ·

decorative finishes
by jennifer poe

jennifer poe
www.fleurdefini.com
Baton Rouge, LA
P 225.677.7001
C 225.247.4151

8.

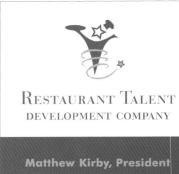

RESTAURANT TALENT
DEVELOPMENT COMPANY

Matthew Kirby, President
2020 Howell Mill Road
Suite 170
Atlanta, GA 30318

P 404.355.3401
F 404.745.8012
E mkirby@restauranttalent.com
restauranttalent.com

restauranttalent.com

1.

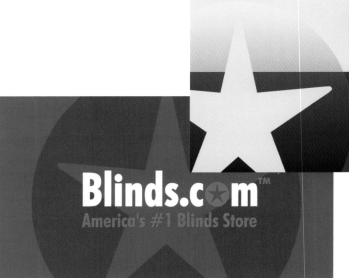

Blinds.com™
America's #1 Blinds Store

JAY STEINFELD
President & CEO
4660 Beechnut - Ste. 218
Houston, TX 77096
T 713-838-3030
F 713-838-1035
jay@Blinds.com

Blinds.com™
America's #1 Blinds Store

2.

Future Kids

p. o. box N-511
nassau, bahamas
tel: (242) 364-8406
fax: (242) 393-5645
eml: info@futurekids.org
web: www.futurekids.org

3.

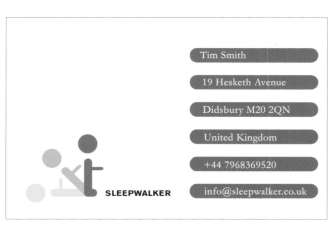

Tim Smith

19 Hesketh Avenue

Didsbury M20 2QN

United Kingdom

+44 7968369520

info@sleepwalker.co.uk

SLEEPWALKER

4.

5.

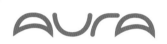

Suzanne Khattari
BA PGD M Phil
Director

Aura Castings
1 Floor, 126 Long Acre
Covent Garden
London WC2E 9PE
t 020 7379 1901
t 020 7379 5893
f 020 7240 5150
info@aura.co.uk

6.

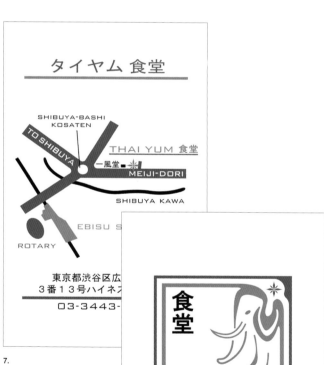

7.

(1,2)
Design Firm **Design Candy**
(3)
Design Firm **Smith + Benjamin Art + Design**
(4-6)
Design Firm **Metorical**
(7)
Design Firm **SIMC Co. Ltd.**

1.
Client   RTD
Designer   Erin Dunn
2.
Client   Blinds.com
Designer   Erin Dunn
3.
Client   Future Kids
Designer   Dionne Benjamin-Smith
4.
Client   Sleepwalker
Designer   Marcus Tonndorf

5.
Client   Metorical
Designer   Marcus Tonndorf
6.
Client   Aura
Designer   Marcus Tonndorf
7.
Client   Thai Yum Shop
Designer   Hidekazu Tsutsui

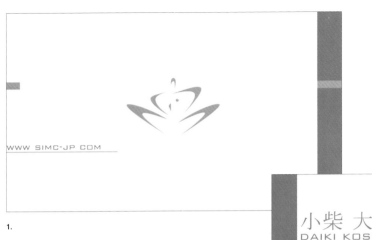

WWW.SIMC-JP.COM

1.

小柴 大樹
DAIKI KOSHIBA

SIMPLE INNOVATIVE MODERN CONCEPT
代表取締役 MANAGING DIRECTOR

📞 03-3475-5720

📱 080-5077-6676

✉ DKOSHIBA@SIMC-JP.COM

SIMC CO., LTD.
1-10-6 MINATO-KU NISHI-AZABU
NISHI-AZABU 1106 BLDG. B1
〒106-0031
東京都港区西麻布 1-10-6
NISHI-AZABU 1106 BLDG. B1
〒106-0031

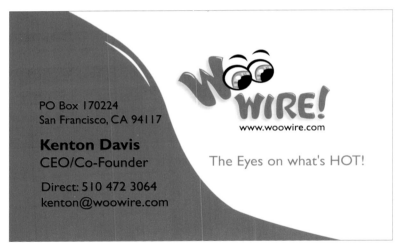

PO Box 170224
San Francisco, CA 94117

Kenton Davis
CEO/Co-Founder

Direct: 510 472 3064
kenton@woowire.com

www.woowire.com

The Eyes on what's HOT!

2.

Robert Kaye

MetaBrainz Foundation
Mayhem & Chaos Coordinator

rob@eorbit.net
805.459.0815

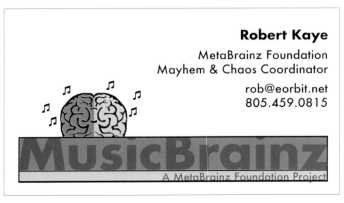

A MetaBrainz Foundation Project

3.

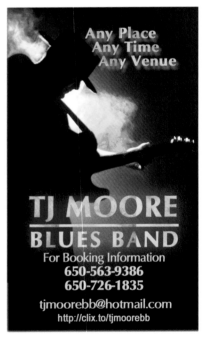

4.

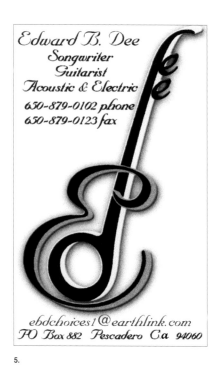

5.

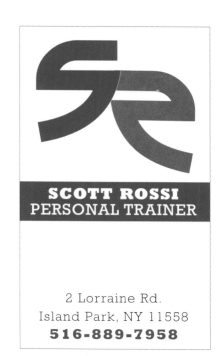

SCOTT ROSSI
PERSONAL TRAINER

2 Lorraine Rd.
Island Park, NY 11558
516-889-7958

6.

John Stevens

70 Oaklawn Avenue Farmingville, NY 11738
Phone/Fax: 631.732.9672 E-mail: john@infourdesign.com

infourdesignstudio ▪▪
GRAPHIC DESIGN.WEB DEVELOPMENT.ADVERTISING ART

7.

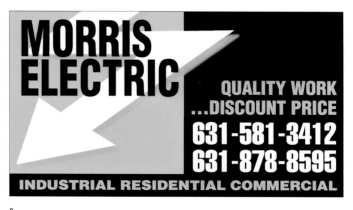

8.

(1)
   Design Firm **SIMC Co. Ltd.**
(2,3)
   Design Firm **elf design**
(4,5)
   Design Firm **Randie Marlow**
(6-8)
   Design Firm **infour design**

1.
   Client   SIMC
   Designer   Hidekazu Tsutsui
2.
   Client   Woowire
   Designer   Erin L. Ferree
3.
   Client   MetaBrainz Foundation
   Designer   Erin L. Ferree
4.
   Client   T.J. Moore
   Designer   Randie Marlow

5.
   Client   Edward B. Dee
   Designer   Randie Marlow
6.
   Client   Scott Rossi
   Designer   John Stevens
7.
   Client   infour design
   Designer   John Stevens
8.
   Client   Morris Electric
   Designer   John Stevens

Generation Smart is dedicated to child

The new **"Scholastic sing-a-longs"** CD
fun educational lyrics and memorable m
Valuable lessons and facts are revealed a
discovers the joy of each song.

Broaden your child's knowledge. Provide
background for math, science, and readin
www.generationsmart.com for more in

1.

G E N E R A T I O N S M A R T

www.generationsmart.com

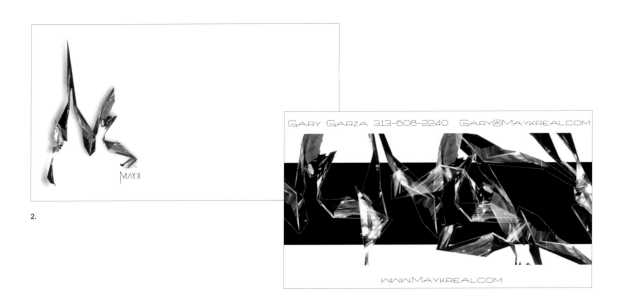

2.

3.

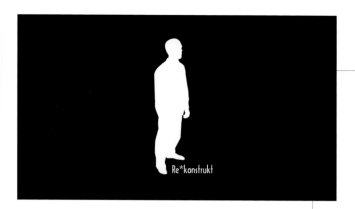

Design & Experimental Medium
www.Rekonstrukt.com

Dorian J. Compo   248.224.3477
Designer   dorian@rekonstrukt.com

4.

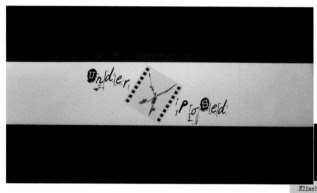

5.

Elizabeth Courtney Raley   Phone: 248-224-3306

WWW.UnderXposed.com

Elizabeth@Underxposed.com

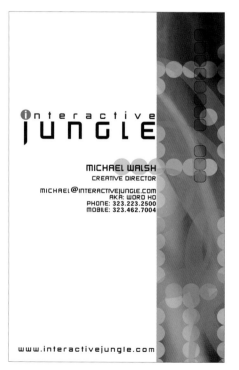

6.

(1)
Design Firm **infour design**
(2-5)
Design Firm **Mayk**
(6)
Design Firm **Jungle 8**

1.
Client   Generation Smart
Designer   John Stevens
2.
Client   Mayk
Designer   Dorian J. Compo
3.
Client   Porcelain Monkey
Designer   Dorian J. Compo
4.
Client   Rekonstrukt
Designer   Dorian J. Compo

5.
Client   UnderXposed
Designer   Dorian J. Compo
6.
Client   Interactive Jungle
Designer   Lainie Siegel

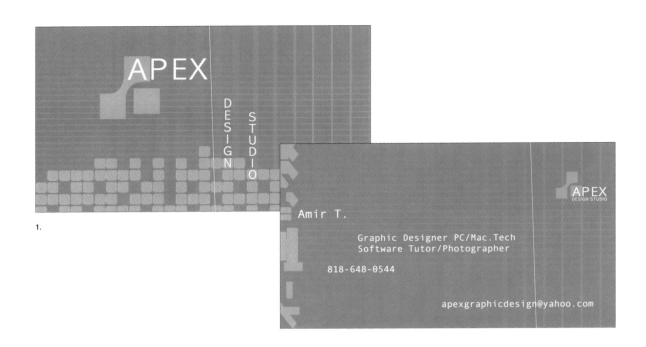

1.

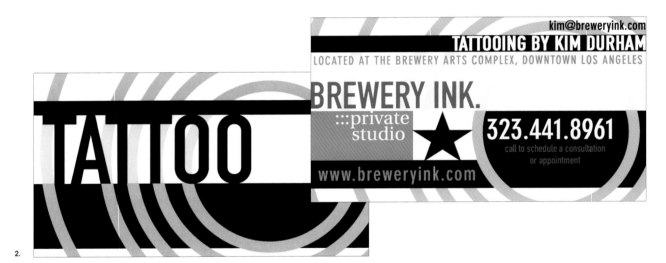

2.

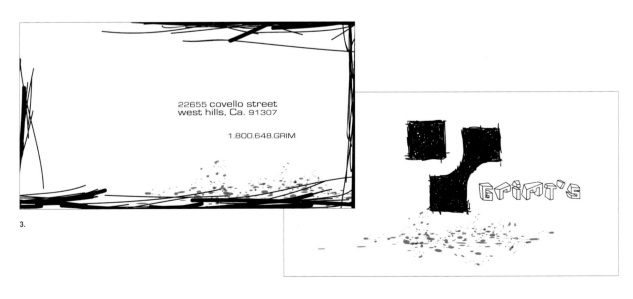

3.

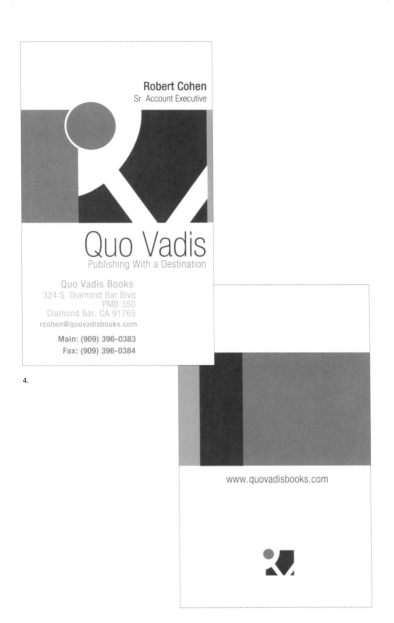

Robert Cohen
Sr. Account Executive

Quo Vadis
Publishing With a Destination

Quo Vadis Books
324 S. Diamond Bar Blvd
PMB 350
Diamond Bar, CA 91765
rcohen@quovadisbooks.com

Main: (909) 396-0383
Fax: (909) 396-0384

4.

www.quovadisbooks.com

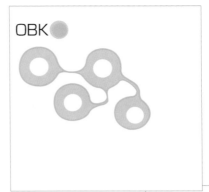

OBK

5.

www.obk.org

Robert James
Vice President of sales
rjames@obk.com

The Michelin Building
20 Shorbard Court NE Suite 8000
Cincinnati, Ohio 80662-0994
912.538.8851

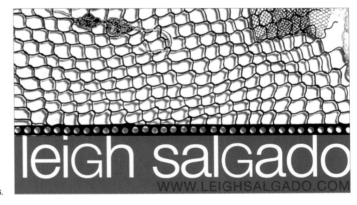

leigh salgado
WWW.LEIGHSALGADO.COM

6.

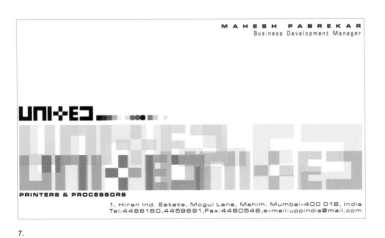

MAHESH PABREKAR
Business Development Manager

UNI+E⊐

PRINTERS & PROCESSORS

1, Hiren Ind. Estate, Mogul Lane, Mahim. Mumbai-400 016, India
Tel:4466160,4459691,Fax:4460546,e-mail:uppindia@mail.com

7.

Jaspal Singh

1 Wood Rose, Near HDFC Bank, Lokhandwala Complex, Andheri (W), Mumbai - 53 Tel : 6350223

1.

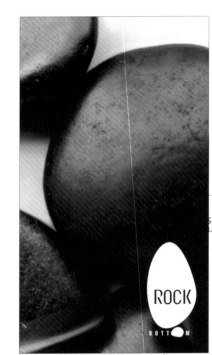

SY GOW
LATIONS • EVENTS MANAGEMENT

ROCK
BOTT M

ROCK BOTTOM
@ HOTEL RAMEE GUESTLINE
A B NAIR ROAD JUHU, MUMBAI

TEL 022 56935550   FAX 022 26202821
EMAIL ROCKBOTTOMINDIA@REDIFFMAIL.COM

2.

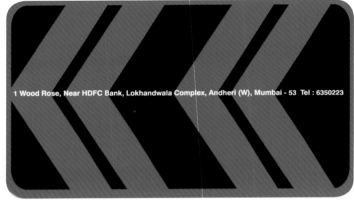

VITAMIN TALENT MANAGEMENT

Sucharita Nar

#6, 10th Main, 1st Cross, Indiranagar 2nd Stage, Bangalore-560038,
Phone: 91-80-5202818, Email: suchi@vitamintalent.com, www.vitamintalent.com

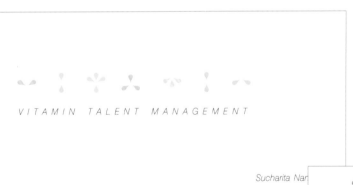

3.

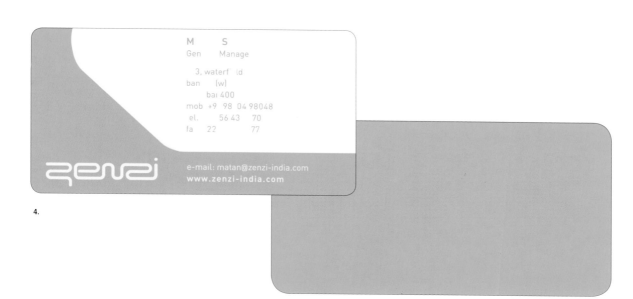

4.

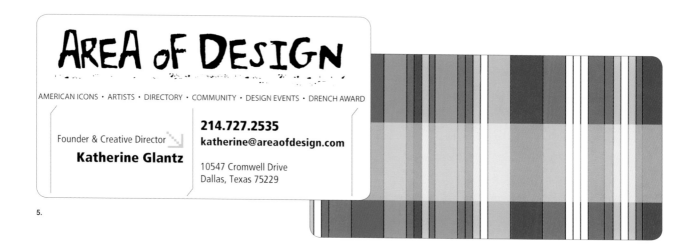

AREA of DESIGN

AMERICAN ICONS · ARTISTS · DIRECTORY · COMMUNITY · DESIGN EVENTS · DRENCH AWARD

Founder & Creative Director
Katherine Glantz

214.727.2535
katherine@areaofdesign.com

10547 Cromwell Drive
Dallas, Texas 75229

5.

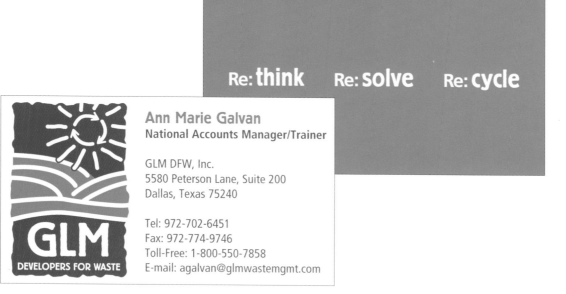

Re: **think**   Re: **solve**   Re: **cycle**

Ann Marie Galvan
National Accounts Manager/Trainer

GLM DFW, Inc.
5580 Peterson Lane, Suite 200
Dallas, Texas 75240

Tel: 972-702-6451
Fax: 972-774-9746
Toll-Free: 1-800-550-7858
E-mail: agalvan@glmwastemgmt.com

6.

GLM
DEVELOPERS FOR WASTE

(1-4)
Design Firm **Grandmother India**
(5,6)
Design Firm **Jabeye**

1.
Client   Neon 69
2.
Client   Rock Bottom
3.
Client   Vitamin
4.
Client   Zenzi
5.
Client   Area of Design
6.
Client   GLM DFW

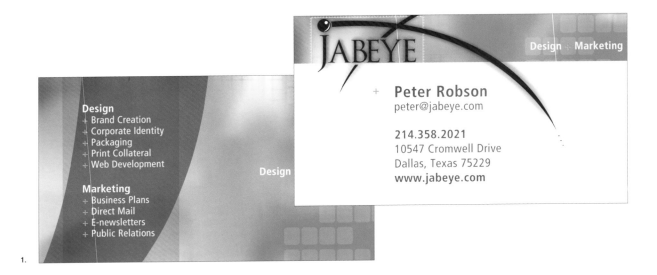

Design
+ Brand Creation
+ Corporate Identity
+ Packaging
+ Print Collateral
+ Web Development

Marketing
+ Business Plans
+ Direct Mail
+ E-newsletters
+ Public Relations

JABEYE Design + Marketing

+ Peter Robson
peter@jabeye.com

214.358.2021
10547 Cromwell Drive
Dallas, Texas 75229
www.jabeye.com

1.

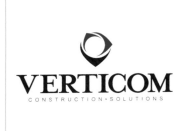

Jeff Lewis
President

m - 214.850.3042
w - 214.741.6898
f - 214.741.6899
jeff.lewis@verticom.net

2142 Irving Boule
Suite 100
Dallas, Texas 752

www.verticom.ne

VERTICOM
CONSTRUCTION·SOLUTIONS

2.

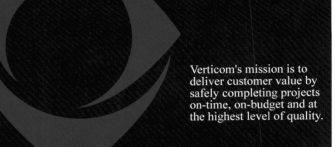

Verticom's mission is to
deliver customer value by
safely completing projects
on-time, on-budget and at
the highest level of quality.

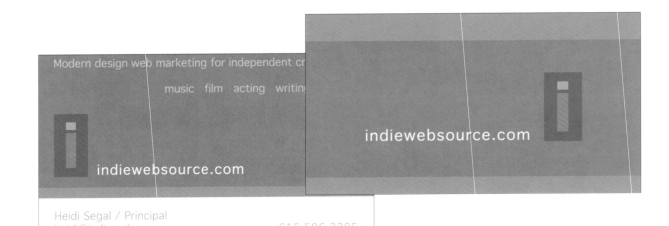

Modern design web marketing for independent cr

music   film   acting   writin

indiewebsource.com

indiewebsource.com

Heidi Segal / Principal
heidi@indiewebsource.com   615 586 2285

3.

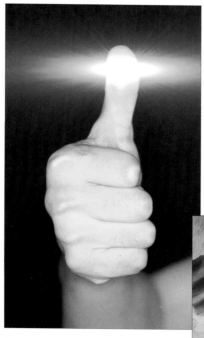

4.

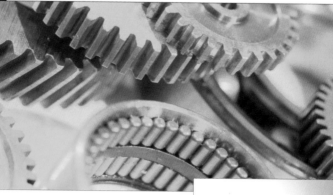

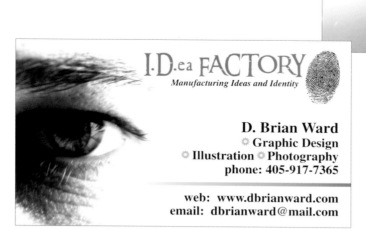

I.D.ea FACTORY
Manufacturing Ideas and Identity

D. Brian Ward
☼ Graphic Design
☼ Illustration ☼ Photography
phone: 405-917-7365

web: www.dbrianward.com
email: dbrianward@mail.com

(1,2)
Design Firm **Jabeye**
(3)
Design Firm **Inestudio**
(4)
Design Firm **D. Brian Ward**

1.
Client   Jabeye
2.
Client   Verticom
3.
Client   Indiewebsource.com
Designer   Heidi Segal
4.
Client   Idea Factory
Designer   D. Brian Ward

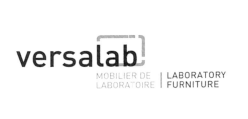

1.

Patrick Deschênes
deschenes.p@versalab.ca

VERSALAB INC.
MOBILIER DE LABORATOIRE
LABORATORY FURNITURE

539, RUE ST-AMABLE STREET
ST-BARNABÉ-SUD (QUÉBEC) J0H 1G0

TÉL. / PHONE (450) 792.2442
MONTRÉAL (514) 861.4577
TÉLÉC. / FAX (450) 792.3608

michelle paré
michelle@ardoise.com

24, AVENUE DU MONT-ROYAL OUEST

BUREAU 601 | MONTRÉAL (QUÉBEC) | H2T 2S2

TÉL.: 514.287.1002 | FAX: 514.287.1040

ardoise design communications inc.
www.ardoise.com

ardoise

2.

EBC*L

European Business
Competence*
Licence

International Centre of EBC*L

Mag. Andrea Setznagel
Project Management

EBC Licencing GmbH

Aichholzgasse 4/8
A-1120 Wien

Tel. +43-1-813 997 745

a.setznagel@ebcl.info
www.ebcl.info

3.

liesbet vandebroek & dieter dubkowitsch

NEUSTIFTGASSE 34/9, A-2500 BADEN

TEL: +43 2252 206 792 FAX: +43 2252 206 931

mobil: LIESBET: +43 664 392 75 75 mobil: DIETER: +43 664 308 22 02

email: l.vdb@flandern.co.at email: dubkowitsch@bahntours.at

4.

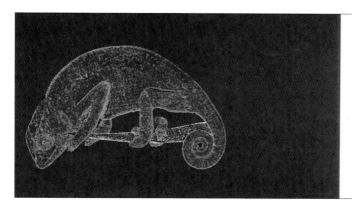

Martin Widtmann | Produktionsleitung

Niederösterreichische | Fon +43(0)1-889 33 62-31
Audiovision Ges.m.b.H. | Fax +43(0)1-889 28 31
Filmstadt Wien | Mobil +43(0)664-412 11 06
Speisinger Straße 121–127 | e-mail: office@nav.at
A-1238 Wien | http://www.nav.at/nav

5.

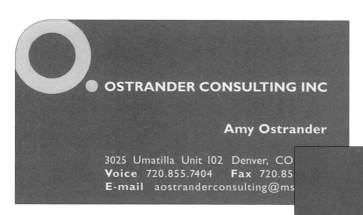

OSTRANDER CONSULTING INC

Amy Ostrander

3025 Umatilla Unit 102 Denver, CO
Voice 720.855.7404 **Fax** 720.85
E-mail aostranderconsulting@ms

6.

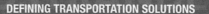

DEFINING TRANSPORTATION SOLUTIONS

OSTRANDER CO

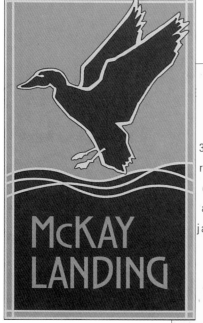

ric Jaeger

3975 ½ Zuni Street
roomfield Co 80020
el 720.872.1891
ax 720.872.1897
jaeger@englehomes.com

ENGLE
HOMES
COLORADO

McKAY LANDING

7.

PENTERRA PLAZA

8110 East Union Avenue   Denver Colorado 80237
Telephone 303.783.6633   Facsimile 303.789.0672
dgregory@penterraplaza.com   www.penterraplaza.com

DAWN GREGORY
York Management, Inc.

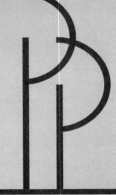

1.

FORD
CRIMINAL
LAWYERS

Chris Ford BEc LLB

Ford Criminal Lawyers Suite 201, 370 Pitt St
T 02 9261 2982 F 02 9261 2989 M 0418 40⁄
chris@criminallaw.net.au **www.criminallaw**

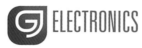

FORD

2.

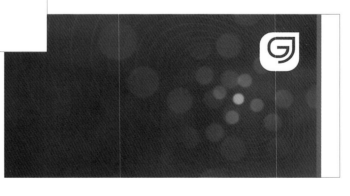

⊙J ELECTRONICS

Richard Jefferson *Managing Director*

GJ Electronics Ltd, Units 8-10, Wembdon Business Centre,
Bower Road, Smeeth, Ashford, Kent TN25 6SZ U.K.

tel. +44 (0)1303 814224   fax. +44 (0)1303 814073
richard@gjelectronics.co.uk mob. 07785 947962

3.

Andrew Hasler
Director

AJH Studios, Suite 206   **T:** +61 2 9331 0902
20-22 Bayswater Road   **F:** +61 2 9331 0807
Potts Point, NSW 2011   **M:** 0412 818 858
Australia   **E:** andrew@ajhstudios.com.au

ABN: 47 440 826 525   www.ajhstudios.com.au

4.

NAME
Martin J. McNeese

JOB
CREATIVE DIRECTOR

ADDRESS
**2151 HAWKINS STREET
SUITE 100
CHARLOTTE, NC 28203**

PHONE   FAX
704 343 9280   **704 343 9285**
EMAIL
MMCNEESE@TECHNIKONE.COM

5.

Research

Brand Management

Strategic Planning

Corporate Identity

Media Service

6.

Karl Peters
Senior Art Director

BRANDSAVVY

BrandSavvy, Inc.
66 West Springer Drive
Suite 206
Highlands Ranch, CO 80129
303.471.9991 **Tel**
720.344.2394 **Fax**
720.205.2048 **Cell**
peters@brandsavvyinc.com
www.brandsavvyinc.com

**American
Water Works
Association**

Jon R. Runge
Communications and Marketing Director

6666 West Quincy Avenue
Denver, CO 80235-3098
M 303.794.7711
F 303.795.1989
D 303.347.6232
jrunge@awwa.org
www.awwa.org

7.

Advocacy

Communications

Conferences

Education and Training

Science and Technology

Sections

(1)
   Design Firm **Noble Erickson Inc.**
(2-4)
   Design Firm **Ident**
(5)
   Design Firm **TechnikOne**
(6,7)
   Design Firm **Brand Savvy**

1.
   Client   Penterra Plaza
   Designer   Steven Erickson
2.
   Client   Ford Criminal Lawyers
   Designer   Jeremy Tombs
3.
   Client   GJ Electronics
   Designer   Jeremy Tombs
4.
   Client   AJH Studios
   Designer   Jeremy Tombs

5.
   Client   TechnikOne
   Designer   Martin McNeese
6.
   Client   Brand Savvy
   Designer   Karl Peters
7.
   Client   American Water
              Works Association
   Designer   Karl Peters

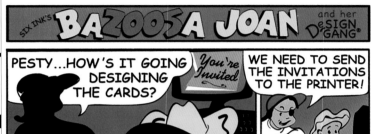

1.

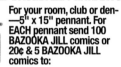

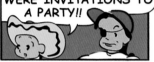

3.

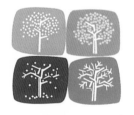

rising sun catering

2.

Heather Harris
EVENT DESIGNER

...@risingsuncatering.com

...aw road
...francisco, ca 94080
(650) 589-0157 (tel)
(650) 589-6783 (fax)
www.risingsuncatering.com

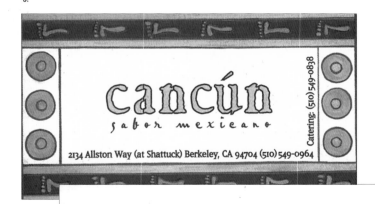

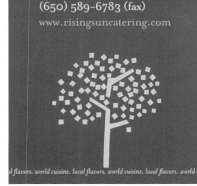

cancún
sabor mexicano

Catering: (510) 549-0838

2134 Allston Way (at Shattuck) Berkeley, CA 94704 (510) 549-0964

gastronomia mexicana

prepared in the ancient tradition

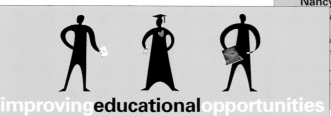

east bay consortium
of educational institutions, inc.

Nancy Chou, *Associate Director*

@eastbayconsortium.org

st 10th Street, Room 9
d, CA 94606

879-8367
879-8301   **www.eastbayconsortium.org**

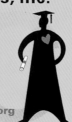

improving educational opportunities

A California Student Opportunity and Access Project (Cal-SOAP)

4.

SHARP
E V E N T S

415-781-1141 PHONE
415-345-0809 DIRECT
415-626-4493 FAX

One Daniel Burnham Court
Suite #350c
San Francisco, CA 94109

Danielle Slanina
Operations Coordinator

dslanin
www.sh

5.

[sharp ideas. sharp solutions.]

Form ation

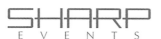

Ideas ➡ Sources ➡ Products

Mark Towery
President

888 Brannan Street,   Suite 349
San Francisco, California 94103 **USA**
Phone: 4 1 5 . 4 3 7 . 6 4 2 0
Fax: 4 1 5 . 8 6 1 . 0 6 9 6
E-mail: mtowery@formationinc.com
w w w . f o r m a t i o n i n c . c o m

6.

(1-7)
Design Firm **Six·Ink**

1.
Client   Six·Ink
Designer   Judy Lichtman
2.
Client   Rising Sun Catering
Designer   Judy Lichtman
3.
Client   Cancún Sabor Mexicano
Designer   Judy Lichtman
4.
Client   East Bay Consortium of
                Educational Institutions, Inc.
Designer   Judy Lichtman
5.
Client   Sharp Events
Designer   Judy Lichtman

6.
Client   Formation
Designer   Judy Lichtman

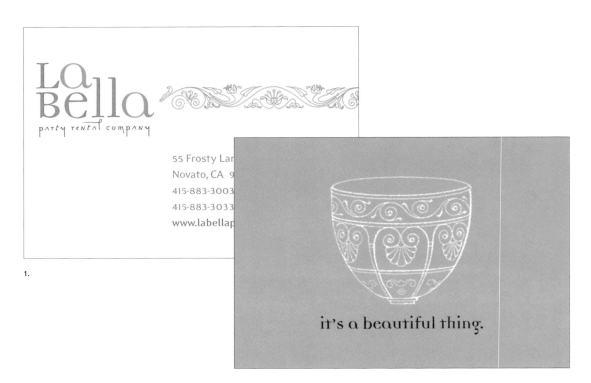

La bella
party rental company

55 Frosty Lar
Novato, CA 9
415·883·3003
415·883·3033
www.labellap

1.

it's a beautiful thing.

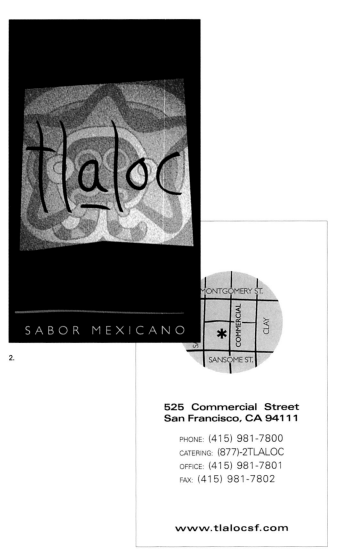

tlaloc

SABOR MEXICANO

2.

MONTGOMERY ST.

COMMERCIAL

CLAY

*

SANSOME ST.

525 Commercial Street
San Francisco, CA 94111

PHONE: (415) 981-7800
CATERING: (877)-2TLALOC
OFFICE: (415) 981-7801
FAX: (415) 981-7802

www.tlalocsf.com

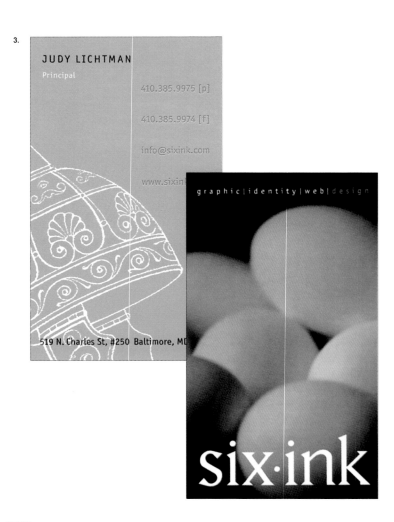

3.

JUDY LICHTMAN

Principal

410.385.9975 [p]

410.385.9974 [f]

info@sixink.com

www.sixin

graphic|identity|web|design

519 N. Charles St, #250 Baltimore, MD

six·ink

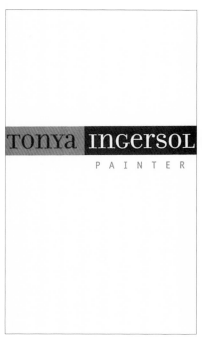

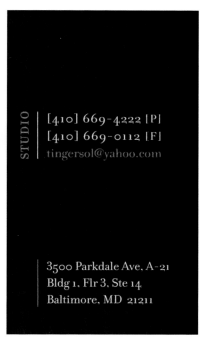

tonya INGERSOL
P A I N T E R

STUDIO

[410] 669-4222 [P]
[410] 669-0112 [F]

tingersol@yahoo.com

3500 Parkdale Ave, A-21
Bldg 1, Flr 3, Ste 14
Baltimore, MD 21211

4.

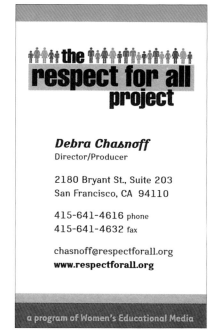

the **respect for all** project

Debra Chasnoff
Director/Producer

2180 Bryant St., Suite 203
San Francisco, CA 94110

415-641-4616 phone
415-641-4632 fax

chasnoff@respectforall.org
www.respectforall.org

a program of Women's Educational Media

5.

Heather A. Hiles, MBA
President & CEO

415|848|4488 [P]
415|309|7704 [C]

52 Coleridge Street
San Francisco, CA 94110
415|268|4234 [F]

heather@hilesgroup.com
www.hilesgroup.com

T H E   H I L E S   G R O U P

6.

J.B. Enterprise & Associates, LLC

Roger Busch
Commercial Sales Manager

Kihei Self Storage, 300 Ohukai Rd, # I-3, Kihei-Maui, HI 96753
phn: (808) 891-2319 / (800) 504-2011
cell: (808) 870-5997 / fax: (808) 891-0382
email: info@jbpool.com / web: www.jbpool.com

7.

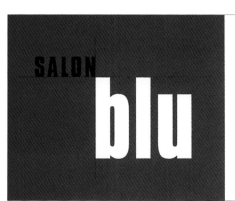

SALON
blu

Barbara Fuller

2510 Main Street
Suite D
Santa Monica
California 90405

310.392.3331 tel
310.392.4811 fax

8.

(1-6)
   Design Firm **Six·Ink**
(7,8)
   Design Firm **Treehouse Design**

1.
  Client   La Bella
  Designer Judy Lichtman
2.
  Client   Haloc
  Designer Judy Lichtman
3.
  Client   Six·Ink
  Designer Judy Lichtman
4.
  Client   Tonya Ingersol
  Designer Judy Lichtman

5.
  Client   Women's Educational Media
  Designer Judy Lichtman
6.
  Client   The Hiles Group
  Designer Judy Lichtman
7.
  Client   J.B. Enterprise &
             Associates, LLC
  Designer Tricia Rauen
8.
  Client   Salon Blu
  Designer Tricia Rauen

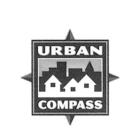

Don Morgan
President,
Board of Directors

11100 South Central Ave.
Los Angeles, CA 90059
323-383-7588 phn
323-564-9009 fax
www.urbancompass.org
info@urbancompass.org

1.

Guiding Youth Toward a Hopeful Future

●●● LILLIAN VERNON®
C O R P O R A T E   S A L E S

BETH V. DRAGOO   ASI 67520
ACCOUNT EXECUTIVE

10720 SAND KEY CIRCLE
INDIANAPOLIS, IN 46256

TEL: 317.577.3610   FAX: 317.577.3615
E-MAIL: bdragoo@lillianvernon.com
WWW. LILLIANVERNON.COM

2.

John Coates
President
Codel Enterprises Burns USA
P.O. Box 269
Bethel, CT 06801

ph: 203 205 0056
fx: 203 205 9062

john@Burnsusa.com

3.

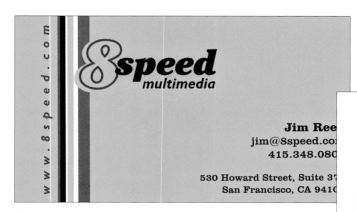

8speed
multimedia

Jim Ree
jim@8speed.co
415.348.080

530 Howard Street, Suite 3
San Francisco, CA 941

4.

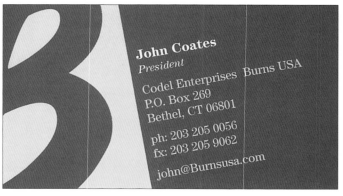

SPEAK!

You need to communicate.
We'll make it resonate.

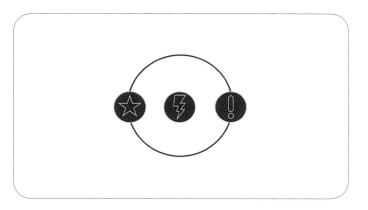

Visual Intelligence Agency, inc.

Darryl Ohrt
Instigator

155 Main Street, Danbury, CT 06810
203.730.6300 ext. 201
fax 203.730.6303
darryl@viaworldwide.com
www.viaworldwide.com

Visual Intelligence Agency, inc.

Kevin Gardner
Slacker

155 Main Street, Danbury, CT 06810
203.730.6300 ext. 202
fax 203.730.6303
kevin@viaworldwide.com
www.viaworldwide.com

5.

Visual Intelligence Agency, inc.

David Plain
Jedi Knight

155 Main Street, Danbury, CT 06810
203.730.6300 ext. 206
fax 203.730.6303
dave@viaworldwide.com
www.viaworldwide.com

Visual Intelligence Agency, inc.

Justus Johnson
High Roller

155 Main Street, Danbury, CT 06810
203.730.6300 ext. 207
fax 203.730.6303
justus@viaworldwide.com
www.viaworldwide.com

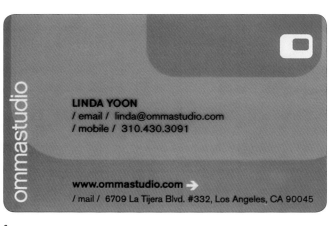

ommastudio

LINDA YOON
/ email / linda@ommastudio.com
/ mobile / 310.430.3091

www.ommastudio.com →
/ mail / 6709 La Tijera Blvd. #332, Los Angeles, CA 90045

6.

(1)
Design Firm **Treehouse Design**
(2-4)
Design Firm **Visual Intelligence Agency, Inc.**
(5)
Design Firm **8 Speed Multimedia**
(6)
Design Firm **Ommastudio**

1.
Client   Urban Compass
Designer Tricia Rauen
2.
Client   Lillian Vernon
Designer Kevin Gardner

3.
Client   Burns USA
Designer Kevin Gardner
4.
Client   8 Speed Multimedia
Designer Jim Reed
5.
Client   Visual Intelligence Agency, Inc.
Designer Judy Lichtman
6.
Client   Ommastudio
Designer Linda Yoon

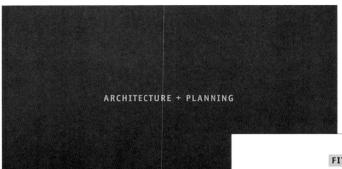

1.

FITSCHEN + ASSOCIATES INC.

JON GREGORY, *designer*
560 SUTTER ST. NO: 210 SAN FRANCISCO, CA 94102·1104

telephone NO:

415·788·0220

FAX 415·788·0112
EMAIL *jon@fitschendesign.com*
www.fitschendesign.com

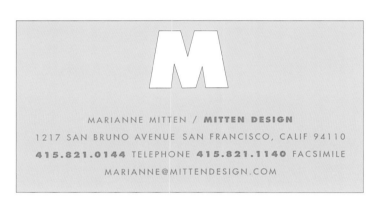

MARIANNE MITTEN / **MITTEN DESIGN**
1217 SAN BRUNO AVENUE SAN FRANCISCO, CALIF 94110
415.821.0144 TELEPHONE **415.821.1140** FACSIMILE
MARIANNE@MITTENDESIGN.COM

2.

THREE GOLDEN APPLES
F I N E   J E W E L R Y

3.

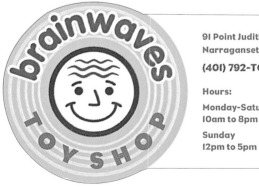

91 Point Judith Road
Narragansett, RI 02882

(401) 792-TOYS (8697)

Hours:

Monday-Saturday
10am to 8pm

Sunday
12pm to 5pm

4.

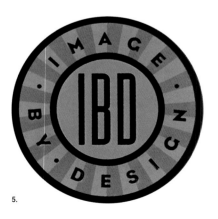

5.

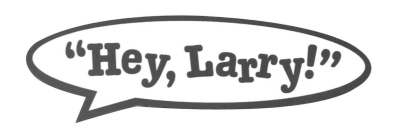

6.

Herip Associates

5995 Center Street
P.O. Box 113
Peninsula, Ohio 44264-0113

330 **657·2231** Akron
330 **467·8583** Cleveland
330 467·8507 Fax
www.HeripDesign.com

Walter M. Herip   *President & Creative Director*

Brand Management &
Marketing Communications

Visitors Expected. For a map visit www.HeripDes...

7.

The James/Gregory Group Inc.   P. O. Box 434

Cleveland

Ohio

James G. Dalessandro

President   44040-0434

• • •   216.461.1109

8.

R E D
R E E D E R
D E S I G N
I N C.

JR

Rachelle E. Reeder
P r e s i d e n t
Design Consultant

Surface Design,
Colorations and
Styling Services

244 Kelso Road E.
Columbus, Ohio
4 3 2 0 2
614/267.4337

9.

(1,2)
    Design Firm **Mitten Design**
(3-6)
    Design Firm **Creative Vision Design Co.**
(7,8)
    Design Firm **Herip Associates**
(9)
    Design Firm **Rickabaugh Graphics**

1.
    Client   Fitschen + Associates, Inc.
    Designer   Marianne Mitten
2.
    Client   Mitten Design
    Designer   Marianne Mitten
3.
    Client   Three Golden Apples
    Designer   Greg Gonsalves
4.
    Client   Brainwaves Toyshop
    Designer   Greg Gonsalves
5.
    Client   Image By Design
    Designer   Greg Gonsalves

6.
    Client   "Hey, Larry!"
    Designer   Greg Gonsalves
7.
    Client   Herip Associates
    Designer   Walter M. Herip
8.
    Client   The James/Gregory
             Group Inc.
    Designer   Walter M. Herip
9.
    Client   Rachelle E. Reeder
    Designer   Eric Rickabaugh

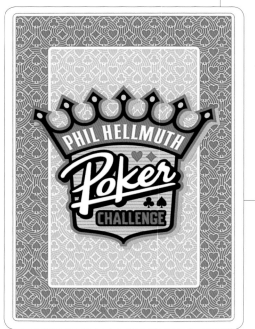

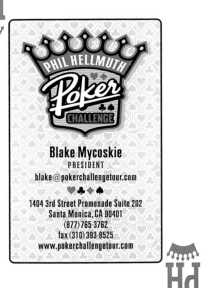

Blake Mycoskie
PRESIDENT
blake@pokerchallengetour.com
♣♠♣♠
1404 3rd Street Promenade Suite 202
Santa Monica, CA 90401
(877) 765-3762
fax (310) 393-9525
www.pokerchallengetour.com

1.

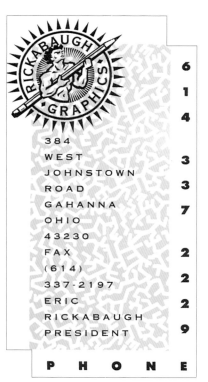

384
WEST
JOHNSTOWN
ROAD
GAHANNA
OHIO
43230
FAX
(614)
337-2197
ERIC
RICKABAUGH
PRESIDENT

6
1
4
3
3
7
2
2
2
9

P H O N E

2.

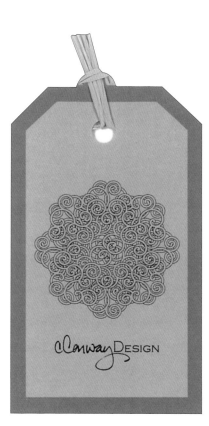

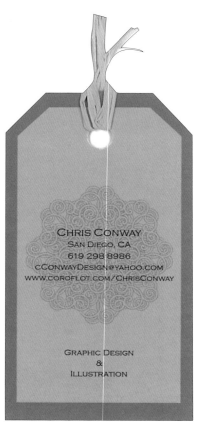

CHRIS CONWAY
SAN DIEGO, CA
619 298 8986
CCONWAYDESIGN@YAHOO.COM
WWW.COROFLOT.COM/CHRISCONWAY

GRAPHIC DESIGN
&
ILLUSTRATION

3.

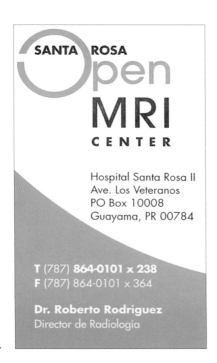

SANTA ROSA **Open MRI CENTER**

Hospital Santa Rosa II
Ave. Los Veteranos
PO Box 10008
Guayama, PR 00784

T (787) **864-0101 x 238**
F (787) 864-0101 x 364

Dr. Roberto Rodríguez
Director de Radiología

4.

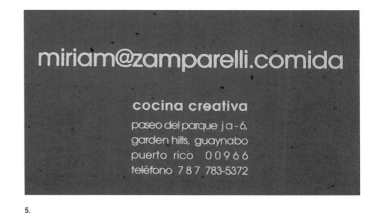

miriam@zamparelli.comida

cocina creativa
paseo del parque j a - 6,
garden hills, guaynabo
puerto rico 00966
teléfono 787 783-5372

5.

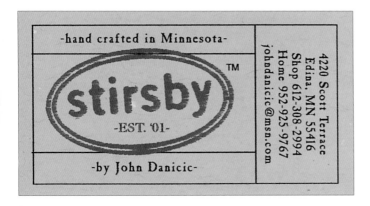

-hand crafted in Minnesota-
stirsby
-EST. '01-
-by John Danicic-
™

4220 Scott Terrace
Edina, MN 55416
Shop 612-308-2994
Home 952-925-9767
johndanicic@msn.com

6.

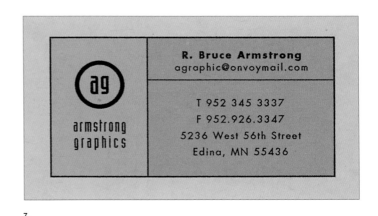

ag
armstrong graphics

R. Bruce Armstrong
agraphic@onvoymail.com

T 952 345 3337
F 952.926.3347
5236 West 56th Street
Edina, MN 55436

7.

Dr. Melissa Viker
Optometrist
952.829.9024

T H E EYE DOCS

Dr. Britt Gustafson
Optometrist
952.829.9024

The Eye Doctors Inc
See The Difference

12195 Singletree Lane Eden Prairie, MN 55344 @ Wal-Mart

8.

(1,2)
Design Firm **Rickabaugh Graphics**
(3)
Design Firm **Conway Design**
(4,5)
Design Firm **Maremar Graphic Design**
(6-8)
Design Firm **Armstrong Graphics**

1.
Client Phil Hellmuth Poker
Challenge
Designer Eric Rickabaugh
2.
Client Rickabaugh Graphics
Designer Eric Rickabaugh
3.
Client Conway Design
Designer Christina Conway
4.
Client Santa Rosa
Open MRI Center
Designer Marina Rivón

5.
Client Cocina Creativa
Designer Marina Rivón
6.
Client Stirsby
Designer R. Bruce Armstrong
7.
Client Armstrong Graphics
Designer R. Bruce Armstrong
8.
Client The Eye Doctors Inc.
Designer R. Bruce Armstrong

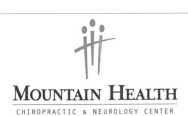

a b c d e
f g h i j
k l m n o
p q r s t
u v w x **y z**

young zeck image communications

greg zeck

7038 lake shore drive
minneapolis, mn 55423
phone: 612-243-9090
fax: 612-243-9091
www.youngzeck.com
gregzeck@youngzeck.com

1.

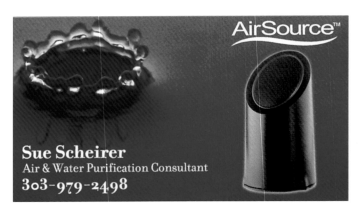

Sue Scheirer
Air & Water Purification Consultant
303-979-2498

AirSource™

2.

MOUNTAIN HEALTH
CHIROPRACTIC & NEUROLOGY CENTER

DAVID G. ARTHUR, DC, CCCN
Certified Chiropractic Clinical Neurologist

3646 South Galapago Street, Englewood, CO 80110 • **303 781 5617**
Fax 303 781 1045 • www.mountain-health.com • doctor@mountain-health.com

www.mountain-health.com

3.

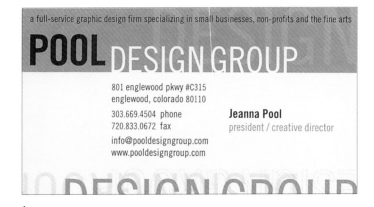

a full-service graphic design firm specializing in small businesses, non-profits and the fine arts

POOL DESIGN GROUP

801 englewood pkwy #C315
englewood, colorado 80110

303.669.4504 phone
720.833.0672 fax

info@pooldesigngroup.com
www.pooldesigngroup.com

Jeanna Pool
president / creative director

4.

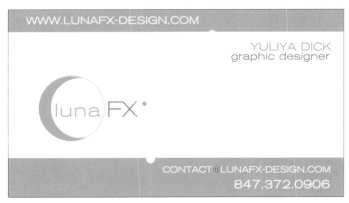

WWW.LUNAFX-DESIGN.COM

YULIYA DICK
graphic designer

luna FX

CONTACT@LUNAFX-DESIGN.COM
847.372.0906

5.

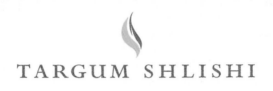

ANDREA GOLLIN

3300 Northeast 191 Street, S
Aventura, Florida 331
305/285-9848 tel/fax
andrea@targumshlishi.org   www.tar

6.

TARGUM SHLISHI

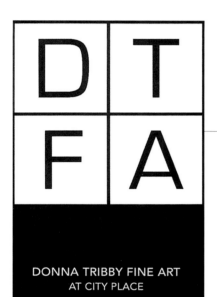

DTFA

DONNA TRIBBY FINE ART
AT CITY PLACE

7.

DONNA TRIBBY
477 S. ROSEMARY AVE
SUITE 193
WEST PALM BEACH, FL 33401

T: 561_833 4001
F: 561_833 4006
E: dtfadonna@aol.com
W: donnatribbyfineart.com

DONNA TRIBBY FINE ART
AT CITY PLACE

Andrew Kelly
akelly@urbanusfurniture.com

URBANUS 305/576-9510 ext 102
305/576-4735 fax
89 northeast 27 street miami, fl 33137

www.urbanusfurniture.com

8.

(1)
Design Firm **Armstrong Graphics**
(2-4)
Design Firm **Catalyst Creative**
(5)
Design Firm **LunaFX**
(6-8)
Design Firm **Inkbyte Design**

1.
   Client   Young Zeck Image
               Communications
   Designer R. Bruce Armstrong
2.
   Client   AirSource
   Designer Jeanna Pool
3.
   Client   Mountain Health
   Designer Jeanna Pool
4.
   Client   Pool Design Group
   Designer Jeanna Pool

5.
   Client   LunaFX
   Designer YuLiya Chepuznaya
6.
   Client   Targum Shlishi
   Designer Peter Roman
7.
   Client   DTFA/Donna Tribby
               Fine Art
   Designer Peter Roman
8.
   Client   Urbanus
   Designer Peter Roman

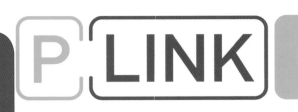

Celia Domenech

305.665.0892 | celia@celiadomenech.com

1.

www.sportsartfitness.com

SportsArt *FITNESS*

19510 144th Avenue NE, Suite A1
Woodinville, WA 98072
corp phone: 800.709.1400
corp fax: 425.488.8155
customer service: 866.709.1750

2.

Gloria W Chen
Senior Graphic Designer

SportsArt *FITNESS*

t: 425.481.9479~130
f: 425.488.8155
gloria@sportsartamerica.com

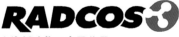

上海耀迪化工有限公司

羅培貽 博士

上海市浦东向城路15号锦城大厦22楼D座
电话: 86-21-58300131 • 86-21-58300132
传真: 86-21-58300770

3.

Shanghai Radcos Chemical Co., LTD

o, Ph.D

Building 22F/D
No. 15 Xiangheng Road • Pudong, Shanghai, PRC
t: 86-21-58300131 • 86-21-58300132 • f: 86-21-58300770

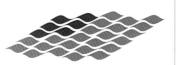

Rob Butterworth
Director, Operations & Administration

Boston ★ 2004
Nothing conventional about it.

Three Copley Place, Suite 501 | Boston, MA 02116 | rbutterworth@boston04.com
PHONE 617.247.2004 | FAX 617.247.1430 | CELL 617.594.1586

4.

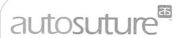

autosuture

Rosetta Mazzei
Marketing Coordinator
203-845-1373 (direct)
203-845-4257 (fax)
rosetta.mazzei@tycohealthcare.com

www.autosuture.com

United States Surgical
150 Glover Avenue
Norwalk, CT 06856
203-845-1000 (main)
800-722-8772 (toll free)

tyco
Healthcare

5.

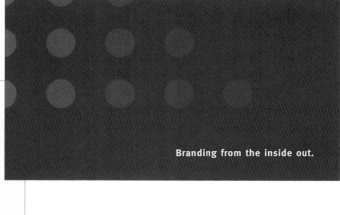

brand therapy™

Branding from the inside out.

Sherry Paul   **Tel:** 415.388.7575   **Fax:** 415.388.7979
Email: sherry@brandtherapy.com

6.

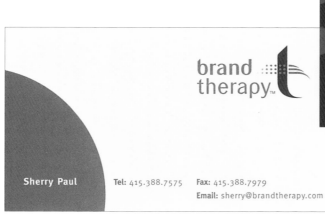

BLENDE
DENTAL GROUP

DANA G. KEILES, D.M.D.
SPECIAL NEEDS DENTISTRY

390 LAUREL STREET, SUITE 310
SAN FRANCISCO, CA 94118
TEL 415.563.4261
FAX 415.563.1476
EMAIL MAIL@DRBLENDE.COM
WEB WWW.DRBLENDE.COM

7.

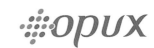

PH: 925.275.1626   FX: 925.215.2531
info@opux.com   3058 Fostoria Circle, Danville, CA 94526
www.opux.com

1.

Elizabeth Chyr
Marketing Coordinator

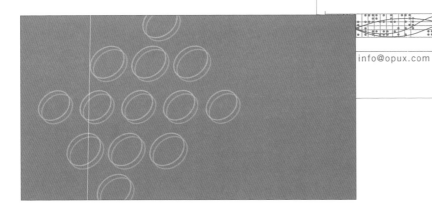

ACADEMY STUDIOS

70 Galli Drive
Novato, CA 94949 USA

T 415.883.8842
D 415.883.8999 x109   echyr@academystudios.com
F 415.883.1031   www.academystudios.com

2.

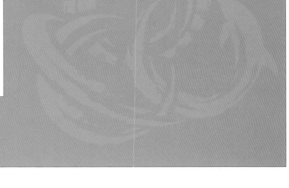

www.leapgroup.com

3.

Martha Olsen

THE leap GROUP

Tel: 415.456.7404 Fax: 415.459.4613
E-mail: marols@leapgroup.com
38 Knoll Road, San Anselmo, California 94960

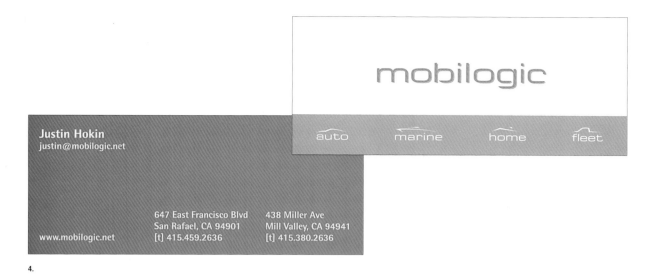

Justin Hokin
justin@mobilogic.net

www.mobilogic.net

647 East Francisco Blvd
San Rafael, CA 94901
[t] 415.459.2636

438 Miller Ave
Mill Valley, CA 94941
[t] 415.380.2636

4.

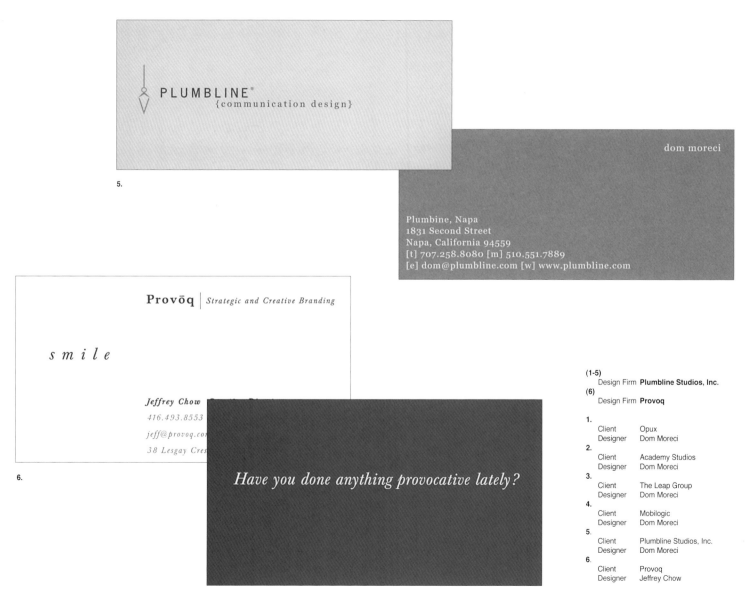

PLUMBLINE®
{communication design}

5.

dom moreci

Plumbine, Napa
1831 Second Street
Napa, California 94559
[t] 707.258.8080 [m] 510.551.7889
[e] dom@plumbline.com [w] www.plumbline.com

Provōq | *Strategic and Creative Branding*

s m i l e

Jeffrey Chow

416.493.8553

jeff@provoq.co

38 Lesgay Cres

6.

Have you done anything provocative lately?

(1-5)
Design Firm **Plumbline Studios, Inc.**
(6)
Design Firm **Provoq**

1.
Client   Opux
Designer   Dom Moreci
2.
Client   Academy Studios
Designer   Dom Moreci
3.
Client   The Leap Group
Designer   Dom Moreci
4.
Client   Mobilogic
Designer   Dom Moreci
5.
Client   Plumbline Studios, Inc.
Designer   Dom Moreci
6.
Client   Provoq
Designer   Jeffrey Chow

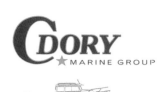

Jeff Messmer
V.P. Sales & Marketing

25 37th Street NE
Auburn, WA 98002

253.839.0222 phone
206.940.0571 cell
253.839.5544 fax

jeffmessmer@c-dory.com
www.c-dory.com

1.

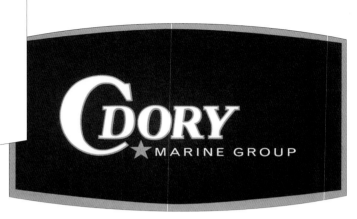

PESTO | CHEESE SPREADS

622.1016
622.7410 FAX

GLENN NEASE

SO NATURALS

1914-A OCCIDENTAL AVE. S.

SEATTLE, WA | 98134

http://www.cibonaturals.com

glenn@cibonaturals.com

2.

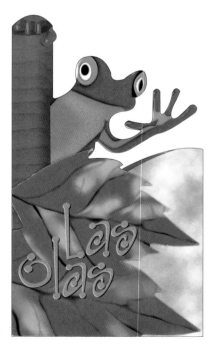

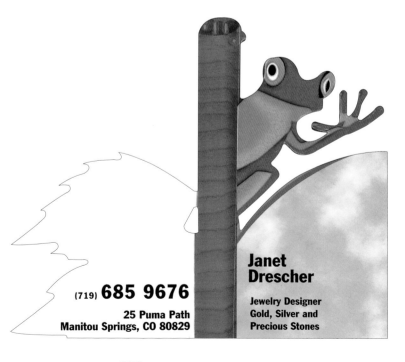

(719) **685 9676**

25 Puma Path
Manitou Springs, CO 80829

Janet
Drescher

Jewelry Designer
Gold, Silver and
Precious Stones

3.

Tony Scoringe

206.669.6645 Cell
tscoringe@travel2events.com

Seattle
123 NW 36th St.
Suite 201
Seattle, WA 98107

206.545.0272 Ext 228
206.545.0273 **Fax**

Los Angeles
8055 W. Manchester Blvd.
Suite 455
Playa del Rey, CA 90293

310.578.8453 **Tel**
310.821.6972 **Fax**

4.

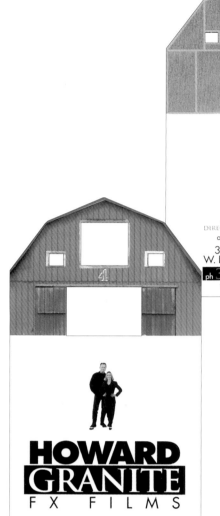

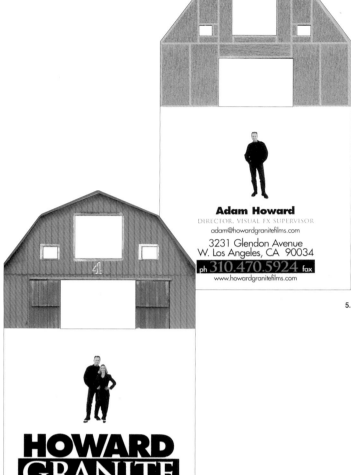

Adam Howard
DIRECTOR, VISUAL FX SUPERVISOR
adam@howardgranitefilms.com
3231 Glendon Avenue
W. Los Angeles, CA 90034
ph **310.470.5924** fax
www.howardgranitefilms.com

5.

**HOWARD
GRANITE
F X F I L M S**

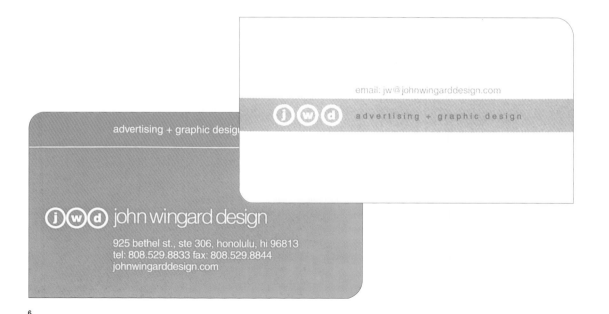

advertising + graphic design

email: jw@johnwingarddesign.com

(j)(w)(d) advertising + graphic design

(j)(w)(d) john wingard design

925 bethel st., ste 306, honolulu, hi 96813
tel: 808.529.8833 fax: 808.529.8844
johnwingarddesign.com

6.

(1-3)
Design Firm **Daigle Design**
(4,5)
Design Firm **Carlow Design**
(6)
Design Firm **John Wingard Design**

1.
Client   C-Dory
Designer Candace Daigle
2.
Client   Cibo Naturals
Designer Candace Daigle
3.
Client   Las Olas
Designer Candace Daigle
4.
Client   travel2events.com
Designer Richard Carlow
5.
Client   Howard Granite
Designer Richard Carlow
6.
Client   John Wingard Design
Designer John Wingard

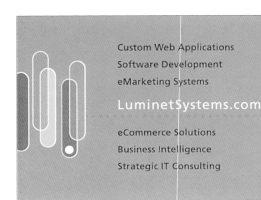

Custom Web Applications
Software Development
eMarketing Systems

LuminetSystems.com

eCommerce Solutions
Business Intelligence
Strategic IT Consulting

1.

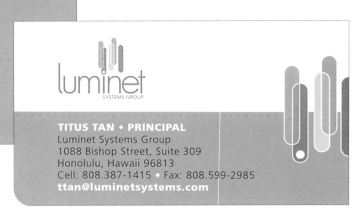

luminet
SYSTEMS GROUP

TITUS TAN • PRINCIPAL
Luminet Systems Group
1088 Bishop Street, Suite 309
Honolulu, Hawaii 96813
Cell: 808.387-1415 • Fax: 808.599-2985
ttan@luminetsystems.com

ARTISENT

Scott Doiron

374 Con
Boston,
Tel 617
Fax 617
scott@a

www.artisent.com

2.

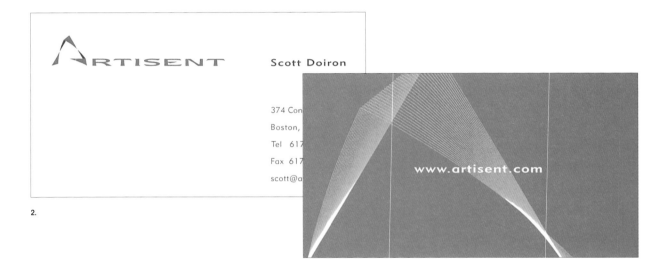

**HEATING, COOLING, AIR
AND WATER SYSTEMS**

Darrell L. Leach
Service Technician

1235 S. SANTA FE
WICHITA, KS 67211
TEL 316 264 2299
TEL 888 4 MANNYS
FAX 316 264 0903
mannys@feist.com

3.

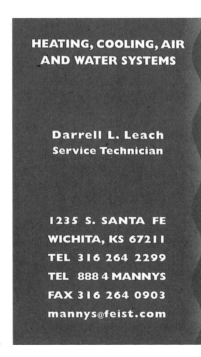

MANNY'S™
Tame Your
Environment.

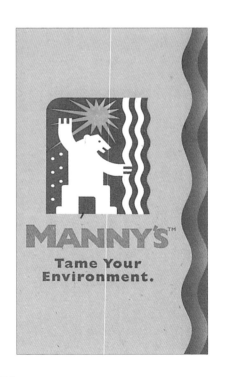

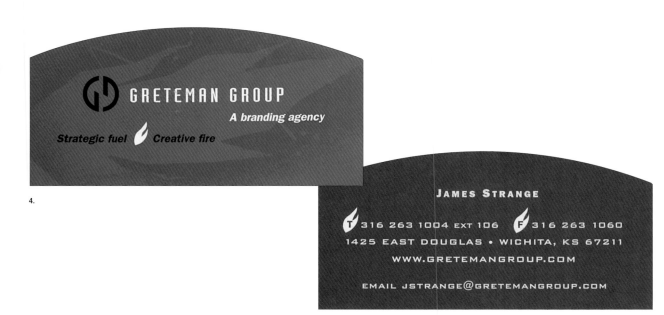

4.

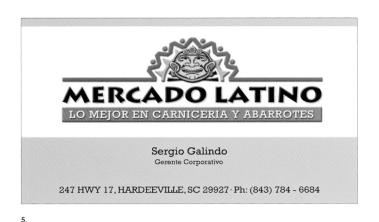

5.

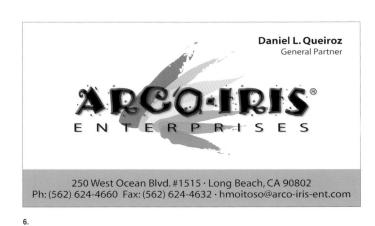

6.

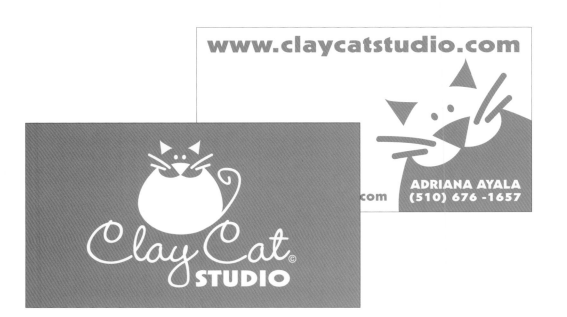

7.

1.

Anthony Nex Photography
8749 West Washington Boulevard
Culver City California 90232
tel 310.836.4357 fax 310.837.2646

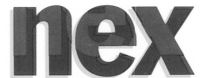

2.

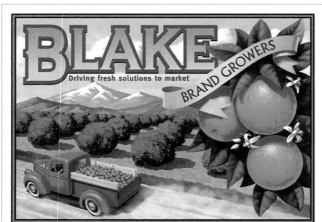

Jeff Blake
Proprietor

jblake@brandgrowers.com
brandgrowers.com

600 W. Olive Ave, 5th Floor
Burbank, CA 91505
t 818-333-5005
f 866-209-4190

9457 S. University Blvd, #350
Highlands Ranch, CO 80126
t 720-320-7656
f 866-209-4190

branding marketing naming • concepts copy design • broadcast print web

3.

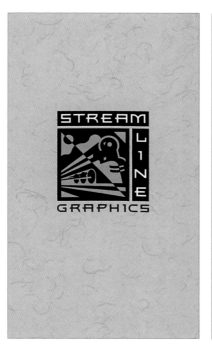

STREAMLINE GRAPHICS

2639 TWENTY-NINTH STREET

SANTA MONICA CA 90405

TELEPHONE 213.452.7828

FAX NUMBER 213.452.4997

CARLOS QUIROGA

GENERAL MANAGER

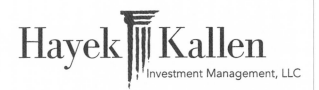

Eric O. Kallen
Managing Director
Eric@HayekKallen.com

121 Fairhope Avenue
Fairhope, Alabama 36532
251.928.8999   251.928.8991 Fax

www.HayekKallen.com

4.

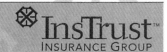

Michael G. Myles, President

mgmyles@InsTrustInsurance.com | www.InsTrustInsurance.com

251.665.2400 | 251.660.7051 Fax

P.O. Box 190339 | Mobile, Alabama 36619

5.

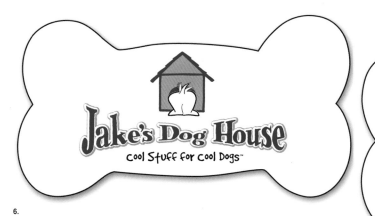

6.

Jeane P. Stein
Jake's Owner
jeane@jakesdoghouse.com

P.O. Box 3748, Cherry Hill, NJ 08034
Phone: 856-751-5905   Fax: 856-751-8511
www.jakesdoghouse.com

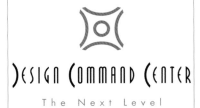

The Next Level

David Girgenti
Chief Commanding Officer

•

www.designcommandcenter.com

7.

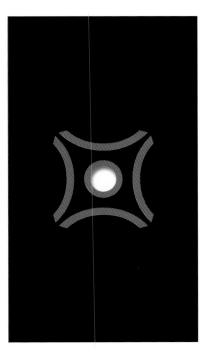

(1-3)
  Design Firm **Evenson Design Group**
(4,5)
  Design Firm **Pixallure Design**
(6,7)
  Design Firm **The Star Group**

1.
  Client   Nex Photography
  Designer   Stan Evenson
2.
  Client   Brand Growers
  Designer   Stan Evenson
3.
  Client   Streamline Graphics
  Designer   Stan Evenson
4.
  Client   Hayek Kallen
  Designer   Terry Edeker
5.
  Client   InsTrust Insurance Group
  Designer   Terry Edeker
6.
  Client   Jake's Dog House
  Designer   Dave Girgenti
7.
  Client   Design Command Center
  Designer   Dave Girgenti

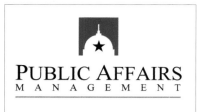

PUBLIC AFFAIRS
M A N A G E M E N T

Dennis F. Marco
Managing Director
dmarco@publicaffairsmgt.com

p | 609-39
f | 609-39

Capitol Complex
Suite 108 | 172 W
Trenton, N

www.publicaff

1.

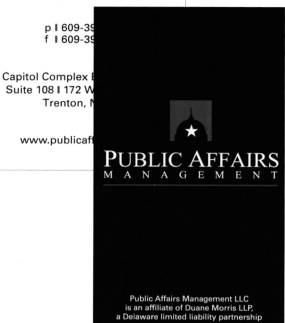

PUBLIC AFFAIRS
M A N A G E M E N T

Public Affairs Management LLC
is an affiliate of Duane Morris LLP,
a Delaware limited liability partnership

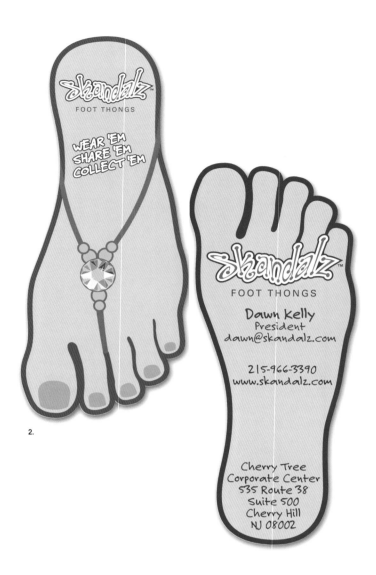

Skandalz
FOOT THONGS

WEAR 'EM
SHARE 'EM
COLLECT 'EM

Skandalz
FOOT THONGS

Dawn Kelly
President
dawn@skandalz.com

215-966-3390
www.skandalz.com

Cherry Tree
Corporate Center
535 Route 38
Suite 500
Cherry Hill
NJ 08002

2.

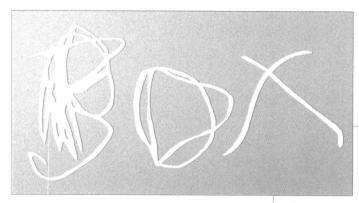

3.

Box cafe restaurant
189 Collins Street Melbourne Victoria 3000. T 03 9663 0411. F 03 9663 0422

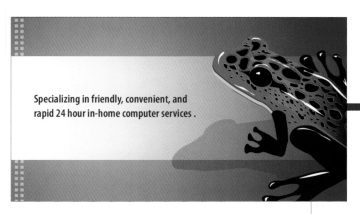

Specializing in friendly, convenient, and rapid 24 hour in-home computer services .

4.

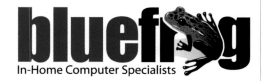

bluefrog
In-Home Computer Specialists

Frank Sheron
President/CEO

260.432.5636
franklin@bluefroginhome.com

www.bluefroginhome.com

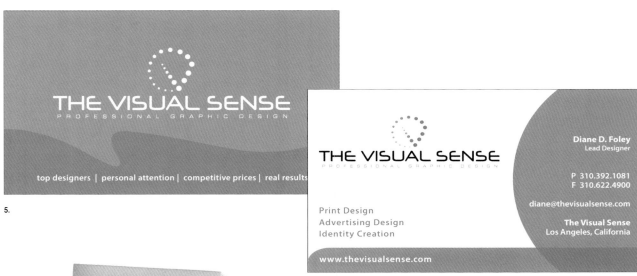

THE VISUAL SENSE
PROFESSIONAL GRAPHIC DESIGN

top designers | personal attention | competitive prices | real results

5.

THE VISUAL SENSE
PROFESSIONAL GRAPHIC DESIGN

Print Design
Advertising Design
Identity Creation

www.thevisualsense.com

Diane D. Foley
Lead Designer

P 310.392.1081
F 310.622.4900

diane@thevisualsense.com

The Visual Sense
Los Angeles, California

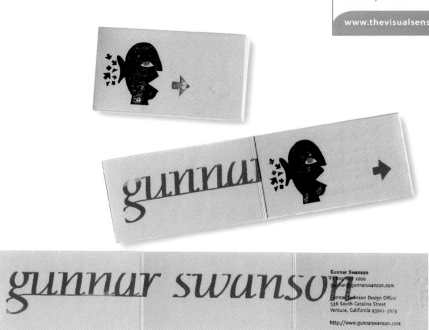

gunnar swanso

Gunnar Swanson
1 800 002 2200
gunnar@gunnarswanson.com

Gunnar Swanson Design Office
536 South Catalina Street
Ventura, California 93001-3625

http://www.gunnarswanson.com

6.

(1,2)
Design Firm **The Star Group**
(3)
Design Firm **Mia & Jem**
(4,5)
Design Firm **The Visual Sense**
(6)
Design Firm **Gunnar Swanson Design Office**

1.
Client   Public Affairs
Designer   Dave Girgenti
2.
Client   Skandalz
Designer   Dave Girgenti
3.
Client   Box Restaurant
Designer   Mia & Jem
4.
Client   Blue Frog
Designer   Diane Foley
5.
Client   The Visual Sense
Designer   Diane Foley
6.
Client   Gunnar Swanson
              Design Office
Designer   Gunnar Swanson

Index